This is a further volume in a series of companions to major philosophers. Each volume contains specially commissioned essays by an international team of scholars together with a substantial bibliography and will serve as a reference work for students and nonspecialists. One aim of the series is to dispel the intimidation such readers often feel when faced with the work of a difficult and challenging thinker.

This is one of the most comprehensive and up-to-date surveys of the philosophy of Sartre, by some of the foremost interpreters in the United States and Europe. The essays are both expository and original, and cover Sartre's writings on ontology, phenomenology, psychology, ethics, and aesthetics, as well as his work on history, commitment, and progress; a final section considers Sartre's relationship to structuralism and deconstruction. Providing a balanced view of Sartre's philosophy and situating it in relation to contemporary trends in Continental philosophy, the volume shows that many of the topics associated with Lacan, Foucault, Lévi-Strauss, and Derrida are to be found in the work of Sartre, in some cases as early as 1936. A special feature of the volume is the treatment of the recently published and hitherto little studied posthumous works.

New readers and nonspecialists will find this the most convenient, accessible guide to Sartre currently available. Advanced students and specialists will find a conspectus of recent developments in the interpretation of Sartre.

D1223571

THE CAMBRIDGE COMPANION TO
SARTRE

The Cambridge Companion to
SARTRE

edited by Christina Howells

PUBLISHED BY THE PRESS SYNDICATE OF THE UNIVERSITY OF CAMBRIDGE
The Pitt Building, Trumpington Street, Cambridge, United Kingdom

CAMBRIDGE UNIVERSITY PRESS
The Edinburgh Building, Cambridge CB2 2RU, UK   http: //www.cup.cam.ac.
40 West 20th Street, New York, NY 10011-4211, USA   http: //www.cup.org
10 Stamford Road, Oakleigh, Melbourne 3166, Australia

First published 1992
Reprinted 1994 (twice), 1995, 1997, 1998, 1999

Printed in the United States of America

Typeset in Trump Mediaeval

A catalogue record for this book is available from the British Library

Library of Congress Cataloguing-in-Publication Data is available

ISBN 0-521-38812-0 paperback

CONTENTS

v

CONTRIBUTORS

RONALD ARONSON teaches at Wayne State University. He has published widely on Sartre, including *Jean-Paul Sartre – Philosophy in the World* (Verso, 1980) and *Sartre's Second Critique* (University of Chicago Press, 1987); he also edited *Sartre Alive* (Wayne State University Press, 1991) with Adrian van den Hoven.

HAZEL E. BARNES is Professor of Philosophy Emerita at the University of Colorado. She is the translator of Sartre's *Being and Nothingness* and the author of *Sartre and Flaubert: An Existentialist Ethics,* and *Humanistic Existentialism: The Literature of Possibility.*

PETER CAWS is University Professor of Philosophy at the George Washington University. He is the author of *Sartre* (Routledge and Kegan Paul, 1979 and 1984) and *Structuralism: The Art of the Intelligible* (Humanities Press, 1988 and 1990); he also edited *Current French Philosophy* (a special issue of *Social Research*, Summer 1982) and *The Causes of Quarrel* (Beacon Press, 1989).

ROBERT D. CUMMING is the Woodbridge Professor of Philosophy Emeritus at Columbia University, where he also taught in the graduate department of Political Science. He is the author of *The Dream Is Over* (on the "end-of-philosophy" argument). His *Method and Imagination* (on Sartre's relation to Husserl) will be published in 1992.

THOMAS R. FLYNN is Samuel Candler Dobbs Professor of Philosophy at Emory University. He is the author of *Sartre and Marxist Existentialism: The Test Case of Collective Responsibility* (University of Chicago Press, 1984) and has published widely on Sartre and on Foucault. He is completing a book-length study of Sartre, Foucault, and reason in history.

vii

LEO FRETZ teaches philosophy at the University of Technology of Delft (The Netherlands). He has published on Sartre's philosophy in several European countries and in the United States. He also writes on ethics, bio-ethics, and political philosophy.

RHIANNON GOLDTHORPE is Fellow and Tutor in French at St. Anne's College, Oxford. She is the author of *Sartre: Literature and Theory* (Cambridge University Press, 1984) and of *La Nausée*, a monograph on Sartre's novel for the Unwin Critical Library series (Harper Collins, 1991).

CHRISTINA HOWELLS is Fellow and Tutor in French at Wadham College, Oxford. She is the author of *Sartre's Theory of Literature* (Modern Humanities Research Association 1979) and *Sartre: The Necessity of Freedom* (Cambridge University Press, 1988). Her research interests center on Continental philosophy, literary theory, and modern French literature.

DAVID A. JOPLING is a Mellon Post-Doctoral Fellow at the Department of Psychology, Emory University, in association with the Emory Cognition Project's Colloquium on the Self; he is also Assistant Professor of Philosophy at Emory University. He has published articles on philosophical issues in Sartre, Levinas, interpersonal relations, and biography, and is currently working on a book on reflective self-evaluation and self-knowledge.

JULIETTE SIMONT is Researcher at the National Fund for Scientific Research in Belgium. She has written numerous articles about Sartre's philosophy. She contributes frequently to the review *Temps modernes*. She is the Secretary of the *Groupe d'études sartriennes*, an international association dedicated to the study of Sartre.

PIERRE VERSTRAETEN is Professor of Philosophy at Brussels University. He is the author of *Violence et éthique, esquisse pour une morale dialectique à travers le théâtre de Sartre* (Gallimard, 1972). He has published numerous articles on Sartre's thought. He was co-director with Sartre of the collection *Bibliothèque de Philosophie* at Gallimard.

CHRONOLOGICAL BIOGRAPHY

1905	June 21. Birth of Jean-Paul-Charles-Aymard Sartre in Paris, 13, rue Mignard, XVIᵉ.
1906	Father dies.
1906–11	Lives with mother and grandparents in Meudon.
1911–15	Moves to Paris, 1, rue Le-Goff, Vᵉ.
1913	Lycée Montaigne.
1915	Lycée Henri IV.
1917	Mother remarries (Joseph Mancy). The family moves to La Rochelle, where Sartre is unhappy at school.
1920	Returns to Lycée Henri IV.
1921–2	Baccalauréat.
1922–4	Lycée Louis-Le-Grand to prepare entrance to École Normale Supérieure.
1923	Publishes short story "L'Ange du morbide" and several chapters of "Jésus la Chouette" in *La Revue sans titre*.
1924–9	École Normale Supérieure.
1928	Fails *agrégation*.
1929	Meets Simone de Beauvoir. Passes *agrégation* in first place, having reconciled himself to presenting more traditional philosophical ideas.
1929–31	Military service.
1931–6	Teaches philosophy at *lycée* in Le Havre. Starts first version of *La Nausée*.
1933–4	Obtains grant to study at the French Institute in Berlin, where he discovers phenomenology, writes *La*

	Transcendance de l'ego and a second version of *La Nausée*.
1935	Tries mescalin, which produces depression and hallucinations.
1936	Publication of *L'Imagination* (Alcan).
	He and Simone de Beauvoir incorporate Olga Kosakiewicz into their life together to form a *ménage à trois*. Its failure is recounted in de Beauvoir's novel *L'Invitée*.
	Gallimard refuses *Melancolia* (*La Nausée*).
1936–7	Teaches in Laon.
1937	*La Nausée* accepted by Gallimard after some pressure.
1937–9	Teaches in Lycée Pasteur in Paris.
1938	Writes *La Psyché*, from which *L'Esquisse d'une théorie des émotions* is drawn.
	Publication of *La Nausée*.
1939	Publication of *Le Mur* and *L'Esquisse*.
	Conscripted on September 2 to 70th Division in Nancy, later transferred to Brumath and then Morsbronn. Meanwhile working on *L'Age de raison* and *L'Être et le néant*.
1940	Publication of *L'Imaginaire*.
	Prix du Roman Populiste for *Le Mur*.
	Imprisoned in Padoux, then Nancy, then Stalag XII D in Trèves.
	Teaches Heidegger to fellow prisoners.
	Writes and directs *Bariona* in prisoner-of-war camp.
1941	Obtains his freedom from prisoner-of-war camp by dint of posing as a civilian.
	Founds a short-lived intellectual Resistance group, Socialisme et Liberté, with Merleau-Ponty.
	Teaches in Lycée Condorcet until 1944.
1943	Publication of *Les Mouches* and *L'Être et le néant*.
	Writes articles of literary criticism on, among others, Camus, Blanchot, and Bataille.
1944	Meets Genet.
	Sets up editorial board for *Les Temps modernes*.
1945	Publication of *Huis clos*, *L'Age de raison*, *Le Sursis*.
	Refuses Legion of Honor.

Goes to the United States as a special representative
of *Combat* (Camus's journal) and *Le Figaro,* and again
later in the year to give a series of lectures in
American universities.
The first number of *Les Temps modernes* appears.
Gives the (in)famous lecture "L'Existentialisme est
un humanisme." This is at the start of the great
vogue for existentialism and of Sartre's notoriety.

1946   Publication of *L'Existentialisme est un humanisme,
        Morts sans sépulture, La Putain respectueuse,
        Réflexions sur la question juive, Les Jeux sont faits.*
        First quarrel with Camus.

1947   Publication of *Situations I, Baudelaire, Théâtre I.*
        Qu'est-ce que la littérature? is serialized in *Les
        Temps modernes.*

1948   Publication of *Les Mains sales, Situations II,
        L'Engrenage.*
        Participates in the founding of the Rassemblement
        Démocratique Révolutionnaire (RDR)
        The Catholic Church puts all Sartre's works on the
        Index.
        Sartre is working on his *Morale* and a long study of
        Mallarmé (parts of both will be published
        posthumously).

1949   Publication of *La Mort dans l'âme, Situations III,
        Entretiens sur la politique.*
        Disaffection with and abandonment of RDR.
        Controversy with Mauriac.
        Visits Guatemala, Panama, Curaçao, Haiti, and
        Cuba.

1950–1 Publication of *Le Diable et le Bon Dieu* (1951).
        Studies history and economy and rereads Marx.
        Part of the study of Genet is published in *Les Temps
        modernes.*
        Sartre and Merleau-Ponty denounce the Soviet
        concentration camps.
        Travels in Sahara and Black Africa.
        Significant differences of opinion with Merleau-Ponty
        over the Korean war.

1952–5   Publication of *Saint Genet, comédien et martyr* (1952), *Kean* (1954).
          For the next four years Sartre's concerns are primarily political; he writes *Les Communistes et la paix*; signs a manifesto against the Cold War; forbids a production of *Les Mains sales* in Vienna; speaks on behalf of the peace movement; visits Heidegger; protests against the execution of the Rosenbergs (1953); participates in an extraordinary meeting of the World Council for Peace in Berlin (1954); visits the Soviet Union and describes his experiences there in *Libération* and *L'Unità*; is named vice-president of the France–USSR association; visits China (1955); returns to the Soviet Union.

1956   Publication of *Nekrassov*.
          The Soviet intervention in Hungary is condemned by Sartre who leaves the France–USSR association, writes *Le Fantôme de Staline*, and produces a special number of *Les Temps modernes* devoted to the Hungarian question.

1957   Begins writing the *Critique de la raison dialectique*. Protests against the Algerian war and torture.

1958–9   Writes a commentary on Henri Alleg's *La Question* for *L'Express* and the journal is seized. Various subsequent issues of *Les Temps modernes* are also seized. Participates in demonstrations against de Gaulle; speaks at an antifascist rally; gives a press conference on the violation of human rights in Algeria.

1960–6   Publication of *Les Séquestrés d'Altona* and *Critique de la raison dialectique*. Visits Cuba, meets Castro and Che Guevara.
          Gives lecture on theater in the Sorbonne.
          Visits Yugoslavia, meets Tito, gives a lecture in Belgrade.
          Participates in further debates on Algeria, signs manifestos, gives press conferences.

1962   Further political activity. Visits Poland and the Soviet Union; meets Khrushchev.

John Huston's film *Freud* is released. Sartre's scenario
has been changed and he withdraws his name from
the titles.

1963   Publication of *Les Mots*.
        Participates in political press conferences, gives an
        antiapartheid lecture, visits Czechoslovakia.

1964   Publication of *Situations IV, V,* and *VI*.
        Speaks at UNESCO Kierkegaard conference and at
        Conference on Ethics in Gramsci Institute in Rome.
        Is awarded and refuses the Nobel Prize (about
        £25,000).

1965   Publication of *Situations VII, Les Troyennes*. Refuses
        to lecture in Cornell University in States. Visits the
        USSR.
        Supports Mitterrand as presidential candidate.

1966   Publishes extracts from his study of Flaubert in *Les
        Temps modernes*.
        Joins the Russell Tribunal investigating American
        war crimes in Vietnam.
        Gives series of lectures in Japan.

1967   Lectures in Egypt, meets Nasser, visits refugee camps.
        Travels in Israel in a less formal capacity.
        Correspondence with de Gaulle over the Russell
        Tribunal.
        Sartre and Aragon refuse to participate in the Tenth
        Congress of Soviet Writers in protest against the
        Sinyavsky–Daniel trial.
        Supports Israel over opening of the Gulf of Aqaba.
        Gives lecture on Vietnam in Brussels.

1968   Supports student movement in May uprising.
        Accuses Communist party of betraying the May
        revolution.
        Condemns intervention of Soviet troops in
        Czechoslovakia.

1969   Sartre's mother dies.
        Protests against expulsion of thirty-four students
        from University of Paris.
        Asks for release of Régis Debray.
        Gives television interview on Vietnam War.

1970   Signs declaration on Biafra.
              Takes over as editor of *La Cause du peuple*, whose
              previous two editors have been imprisoned.
              Meets Pierre Victor, with whom he later collaborates
              in ethical discussions.
              Participates in founding of Secours Rouge.
              Is made nominal director of several minor
              publications of the extreme Left.
              Blames the State as employer for fatal accidents at
              Lens colliery.

1971   Publication of *L'Idiot de la famille*, vols. I and II. Has
              mild heart attack.
              Supports a hunger strike in favor of political
              prisoners. Participates in abortive occupation of Sacré
              Cœur.
              Breaks off relations with Cuba over Padilla affair.
              Demonstrates against racism.
              Signs petition asking for right to emigrate for Soviet
              citizens.

1972   Publication of *Situations VIII* and *IX* and of *L'Idiot
              de la famille*, vol. III.
              Start of film on his life and works by Astruc and
              Contat. Disaffection with oversimple line of class-
              hatred of *La Cause du peuple*.
              Agrees to edit new daily paper, *Libération*.

1973   Further, more serious heart attack.
              Moves from boulevard Raspail to boulevard Edgar-
              Quinet. Semiblindness after two hemorrhages in his
              good eye.
              Pierre Victor reads to Sartre, who can no longer see
              sufficiently well.
              Takes side of Israel in war of Yom Kippur.

1974   Publication of *On a raison de se révolter*.
              Abstains in presidential elections.
              Gives up editorship of various left-wing journals on
              health grounds.
              Meets Marcuse for discussion about the situation of
              the intellectual.

Starts autobiographical dialogues on tape with S. de Beauvoir.

With three others Sartre prepares a series of television programs on the last seventy years of history. The project is never produced.

Dissociates from UNESCO as a protest in defense of the State of Israel.

Goes to Stuttgart to meet the terrorist A. Baader and denounces his conditions of imprisonment.

1975   Visits Portugal.

Signs petitions condemning Soviet repression.

In an interview with M. Contat declares himself in favor of "libertarian socialism."

Decides to reduce his public activities and spend more time on the preparation for the book on ethics, *Pouvoir et liberté*, with Pierre Victor.

1976   Publication of *Situations X*.

Sartre par lui-même (film) appears.

Accepts doctorate from University of Jerusalem.

Signs various political petitions and articles.

1977   Publication of *Sartre* – text of the film.

Takes up position against the "nouveaux philosophes," and also declares "Je ne suis plus Marxiste" (in an interview in *Lotta continua*).

Calls on Israel to respond to President Sadat's peace initiative.

1978   Goes to Israel to try to further the peace initiative.

Participates in film on S. de Beauvoir.

Appeals for return to France of D. Cohn-Bendit.

1979   Participates in Israeli–Palestinian conference organized by *Les Temps modernes* in Foucault's house. Extract from *Mallarmé* appears in *Obliques*.

Participates in press conference for Boat People from Vietnam.

1980   Continues interviews with Pierre Victor.

Supports boycott of Olympic Games in Moscow.

March 20 hospitalized for edema of the lungs.

April 13 goes into a coma and dies on April 15.

April 19. Funeral procession from hospital to cemetery of Montparnasse, where his ashes are buried.

Further biographical details may be obtained from the seventy-page chronology introducing the Pléiade edition of Sartre's *Oeuvres romanesques; Les Écrits de Sartre,* ed. M. Contat and M. Rybalka; F. Jeanson, *Sartre dans sa vie,* Seuil, 1974; S. de Beauvoir, *La Force de l'âge, La Force des choses, Tout Compte fait, La Cérémonie des adieux;* A. Cohen-Solal, *Sartre 1905–1980;* R. Hayman, *Writing Against: A Biography of Sartre,* 1986.

ABBREVIATIONS

For full bibliographical details, see the Bibliography.

AS	*Confrontation, 20, Après le sujet qui vient*
BN	*Being and Nothingness* (Sartre)
CDG	*Carnets de la drôle de guerre* (Sartre)
CDR	*Critique of Dialectical Reason* (Sartre)
CM	*Cahiers pour une morale* (Sartre)
CRD	*Critique de la raison dialectique* (Sartre)
E	*Écrits* (Lacan)
EN	*L'Être et le néant* (Sartre)
Enc	*The Logic of Hegel* (Hegel)
Enz	*Enzyklopädie* (Hegel)
Ge&S	*Genèse et structure* (Hippolyte)
GS	*Gesammelte Schriften* (Dilthey)
IF	*L'Idiot de la famille* (Sartre)
Im	*L'Imaginaire* (Sartre)
M	*Marges* (Derrida)
MC	*Les Mots et les choses* (Foucault)
Méd	*Méditations Cartésiennes* (Husserl)
OR	*Œuvres romanesques* (Sartre)
ORR	*On a raison de se révolter* (Sartre)
Ph Sp	*Phenomenology of Spirit* (Hegel)
PS	*La Pensée sauvage* (Lévi-Strauss)
Sc L	*Science of Logic* (Hegel)
SG	*Saint Genet* (Sartre)
Sit II–X	*Situations*, Vols. II–X (Sartre)
SM	*Search for a Method* (Sartre)
TE	*La Transcendance de l'ego* (Sartre)
VP	*La Voix et la phénomène* (Derrida)

Introduction

This collection of essays, by some of the foremost interpreters of Sartre from Europe and the United States, was composed specifically for the new series of Cambridge Companions to Major Philosophers. None of the essays has been published previously elsewhere. The contributors range from the most senior and established Sartrean scholars to some of the most promising and lively of the younger generation of critics. As editor, my task was to commission a broad range of essays, covering the major aspects of Sartre's philosophical work and its implications, in line with the purpose of the new Cambridge series. What struck me most forcibly on receipt of the typescripts, was the originality, density, and cohesion of the interpretations. They not only present a generous and balanced view of the wide variety of Sartre's philosophy, but also all make a contribution to the "new" Sartre, that is to the view of Sartre which has been gradually emerging since his death in 1980, as a figure whose diversity was far from being mastered, who could not, without distortion and impoverishment, be identified with the "classical existentialist" of the 1940s, and whose relationship to Structuralism and Post-Structuralism, as well as to psychoanalysis, Marxism, and literary theory, was far more complex than had been generally supposed. Suffering, since the 1960s, from the backlash of rejection that exceptional popularity and fame brings in its wake, Sartre was commonly used as the humanist target against whom nascent Structuralist, Marxist, and Deconstructionist critics could test their arms. But their weaponry was not furnished with quite the anti-Sartrean ammunition that they imagined: Sartre's gradual incorporation of Marxism since the 1950s was not exhibited solely in his difficult and little read *Critique of Dialectical Reason* (1960), nor could his relationship to Freud be reduced to the critique to be found in *Being and Nothingness* (1943) or to the elaborate Freud scenario, relic of his abortive collaboration with John Huston. The *Idiot of the Family* (1971–2) is certainly the text that reveals most clearly the extent and fruitfulness of Sartre's constantly evolving relationship with the other major thinkers of his age. Its implications are only now starting to be thought through, and its mark is evident in many of the essays in this collection. But this is still only half the picture. Not only did Sartre's critics of the sixties and seventies attempt, unwittingly perhaps, to fossilize him in the classical works he had himself by then outgrown, but they did not accord those works themselves a fair reading. The decentered subject, the rejection of a metaphysics of presence, the critique of bourgeois humanism and individualism, the conception of the reader as producer of the text's multiple meanings, the recognition of language and thought structures as masters rather than mastered in most acts of discourse and thinking, a materialist philosophy of history as detotalized and fragmented, these are not the inventions of Lacan, Foucault, Lévi-Strauss and Derrida; nor are they to be found merely in Sartre's later works such as the *Critique* (1960), *Words* (1966) or the *Idiot of the Family* (1971–2) where it could be argued that they should be attributed to his receptivity to the major trends of his age (though the *Critique of Dialectical Reason* would still predate most of the French Structuralists' major works). The notions are, rather, present from the outset: in the *Transcendence of the Ego* (1936), in *Sketch for a Theory of the Emotions* (1940), in *Nausea* (1941), in *Being and Nothingness* (1943), and even in his most polemical theoretical work, *What Is Literature?* (1948). This preoccupation with the deconstruction as well as the reconstruction of the human is also to be found in the posthumously published works, ranging from the early *Cahiers pour une morale* (1983), *Carnets de la drôle de guerre* (1983), and *Vérité et existence* (1989), through to the notes for volume IV of the *Idiot of the Family*, the second volume of *Critique*, and the later meditations on ethics. All these have informed, and indeed in some cases form the focus of, the contributions to this *Companion*.

Part I of this book concentrates primarily, but not solely, on the works of the thirties and forties. Hazel Barnes gives an illuminating presentation of Sartre's ontology, with a particularly subtle account of the relationship between consciousness, being-for-itself, and nothingness, as well as of that between consciousness and body and consciousness and world. She draws primarily, of course, on *Being and Nothingness*, but also makes use of the *Critique*, *The Psychology of the Imagination*, the *Idiot of the Family*, the *Carnets*, and the *Cahiers*. A substantial and controversial final section is devoted to the role and reality of the ego. Here Professor Barnes goes beyond what has until now been Sartrean orthodoxy, to argue that the ego is not merely an inevitable fabrication, but a necessary and healthy part of personal existence, a bulwark against irresponsibility and meaninglessness. The systematic reader who compares the opinions held by the various contributors to this book will not fail to note that this view is somewhat different from my own interpretation in the final chapter, which aligns Sartre's attitude to the ego with Lacan's well-known hostility to ego psychology. But Professor Barnes's paper certainly led me to reconsider my interpretation, and think out how I would defend it, and I hope the reader of this *Companion* will relish the heterogeneity and occasional heterodoxy of its contributions as a sign of the lively state of Sartre studies in the 1990s.

Robert Cummings's essay on Sartre and Husserl focuses on their respective interpretations of role-playing as a base for a wide-ranging analysis of the specificity of Sartrean phenomenology. The chapter starts, naturally, from *The Psychology of the Imagination*, and includes not only the *Transcendence of the Ego* and *Being and Nothingness*, but also *Saint Genet*, the *Critique*, *Words*, the *Carnets*, and a considerable section on the *Idiot of the Family* as well as several references to Sartre's fiction. The analysis of the role of affectivity and affective meaning for Sartre is used to show his difference from as well as his debt to Husserl, and concludes with a sharp reminder of the inappropriateness of attempting to discuss Sartre's philosophy in isolation from his creative literature. Professor Cummings's own work has certainly avoided that pitfall in both its judicious intermingling of primary texts and its excursions outside philosophy into psychoanalysis, drama, and Marxism.

Leo Fretz's chapter traces the development of the notion of the individual in Sartre's philosophy from the *Transcendence of the Ego* through *Being and Nothingness* to the *Critique*, and argues that the "epistemological break," if there is one, should be located not, as is generally thought, between *Being and Nothingness* and the *Cri-*

tique, but rather between the *Transcendence* and *Being and Nothingness.* In the *Transcendence of the Ego* consciousness is individuated but impersonal, at least on a primary level; the attempt in *Being and Nothingness* to follow Heidegger and locate consciousness *in* the world gives consciousness a personal structure as *pour soi, ipséité,* and, Fretz argues, poses afresh the problem of solipsism. The *Critique* resolves this problem by envisaging the *cogito* as dialectical and "historical man" in necessary relation to other men. Fretz sees this final position as synthesizing the two different kinds of transcendental consciousness of the *Transcendence* and *Being and Nothingness.* In an unexpected and provocative conclusion he returns to the last page of the *Transcendence,* where Sartre states that the conception of the ego as a transcendental object in the world lays the foundation for an ethics and politics that are entirely positive. In the light of Hazel Barnes's rehabilitation of the ego this relating of the ego to ethics is particularly suggestive.

Part II of the *Companion* continues the ethical meditation opened by Leo Fretz's chapter. David Jopling's essay on Sartre's moral psychology gives a lucid and sympathetic account of the implications of the existential conception of freedom for morality. He focuses on the issues of self-determination and self-knowledge – how we make of ourselves the kinds of people we want to be – rather than on the more popular and contentious questions of free choice of action and the rejection of absolute moral laws. He explores some of the most fundamental questions raised by the radical claims of *Being and Nothingness,* in particular with respect to the project, arguing that, in its all-embracing nature, it is ultimately at odds with Sartre's claim that we are all self-determining agents. How can we ever change at all, if our whole lives are globally governed by our project, which can only be altered by a "radical conversion"? Jopling shows how the answers to questions such as this are to be found in Sartre's later works, in the *Critique* and more especially the *Idiot of the Family,* in which a Marxist theory of social conditioning together with a theory of childhood development and of social "predestination" mean that we are no longer envisaged as making ourselves "from the ground up" as it were, but rather as reworking and integrating already existing dispositions, character traits, emotional patterns, and so on. In this way self-determination still involves total responsibility, but it is rather that of *assuming* responsibility for ourselves – selves to whose characteristics, coherence, and purpose we have contributed, but on the basis of the given, not, like gods, ex nihilo.

Rhiannon Goldthorpe continues the emphasis on the importance of the *Idiot of the Family* as a response to the questions posed by Sartre's early works, this time in the domain of literary commitment. She also draws on a wide range of other texts, from *What Is Literature?* and *Saint Genet* to the posthumously published *Engagement de Mallarmé*, the *Cahiers*, the *Carnets*, and volume II of the *Critique*. She uses *Search for a Method*, with its theory of the individual as a kind of *universel singulier*, totalizing and totalized by his or her epoch, to supplement and resolve some of the uncertainties of the earlier, unsystematic *What Is Literature?*, in particular with respect to the relationship between subjective and objective and to the problem of alienation. One of the most intriguing aspects of her essay is the discussion of Sartre's debt to Dilthey's notion of *verstehen* (*compréhension*), which envisages understanding as a form of hermeneutic circle moving between complex wholes and their parts in a continuing attempt at totalization. In the domain of literary commitment, *compréhension* further suggests the possibility of transcending conflict by grasping the other as subject rather than object, a notion that is vital to works such as *Saint Genet* and *Black Orpheus*, and which allows poetry to come into its own as an indirect suggestion of what prose fails to say. Flaubert is perhaps a test case of this in several senses; and Goldthorpe shows the complexity of Sartre's conception of the novelist's commitment, culminating in an analysis of *Saint Julien l'hospitalier* as concentrating in itself the social, historical, and personal contradictions of Flaubert's life story. Here Sartre's own reading is shown as a dynamic transcendence of the contradictions of the *Esprit objectif*, and itself a form of *littérature engagée*.

Juliette Simont completes this section with a chapter centrally devoted to tracing the development of Sartre's ethical positions. Her essay is bold and comprehensive, drawing not only on *Being and Nothingness*, *Saint Genet*, the *Critique*, and the posthumous *Cahiers pour une morale*, but also on the as yet unpublished notes, dating from 1964–5, for lectures given at the Gramsci Institute in Rome, and for a lecture scheduled for Cornell, but canceled in protest against American bombings in Vietnam. Simont traces the fortunes of the notion of *value* from the 1940s to the 1960s. *Being and Nothingness* asks if value is necessarily alienating, or if it only produces alienation when it is imbued with the *esprit de sérieux*. The *Cahiers* argue that value itself is not alienating, alienation comes from other people, from value transformed into obligation, and from the counterfinality of the material world, which distorts one's intentions. The *Critique* continues the opposition between value and obligation, now described as imperative, but with a reversal of interpretation: The imperative is perceived as external and can therefore be potentially resisted, value is now seen as more noxious because it is obligation internalized and imperceptible. The Rome and Cornell lectures shift the locus of opposition to that between need and desire: *Desire* involves alienation to the others on whom it makes me dependent, *need* might provide the foundation for a materialist, humanist ethics that would involve the rejection of all behavior that increased human alienation to the practico-inert.

Like Leo Fretz and David Jopling, Juliette Simont sees in the works of the sixties not merely a radicalization of perspective under the influence of Marxism, but also, and more surprisingly, a humanist materialism that, in its recognition of objective alienation, makes possible a moderate optimism concerning the possibility of a positive historical ethics.

The third part continues the focus on Sartre's later and posthumously published works. Tom Flynn's essay on the poetics of history takes the unusual approach of using Sartre's philosophy of the imagination to illuminate his philosophy of history. Just as Juliette Simont showed Sartre in the forties envisaging the work of art as a paradigm for ethical structures, so Tom Flynn shows him likening the intelligibility of history to that of an art work in so far as both are products of creative freedom. His chapter is wide-ranging, focusing in detail on *The Psychology of the Imagination*, the *Carnets*, the *Cahiers*, the *Critique*, and the *Idiot of the Family*. He discusses the question of understanding (*verstehen*) in respect of history, which picks up Rhiannon Goldthorpe's analysis earlier in this collection, and uses Sartre's distinction between *sens* and *signification* to show how the *meaning* of history may be understood in an aesthetic sense as the product of human totalization. The problem, of course, remains of how individual totalizations may themselves be totalized: Can there be a grand totalization without a totalizer? This question is raised in both the *Idiot* and the first volume of the *Critique* and its discussion continues in volume II of the *Critique* as the problem of "enveloping totalization." Flynn describes Sartre's ideal as existential and committed history, but one that, it seems, remains in some sense imaginary. His massive study of Flaubert is, we are reminded, "a novel that is true." Since, for Sartre, truth is always human, history too, in this sense, must be a *roman vrai*.

Ronald Aronson's essay continues the analysis of Sartre's theory of history, focused now on the precise question of the nature of progress. He draws primarily on the *Cahiers* and volume II of the *Critique* as well as on *Existentialism Is a Humanism, Search for a Method*, and the *Idiot of the Family*. Aronson traces the complexities of Sartre's position, analyzing the early outright rejection of the myth of progress that Sartre still maintained in the *Idiot of the Family* (where progress is described as a ruling class mystification designed to stave off social change) in conjunction with his acknowledgment of scientific and technological progress. The chapter explores Sartre's meditations on detotalized totalities (which mean that progress, like history, can have no single subject) and examines the undoing of progress by alienation and the practico-inert. Ronald Aronson not only guides the reader through the evolving intricacies of Sartre's argument, and shows the implications for it of other aspects of his theory of history, he makes a contribution of his own in the final section, which uses Sartre's thinking in a way he did not perhaps foresee, with the suggestion of progress as a *positive* practico-inert, embodied, for example, in civil rights legislation or other forms of democratization.

Peter Caws's exploration, in his controversially titled essay, of the relationship between Sartre and Structuralism, also argues that there is considerably more to be made of the notion of the practico-inert for twentieth-century social philosophy than has so far been realized. His chapter contains an excellent portrayal of the "new Sartre" which I referred to at the beginning of this Introduction. For it shows a Sartre who is not necessarily at odds with Structuralism, a Sartre who was perhaps driven to oppose it both by public pressure and by the more outlandish of Structuralist positions but whose own work showed plentiful evidence of an understanding, and indeed serious use, of Structuralist theory. The major disagreement concerned the question of *agency:* Were structures originally produced by subjects, or not? Caws sides with Sartre in seeing the objective, impersonal vision of radical Structuralism as a non-sense: It is surely more implausible to attribute agency to structures than to people. How can myths "think themselves" or produce themselves in any real sense? And he sees Sartre's own positions in the *Critique* and the *Idiot of the Family*, especially volume III, as exemplary of the best kind of Structuralism, one that does not attempt to ignore the human subject but takes fully into account its inability to control the complex, semi-inert structures that traverse it. This is the moment for a renewed study of the practico-inert and the *esprit objectif* of volume III of the *Idiot*, seen now not merely as restricting but also as potentially liberating and facilitating. Peter Caws concludes with a convincing call for not only a renewed picture of Sartre, but also a renewed vision of Structuralism, one that would not reject everything because of the excesses and aberrations of a few.

The reconsideration of Sartre's relationship with Structuralism continues in my own chapter, focused specifically on the question of the subject, and extending also to Post-Structuralism and Deconstruction. In it I pursue a double line of argument, showing first that the subject for Sartre is not the autonomous, self-sufficient foundation his opponents portray it as, but rather divided, non-egoic, never self-identical, and second that the major opponents of a philosophy of the subject in France are now withdrawing from their previous radical positions and attempting to construct a notion of subjectivity that would be compatible with what has been learned from Structuralism and Deconstruction. I argue that their efforts so far are producing a subject that is remarkably, though unacknowledgedly, akin to that of *Being and Nothingness*. The disregard of Sartre's early writings on the subject constitutes an intellectual blind spot that undermines the insights of much recent French philosophy.

There is, in fact, notably no contribution from a French philosopher in this *Companion*, though there are two by French speakers, Juliette Simont and Pierre Verstraeten, and the latter closes the collection with a dense essay on Sartre and Hegel. That contribution appears in an appendix because it exhibits a degree of technical complexity unlikely to be assimilable by nonspecialists, for whom, in part at least, this book is intended. However, it provides precisely a striking example of a certain kind of French philosophy, carried out here moreover by a Belgian, for few serious philosophers in France in recent years have concerned themselves with the exegesis of Sartre.

Pierre Verstraeten undertakes a comparison of Sartre and Hegel through an interpretation of their conceptions of the difficult notions of infinity and limits, and the better known question of being-for-others, and argues that the affinities between them in these significant areas are far closer than Sartre himself would have been prepared to admit. Verstraeten focuses the references to Hegel dispersed throughout previous essays in the collection – notably in Goldthorpe, Simont, Flynn, and Aronson – and provides a concluding reminder of both the still insuperable differences between Anglo-American and French philosophy, and of Sartre's own continuing resistance to recuperation.

I Phenomenology and existentialism

1 Sartre's ontology: The revealing and making of being

In Sartre's ontology what differentiates human being from all other being is precisely nothing. Or more accurately, it is a nothingness. In rewriting the sentence I have subtly changed it. Human being is not the same as the rest of being but is distinguished from it by a separating nothingness. Have I merely effected a sleight of hand? Is this nothingness a futile hypostatization? Or is it in reality a disguised something?

When the Greek Atomists declared that reality consisted of atoms and void, it was easy to grasp that the void was real without being a substance. We can see a hole. Clearly, emptiness was necessary if atoms were to group and regroup themselves in the forms that make up the universe. But the Atomist's nonbeing does not *do* anything; it is being in the form of self-moving atoms that is responsible for both relative permanencies and change. By contrast, Sartre puts all signifying activity where there is nothingness. And where is this nothingness? He tells us that "Nothingness lies coiled in the heart of being – like a worm" (p. 56).[1] But this metaphor is something of an enigma and requires explanation. One thing is sure: Where there is nothingness, there is consciousness, but the two are not quite synonyms. And in one context Sartre speaks of "little pools of non-being" existing out there in the world (p. 53). Consciousness and nothingness are dependent on being, but they are not being. Sartre's ontology is a phenomenological description of the relation of this no-thing, which is consciousness, to the being on which it depends.

Being, in Sartre's view, if we describe it abstractly, is the condition of all revelation. For anything to be revealed, for it to be there, it must *be*. Consciousness *reveals* being. Both the revealed and the revealer have a certain transphenomenality. As an "ontological

13

proof" of the transphenomenality of being, Sartre offers the defini-
tional statement that "consciousness is born *supported by* a being
which is not itself" (p. 23). An object is revealed by – that is, appears
to – consciousness in a series of what the phenomenologists call
Abschattungen, a succession of glimpses, shadings, profiles, but the
object is not exhausted by its appearances, which are infinite. Other
ways of looking at it are always possible. Equally, but differently,
consciousness is transphenomenal. To be aware of an object is not to
be the object. The object does not enter into consciousness any more
than consciousness enters into it. Consciousness is not a thing, not
an entity, not a substance. Sartre calls it a "nonsubstantial absolute." It is absolute because it is nonsubstantial.

> Conscience has nothing substantial, it is pure "appearance" in the sense
> that it exists only to the degree that it appears. But it is precisely because
> consciousness is pure appearance, because it is total emptiness (since the
> entire world is outside it) – it is because of this identity of appearance and
> existence within it that it can be considered as the absolute. (p. 17)

Its existence is only the activity of revealing. Sartre adopts fully the
phenomenological declaration: "All consciousness is consciousness
of something" (p. 11).

We might put Sartre's basic meaning in everyday, nonphilosophi-
cal terms if we said something like the following: We as human
beings confront a brute, concrete reality that existed before the evolution of conscious life. Into this undefined being, what we call
consciousness introduces significance, differentiation, form, meaning, and our own purposes. Through our bodies we can use this
universe, but there is nothing there that could properly be said to be
responsive to us – only indifferent. Insofar as Sartre holds that consciousness is not itself a being but is the source of all determination,
of everything that "happens" to being, his position has been considered by many critics to be both idealist and dualist. Yet Sartre himself finally said that what he wished to establish was a monistic
materialism.[2] By this term Sartre meant to indicate that there is no
spiritual or mental reality that exists independent of matter. But this
does not mean that conscious processes can be explained by the
same kinds of laws that determine nonconscious chemical and physical reactions. Consciousness is neither thing nor spirit. Somehow
(only a biologist or a psychoneurologist could, theoretically, say how

and only a metaphysician could speculate as to why) there emerged in the mass of being a power of withdrawal, a separation. Consequently, one part of being (although to say "part" is already to have adopted the distinguishing point of view of consciousness) could relate itself to the rest of being. The separation and consequent relating are accomplished by means of this, as it were, crack or hole in being. The splitting apart is the activity we know as consciousness. Thus consciousness is aware of objects and of its own activity by its power of detachment. It enfolds its objects in a shell of nothingness, thus making itself a reflecting of them, a point of view on them. It is this that we mean when we say that consciousness *intends* its objects or that consciousness reveals being or that being appears to consciousness. Nevertheless, we should not say that consciousness is a structured mind or, indeed, any entity whatsoever.

Sartre's position would be incomprehensible except for one thing: Although consciousness reveals being, the fundamental opposition on which he builds his ontology is not that between consciousness and being but the distinction between two regions of being, only one of which is characterized as inextricably associated with consciousness. These are being-in-itself (*l'être-en-soi*) and being-for-itself (*l'être-pour-soi*), but insofar as being-for-itself *is*, it has the same being as being-in-itself. It is distinguished only by the presence in itself of the active negating activity we experience as consciousness. Thus the two regions of being are inseparable except abstractly, and the truth is that the distinction between being-in-itself and being-for-itself is less clearcut and more complex than first appears.

I suppose that it is accurate to say loosely that being-in-itself is nonconscious being and that being-for-itself is conscious being. And, at least pragmatically, we may as well restrict being-for-itself to human being. Although Sartre, in a late interview, hinted that perhaps all living things might be said to share in being-for-itself, his remarks were obviously not carefully thought through.[3] Certainly, the for-itself Sartre had in mind in everything he wrote is not only intentional but radically free self-consciousness, a definition not at all appropriate to instinct-guided animals, let alone plants. Yet, while the conscious/nonconscious distinction always holds, Sartre uses both "being" and "being-in-itself" in ways that obviously have varying referents; moreover, "consciousness" and "being-for-itself," while they are inextricable and sometimes used interchangeably, are not identical. I will try to show how careful discrimination of the various ways in which Sartre uses these basic terms and observation of the degree to which he blurs his original sharp cleavage between the two regions of being will aid us in understanding the connection of consciousness with (1) nothingness, (2) body, (3) external objects, and (4) the ego.

CONSCIOUSNESS AND NOTHINGNESS

We may begin with being-for-itself and consider first of all what Sartre means by the terms "consciousness" and "being-for-itself" and their respective connections with the elusive nothingness. Consciousness is the activity of revealing; that is, of reflecting, of intending. As an activity, consciousness is doubly dependent on being. First, it cannot exist except as there is something to be revealed (all consciousness is consciousness *of* something). And it is the activity of a being; that is, of a being-for-itself. This emphatically does not mean that these are two existences. Neither consciousness nor being-for-itself exists separately from the other. Being-for-itself *is* (self)conscious being. If in the Introduction to *Being and Nothingness* one occasionally feels that a disembodied mind is at work, this illusion is quickly dispelled. The for-itself carries a lack of being at its heart due to the presence of the nihilating (= nothing making) consciousness that is inseparable from it.[4] A corpse is no longer a for-itself but an in-itself. Frequently, by a sort of metonymy, Sartre uses the two terms, "consciousness" and "being-for-itself," interchangeably – in contexts where it makes no difference whether the reader is expected to have in mind a human individual confronting the world or the individual's awareness of the world confronted. But when he wants to be precise about the relation of consciousness to the body, for example, or to the ego, Sartre never substitutes "for-itself." Comparably, there are times when he uses "for-itself" but not "consciousness" synonymously with generic "man" or "human reality" (Sartre's translation of Heidegger's *Dasein*). This last point is especially important. Consider the following examples taken almost at random from the chapter "The Problem of Nothingness":

Man is the being through whom nothingness comes to the world. (p. 59)

A bit later,

It is not given to "human reality" to annihilate even provisionally the mass of being which it posits before itself. Man's *relation* with being is that he can modify it. (pp. 59–60)

And finally,

There must exist a Being (this cannot be the In-itself) of which the property is to nihilate Nothingness, to support it in its being, to sustain it perpetually in its very existence, *a being by which Nothingness comes to things.* (p. 57)

Sartre could not make it more clear that the for-itself (the human individual) is the being that supports the negating activity of consciousness and that consciousness is associated with the lack of being that forces the for-itself to make itself be rather than simply being what it is.

In the *Critique of Dialectical Reason* Sartre says paradoxically that his philosophy is a materialism and that it gives their due weight to both matter and consciousness. Whatever object a consciousness intends, there is always a material substratum, whether it is physical or physiological, engrams in the brain, or the nebulous physical-chemical reaction that is said to accompany all thinking. "Everything points to the fact that living bodies and inanimate objects are made of the same molecules,"[5] Sartre claims. This does not mean that consciousness is made of molecules. Consciousness is an activity dependent on molecules organized in the form of a body, but this is not to reduce it to body. Sartre would surely agree with William James, who claimed that "even if the coming to pass of mind-states depends upon brain states, the nature of mind-states is not necessarily explained by such dependence."[6] But we must be careful that in refusing to give consciousness the status of entity or substance we do not deny its reality. Consciousness is real as activity. Something happens, is done, even if that something is the establishing of a negation. Sartre did not go so far as James and some later phenomenologists in suggesting that because of the all but inevitable danger of treating as a thing that which is pure activity we should avoid the term "consciousness" entirely. I think Sartre is right here. We do not have to invent a verb such as "consciencing" in order to remember that what we are discussing is a doing and not a being. It is possible to describe what seeing is without hypostatizing sight as something that does the seeing. The phenomenological description of consciousness which is the core of Sartre's ontology is the account of how a being-for-itself (each one of us) is conscious, not physiologically but phenomenologically. Consciousness is being aware of. . . . What does it mean to be aware of . . . ?

We have observed that consciousness is doubly attached to being while not being a being. We should now try to determine exactly how consciousness stands in relation to nothingness. Are they synonyms? And if they are, how is this nothingness different from the everyday nothing, which Sartre could not intend without reducing his philosophy to absurdity?

A key passage with which we may begin is the following:

The Being by which Nothingness arrives in the world is a being such that in its Being, the nothingness of its Being is in question. *The being by which Nothingness comes to the world must be its own Nothingness.* By this we must understand not a nihilating act which would require in turn a foundation in Being, but an ontological characteristic of the Being required. (pp. 57–8)[7]

The being that brings nothingness into the world, thereby questioning its own being, is the conscious for-itself. We must not think of consciousness as a sort of empty space within the for-itself. That would be to make it into a passivity. Consciousness is action, the act of detachment, which brings into being a signifying nothingness.

It may be easiest to approach the problem of what consciousness is by asking what consciousness does or what happens when there is consciousness. We will quickly find that terms which at first seem to be different are equivalents: awareness, intentionality, revelation, reflection, nihilation. To be aware of an object is to separate it as an entity from its ground, as one is aware of a tree rather than an undifferentiated, blurred landscape. It is also to be aware that the object is not the same as the awareness. In other words, to be conscious of the tree is to reveal the tree as not the same as the boulder beside it, or the earth in which it is rooted, or the sky above it, and to reveal that the tree is *there*, not within or a part of the perceiving consciousness. Consciousness is a presence *to* its object, a reflection of it. But consciousness is *not* its object. To be aware of something is thus doubly negating. Every intending act is positionally aware of the object it posits and nonpositionally aware of itself as awareness.

Sartre distinguishes the two by putting the second "of" in parentheses: Consciousness of an object is also consciousness (of) itself. To put it another way: All consciousness is consciousness *of* something and at the same time self-consciousness. But we must always remember that there is no substance or content in this self, only the bare fact of the self-awareness. In a sense this consciousness (of) itself *is* the negation. For consciousness could not exist without a separation from its object. If consciousness were one with its object, there would be only the object. When Sartre says that the for-itself nihilates nothingness, he means simply that the act of being conscious is precisely the introduction of the separation of (self)-awareness from its object and of the object from its ground and, of course, the positing of the ground itself as part of the object which the awareness is not.

In this context we are considering the prereflective (that is, nonreflective) consciousness. For Sartre, there is no "I" or "me" in the self of which consciousness is nonpositionally aware, no admixture whatsoever of the personalized, biographical self. Consciousness is subjectivity in that it is awareness (of) being aware as well as awareness of its object, but there is no structured subject. The "I" and the "me" are the result of the work of reflective consciousness, a consciousness that takes its awareness as its direct object. We will find them in the ego but not in translucent prereflective consciousness. Yet we must note that the prereflective consciousness is never confined within a present "now." To be conscious of a particular object (and of not being it) is to be aware that this awareness is not the same as the just past awareness. Consciousness in its very existence is temporal, which means that it is aware of its background of past and future awareness. Sartre speaks of consciousness as a "perpetual flight." We could also call it unbroken activity. Instead of being a succession of "nows," consciousness is awareness (of) itself as always in movement from prior to subsequent awarenesses. On a nonreflective level this means that every conscious intention appears on an internal temporal ground comparable to the spatial ground of a perception. Consciousness is aware (of) itself as revealing in a continuous succession of nihilations.

If we firmly grasp the idea that the introduction of nothingness and intentional consciousness are one and the same, we will not fall into the absurdity of asking whether consciousness *is* nothingness, and if so, how it can act. Insofar as it *is*, consciousness *is* the act of intending objects, which *is* the negation that reveals objects as existing independently of the awareness of them. Consciousness *is* the reflection of objects, and this, in turn, is only the (self)-distancing that Sartre calls nihilation.

EMBODIED CONSCIOUSNESS

Should we then conclude that, as with the Atomists, it is after all being (that is, the body) which acts and not the nothingness? Yes, if by that we mean that consciousness cannot take place without a body, just as it cannot exist without an object. No, if we try to see consciousness as directed by some bodily organ responsible for it. Consciousness is the (self)-directing, not the directed. Consciousness is not the instrument of the body, and Sartre states explicitly that the body is not the instrument of consciousness. Until now we have seen consciousness as not being what it nihilates. But with respect to the body Sartre says that consciousness both is and is not its body. This is because the body is both being-for-itself and being-as-itself. More precisely, the body exists in three dimensions.

The first of these is the body as being-for-itself. Fundamentally, the body is always being-for-itself, whether or not the other two dimensions are being actively realized. The for-itself *is* conscious body. Consciousness exists embodied. Sartre tells us that the body is the facticity of the for-itself, the fact of its being situated in the world. "To say that I have entered into the world, 'come to the world' or that there is a world or that I have a body is one and the same thing" (p. 419). It is the body that individualizes, that serves as a unifying center of reference, which makes it possible to distinguish dream from reality. Sartre forbids us to think of a consciousness as inhabiting a body or as possessing it or as using it, all of which would imply separate existence – and existents – within a for-itself.

Being-for-itself must be wholly body, and it must be wholly consciousness; it cannot be *united* with a body. (p. 404)

The body *is* being-for-itself. And at one point Sartre seems to say that consciousness *is* body:

The body is what consciousness *is*, it is not even anything except body. The rest is nothingness and silence. (p. 434)

Sartre says that "consciousness exists its body." As in its relationship to all other beings, consciousness nihilates the body of which it is aware, distancing itself from it even while dependent on it. The difference here is that body is always present as part of the ground of all intended perceptions, feelings, and so on. Just as "the world" is. The world, in phenomenological terms, is external reality ordered into the unified ground of conscious experience. "To be conscious is always to be conscious of the world, and the world and body are always present to my consciousness, although in different ways" (pp. 439–40).

Experientially, the body is the focus of reference by which consciousness is located in the world. The body is a point of view on the world, but it is the point of view on which I cannot take a point of view. Similarly, it is the master instrument for all other instruments. But it is the instrument we cannot use because we *are* it. Sartre states that "my body is a conscious structure of my consciousness" (p. 434). But this means only that consciousness includes the body as part of the ground of intentional acts, not that body clogs consciousness itself as if with a foreign presence. In sexual desire, for example, consciousness may intentionally try to suffuse itself wholly in body, "incarnating itself," as Sartre puts it. But it can equally well make of its body that which is bypassed, neglected, as a sign is overlooked as itself and treated only as a signifying directive. The body is also "the past," both as the remembered backdrop of other conscious acts and as the being which my consciousness "surpasses."

Insofar as consciousness always "goes beyond" its body, the body must in some way be present as being-in-itself. In both of the other two dimensions this aspect of the body is of central importance. The second dimension is my-body-for-the-Other, though Sartre recognizes that we may discuss it more conveniently as "the Other's body" – that is, a body as it appears to another consciousness. The Other's body (like mine for the Other) is a material object in the world which I perceive from the outside. But it is unlike any other object, for I can understand its movements and utterances only by reference to a controlling subjectivity. Therefore, all my relations to that in-itself are colored by my awareness of the hidden, governing presence of a for-itself. I cannot grasp that for-itself directly, but its undeniable existence dominates my relations with the Other's body. Although Sartre's presentation of the body's second dimension does not dwell on the human possibilities inherent in it, I will try to show a bit later that it is of great significance in other contexts. For the moment I will merely point out that it is within the compass of this dimension that any genuine personal encounter must occur. It is here that the subject–object conflict of consciousness can be, to a significant degree, replaced by empathy and reciprocity.

If the body-as-being-for-itself corresponds roughly to first person experience and if the other's body at least allows for the "you" of the second person, Sartre's third bodily dimension, my-body-as-known-by-the-Other is wholly third person. Here the body comes close to being pure in-itself. It is in this dimension, for example, that I acknowledge my body as a thing capable of being diagnosed as infected, diseased, and so forth, comparably to other body-things. It represents to my consciousness a vulnerability, dependent on external circumstances out of my control.

In the relation of consciousness to its body we can see at close hand the original relation of the for-itself to the in-itself. Sartre writes:

The for-itself is the in-itself losing itself as in-itself in order to found itself as consciousness. Thus consciousness holds within itself its own being-as-consciousness [i.e., its (self)-awareness], and since it is its own nihilation [i.e., takes itself as not being what it intends], it can refer only to itself; but *that which* is nihilated in consciousness – though we cannot call it the foundation of consciousness – is the contingent in-itself. (p. 130)

"The in-itself is what the for-itself was *before*" (p. 198). Similarly, the body cannot be called the foundation of consciousness because it does not determine consciousness nor make it what it is. But the body is always present as that which consciousness nihilates, goes beyond. Thus to say that my body is my past is to make an ontological statement as well as to recognize a psychological reality.

CONSCIOUSNESS AND ITS EXTERNAL OBJECTS

Consciousness reveals being, is dependent on being, does not create being. Sartre states this emphatically in the Introduction to *Being and Nothingness.* Yet in the chapter that follows he says that "man's relation to Being is that he can modify it" (pp. 59–60). In other contexts he discusses ways in which the intentions of consciousness are inscribed in matter. And the ego, which he tells us is being-in-itself, is actually the product – the creation – of consciousness. Rather than accuse Sartre of inconsistency, we should recognize that according to context, he uses the word "being" (sometimes but not always synonymously with being-in-itself) with three different referents.

First comes that being which we meet on page 1 of *Being and Nothingness,* that being which is "disclosed to us by some kind of immediate access – boredom, nausea, etc." This being is what is meant when we say that anything *is* existentially. Even consciousness must be in some way caught up in this being, in the sense that we can say that Descartes's consciousness was but is no longer. In the ordinary sense of the words, we can say that there is nothing that is not included in this being. But again we must be careful. For to be precise, the being that is the object of consciousness cannot be said to include nothingness. This is the being of which Sartre tells us that we can conclude only that "Being is. Being is in itself. Being is what it is." (p. 29) Sartre's choice of nausea and boredom as examples of ways of access to being is not random. Both are major motifs of Sartre's novel *Nausea* and serve equally, though differently, to disclose to Roquentin the contingence of all existents, including himself. Nausea is the recognition by consciousness of its embodiment, the realization that its existence is dependent on body. It is consciousness's apprehension of itself as *having to* reveal being, as existing only as an endless activity of revealing. In boredom consciousness apprehends itself as freedom without a given that it is *for,* a freedom without a goal. Or, to put it differently, the for-itself grasps the fact that making itself be is its only goal. In both of these primitive encounters, being is revealed to the for-itself as both the condition and the necessity of revelation.

With respect to being-in-itself as the external, material universe, consciousness's revelation is also a discrimination, an ordering. Consciousness's intending of being becomes a focus on object and ground. The world "is revealed simultaneously as a synthetic totality and as a purely additive collection of all the 'thises' " (p. 253). With respect to consciousness as simply the observer of individual things, Sartre does not greatly differ from his phenomenological predecessor except in his care to avoid what he considers to be a Kantian taint in the later work of Husserl. In perceiving a lemon, for example, Sartre would argue that the reality of the lemon is its being, not its essence, and that I confront this being directly. All of the lemon is present to me in each of its appearances to consciousness, even though it is not exhausted by its appearances. Similarly, all of the lemon is present in each of its qualities, whether I focus on one of those (color, taste, smell) rather than the others or combine them in a process of abstracting that enables me to establish the essence of "lemon." This kind of perception of an object is a nontemporal revelation except insofar as awareness of the object as already there or as continuing to be there is an extension of consciousness's own sense of "before" and "after."

There are other occasions when consciousness projects into the world its own temporality, thus introducing something new into being. It is in connection with destruction, in particular, that Sartre sounds most like an idealist. Destruction, he says flatly, does not exist except through consciousness. This is because only a consciousness can introduce the negation establishing that what was is no longer. Sartre's explanation of potentiality shows still more clearly a reality that exists in being-itself although revealed by a consciousness. We look at a clouded sky and say, "It is going to rain." The for-itself reads the threat or promise in the leaden clouds. But apart from the for-itself there is no potentiality. If restricted to the present, there is only a measurable humidity, for example. The temporalizing consciousness goes beyond what is not yet but may be in the future, thus revealing a potentiality as in truth existing in these clouds, one that consciousness could not have revealed in yesterday's sun-filled sky. Understanding Sartre's view of potentiality may help us grasp more easily what he means by saying that the for-itself brings nothingness into the world. For in addition to the fact that all intentionality evokes a nothingness in the double sense that consciousness makes itself not be its objects and determines one object as not being either another or its own surrounding ground, Sartre declares that there are, so to speak, "little pools of non-being" outside, in the world (p. 53). These he calls *négatités*, negativities – such things as absence, distance, regret. These, like quality and quantity, destruction, and potentiality, are in the world but revealed by consciousness.

In the relations to being-in-itself that I have mentioned so far, the terms "consciousness" and "for-itself" could be used interchangeably. This is because the revealing has modified being solely in terms of determination, mentally. Material modification of the world can be carried out only by a being-for-itself. Consciousness as such cannot, for instance, eat an apple, but it would be just as wrong to speak of the body eating without or in separation from consciousness. It is, of course, the body-as-being-for-itself that eats. As for the apple, by itself it is merely an indeterminate being-in-itself. This is shown by the fact that one can on occasion ignore its edible quality and use it as an ornament, a paperweight, or a ball. I can do the same with a small stone. But in all these cases, I will discover that the apple, but not the stone, is perishable, and this characteristic of the apple does not depend on me. Material things have a "coefficient of adversity," of resistance (p. 619). One cannot do just whatever one wants with being-in-itself.

If I have belabored the obvious here, it is to point up the basic thrust of Sartre's attempt in *Being and Nothingness* to find a position midway between Berkeleian idealism, which argued that objects exist only insofar as they are perceived, and Cartesian realism, which claimed that the mind somehow holds within itself representations of objects existing external to it. Consciousness does not create material being, and it is not – as consciousness – determined by it. But in revealing being, consciousness introduces differentiation and significance. Consciousness bestows meaning on being.

Finally, Sartre uses "being-in-itself" (and sometimes just "being") in a third way, hinted at in the Introduction, fully discussed in later sections of *Being and Nothingness* and, indeed, in most of his philosophical works, both before and after that book. "Being-in-itself" is a term that can be applied to anything whatsoever that is the object of consciousness. Suddenly the domain of being-in-itself is infinitely enlarged, and we find a complex relation of consciousness to being, one that results in the production of a distinctive type of being-in-itself, one that so totally reflects the modification imposed by intentional consciousness that we may say consciousness has created it. Naturally, this is not a material being created ex nihilo as if by a magical fiat on the part of consciousness. Rather it is those kinds of being in which psychic overlay and matter have been melded in varying proportions. Included here are worked-matter, the work of art (which, strictly speaking, is a special kind of worked-matter), and the ego. Oreste Pucciani has called the first two of these beings psychic in-itselfs.[8] I would extend the term also to the third. (Sartre, indeed, says specifically that the ego is the product of consciousness and that it is being-in-itself.)

Worked-matter, first mentioned by Sartre in the *Critique*, derives from his discussion of the practical engagement of the for-itself with being-in-itself, something missing and badly needed in *Being and Nothingness*. He points out that the human organism is able to inter-act with the material environment only insofar as it makes itself matter. In need of external physical matter (air, water, food), the human organism takes on an inorganic dimension; in turn, the organism imposes on the environment a structure that reflects the organic. The body-for-itself makes itself a tool in order to render external things instrumental to its needs. The body, made tool, fashions tool-things to work in matter. There occurs a "transubstantiation."[9] The thing becomes human to the exact degree that the human becomes a thing. Obviously, we live in a world of worked-matter that is psychic in-itself. Everyday examples abound. A gun, to anyone except a baby or a primitive, is not an undefined material thing; it holds inscribed in it intentions, possibilities, and meanings. A ticket is a ticket rather than a pasteboard rectangle only insofar as it is supported by consciousness, but you cannot get into the theater without it. By means of worked-matter we individually and collectively carve out our being in the world by our concrete actions or praxis. The world of worked-matter, which Sartre dubs the practico-inert, may steal my action from me. This may happen indirectly as in the numerous instances when what I have put into the world is used by others against me. Or it may come as the consequence of my actions in the natural environment. A collective example today of this kind of "counterfinality"[10] would be the "greenhouse effect." The necessity for us to objectify our projects in matter Sartre views as a permanent threat of alienation, certain to be realized to greater or lesser degree. Through material objectification the for-itself becomes the victim of its own devising. Nevertheless, it is only through inscribing its intentions in matter that the for-itself can have a history. "It is not the act of understanding that fixes meanings; it is Being."[11] And here "Being" equals "matter." Worked-matter finally includes all of the human stamped physical and cultural environment (bus routes,

institutions, customs, and so on) in which we live. It comes closest
to being predominantly psychic in what Sartre terms the "objective
Mind" (or Spirit, *l'Esprit objectif*), which is reminiscent of but by no
means the same as Hegel's objective Spirit. It is the cluster of ideas,
beliefs, attitudes, and the like that dominate a given area in a given
era. It includes literature and the other arts along with the definition
of art. But this point brings us to a special category of psychic in-itself
that is significantly differentiated from other forms of worked-
matter – the work of art.

The work of art combines not only matter and psychic intention
but the juxtaposition of the real and the unreal, the tangible and the
imaginary.

In *The Psychology of Imagination* Sartre had argued that the aesthetic object is unreal, but that as an unreal object it exists so long as
and only when it is brought into being by a consciousness. The events
and characters of a novel exist only as they are sustained by the act of
reading. In *The Family Idiot* Sartre elaborated still further his distinction between the printed book, painted canvas, or whatever and the
aesthetic object evoked by it. The former is "a real and permanent
center of derealization."[12] It differs from ordinary worked-matter in
that it has been designed not primarily to modify or to elicit action in
the real world but to cause whoever encounters it to create unreal
images. Sartre applies a new term to such things as Hamlet or Venus.
They are "social imaginaries," and they have real effects. For those
who created them, the results may even be counterfinalities – for
example, the death sentence passed against Salman Rushdie, or the
fact that for Flaubert the success of *Madame Bovary* was based on a
realistic reading of the novel which he had never intended. For readers, too, literature can be dangerous. Once a social imaginary has
been introduced into the psyche, it exists there – as an unreal in the
beginning, but, as Sartre has pointed out, memory often confuses real
and imagined experiences. And sometimes the latter, more than the
former, determine how the world appears to us. The ego as the unity
of the psychic will reflect both.

THE REALITY AND ROLE OF THE EGO

Any well-read student of philosophy is aware that Sartre's independence from Husserl began with his denial of the existence of a tran-

scendental ego. Edmund Husserl was the founder of the phenomenological movement, one of the philosophical traditions out of which
existentialism evolved. The transendental ego, he believed, was an
innate I-subject present in all conscious activity, contributing to the
structuring of our experience. For Sartre, consciousness exhibits no
trace of such a transcendental ego. A fortiori consciousness is not
inhabited by the empirical ego, popularly thought of as a determined
and determining personality structure. There is always a separation
between consciousness and ego.

What exactly, properly understood, are the role and the reality of
the ego in Sartre's ontology? The fact is that the question of the
reality of the ego, as Sartre conceived it, is problematic. The role of
the ego was never fully spelled out by him, and its importance has
certainly not been recognized by Sartre's critics. Consequently, I
think it is advisable to determine what is implicit as well as explicit
in what he has written about the ego and to see how the ego as
presented in his first essay on the subject fits in with his later discussion of other aspects of our psychic life.

The Transcendence of the Ego[13] is very clear as to how the ego
comes into being. It has been constituted by a consciousness reflecting on its own activities, ordering them in terms of imposed meanings and unifying them. The ego is fabricated out of the psychic
residue of earlier experiences, and it is their unity. But it is consciousness that establishes this unity. Most important, consciousness *is
not* the ego. The ego is not inside consciousness but outside it.
Consciousness is separated from the ego in the same kind of
nihilating withdrawal that consciousness effects with respect to all
of its objects. The ego is the object of consciousness.

Sartre describes the formation of the ego by listing its components. Consciousness makes the ego by unifying its own actions
(past and presently projected), its qualities (more exactly, the qualities that the actions seem to indicate), and its states. The actions
carry, of course, the interpretations imposed by the consciousness
that initiated them. Qualities are, as it were, the labels consciousness attaches to its accumulated acts. A state (to use Sartre's examples of love and hatred) is a psychic structure constituted by consciousness's resolve to impose a continuity between past, present,
and future affective responses to another person. As such, love or
hatred, in contrast to spontaneous impulses of erotic desire, tender-

ness, or repugnance, stands midway between a vow and a latent charge since it is held to exist even when consciousness does not hold it in a field of awareness, has not at the moment "awakened" it. Nevertheless, Sartre says that the state is real.

Is the ego real? The short answer is definite enough: The ego is real, but it is not what it seems – at least not as it is popularly regarded. But if we try to establish in exactly what way it is real, the answer is surprisingly difficult, particularly if we limit ourselves to what Sartre said in *The Transcendence of the Ego*. Placed side by side, some of his statements in that work appear to be, if not contradictory, at least somewhat confusing. Consider the following:

Besides telling us that the ego is the unity of actions, states, and qualities, and that it is "nothing outside of the concrete totality of states and actions it supports" (p. 74), Sartre enlarges the concept by saying that the ego "constitutes the ideal and indirect (noematic) unity of the infinite series of our reflected consciousnesses" (p. 60). But this "ideal" unity is real. The ego "has a concrete type of existence, undoubtedly different from the existence of mathematical truths, of meanings, or of spatio-temporal beings, but no less real" (p. 52). Sartre tells us that the ego is opaque. It is like a pebble, but not like a stone one can pick up and examine; rather it is like a pebble seen indistinctly, at the bottom of the stream, beneath the moving water (pp. 51–2). Again, the ego resembles a melody that must be supported by a consciousness. (Incidentally, Roquentin in *Nausea* says explicitly that the melody is not an existent but has being, like the mathematical circle.) Finally, the ego exists outside, like the world (pp. 105–6) or, as Sartre will put it later, on the side of being-in-itself. But disconcertingly Sartre says also that the ego appears only when one is not looking at it (p. 88).

We may note that we find in these statements hints that in some respects the status of the ego has some things in common with that of each of the other two kinds of psychic in-itself, as well as sharp dissimilarities. The ego's reality is not wholly unlike that of worked-matter. Sartre, to be sure, compares it to a pebble, which is a thing in nature, but his point is to emphasize that the ego is external to consciousness, which cannot get inside it. This is true also of the worked-matter that makes up the practico-inert. The ego is a psychic being, the result of consciousness' "working" its own past. Its qualities exist for consciousness to focus on in somewhat the same way that qualities are present in any man-made object – revealed, abstracted, ordered. But contrary to what the Freudians might argue, the unified psychic cannot take on a life of its own. It cannot by itself turn back on a consciousness as a counterfinality. Nor is the ego subject to deviation at the hand of other persons and the forces of nature. The reality of the ego is much closer to that of the aesthetic object. It is like a melody that is composed out of separate sounds but is heard as a pattern. (We may note also that the melody does not create itself.) But the ego, even more than social imaginaries, is subject to change, not by others, but by its author. At this point I think we can more easily understand how Sartre can compare the ego both to a melody and to a pebble at the bottom of the stream. For it is in one sense an object out there, with a certain opaqueness, something that we can't get inside of. At the same time it must be constituted by a consciousness, like any unreal social imaginary. We can understand why Sartre can call it both a real existence and an ideal unity.

There still remains that final pair of seemingly contradictory statements: that the ego appears only indirectly when one is not looking at it, and that my ego – like, say, Bob's – is out there in the world, an object for each of us and with no privileged access for me. Sartre explains the first statement by pointing out that the ego disappears if consciousness confronts it directly because such a consciousness is nonreflective and the ego is the product of a reflective consciousness. But when Bob and I each look at each of our egos out there in the world, do we, each one, have to be in the reflective mode? Or do I look at Bob's ego nonreflectively and at my own reflectively? If so, there is no longer the same status or the same access for the two egos. (Sartre never denies, of course, that for me my ego offers a greater feeling of intimacy, but that is only because my ego and its components are more familiar to me, as my house would be as compared with Bob's, unless I have also lived there.)

Departing here from what Sartre has said explicitly, but without, I think, distorting it, let us look more closely and with the aid of what he has written in other contexts. If I look at my ego in the same way that I look at Bob's or he at mine, I am in fact assuming the point of view of the Other. Recall the third dimension of the body – my body as known by the Other and my own assumption of the role of Other when I try to see what's wrong with my sore toe, or observe along with the doctor the abnormal condition of my stomach projected on the screen. I think it is only very rarely that I try to adopt the point of view of the Other on my own ego, but it may happen occasionally – as when I look at my old diary to see what kind of person wrote it, or try to describe to Bob the sort of person I am, which I do by means of anecdote and a rehearsal of my past states and revealed qualities. I believe that in both these instances we are dealing with past egos as established by a reflective consciousness, and I think that Sartre would have to allow this. But the present consciousness is non-reflective. If I look at – or for – Bob's ego, the parallel with the second dimension of the body, my body for the Other or the Other's body for me, is still more striking. Just as I interpret every bodily gesture of Bob's "in situation," so I may try to discover in his behavior the expression of psychic states and qualities and their unifying theme or ego. With patience, intelligent empathy, and good luck, I may nonreflectively grasp Bob's ego, at least as clearly as I see the pebble beneath the water. But this, as much as any observed movement of his body, points ultimately to the out-of-reach consciousness that has effected the discernible psychic unity of Bob as I find him now. The case is the same with respect to my own ego, if I look at it reflectively.

Can we say that there is any parallel between the situation of the ego and the body's first dimension? I think there is, but we cannot press it too far. For the first dimension is the body as being-for-itself, and the ego is being-in-itself. Still I think that just as Sartre says that consciousness exists its body, so we may say that consciousness must live its relation to its ego. I believe that it is in this respect that Sartre says that the ego as the object of a reflective consciousness appears when one is not looking at it. Consciousness, of course, has not created its body, and we saw that for consciousness, the body is the past. Consciousness does create the ego, but here we should keep the present tense. For the ego changes as consciousness changes it. That is why the ego is elusive but not illusive.

Before we try to pinpoint what the role of the ego may properly be said to be, I want to raise two questions, one possibly a bit frivolous, the other serious and important.

Can we meaningfully speak of an ego as being true or false? When I asked myself this, I somewhat surprised myself by concluding that one could. As I said at the beginning, the ego is fabricated by consciousness. I used the word "fabricated" advisedly because of its ambiguity. As the product of consciousness, the ego has indubitably been made by consciousness and is what it is. Whatever kind of unity consciousness has imposed on its worked psychic matter, this unity is truly what consciousness has in fact constituted. But if a for-itself has lived and is living a life in bad faith, then the ego can hardly be other than a fabrication of self-deception, a false ego.

My point will be clearer and perhaps more worthy of consideration if we ask in connection with it a subsidiary question: What is the relation between the ego and the Sartrean fundamental project? If the fundamental project is the for-itself's chosen orientation toward being, its way of making itself be, its nonreflective creation and pursuit of values, the process whereby it chooses to make itself, a "plan aware of itself," to use Sartre's own expression,[14] then the ego is the crystallized reflection of what consciousness considers or imagines its fundamental project to be. Or if this is going too far, then the ego is consciousness's interpretation of the traces left by the fundamental project.

A second and more consequential question involving truth and falsity concerns not the quality of the ego that a consciousness may create, but what a for-itself conceives to be the proper relation between consciousness and the ego it has produced. With regard to the wrong attitude, Sartre has been so explicit that there is no need to speculate. The false assumption is the one that is most commonly held. We reverse the true order of the ego's formation and assume that an underlying ego-pattern (like a genetic code) generates our psychic states, and so on, which as givens determine the nature of our conscious choices and the behavior consequent to them. Actually, the ego does nothing. Its apparent spontaneity is part of the self-deception. When Sartre speaks of the ego as seeming to us to produce results, he means that we want to use the same incorrect language that novelists – and ordinary people, too – use when they say that love or hatred *causes* somebody to do something.

How then, if we are willing to accept Sartre's phenomenological description, *should* consciousness live with its ego? Sartre says not only that the ego is the product of a reflective consciousness, but that it is the result of impure reflection. The connotations of "impure" suggest that somehow the ego is tainted, that it is something which ought not to have been brought into existence. If that is so, then, indeed, we are all guilty of original sin and there is no Grace to save us. But need this be the case? A key concept of Sartre's that is relevant here is "bad faith" (*la mauvaise foi*). This is a special form of self-deception, a lie to oneself, by which a person shifts conveniently from one to the other of the two ways in which we can say that a human being "is." As free self-consciousness, we are not made-to-be by determined or instinctual forces, not like waterfalls or butterflies. We are not destined; we are self-determining. Yet since we exist as conscious bodies, we interact with the world and are responsible for what we do in and to it. Obviously, if we regard the ego and its components as things that make us what we are, we have fallen into one of the traps of bad faith by denying our transcendence, by refusing to acknowledge that our being is not like that of things in the world. But the second aspect of bad faith, as Sartre presents it, lies in refusing to accept responsibility for our facticity; that is, by pretending that since we are free, we can no longer be defined by our actions at all – though I could steal without being a thief, even at the moment when I am stealing. Nonreflective responses are not the only expressions of our freedom. Perhaps a consciousness in good faith is *obliged* to practice the kind of self-reflection that produces the ego. In an interview in 1971 Sartre said that pure reflection is achieved by a critical praxis we perform on ourselves, one that he had never described.[15] However that may be, his discussion of pure reflection in *Being and Nothingness* seemed to indicate that what pure reflection reveals – glimpsed over the shoulder, as it were, and only as a pseudo-object – is our perpetually active, impersonal intentional consciousness. He appeared to refer not to a philosophical method but rather to a more common sort of experience, one that I personally find comes most often in fatigue, slight insobriety, or a sudden return to focusing on immediate surroundings after intense involvement in sustained nonreflective activity focused elsewhere. It manifests itself in a feeling that what is happening now is no more real than what was happening yesterday or will be tomorrow and that at the core of the experience there is no stable and enduring "I." To interpret pure reflection as the evidence of the presence in us of an impersonal, though individual, consciousness, is for Sartre both correct phenomenological procedure and the revelation of our existential freedom. It is this that makes it possible for human reality to effect even a drastic modification of the fundamental project. But I do not see how it would be possible or even meaningful to effect a change of project without the ego. Whatever the catalytic event precipitating a new choice of oneself or – if you prefer – of one's way of being, any enduring change must surely involve the kind of reflection that takes a point of view on what the activities of a free consciousness have been. Temporal consciousness does in fact, Sartre claims, exist as a perpetual totalizing of its experiences. Therefore, the ego as their ideal unity must be always conceivable for a consciousness, though a consciousness in good faith will perpetually recreate it – just as we recreate our pasts in projecting our futures.

Inasmuch as the for-itself, which each one of us is, is described as a pursuit of being and a self-making, the image of what seems to be the self that has been made up until now must be among the more significant data of our conscious life. Sartre says that by my actions I carve out my being in the world. We can read this in either of two ways: either that by my actions in the world I carve out my being, or that by my actions I carve out my (hyphenated) being-in-the-world. In either case this is my final self-image, though, like any inscription in matter, the image is precarious and vulnerable to defacement by other persons. Still, as a self-image it is legitimate as contrasted with "I am what I possess," or "I am my professional title." The difference is the same as that between a consciousness's authentic relation to its ego and one in bad faith.

At this point I should like to make another comparative reference to Sartre's ontology of the body. Sartre writes, "We could define the body as *the contingent form which is assumed by the necessity of my contingency*" (p. 408). It was not necessary that there should be this consciousness in this body, but it is necessary that a consciousness should have – or more properly should exist – a body. In the same way, consciousness need not create or sustain any particular ego, but it must make *an* ego – at least, if a person is to lead anything at all resembling a normal life. This conclusion will be reinforced if we consider the role of the ego apart from its susceptibility to utilization as a device in bad faith. Consider once again the Other's body for me and the Other's ego for me.

In the posthumous *Cahiers pour une morale* Sartre claims that authentic love, which no longer wants to appropriate the Other as an object, respects the Other's subjectivity, but does not originate in direct response to the Other's consciousness as a free upsurge. Specifically, he writes:

Freedom as such is not lovable, for it is nothing but negation and productivity. Pure being, in its total exteriority of indifference, is not *lovable* either. But the Other's body is lovable inasmuch as it is freedom in the dimension of being.[16]

Since Sartre speaks here of love, not simply sexual desire, it is the Other's body as the expression of his psyche, or as we say more naturally of his personality, that I love. And when one feels that what one loves in the Other is not this or that trait as manifested in particular actions, but somehow the Other's person, it is the ego that is intended, along with the free consciousness that created it. Even outside the erotic context, as in friendship, it is my feeling toward the self which the Other is making that makes me wish to make room in my own project for his or hers, so as to shelter or lend assistance to it.

Obviously, as the Other is to me, so am I to the Other. I am aware of this, and insofar as I am not merely trying to offer to the Other an artificial self to be admired, it is the quality of my being that I try to communicate, not the abstract reality of my impersonal consciousness. "Why is it not my fundamental project?" someone may ask. The project is, of course, the ultimate reference point, but I myself cannot grasp it except as it has been reflected and objectified and inevitably, to some degree, transformed. At best I can try to reveal to the Other only what I believe that I have made of myself. As I remarked earlier, some sense of the sort of ego I have structured is necessary if I am to change significantly, that is, to assume responsibility for my life. Sartre himself acknowledged as much in the *War Diaries*. After concluding that his earlier attempt to identify authenticity with pure spontaneity was mistaken, he began to stress instead the importance of taking one's own actions and situation into account and engaging oneself. This, he concluded, did not entail introducing once again a determining ego. But he recognized the importance of the personal aspect. He wrote:

Does that mean I'm going to allow the Self back in? No, certainly not. But though the ipseity or totality of the for-itself is not the Self, it's nevertheless the *person*. I'm in the course of learning, basically, to be a person.[17]

If the ego is the product of consciousness, it has at least the value of a creative work in which external ingredients display the stamp of consciousness. Consider what it would mean to be a consciousness without an ego. In a very modified form, one could perhaps live as a sort of weather vane, creating no personal value system, certainly not responsibly and not very meaningfully. If taken to its literal and logical extreme, the condition of conscious life without an ego could only be pathological.[18]

CONCLUSION

Sartre's ontology is phenomenological – that is, descriptive – as indicated by the subtitle of *Being and Nothingness*. It does not ask *why* being should be or why there should be consciousness. In Sartre's nonteleological universe, purpose and goal appear only with the for-itself, which Sartre describes as "a plan aware of itself."[19] One might still ask *why* consciousness emerges at a particular stage of evolution, why there should be consciousness or a for-itself (and here, I believe, the term might be extended to nonhuman beings). Interestingly enough, although Sartre tacitly assumes the validity of some theory of biological evolution, he holds that the answer to this "why" should be sought, not in scientific explanations, but in metaphysical hypotheses. He himself is careful to avoid any taint of metaphysical speculation except for one never fully developed suggestion. This stems from his discussion of motion, in *Being and Nothingness*. In motion (when it is revealed to a consciousness, of course) Sartre sees a peculiar property of objects that is difficult to classify ontologically. Motion has a hybrid sort of being, one that "cannot be derived ontologically from the nature of the For-itself, nor from its fundamental relation to the In-itself, nor from what we can discover originally in the phenomenon of being" (pp. 285–6). Sartre advises the metaphysician to investigate motion as a clue for understanding the first emergence of being-for-itself from being-in-itself:

In particular it is the task of the metaphysician to decide whether motion is or is not a first "attempt" on the part of the in-itself to found itself, and to determine what are the relations of motion as a "disorder of being" with the for-itself as a more profound disorder pushed to nihilation. (p. 790)

In my opinion, reasonable hypotheses as to the why of consciousness are more likely to be found by persons capable of bringing
together the discoveries of evolutionary biology and the insights of a
phenomenological-existentialist study of consciousness as an epiphenomenon (though without the reductionist overtones which
that term usually carries). It is interesting, however, to note that
Sartre would search for affiliations between consciousness and
those things in nature that are bound up with movement. Whatever
else it may or may not be, consciousness is activity.

Consciousness is not a being but the activity whereby a human
being recasts an impersonal universe in the form of the human life
world. Its revelation of being is a creative revealing, but consciousness never becomes its creations. It is the interplay of the structuring by consciousness and its free transcending of structures that
provides the unity of Sartre's philosophy.

NOTES

1 Jean-Paul Sartre, *Being and Nothingness. An Essay on Phenomenological
  Ontology*, tr. Hazel E. Barnes (New York: Washington Square Press, 1972).
  Unless clearly indicated in the context or in the Notes, all page references
  refer to this text. In a few instances I have slightly modified my earlier
  translation but never so as to change the meaning. Sartre is inconsistent
  in his capitalization of ontological terms. Here I have chosen not to capitalize any of them except in quotations.
2 Jean-Paul Sartre, *Critique of Dialectical Reason. Vol. I. Theory of Practical Ensembles*, tr. Alan Sheridan-Smith, ed. Jonathan Ree (Atlantic Highlands, N.J.: Humanities Press, 1976), pp. 180–1. I have discussed Sartre's
  philosophy as a materialism in an article, "Sartre as Materialist," *The
  Philosophy of Jean-Paul Sartre*, ed. Paul Arthur Schilpp (La Salle, Ill.:
  Open Court, 1981), pp. 661–84. That article also contained material on
  Sartre's view of the body and of motion that is partially repeated here.
3 Barnes, "Sartre as Materialist," p. 40.
4 Sartre's relevant terms in French are *néant* (nothingness), *néantir* (to
  nihilate), *neantisation* (nihilation).
5 *Critique*, p. 81.
6 The wording is that of Gerald E. Myers, summing up James's position on
  the relation of brain and consciousness. *William James: His Life and
  Thought* (New Haven, Conn.: Yale University Press, 1986), p. 55.

7 Christina Howells takes this passage as evidence that Sartre does in fact hypostatize consciousness as a nothingness. But the "being" referred to is the for-itself – i.e., human being – not consciousness. To give ontological status to the nothingness that consciousness as an activity brings into the world is not, in my opinion, to hypostatize it. "Sartre and Negative Theology," *The Modern Language Review* (July 1981): 552.

8 Oreste Pucciani points out that the concept of worked matter provides the necessary link between Sartre's rudimentary aesthetic theory in *The Psychology of Imagination* and its full development in *The Family Idiot*. "*Cet objet sartrien neuf: 'Un centre réel et permanent d'irréalisation'*," *Dalhousie French Studies* (October 1983): 84–97.

9 *Critique*, p. 178.

10 *Critique*, pp. 124 and 162.

11 *Critique*, p. 182. I have somewhat modified Sheridan's translation.

12 Jean-Paul Sartre, *The Family Idiot*, tr. Carol Cosman (Chicago: University of Chicago Press, 1987), vol. II, p. 130.

13 Jean-Paul Sartre, *The Transcendence of the Ego. An Existentialist Theory of Consciousness* (New York: Farrar, Straus and Giroux, n.d.).

14 Jean-Paul Sartre, *Existentialism*, tr. Bernard Frechtman (New York: Philosophical Library, 1947), p. 19.

15 "On The Idiot of the Family," an interview with Michel Contat and Michel Rybalka, in *Life/Situations/Essays Written and Spoken*, tr. Paul Auster and Lydia Davis (New York: Pantheon Books, 1977), p. 122.

16 Jean-Paul Sartre, *Cahiers pour une morale* (Paris: Gallimard, 1983), p. 523. For a fuller discussion of the ego in this connection, see my article, "The Role of the Ego in Reciprocity," *Sartre Alive*, edited by Ronald Aronson and Adrian van den Hoven (Detroit: Wayne State University Press, 1991), pp. 151–9.

17 Jean-Paul Sartre, *The War Diaries of Jean-Paul Sartre, November 1939/ March 1940*, tr. Quintin Hoare (New York: Pantheon Books, 1984), pp. 324–5.

18 Freudian and post-Freudian psychologists have held that loss or weakness of ego is frequently the key to serious psychic disorders, but their claim is accompanied by mechanistic and biological implications to which Sartre strongly objected. One could easily adapt the Sartrean view of the ego to the study of pathological psychic manifestations while still holding that an unstructured free consciousness, not the personalized psyche, remains as the core of our human being.

19 *Existentialism*, p. 19.

2 Role-playing: Sartre's transformation of Husserl's phenomenology

INTENTIONAL ANALYSIS

The title of one of Sartre's essays, *Questions of Method*, is perhaps a sufficient reminder of how remote from us he was as a philosopher. Questions of methodology, Charles Taylor long ago pointed out, are "usually thought to be a waste of time" in England, where most philosophers prefer to adopt "the stance of the inarticulate gardener with a green thumb being interrogated by the agronomist – I just plants it and it grows."[1]

Sartre takes over from Husserl's phenomenology two methodological procedures, "intentional analysis" and "eidetic analysis." Intentional analysis is a procedure for analyzing consciousness with respect to its "meaning-endowing" acts, by which I identify something as being what it is. Thus I am conscious of it as "a triangle," as "a table," as "anger." Phenomenological analysis is *in-tentional* in the etymological sense that it follows out the identifying reference of the "act" to the object "aimed at" as the "target" of the reference.[2] Sartre's dedication to intentional reference is manifest in the succession of two titles: Having reviewed traditional theories of the imagination under the title *L'Imagination*, he conducts his own analysis under the title *L'Imaginaire*. The difference in title indicates a change from the traditional analysis in which the imagination is one of the faculties of the mind, to an intentional analysis in which characteristics of the imagination are determined by following out the reference to the imaginary object. I shall offer an example of this intentional analysis as soon as I have brought out how an intentional analysis is also "eidetic."

First, however, it should be observed that phenomenology, as the outcome of employing an intentional analysis, should not be confused with the once fashionable epistemological position in Anglo-American philosophy, "phenomenalism," in accordance with which what are immediately given as the objects of my consciousness are sense data. These are merely subjective, and Husserl protests against phenomenalism on behalf of the objectivity of what an intentional act of consciousness immediately refers to: "I do not see color-sensations but colored things, I do not hear tone-sensations but the song of the singer, etc."[3]

EIDETIC ANALYSIS

So far we have remained at the lower level of a phenomenological analysis. The objects that come within its scope as an "eidetic analysis," are not only the intentional objects I have been citing, but at a higher level "essences." (*Eidos* is Greek for "essence.") When the phenomenologist follows out an act of intentional reference to its object, he is not interested in the particular table that he may be remembering in his parents' dining room or in his anger at government policies. These are just examples. What he would analyze by analyzing such examples are the "essences" they exemplify: the essential structure of an act of perception, of an act of remembering, and so forth, but above all of an act of intentional reference itself, in its correlation with its object. Even the term "act" picks out an essential structure, abstracting from the vagaries of particular psychological activities.

Anglo-American philosophy sometimes accommodates some version of intentional reference, and often relies on examples and on counterexamples to advance an analysis. But it is intolerant of essences. Gilbert Ryle was more exposed to Continental philosophy than most of his generation, and he comments on Husserl that the "intuition of essences [was not] the sort of accomplishment of which any Anglo-Saxon could boast with a straight face."[4]

Let us try to straighten our faces. The claim conveyed by the term "essence" is that any example Husserl uses exemplifies what it is an example of: I cannot perceive, and so on without concomitantly recognizing that I am perceiving, and so on.

Sartre has characterized his major work, *L'Être et le néant* (*Being and Nothingness*) as an "eidetic analysis of self-deception."[5] But the essential structure of self-deception is complicated. So I begin with a prominent earlier effort of Sartre's – to distinguish the essential structure of an act of imagination from that of perception, by following out the intentional references.

This procedure is illustrated by one of Sartre's examples. If I am standing in front of the Pantheon in Paris, it is an object that I can perceive. I can observe its columns and acquire knowledge as to how many they are. But if I am in London, imagining the Pantheon, I cannot determine the number of its columns by observing the object I am imagining. Of course, if I already know how many columns it has, as a result of having previously observed it (and I also happen to be skillful at concocting images), I may be able to incorporate this knowledge in my image of the Pantheon. This does not, however, render my now imagining it bona fide observation, for I am not acquiring any knowledge from imagining the object. My previously acquired knowledge has already been expended in constituting my image. Such pseudo-observation (Sartre's term, which he derives from Husserl, is "quasi-observation") is an essential characteristic of the process of imagining, as opposed to the bona fide observation that is essentially characteristic of the process of perception.[6]

If phenomenology is sometimes confused with phenomenalism, because its commitment to intentional analysis is overlooked, it is also often confused with introspection, because its commitment to eidetic analysis is overlooked. Introspection is a familiar, rudimentary way of compiling empirical facts. I ask myself, "Do I love her?" Usually I attempt to answer the question by introspection: I did miss her on Monday, but on Tuesday she slipped my mind, and on Wednesday I was susceptible to another woman. As a compilation of such facts (positive and negative) my introspection is comparable to my observing the Pantheon, and to the more rigorous inductive procedure of the empirical scientist. Like him, I proceed from the particular facts to whatever generalization they may warrant. Presumably presiding over this procedure in my example is some general sense as to what love is. This general sense may be merely, largely, or entirely, the outcome of previous crude inductive generalizations by myself or others. It is quite possible that love is so variable a phenomenon from one individual to another, from one culture to another, that an eidetic analysis cannot arrive at an essence – at what love is essentially. It may be more feasible to determine what a higher level phenomenon such as an emotion is – as Sartre tries to do in his *Esquisse d'une théorie des emotions*. It may be even more feasible to determine what an act of perception or imagination is. But the crucial instance is intentional reference itself. As Husserl argues, "In perception something is perceived, in imagination, something imagined . . . in desire something is desired, in love, something is loved, in hatred, hated."[7]

This argument illustrates how an eidetic analysis is not an inductive generalization from as many particular cases as can be found; it is instead an "eidetic re-duction" in the etymological sense that consciousness is "led back" from particular examples to what is essential, which any of them exemplifies. This reduction Husserl also calls "free variation." In the argument he has just given, what is variable in the examples (perception, imagination, desire, love, hatred) is eliminated in favor of what remains invariant, and so is to be acknowledged essential – the intentional reference to the object. The phenomenologist thus arrives at the formulation, "Every act of consciousness is consciousness of something."

Husserl makes a comparison with geometry, which is also an "eidetic science." The geometer may draw as an example a particular triangle on the blackboard each time he conducts a demonstration. His lines may wobble differently each time, but these differences must be eliminated, if we are to follow the demonstration, in favor of what these particular triangles ideally exemplify – what a triangle essentially is.

IMPERSONATION

Lumping phenomenologists together is as silly as lumping together Anglo-American philosophers, whatever brief justification such lumping together may have as a preliminary. Sartre takes over his procedure of eidetic analysis from Husserl, but he modifies it, apparently without recognizing that he is doing so. If matters were as simple as Husserl's analogy to geometrical figures suggests, some of the differences between Husserl and Sartre would not show up as differences in the examples each relies on to advance an eidetic analysis.

Husserl has a general preference for examples from perception, for reasons that I shall examine later. Sartre goes on to analyze the imagination as opposed to perception, in the fashion I have illustrated by his example of the Pantheon. Sartre's longest example, in *L'Imaginaire*, is one which not only Anglo-American philosophers would be unlikely to accord such prominence, but is also not an example Husserl ever used. The length of Sartre's analysis of it suggests that there was for him a lot of philosophical mileage in it. In fact it will prepare us for the later "eidetic analysis of self-deception" of *Being and Nothingness*.

Sartre begins by summarizing the problem posed by the example: "On the stage of the music hall, the impersonator (*fantaisiste*) is doing impersonations" (*fait des imitations*). I recognize the performer she is impersonating: it is Maurice Chevalier. I appraise the impersonation: "It really is Chevalier" or "It doesn't come off." The phenomenological problem is "What is going on in my consciousness?"[8]

Sartre's answer is in terms of what Husserl analyzed as the "synthesis of identification." We have seen that intentional reference is a "meaning-endowing" act – that is, it identifies what I am conscious of as "a triangle," a "table," "anger," and so forth. In the case of perception at least, identification further involves a "synthesis of identification" in that I identify "aspects" (*Abschattungen*) of what I perceive as belonging to what I perceive. For example, I identify the table as oblong, as brown, as rickety.

The example of the impersonator's portrayal of Chevalier follows in Sartre the example of a portrait, which is an example Husserl does frequently use in analyzing the imagination. The differences between the two "syntheses" involved indicate that Sartre is proceeding in a different fashion from Husserl:

> The difference between consciousness of an impersonation and consciousness of a portrait derives from the materials. The material of the portrait itself solicits the spectator to carry out the synthesis, inasmuch as the painter knows how to endow it with a complete resemblance with its model. The material of the impersonation is a human body. It is rigid, it resists. (Im., p. 57)

Sartre concedes that "an impersonation can be as close a resemblance as a portrait, for example when the impersonator uses make-up" (p. 58). But a close resemblance would not yield the kind of analysis Sartre wants to carry out in which the portrayal by the impersonator is to be opposed to the portrait. His assumption that in the portrait the resemblance can be so close as to be "complete" (*parfaite*), seems rather implausible, but the implausibility betrays his effort tc ɔush the differences between the two examples until they amount to an opposition.

Consider the juncture at which he maintains this opposition with respect to the two syntheses. While I identify what I perceive in the portrait with what I imagine are "aspects" of the person portrayed, many of the aspects I can perceive of Franconay, the impersonator, are themselves opposed to those of Chevalier, the impersonated I am to imagine. What I perceive is short, plump, dark-haired, curvacious, female; what I am to imagine is tall, thin, blond, male. This is why there is a risk of the impersonation not coming off: I may merely see "a short woman making faces."

How are these oppositions to be overcome, so that our reaction will be the identification: "It really is Chevalier"? Sartre stresses first the function of signs: "She is sticking out her lower lip, she is keeping her head forward. I stop perceiving, I read these signs. . . . The straw hat is initially a simple sign. . . . I recognize that the hat of the impersonator refers to Chevalier" (p. 58).

Again Sartre compares what is going on in my consciousness here with what goes on in the example of the portrait as "a faithful rendering of its model in all its complexity. . . . In an impersonation a model has already been thought through and reduced to formulae. . . , to schemata – the rakish angle of the straw hat, the jut of the jaw" (p. 59). The contribution these schemata make is what we have already encountered, Sartre explains, as "the phenomena of quasi-observation." What I am to imagine while perceiving Franconay is what I already know about Chevalier.

This knowledge that Franconay is impersonating Chevalier is not sufficient in itself to constitute the image of Chevalier. All we have so far are "schemata," which are "arid," "rigid," and "abstract." What is still required is that "into these conventional formulae . . . an imaginative intuition" must "flow" (p. 59).

In explaining how this takes place, Sartre recognizes that my originally perceiving Chevalier himself on the stage or screen was "accompanied by an affective reaction" (p. 61) and that this reaction is itself intentional – "a feeling for something," and so "projects on his face a certain indefinable quality which might be called his 'meaning'" (p. 62). When I am later watching Franconay and read the signs, this affective reaction is "reawakened and incorporated in the intentional synthesis" (p. 62). In correlation,

the affective meaning of the face of Chevalier is going to appear on the face of Franconay. It actualizes the synthetic unification of the different signs, animates their rigid aridity, and gives them life and a certain density. (p. 62)

Sartre would seem to be acknowledging a terminological debt here to Husserl's phenomenology by putting quotation marks around "meaning." The preceding "might be called" is then precautionary and alerts us to a crucial adjustment he is making in Husserl's analysis. A meaning that is "indefinable" Husserl would find a contradiction in terms. For him something is endowed with a meaning by an act of consciousness that identifies, and in this sense defines, what the something is. Meaning can become indefinable in Sartre to the extent it is not cognitive but affective, and equatable (to go on with Sartre's analysis of the example) with "the essence, as it were, of Chevalier . . . " (p. 61).

Like the "might be called" the "as it were" betrays the extent to which Sartre is measuring his analysis, not just directly against the experience being analyzed (as a phenomenologist should, since he is committed to describing what is immediately given to consciousness by its intentional reference), but against the terminology Husserl had elaborated in his own analysis of what is immediately given. There is thus a very specific justification for my comparison, even for the purpose of an exposition of Sartre.

Chevalier as merely a particular person could not have an "essence" in Husserl. Indeed Husserl asserts that phenomenology does not "deal with the experiences of empirical persons" and "knows nothing . . . of my experiences or those of others."[9] Again the analogy to geometry as an eidetic science holds: In grasping the essential structure of a triangle or other shape, I am not concerned with the idiosyncracies of the geometer's own performance in drawing it on the blackboard, any more than with the wavering lines of the particular triangle he draws.

In Sartre, however, there is no longer the same sharp distinction of level between an essence and particular facts or particular persons that Husserl sought by his "eidetic analysis."[10] This difference between them is perhaps implicit in Sartre's dropping Husserl's term "eidetic reduction" while retaining the more noncommittal term "eidetic analysis." But consciousness in Sartre's example is still "led back," if in a more casual fashion: What in Husserl was a distinctively methodological procedure has become in Sartre embedded in a more ordinary experience. Thus as we watch the impersonation, we overlook certain particular "aspects" of Franconay: "This dark hair, we do not see as dark, this body, we do not perceive as a female body, we do not see its pronounced curves. . . . The hair, the body are perceived as indeterminate masses . . ." (p. 60). However, these particular "aspects" are not entirely eliminated from the "synthesis of identification," since they are still needed to "represent the indeterminate body, the indeterminate hair of Chevalier" (p. 60).

In fact, instead of maintaining a definite distinction between the imagined "essence as it were of Chevalier" and the perceived characteristics of Franconay, the point of this example for Sartre is the interplay:

It often happens that the synthesis is not entirely achieved: the face and body of the impersonator do not lose all their individuality, and yet, on this face, on this female body, the expressive nature "Maurice Chevalier" is about to appear. A hybrid state develops, which is neither altogether perceptual nor altogether imaginative and which deserves being described for its own sake. These unstable and transitory states are obviously what is most entertaining for the spectator about an impersonation. (p. 63)

CRITERIA

What is at issue in the differences from Husserl that are illustrated by Sartre's exploiting, as crucial to his eidetic analysis, an example that Husserl never used?

Unlike Sartre, Husserl is explicit about his criteria for selecting examples: "Outer perception . . . provides clear and stable examples." There is an alternative candidate he would disqualify:

Anger, when reflected on, may dissipate, or its content may be rapidly modified. . . . The process, to be sure, is not without meaning, but is perhaps not what should be investigated. In contrast, outer perception . . . is not dissipated by reflection. . . . Clear perception is always at our disposal when we need it as an example.[11]

Sartre must have had different criteria in selecting examples to advance his eidetic analysis, for though Husserl may disqualify an emotion as "not what should be investigated," Sartre did investigate the emotions. In fact it was his "Theory of the Emotions" that he was able to salvage when he discarded as "pure Husserl" the rest of a comprehensive phenomenological psychology that he had written.[12] But it is not just an arbitrary matter of Sartre's happening to be interested in the emotions (and so in affective reactions and affective meanings) on which Husserl pretty much turns his back.

On the one hand, we have seen that there are criteria that promote Husserl's interest in outer perception. His statement of these criteria I have quoted from a section of *Ideas I* titled, "The Role of Perception in the Method of Eidetic Clarification." The function of an eidetic analysis for Husserl is to clarify, and he accordingly prefers to apply this analysis to examples that themselves are clear. The achievement of this clarity depends in turn in Husserl (as in Descartes) on satisfying another criterion, distinctness. We have taken note of his concern to distinguish sharply, with his eidetic analysis as a "reduction," the level of "essence" from the level of particular facts. But to achieve clarity another criterion besides distinctness must be satisfied, stability: What "must . . . be made perfectly clear" is that which "floats before us in fluid unclarity."[13]

On the other hand Sartre's analysis of the impersonation uses different criteria. Because the "schemata" are "arid," "rigid," and "abstract," the "imaginative intuition" that is needed to supplement them "must flow." More generally his analysis must be fluid because he takes its subject matter to be fluid: "The image is not given to us as a piece of wood which floats [*flotte*] on the ocean, but as a wave [*flot*] among waves."[14] The most influential of these other waves are emotions. Husserl finds an emotion unsuitable as an example because "its content may be rapidly modified." But Sartre is not similarly dissuaded from investigating the example of the impersonation because the image induced is "an unstable and transitory state."

SELF-DECEPTION

The example of impersonation, if taken by itself, may still seem too idiosyncratic for its prominence in *L'Imaginaire* to be justifiable. But move on to Sartre's later *Being and Nothingness*, which (I have anticipated) he designated an "eidetic analysis of self-deception." In characterizing "self-deception" Sartre uses one of the few technical terms that he does not borrow from another philosopher. This suggests it may have an intimate involvement with Sartre's own distinctive philosophy. The term is "metastable," and Sartre explains that it describes "the kind of mental structure" that is "precarious and liable to disintegrate." There is an "evanescence of self-deception [*mauvaise foi*] which . . . vacillates constantly between good faith and cynicism."[15]

We recognize in retrospect that the structure of the image induced by the impersonation is also metastable in that it is a "hybrid state" that is "unstable and transitory." In *Starting Point* I have generalized that any full-fledged phenomenon in Sartre has the kind of structure that he defines as metastable. It is a "contradictory composite" (Sartre's dissection of the structure of the "self"). It is a structure that Sartre undertakes with his analysis to exhibit as "ambiguous, contradictory, and unstable" – that is, it first emerges in this analysis as a phenomenon which is ambiguous; the ambiguity sharpens (in a fashion Sartre's analysis follows out) into an opposition or contradiction, which renders the composite unstable.[16]

Husserl never undertook an eidetic analysis of such a phenomenon – not of self-deception any more than of an impersonation. For with him an essence (of intentional reference, of an act of perception, and so forth) emerges from an eidetic reduction as an invariant structure comparable to that of triangle: It is not a "hybrid state" or "unstable and transitory" and it does not "vacillate" between opposites. Consciousness as analyzed by Husserl provides no leeway for "opposition, illusory appearance, being other [*Widerstreit, Schein, Andersein*]."[17]

In *Starting Point* I have described Sartre's analysis as "dialectical" (rather than purely phenomenological) to the extent that it latches on to the movement engendered by the relation between opposites – such as the interplay between perception and imagination in the case of impersonation, or between good faith and cynicism in the case of self-deception.

REFLEXIVITY

Of course there is a salient difference between the mental state produced by the impersonation and self-deception. I may in some mild sense be deceived for a moment by Franconay's impersonation. But Sartre's analysis of the impersonation is an analysis of what is going on in my consciousness as a member of her audience, not of what is going on in Franconay's own consciousness. In contrast self-deception is a reflexive phenomenon. Franconay is not deceived as to who she is or as to what she is about in the impersonation.

Sartre makes the transition in *L'Imaginaire* itself from his initial orientation toward the object of intentional reference to self-reference. I cite one example: I am imagining someone I hate. He is an imaginary object that is "out of reach," as opposed to a real object I perceive. Sartre explains, "I cannot touch it, change its place," as I can a real object. "Or rather I can, but . . . unreally, by not using my own hands but phantom hands that administer unreal blows. . . . To act upon these unreal objects. I must double myself, make myself unreal."[18]

The doubling that reflexive reference secures is associated in Sartre with his phenomenology eventually becoming "existential." Husserl's phenomenology is an intentional analysis in that the "meaning-endowing" act is an act of identification whereby I am conscious of something as what it is – a triangle, a table, anger. What is at stake in the impersonation in Sartre is still the identification of someone else: "It really is Chevalier." But when Sartre's analysis becomes reflexively reoriented toward the "existential" problem of self-identity – of who it is I really am, the problem becomes the problem of my "choice of myself" in *Being and Nothingness*.[19]

This reflexive reorientation is the warrant for my having translated *mauvaise foi* by "self-deception." *Mauvaise foi* in French, like "bad faith" in English, ordinarily carries a reference to interpersonal relations. When I deceive another person, Sartre explains, I may flaunt my intention of telling her the truth ("I would never deceive you"). My intention then "is play-acted, mimicked [*jouée, mimée*]; it is the intention of the character [*personnage*] that I am playing in the eyes of my questioner, but this character . . . does not exist. . . ." (*EN*, p. 86). I have doubled myself, and made myself into an unreal, an imaginary object. But the lie I am telling "does not involve the inner structure of [my] present consciousness." As opposed to such a lie to the other – to this effort to hide the truth from the other – it is, in the instance of self-deception, "from myself that I am hiding the truth."[20]

Self-deception is a phenomenon that Husserl never found it appropriate to treat. His generalization, "We shall always presume sincerity"[21] suggests he might find even interpersonal deception philosophically irrelevant. Thus he does not equip himself philosophically to analyze this phenomenon, at least if it has the structure that it exhibits in Sartre's analysis. He does not envisage an intention being "play-acted," "mimicked," since an "intention" (in the technical sense he gave the term) is inextricably locked into its reference to the "something" it is "consciousness of."

PLAY-ACTING

In Sartre's "eidetic analysis of self-deception," the idiom of play-acting or role-playing is pervasive. There is the example of the waiter who attempts "to imitate in his walk the inflexible stiffness of some kind of automaton, while carrying his tray with the recklessness of a tightrope walker, by putting it in a perpetually unstable, perpetually broken equilibrium, which he perpetually reestablishes by a little movement of the arm and hand. All this conduct seems to us play. . . . He is playing with himself. . . . He is playing at being a waiter" (*EN*, pp. 98–9).

This would seem a banal example of an individual fitting himself into a social role, were it not for Sartre's reflexive emphasis, "He is playing with himself." Another respect in which Sartre shows his own philosophical hand is with respect to how the waiter is play-acting. His playing with the tray is the physical embodiment of the structure that Sartre characterizes as metastable. We first discerned it in the "unstable and transitory" fashion in which, as we watched Franconay, an image of Chevalier was established, only to have it slide back into our perception of Franconay, until the image was again momentarily reestablished.

Self-deception is at least marginally involved for Sartre in the waiter's performance in that no one, however mechanical his gestures, can make himself into an "automaton," fitting himself exactly to the requirements of his social role. Thus Sartre insists that in the waiter's performance more "is at stake than social conditions." I am "aiming at myself as an imaginary café waiter."[22]

The fashion in which Sartre's analysis of self-deception is structured emerges even more definitely in another famous example from

Being and Nothingness – the woman who is about to be seduced. The example of seduction, like that of a waiter, may seem merely a banal social ritual. The usual perspective in considering it is on the interpersonal relation between the seducer and the seducee. But Sartre shows his hand by certain departures. The seducer's intentions are held fixed, to be left outside his analysis: "She knows very well the intentions that the man who is speaking to her cherishes" (*EN*, p. 94). No interest attaches to how he might be deceiving her; only to how she deceives herself.

A complication is that she is playing two roles: One is the self she is conscious of as being a sex object; the other the spiritual self for which she solicits his "admiration and esteem" as "she draws her companion up to the most elevated regions of sentimental speculation" (*EN*, p. 95). In the case of Franconay's performance, what attracted us in the audience was the interplay between our arriving at the level of the image and our sliding back to the level of what is actually perceivable, and then our regaining of the image. Similarly in the case of the woman about to be seduced, what attracts her is the interplay between the two roles she is playing, so that "her aim is to postpone the moment of decision as long as possible."[23]

Thus Sartre's eidetic analysis of self-deception is couched in the idiom of play-acting or role-playing. The example of the impersonation is the first extensive evidence that role-playing will become Sartre's preoccupation. When he used this example, Sartre was still, I suspect, so much in the grip of Husserl's eidetic analysis that he does not describe Franconay as playing the role of Chevalier, but has her instead produce by her performance "the essence, as it were, of Chevalier."

Sartre's retaining Husserl's term does bring out the generality that attaches to a role. If Chevalier were not a well-known performer, a star of stage and screen of some magnitude, whose performances had consolidated their own "formulae" (the rakish angle of the straw hat, the jut of the jaw), Franconay could not bring off her own performance, so that a star is reborn, and we applaud her, "It really is Chevalier." She is not impersonating an ordinary person, but a *personnage,* created by Chevalier's own repeated performances, which render it available for reenactment. An individual's role-playing usually accords more general and more persistent significance to the role played than to his own merely particular and temporary activities.

Anglo-American philosophers have not been much concerned with role-playing, and only with self-deception in more restricted contexts than we find in Sartre. I am not sure that such conduct is so rare that the scope of Sartre's preoccupation is without some justification.

DRAMA

Be this as it may, Sartre provides a further illustration of this preoccupation. In the concluding chapter of L'Imaginaire he introduces his discussion of "the art of the drama" with the statement "It goes without saying that the actor who plays Hamlet makes use of himself, of his whole body, as an analogue of this imaginary character" (p. 367). Distrust a philosopher when he reports what "goes without saying." That Sartre should reduce anything so general as "the art of the drama" to the actor's performance betrays the same preoccupation as his selection of the example of impersonation. But this new example is an advance in reflexivity in that Sartre is now concerned with what is going on in the consciousness, not of the audience but of the actor himself. The problem of "the art of the drama" is posed for Sartre by "the famous paradox of the actor." On the one hand, "certain authorities insist on the fact that the actor does not believe in his role [personnage]." On the other hand, "others demonstrate that the actor is taken in [prise au jeu], the victim in some sense of the hero that he impersonates" (p. 367).

In his resolution of these opposed points of view, Sartre contends on behalf of the second that "the actor may really cry, carried away by his role [rôle]" (p. 367). On behalf of the first point of view, he concedes that "these tears . . . the actor is himself conscious of as the tears of Hamlet – that is, as analogues of unreal tears" (p. 367). Sartre concludes that "it is the actor who renders himself imaginary [s'irréalise] in his role [personnage].[24]

The comparison with acting recurs with the waiter's playing in Being and Nothingness: "I can be the waiter . . . as the actor is Hamlet, by mechanically making the typical gestures of my state, and by aiming at myself as an imaginary café waiter through those gestures taken as an 'analogue'."[25]

I remarked at the outset that it is sometimes regarded as unphilosophical of Sartre to resort to other genres besides philosophy. But the scope of his preoccupation in his philosophy with play-acting or role-playing helps explain why he found it philosophically appropriate to resort to plays. In these plays themselves Sartre is often preoccupied with play-acting. Perhaps the most striking example is his adaptation of Dumas's *Kean* for a very histrionic actor, Pierre Brasseur. Sartre informs his audience that they are to witness a "miracle – you won't know if you are seeing Brasseur playing Kean or Kean playing Brasseur." Again we have a metastable situation involving interplay. But this is not the uncertainty with which we earlier watched Franconay playing Chevalier. The uncertainty is now existential in that Sartre would embroider on the problem of the identity of the person being impersonated. Sartre recalls how Kean, when he heard that an Italian actor was to play him, plastered Paris with posters. "The real Kean is myself." But Kean, Sartre adds, is "an actor who does not stop acting" when he steps off the stage, "who acts out his life, until he no longer recognizes himself, . . . and in the end, is no one."[26]

PSYCHOANALYSIS

Another extraphilosophical genre to which Sartre has resorted is psychoanalysis. In fact he followed up his "eidetic analysis of self-deception" in *Being and Nothingness*, not by publishing the moral philosophy that he had promised as a sequel and that everyone expected from a proper existentialist, but with *Saint Genet, comédien et martyr. The Real Saint Genet (Le véritable Saint Genet)* was the title of a seventeenth-century play about the legendary Saint Genet, who was converted to Christianity during a mock performance in Rome in which he had acted out the ceremony of Christian baptism. At the end of this performance he announced that he really was converted and was martyred on the spot – to become the patron saint of actors. Jean Genet, whom Sartre is psychoanalyzing, is also in a sense not real but the legend whom he imagined himself as being. He is sanctified and marytred by his playing the passive sexual role of a woman, and Sartre's oral pun *saint/seins* equips him with "breasts" for this mock performance. Like Franconay, *il fait une imitation* – he's doing an impersonation.

Sartre's longest work is his psychoanalysis of Gustave Flaubert in *The Idiot of the Family*, which he presents as "the sequel" to *L'Imaginaire*.[27] This is one of Sartre's few assertions on behalf of the continuity of a later work with an early work. To provide a more specific illustration of this continuity, I pull out an example in which Sartre is analyzing what is going on in Flaubert's consciousness, when he is identifying someone as a *personnage*, and is caught up in the interplay, with which we are familiar from the impersonation, between what is imagined and what is perceived:

> If Flaubert was in love with Mathilde, it was in fact, in order not to possess her. The thighs and breasts of a princess are never sufficiently regal except for someone who refrains from touching them and limits himself, as Flaubert did, to desiring a glorious body, the abstract, unrealizable image, the place of coincidence between woman as such . . . and the aristocracy as such. Yet it was necessary that the real body of Bonaparte's cousin should serve as analogue for the image – that is, for Flaubert to exhaust himself in aiming via the cellularity of "this formerly pretty woman," the undivided space, which held her glorious body, via the rough vivacity of "a woman who could equally well have been a whore, who was unreliable and somewhat shopworn." (*IF*, III, p. 540)

There is a tensely twisted reflexive moment in this performance by Flaubert, since he was attempting "to deprive of reality [*déréaliser*] the flesh and conduct of Mathilde by the very desire that pretended to be aroused by her grace and that was in fact feeding on itself. For his primary goal was to transcend the reality that was too commonplace."[28] It is obvious here that Sartre's concern is not with Flaubert's identification of the princess, but with the self-identification that is implicit in how Flaubert identifies the princess.

PERSONALIZATION

Sartre renders Flaubert's self-identification explicit by analyzing the process of "personalization" by which Flaubert first became (in Sartre's titles) an "Imaginary Child" for himself, secondly developed "From the Imaginary Child to the Actor," and thirdly developed "From the Actor to the Author." With respect to the second stage Sartre reports that "At seven years, Flaubert wanted to be a great actor." Thus "the writer in him is to preserve the main characteristics of the actor and his literary style something of his play acting."[29]

That Sartre includes a stage when Flaubert wanted to become an actor may have as much to do with Sartre's own preoccupation with play-acting as it does with Flaubert's own development. Sartre explains that this was a necessary stage in Flaubert's "personalization" in that acting met his "need to escape from his own *persona*, which was shaky and tiresome, by substituting for it the being of a role [*personnage*]."[30] Flaubert is attempting, as it were, to impersonate himself.

Indeed in one stretch of Sartre's analysis of "personalization," he employs an example similar to the example of Franconay impersonating Chevalier:

> With any analogue, one disregards what gets in the way. When an elderly actress skillfully plays the role of a young woman, one lets oneself be carried away; one does not take the wrinkles into account, one "sees" the youthful beauty that she represents. Certainly old age is not suppressed entirely, but remains as a sort of sadness, a "that's all it amounts to" of the secret disillusion that is aroused at this moment, not by the actress in the role but by beauty in general. Thus the masculinity of little Gustave colors the object aimed at . . . with a certain hermaphroditism.[31]

I shall not follow out the implications Sartre pursues with the "Thus" until I have finished with his example of the actress. Observe here the interplay between levels. Just as I disregarded in the impersonation the particularities of Franconay ("This dark hair, we do not see as dark, this body, we do not perceive as a female body") and yet "the hair, the body are perceived as indeterminate masses," so I disregard the wrinkles of the elderly actress, and yet she attains a certain essentiality, whereby "beauty in general" is at stake in her acting. This interplay becomes ambiguous with the concession, "that's all it amounts to," and accordingly "metastable" – liable to disintegrate, like the other precarious structures Sartre favors.

I return from this interplay to the implications that are carried over in Sartre's conclusion, announced by the "Thus." The sexual ambiguity of Franconay's impersonating Chevalier, a *cavalier* (a "ladies' man" to revert to the lingo of a bygone epoch when there were still ladies and men), Sartre did not bring out. But with Flaubert it takes the form of "a certain hermaphroditism," which remains a feature of his adult play-acting – in Flaubert's own words, "I would like to be a woman, in order to be able to admire myself, strip myself naked, . . . to gaze at myself in brooks."³² The "in order to admire myself" is taken by Sartre as "the clue" to the reflexive, masturbation fantasies of "The Imaginary Child":

> It is possible for the child . . . to imagine that he is another who caresses a real woman – himself. . . . His hands are those of another, they descend slowly from his breast to his sides, to his round thighs. . . . From his image he apprehends only the caressed flesh, neglecting the meaningless details, such as his penis. . . .³³

By now Sartre rightly suspects he has outraged the common sense of his reader, who is protesting, "This is impossible." It is to elicit conviction regarding the reductive downplaying of meaningless details that Sartre has interpolated the example of the wrinkled actress.

The reader may renew his protest when Sartre extrapolates to Flaubert's adult behavior: Flaubert "fucks to render himself imaginary" (*baise pour s'irréaliser*).³⁴ I am not sure that this purpose Sartre would acknowledge is all that unusual. But the feature of the process of *déréalisation* that Sartre is arguing is characteristic of Flaubert is his attempt "to identify himself with the woman he is possessing, to steal from her the sensations that she appears to experience: This confused, swooning flesh, it is himself."³⁵ Since Sartre is a little short of empirical evidence in this entire argument, it may be worth observing the support he gains from his own recurrent reflexive shift in identification: What he would account for is the Flaubert who will proclaim, "Mme. Bovary, she is myself."

MARXISM

In bringing out the continuity of Sartre's preoccupation with roleplaying throughout his career, I may seem to be overlooking the moment when his career was disrupted by his conviction that "the fundamental question" had for him become his "relation to Marxism."³⁶ I cannot deal adequately here with a question that was so fundamental for Sartre himself. But I can illustrate briefly how it was for him a question of method. In the *Critique de la raison dialectique*, Sartre retains "the *methodological* principle which holds that certainty starts with reflection" (p. 30) and this is the same principle that he adopted as phenomenological in *L'Imaginaire*. He now claims that this principle "in no way contradicts" the Marxist "principle that defines the concrete person in his materiality. . . . Reflection is a starting point only if it throws us back immediately among things and men, in the world."[37] Where the starting point for the Marxist would be some technological development, the invention or utilization of some tool, Sartre starts out with the individual and his immediately given experience, as constituted by the reflexive experience of his own instrumentality. To spell this out, where the Marxist would start with the lever, the wheel, the stirrup, the pulley, the steam engine, Sartre would start with the moment when the individual leans on a lever, and so on. When the tool that is introduced is a machine, we are dealing with a technological development that is visualized by Sartre, not as lying at the basis of the substructure and generating a sequence of effects that extend into the superstructure, to impose themselves there eventually on individual consciousness. Instead, to cite one of Sartre's examples, "girls working in a factory are ruminating a vague dream," but they are "at the same time traversed by a rhythm external to them," so "it can be said that it is the semiautomatic machine that is dreaming through them."[38]

Even though the impersonation is a much simpler case, we can perhaps still recall Franconay playing the role of Chevalier. In fact Sartre uses the same idiom, which I cannot explore here, since it entails a dialectical reversal that is too remote from Husserl. The relation of impersonation, Sartre concludes, is "a relation of *possession*. An absent Maurice Chevalier chooses, in order to manifest himself, the body of a woman. Thus, originally, an impersonator is someone possessed."[39] Sartre adds in a footnote, "Consciousness of impersonating should be spoken of as certainly a consciousness of being possessed" (*L'Imaginaire*, p. 63). Similarly the girl in the factory gives herself "to the machine," which takes possession of her work, until finally "she discovers herself *the object of the machine.*" (*CRD*, p. 364). One complicating difference is that she cannot slip out of her role. She cannot "take refuge in her most intimate 'privacy'." It is the machine in her which is "dreaming of caresses" (p. 364). The machine is no longer her tool; she has become its tool. But the machine cannot qualify as a subject; while she has become "the object of the machine" she is saddled with the contradiction that she is no longer the subject of her own experiences.[40] This contradiction, though fitted to a more or less Marxist dialectic, is predominantly phenomenological; it is the intentional reference of consciousness to its object which undergoes the reversal.

Consider another less complicated example, where the role-playing is explicit, as in the issue Sartre is taking with orthodox Marxism over the relevance of intentions as opposed to the objective consequences of actions. Sartre complains that "the contemporary utilization" of Marx "by self-styled Marxists" is "superficial and dishonest" (CRD, p. 37). The instance to which he appeals is the claim that "the avowed goal of the Brissotins [during the French revolution] is a mask, that these bourgeois revolutionaries presented themselves as illustrious Romans but that the objective consequences really defined what they were doing" (p. 38).

Sartre demurs, "We should be more careful." He interprets Marx as attempting "a difficult synthesis of intention and consequences" (p. 38). Possibly it is Sartre himself who is attempting a difficult synthesis of phenomenology (as an analysis of intentional, meaning-endowing acts of consciousness) with Marxism. At any rate, Sartre proposes as Marxist

a new idea of human action; imagine an actor who plays Hamlet and is caught up in his play-acting: He crosses his mother's room in order to kill Polonius hidden behind a tapestry. But that is not what he does: He crosses to earn his living, to win fame, and this real activity defines his position in society. But it cannot be denied that these real consequences are not in some fashion present in his imaginary action, . . . or that the way in which he believes himself Hamlet is his own way of knowing himself to be an actor. To return to our Romans of 1789, their way of calling themselves Cato is their manner of making themselves bourgeois. (p. 38)

This reflexive moment of self-identification (when they are caught up in the Roman roles they are playing) is to be incorporated in a Marxist analysis in which it is recognized that "one can halt the revolution more effectively the more one can pose as Brutus or Cato."[41]

If Sartre seems to ride roughshod over the differences between an actor on the stage being "caught up" in a role and the self-deception in which political agents are prevalently enmeshed, this only illustrates how compelling the dramatic analogy remained for him, even when he entered into "relation to Marxism." Indeed the dramatic analogy acquires general scope for him, which in turn justifies his resort literally to plays:

Today I think that philosophy is dramatic. . . . Philosophy is concerned with man, who is at once Agent and Actor, who produces and plays his drama. A play . . . is the most appropriate vehicle for showing man in action.[42]

CONVERSION

I would not have gone to such lengths to bring out anything so obvious as Sartre's preoccupation with role-playing, were it not for its bearing first on the scope gained in his philosophy by his analysis of the imagination and of self-deception, and second on his resort to the seemingly extraphilosophical genres of plays and psychoanalysis. However, Sartre's preoccupation is less with role-playing as such than with role-shifts. Again impersonation provides an elementary example. When Franconay initially steps on to the stage, she is stepping into her own role as an impersonator. Sartre stresses that we do not yet know whom she will be impersonating – that she is going to play the role of Chevalier. The members of the bourgeoisie during the Revolution who particularly interested Sartre do not simply play a bourgeois role, but slide into the further role of Romans. The woman about to be seduced shifts back and forth from the role of sex object to that of a spiritual being. We have watched Flaubert's affective reactions provide Mathilde with a comparable duality.

A more flagrant example, which is closer to home, is *The Respectful Prostitute*. As a prostitute she identifies with the black, another victim. But her image of herself (like our image of Chevalier, as impersonated by Franconay) is "unstable and transitory." She is duped, as herself a Southerner, into respecting mores in terms of which she is beneath respect. This role shift, which is so integral to Sartre's own distinctive phenomenology, he allowed the heavy hand of Stalinist propaganda to halt in the version of the play staged in Moscow, where (he explains) "they could not accept her having a glimmer of consciousness and then becoming completely duped."[43] But "a glimmer of consciousness" is a Sartrean specialty rather than a Marxist one.

What we have seen Sartre analyze as the process of Flaubert's "personalization" is a succession of role shifts. They are lined up by his titles: "From the Imaginary Child to the Actor," "From the Actor to the Author," "From the Poet to the Artist," culminating in the ambiguous, contradictory, and unstable proposition, "Loser Wins," which is presented as "A Conversion."

A "conversion" is philosophically the most significant form of role shift. For philosophy itself has traditionally entailed a conversion to philosophy, ever since Parmenides or the "turning around" (*periagogé*) that takes place in Plato's Cave. Later conversions are usually to philosophy as differently conceived from what it was previously.

Sartre himself underwent three different philosophical conversions: before World War II to Husserl; during the war, to Heidegger; and eventually after the war to his own version of Marxism. The third is the best known of his conversions. But how Marxist is this conversion itself? As a student Sartre had read *Capital* and *The German Ideology*, but he explains, "I had understood everything clearly, and I understood nothing at all. To understand is to transform oneself [*se changer*]."[44] Marx's thesis is that "philosophers have only interpreted the world differently; the point is to change it."[45] But Sartre's conception of understanding imports a reflexive moment of self-transformation into this process of change.

This importation is not simply Sartre's preoccupation with himself. Recall the intrusion of a reflexive moment in the instance of the girl in the factory tending a semiautomatic machine. But one conversion that does preoccupy Sartre throughout his career is the adoption of the role of the writer:

The reason I wrote *The Words* is the reason why I have investigated Genet or Flaubert: How does a man become someone who writes, who wants to speak of the imaginary? This is the question I sought to answer in my own case, as I sought it in the others.[46]

I have already taken note of the "conversion" Sartre attributes to Flaubert. In Sartre's psychoanalysis of Genet, he begins with Genet's "first conversion" which is to crime; his "second" is his self-transformation into an "aesthete," and his "third" is finally into a writer. In Sartre's own literary works themselves conversions are prominent, as Sartre points out:

The characters in my plays and novels reach their decisions suddenly and at a moment of crisis. A moment, for example, is long enough for Orestes to carry through a conversion. (*Les Mots*, p. 199)

Sartre admits, "These characters are fashioned in my image; not as I am, of course, but as I would like to be. . . . I transform a tranquil evolutionism into a revolutionary and discontinuous catastrophism."[47]

The predisposition to conversion, which survives Sartre's successive conversions to other philosophies (to Husserl, to Heidegger, and supposedly to Marxism) is not merely personal, since it assumes the guise of a preoccupation with conversions in his own philosophy. It is illustrated by one of the more exuberant passages in the usually ponderous *Being and Nothingness*, which also illustrates that conversions display his philosophical predilection for structures that are ambiguous, contradictory, and unstable:

These extraordinary and marvelous moments when the previous project collapses into the past in the light of a new project which emerges from its ruins, . . . in which humiliation, anxiety, joy, hope are delicately blended, in which we let go in order to grasp and grasp in order to let go – these have often appeared to furnish the clearest and most moving image of our freedom.[48]

Sartre's philosophy is considered distinctively a philosophy of freedom, but one respect in which it can be distinguished from other philosophies of freedom is by the extent to which the imagination is the agency of our freedom and by the fact that the most moving image of our freedom is a conversion. We are left with the paradox that a philosophical continuity that survives the discontinuities introduced into his philosophy by his successive conversions to other philosophies is his preoccupation with conversion.

AFFECTIVITY

The only one of Sartre's conversions that concerns me directly is the conversion to Husserl that launched his career in philosophy. His conversion was not just sudden, but complete – as conversions are ideally supposed to be: "Husserl had captured me. . . . I saw everything via the perspectives of his philosophy. . . . I was 'Husserlian'."[49]

This conversion has solicited the comparison with Husserl that I have undertaken.

However, I have located a break with Husserl in Sartre's analysis of the impersonation in which Franconay plays the role of Chevalier, and I have suggested that the term "role" in this example should have displaced the Husserlian term to which Sartre still clings, when he refers instead to Franconay's producing our consciousness of "the essence, as it were, of Chevalier."

Yet it should be admitted that Sartre's interest in this example is not just in Franconay's playing the role of Chevalier, but is "eidetic" – it is primarily an interest in "the role of affectivity in [constituting] the consciousness of the impersonation" (*L'Imaginaire*, p. 62). Here, we see, Sartre does employ the term "role." This higher level role involves a role shift (as does the lower level role of Franconay playing the role of Chevalier) with "affectivity taking the place of the strictly intuitive elements of perception in order to actualize the object as an image" (p. 62). Earlier we saw that what perception itself can yield is no longer "intuitive". Perception merely yields what we already know (that Chevalier juts his jaw and wears a straw hat at a rakish angle). But what has to be reawakened, if Franconay's performance is to "come off," is the intuitive "affective reaction" we had when we originally perceived Chevalier, so that the "affective meaning of the face of Chevalier will appear on the face of Franconay" (p. 62).

I have already indicated that Husserl would find "affective meaning" a contradiction in terms. Meaning is cognitive in Husserl's analysis in that the intentional act, which endows the object with meaning, has "the unique function of first providing other acts with represented objects."[50] But Sartre argues against "the primacy of representation," not with any explicit allusion to Husserl, but "as instanced by the traditional assumption that "a representation is always necessary if a feeling is to be provoked." He is blunt, "Nothing is more false" (p. 140).

Sartre offers counterexamples:

If yesterday Peter made an offensive gesture that upset me, what first re-emerges is indignation or shame. These feelings grope blindly for a moment in order to understand themselves; then, illuminated by encountering the relevant knowledge, they produce of themselves the offensive gesture. (p. 272)

Similarly, Sartre reports,

[It has] happened to me . . . that I have felt an extremely precise desire. Affectively its object is strictly determined. . . . Only I do not know what it is. Do I want to drink something cool and sweet; do I want to go to sleep? Is some sexual desire in question? (p. 142)

Sartre explains, "the desire is a blind effort to possess on the representative level what has already been given to me on the affective level."[51]

Moreover, "feeling can be given . . . as a kind of knowledge. If I love the long, delicate white hands of some woman, this love, which is directed on these hands, can be considered one of the ways that they have of appearing to my consciousness. . . . The love projects on the object a certain tonality that could be called the affective meaning of this delicacy, of this whiteness." These conceptions of a feeling that is "a kind of knowledge" and of "affective meaning" are amalgams that would be intolerable to Husserl, with his commitment to the distinctness on which, we earlier saw, meeting the criterion of clarity depends for him.[52]

Doubtless Sartre's conception of the role of "affectivity" was reinforced by his conversion to Heidegger, for whom *Befindlichkeit* is "equiprimordial" with "understanding."[53] *Befindlichkeit* Sartre translates as *affectivité*, but *Befindlichkeit* in Heidegger refers etymologically to how "the being that is there [*Das Dasein*]" "finds itself" there – "in-the-world." It is a "finding of oneself" that is at stake in a conversion. When Sartre was converted to Husserl, he "turned almost pale with emotion," according to Simone de Beauvoir, who was on hand.[54] Or take as an example Sartre's third conversion, which is at once vision and emotion:

The last ties were broken, my vision was transformed: an anticommunist is a dog, I am not leaving from there [*je ne sors pas de là*], I will never leave. . . . After ten years of ruminations, I had reached the point of rupture. . . . In ecclesiastical language it was a conversion. . . . I vowed to the bourgeoisie a hatred that will end only when I do.[55]

I return from Sartre's preoccupation with conversions to his broader conception of a role shift. What is philosophically crucial here is the "eidetic" higher level role shift whereby affectivity can take over, with respect to constituting the meaning of an image, the role that is performed by perception, not just in Husserl, but in the philosophical tradition at large.

This role shift Sartre defends in *L'Imaginaire* with a citation from a novel of Stendhal's: "I cannot see the way things look. I have only my memory from childhood. . . . I see images. I remember their effects on my heart."[56] This accrediting of "affective meaning" is very much Sartre's own commitment as a philosopher. At least it antedates his conversion to Husserl: In the dissertation that he wrote on *L'image* when he was twenty-one Sartre places this citation at a climax, at the beginning of the final section.

Sartre's commitment to affective meaning promotes his transferring, at the very start of his career, a citation from a novel to a philosophical work, and prepares us for his appraisal, at the end of his career, of his longest work – his psychoanalysis of Flaubert – as "a novel that is true." Concomitant with this subversion of the traditional distinction between a genre that perpetrates fictions and the truth claims of philosophy and science is his renunciation: "Husserl's idea of *Philosophy as Rigorous Science* seems to me . . . a crazy idea."[57]

When Sartre found himself being embalmed in *The Library of Living Philosophy*, he was perplexed as to "why among the articles on him [twenty-eight in all] there was only one on literature."[58] Reading Sartre's philosophical works should be accompanied by his own different sense of proportion, and by some alertness to its philosophical implications.

NOTES

1 *Philosophical Review* 73 (1964): 134.
2 The term "intention" derives from medieval usage, but Husserl was sensitive to the secondary classical meanings of *intendere* – "to bend a bow" and "to aim at." (See the fifth of the *Logical Investigations*, §13.)
3 Ibid. §11.
4 *Journal of the British Society of Phenomenology* 2 (1971): 13.
5 *Situations* IV, p. 196. Translations from French are my own.
6. *L'Imaginaire* (1986 ed.), pp. 22, 174.
7 *Investigations* V, §10.
8 *L'Imaginaire*, p. 56 (*The Philosophy of Jean-Paul Sartre*, p. 81). This and subsequent quotations concerning impersonation come from pp. 55–63 of *Idées* edition.

9 *Investigations*, Foreword to 2d ed.

10 Sartre's handling of this example thereby becomes an instance of what Husserl discounts as "picturebook phenomenology" and what I characterize in more general terms as "vulgarization" – a term that I derive from Sartre himself. See *Starting Point*, p. 90, and *Human Nature* 1: 206.

11 *Ideas I*, §70

12 *Entretiens, avec Jean-Paul Sartre* (Simone de Beauvoir), p. 231.

13 *Ideas I*, §66–9.

14 *L'Imaginaire*, p. 36.

15 *L'Être et le néant*, p. 88 (*Philosophy*, p. 140).

16 *Starting Point*, pp. 204, 230.

17 *Ideas I*, §46.

18 *L'Imaginaire*, p. 240 (*Philosophy*, p. 88).

19 *L'Être et le néant*, p. 290 (*Philosophy*, p. 138ff).

20 *L'Etre et le néant*, p. 87.

21 *Investigations* I, §11.

22 *L'Être et le néant*, p. 100 (*Philosophy*, p. 151f).

23 *L'Être et le néant*, pp. 94–5 (*Philosophy*, p. 146ff).

24 *L'Imaginaire*, p. 367f (*Philosophy*, p. 93f).

25 *L'Être et le néant*, p. 100 (*Philosophy*, p. 153).

26 *Les Écrits de Sartre* (Contat and Rybalka), p. 268.

27 *Situations* IX, p. 118.

28 *L'Idiot* III, p. 540. The quotation is from a realistic appraisal of Mathilde provided by the Goncourt brothers.

29 *L'Idiot* I, p. 661f.

30 Ibid., p. 783.

31 Ibid., p. 693.

32 Ibid., p. 684.

33 Ibid. p. 693.

34 Ibid., p. 714.

35 Ibid., p. 705.

36 *New Left Review* 100 (Nov. 76–Jan 77): 144.

37 *Critique*, p. 30.

38 Ibid., p. 364.

39 *L'Imaginaire*, p. 63.

40 *Critique*, p. 364.

41 Ibid., p. 38.

42 *Situations* IX, p. 12.

43 *Les Ecrits de Sartre*, p. 137f.

44 *Critique*, p. 22f.

45 The eleventh of the *Theses on Feuerbach*.

46 *Situations* IX, p. 134f.

47 *Les Mots*, p. 199.
48 *L'Être et le néant*, p. 555 (*Philosophy*, p. 262f). Husserl has interpreted his phenomenological reduction, as "a method of access" (*Zugangsmethod*) to phenomenology, as a conversion (see the final sentence of his *Cartesian Meditations*), and the movement of conversion has been read into Heidegger's "existential analytic" as redemption from inauthenticity. (See Merker's interpretation of this analytic as a *Konversionsgeschichte* – in Merker, *Selbsttäuschung und Selbsterkenntnis: Zu Heideggers Transformation der Phänomenologie Husserls*.) But in Husserl and Heidegger the conversion is a prolonged undertaking, which perhaps can never be completely carried through; it is not an "extraordinary and marvelous," a "metastable," and dialectically balanced moment in which "we let go in order to grasp and grasp in order to let go."
49 *Carnets*, p. 225.
50 *Investigations* V, §41.
51 *L'Imaginaire* [pp. 140ff, 271], p. 142.
52 Ibid., p. 145.
53 *Sein und Zeit*, p. 142.
54 *La force de l'âge*, p. 141.
55 *Situations* IX, pp. 248–9. A simpler example of how for Sartre understanding can be affective is a citation from Merleau-Ponty that Sartre makes his own. Merleau-Ponty is discussing Sartre's interpretation of the anger of Nizan (Sartre's college roommate), and Sartre quotes: "This anger, is it a matter of temperament [*fait d'humeur*]? It is a mode of knowledge [ibid., 241]."
56 *L'Imaginaire*, p. 145.
57 *Situations* IX, p. 70. In the first volume of *The Dream Is Over* I deal with the shifts from Husserl's conception of philosophy as scientific that have punctuated the history of phenomenology: the shift in Heidegger to a conception of philosophy as affiliated with poetry; in Sartre to a conception of philosophy as affiliated with literature; in Merleau-Ponty to a conception of philosophy as affiliated with painting.
58 *The Library of Living Philosophy*, p. 44.

3 Individuality in Sartre's philosophy

In reflecting upon Jean-Paul Sartre's philosophical writings in their entirety, the question arises as to whether these writings constitute a harmonious development or rather provide clear evidence of breaks. Generally, the critical literature assumes that the ontological, epistemological, and anthropological positions that are taken in the early philosophic-psychological writings are further elaborated and deepened in the first major work *Being and Nothingness*. Consequently, there would seem to be no grounds to suppose that in the period between 1934 (the year during which Sartre, in Berlin, worked on *The Transcendence of the Ego*) and 1943 (the year when the first major work was published) alterations in Sartre's philosophical conceptions occurred of such a magnitude as to interfere with the continuity of his thinking.

Matters are quite different with respect to the period between

Although this chapter was especially written for this book, it can nevertheless be considered as a very condensed version of the results of my earlier Sartre research. See for instance the following publications: "Le concept d'individualité" in *Obliques* (Paris 1979), no. 18/19: 221–34. *Het individualiteitsconcept in Sartres filosofie* (The Concept of Individuality in Sartre's Philosophy) (Delft: DUP, 1984). "Sartre et Freud" in Claude Burgelin, ed., *Lectures de Sartre* (Lyon: PUL, 1986), pp. 241–51. "Knappheit und Gewalt: Kritik der dialektischen Vernunft" in Traugott König, ed., *Sartre: Ein Kongress* (Reinbeck bei Hamburg: Rowohlt, 1988), pp. 247–64. This chapter contains therefore several passages translated from some of these publications. Quotes are also taken from the following English translations of Sartre's work: *The Transcendence of the Ego. An Existentialist Theory of Consciousness*, translated and annotated with an introduction by Forest Williams and Robert Kirkpatrick (New York: 1977), cited as TE; *Being and Nothingness. An Essay on Phenomenological Ontology*, translated by Hazel E. Barnes with an introduction by Mary Warnock (London: 1981), cited as BN; *Critique of Dialectical Reason. Vol. I. Theory of Practical Ensembles*, translated by Alan Sheridan-Smith (London: 1976), cited as CDR.

1943 and 1960, the year when the second major work, the *Critique of Dialectical Reason*, was published. Whereas *Being and Nothingness* represents an existentialist conception of man, in which the unique individual – essentially still free even when in chains – is master of his own fate, in the *Critique* the superiority of a historical-materialistic view of man and history is defended, while existentialism is reduced to the status of an enclave within the tenets of Marxism. Evidently, during the course of – and after – the Second World War, Sartre's ideas altered to such a degree as to necessitate a radical revision of his anthropological viewpoints.

Nevertheless, the *homme historique*, that is, the historical-transcendental consciousness that finds itself embedded within the historical and material context of the *Critique*, in many respects calls to mind the liberal *"pour-soi"* of *Being and Nothingness*. This *homme historique* is not just the product of historical and material determinants, but also the free natural agent imparting individual and creative form to history. Whereas interpreters are fairly unanimous in their judgment of Sartre's development until 1943, there is no consensus concerning the subsequent period. This leads Contat and Rybalka to conclude in their bibliography that the question of a possible *"coupure épistémologique"* between *Being and Nothingness* and the *Critique* has not yet been decisively settled.[1] However, Sartre himself did not consider the question to be problematic. During an interview in 1976 he airily rejected such a break:

I think that there is more continuity in thought. I do not believe that there is a break. There are naturally changes in one's thinking; one can deviate; one can go from the one extreme to the other; but the idea of a break, an idea from Althusser, seems to me to be mistaken. For example I do not think that there is a break between the early writings of Marx and *Capital*. Naturally there are changes, but a change is not yet a break.[2]

In this chapter we inquire into the concept of individuality in Sartre's philosophy, that is to say into the position and status of individual consciousness in the various stages of his writings. In such an inquiry it is impossible to circumvent the problem of a possible break, regardless of whether or not such a break would be of an ontological or epistemological nature. It is precisely because Sartrian thinking does not permit any strict division between ontology, epistemology, and anthropology, that ontological and epistemological alterations have immediate consequences for his anthropological positions and vice versa. Both in the early paper *The Transcendence of the Ego*, published in 1936-7 in *Recherches philosophiques*, as well as in the two major works, the individual human being, seeking according to an analysis along Cartesian lines for apodictic certainty, is taken as point of departure. However, the evidence for both the *cogito* and its nature is of a different type in each of the three works. Consequently, an insight into the ontological and epistemological variations wherein the *cogito* becomes manifest is essential to arrive at an adequate characterization of Sartre's concept of individuality in the different phases of his writings.

In the investigation into the possibility of breaks it is essential to eliminate even the slightest traces of prejudice. Both Sartre's views on this matter as well as the current interpretations by others need to be examined and, if necessary, modified. This means that the hypothesis of continuity in the period between 1934 and 1943, often defended, should not be adopted unquestioningly. It may well come to pass that the results of the debate concerning that period will prove to be codeterminant in deciding whether or not the epistemo-logical viewpoints embodied by *Being and Nothingness* and the *Critique* are compatible.

Elucidation with respect to the question of breaks is not only desirable from an anthropological point of view. There are also other issues, apart from the concept of individuality, that would benefit from reflection on this problem. For instance, the question may be posed as to the reason why in *Being and Nothingness* the problem of solipsism is discussed again, while in the "conclusions" to *The Transcendence of the Ego* it had been explicitly eliminated![3] Is it perhaps possible that the problem had to be raised again because the ontologi-cal and epistemological status of the *"pour-soi"* in the first major work is fundamentally different from that of the impersonal *cogito* as it appeared in the early article? Should we consider the solution to this problem furnished in 1943 to be adequate and if not, would it be reasonable to assume that this failure is connected with a fundamen-tal epistemological change of direction in *Being and Nothingness?* Furthermore, why is it that Sartre never published the philosophical ethics heralded at the end of the first major work?[4] Is his own answer to this question adequate or are we faced with other, theoretical reasons, not specified by Sartre, to account for his restrained atti-tude? Is there perhaps a causal connection between Sartre's lifelong struggle with the problem of solipsism and his failure to complete a philosophical ethics? In our elucidation of the various different concepts of individuality used by Sartre during his development, these questions will play an important part. Concerning this process of development, he himself, in the aforementioned interview, states:

Personally I see my life as the life of an anarchistic individualist until '39 . . . and in '39 a certain sort of communication with the people whom I loved during the war and thereafter in captivity; then from '40, under the monstrous conditions that characterized the occupation, the societal comes into my field of vision; I see how people associate with each other and I see that as something that must be changed by the disappearance of the occupying forces, and thus since '45 I began to take part in politics and to think about the social, which terminated, as you know, with the CRD.[5]

It is significant that in this quotation 1939–40 is considered to be a turning point, which leads us to inquire what precisely was the content of the personal experiences and intellectual impulses that brought about such a change and, in addition, to determine whether or not the philosophical positions Sartre held prior to 1940 differ significantly from the viewpoints he defended after 1940 as a consequence of this turning point. Concretely formulated: Can we detect traces of this "anarchistic individualist" in the concept of individuality developed prior to 1940 and, if so, in which ways may these traces be distinguished from the concept of individuality in *Being and Nothingness?* In a confrontation between Sartre's philosophical positions from before and after 1940, greater attention will evidently be paid to *The Transcendence of the Ego* than to the other philosophical-psychological writings of the prewar period, since in this early article the ontological and epistemological foundations are laid for the analyses in *The Emotions* and in *The Psychology of the Imagination.*

It is for this reason that in this chapter a number of important suppositions from *The Transcendence of the Ego* have been reconstructed and the concept of individuality contained therein brought to the focus of attention. This concept, however, underwent such alterations in *The Emotions* and *The Psychology of the Imagination* as would certainly warrant discussion of both of these works. But since this chapter does not permit detailed elaboration a brief examination of a revealing diary entry of 1940 in the *Carnets de la drôle de guerre* will have to suffice. This entry supports the view that Sartre's epistemological and anthropological insights have, in the late thirties, altered to such an extent as to justify the application of the term *"coupure épistémologique."* This digression also provides the transition to a discussion of *Being and Nothingness.* The alteration of epistemological insights that began prior to 1940 is totally realized in this work, with the result that transcendental consciousness, which in *The Transcendence* is still of an entirely *impersonal* nature, here becomes endowed with a *personal* structure.

In the discussion of the concept of individuality in *Being and Nothingness,* Sartre's theory of bad faith is also examined. Furthermore, the "solution" put forward in this work with respect to the problem of solipsism will be questioned. Our discussion of the *Critique* will be limited to parts of *Livre I, Tome I,* where the analysis that seeks apodictic evidence of the dialectic *cogito* is executed. The *homme historique,* embedded in a material and historical situation, appears to be an individual who recognizes "work" as the necessary (insofar as concerns *our* history and *this* world) dialectic relation with the materiality that surrounds him and with the others that similarly work this materiality. Because of this characteristic of the dialectic *cogito,* I will argue that only in the *Critique* does Sartre succeed in formulating a plausible answer to solipsism.

Finally, in the concluding part of this chapter, the problematic question of a Sartrean ethic will, on basis of the insights gained, come up for discussion. Moreover, it will be argued that one of the reasons why Sartre never published an ethic must be attributed to the antagonistic theory of intersubjectivity in *Being and Nothingness,* itself the direct result of Sartre's attempt to refute solipsism, an attempt that, incidentally, did not succeed.[6]

THE TRANSCENDENCE OF THE EGO

The central proposition in the article *The Transcendence of the Ego* is concisely expressed in its title. More elaborately formulated this proposition is as follows: The Ego is not located *within,* but *outside of* consciousness. It is, neither in the formal nor in the material sense, immanent to consciousness. The Ego is transcendent to consciousness. The Ego does not inhabit consciousness; its abode is outside consciousness. It is noteworthy that this challenging proposition is launched precisely following the track of Descartes and Edmund Husserl. The "methodical doubt" of his French and the ἐποχή of his German predecessor are also for Sartre preeminent instruments through which apodictic evidence may be obtained. However, the *cogito* that ultimately emerges in Sartre's writings no longer presents an ego structure. Sartrean transcendental consciousness, though individuated, nevertheless is at the same time wholly *impersonal*. How has this come about? It is because the principle of the so-called intentionality of consciousness has been given its full consequences.

Husserl followed Descartes in his methodical doubt, but similarly radicalized its tenets with the consequence that, for him, transcendental consciousness could no longer be characterized in terms of thinking *matter*, a "*res* cogitans." If, he argued, consciousness only exists as consciousness *of*, that is to say, as an intentional relation to consciousness-transcendent objects, then, in the ἐποχή (Husserl's variant of the "*doute méthodique*"), the psychophysical "I" will perish because this "I" also presents the character of an object. What remains is a transcendental Ego; however, this can no longer in any way be characterized in terms of a "thing," a "res."

Just as Husserl radicalizes Descartes, so in his turn Sartre radicalizes Husserl's principle of intentionality. If one is truly serious with respect to the nonsubstantial character of consciousness and comprehends this in terms of being wholly dynamic in nature, as a being completely directed-at, then, so Sartre claims, the transcendental Ego no longer has any existential right and it evaporates, just as holds true for the psycho-physical I in the ἐποχή.

The settling of accounts with respect to the standard image of the Ego in philosophy and psychology occurs in two stages. In the first part of the article, a phenomenological-transcendental analysis entitled "The I and the Me," Husserl's transcendental Ego is eliminated and the aforementioned impersonal transcendental consciousness generated. In the second part, a phenomenological-psychological analysis titled "The constitution of the Ego," an inventory is made of the elements composing the consciousness-transcendent Ego. The article ends with a number of "Conclusions."

Part I of *The Transcendence of the Ego* consists of three sections. In the first of these Sartre argues that Husserl's phenomenological conception of consciousness as radical intentionality renders a transcendental Ego both impossible and superfluous. When Kant states that "the I Think *must be able* to accompany all our representations,"[7] this does not signify that the I grounds every act of consciousness. The Kantian transcendental consciousness is no *reality*, it *is* nothing other than "the set of conditions which are necessary for the existence of an empirical consciousness."[8] Husserl's transcendental Ego is of a different order. Regardless of how formal and nonsubstantial one may imagine this to be, it will still cloud the absolute transparency of consciousness, which is inherent to its radical intentionality. Whatever way one looks at it, the transcendental Ego is a "center of opacity"[9] *within* consciousness. Not only are a transcendental, intentional, and wholly translucent consciousness on the one hand and a transcendental Ego on the other mutually exclusive; in addition, the latter is in no way a necessary foundation for the unity and the individuality of consciousness. The unity of a series of moments of consciousness does not come about through the agency of a governing I *within* consciousness, such as for example a transcendental Ego "inhabiting" consciousness, but rather, this unity is brought about by the transcendent object at which these moments are intentionally directed. Sartre puts it this way: "The object is transcendent to the consciousnesses which grasp it, and it is in the object that the unity of consciousness is found."[10]

Furthermore, the individuality of consciousness arises from its inherent nature. Consciousness is not only consciousness *of* a transcendent object; it is also and simultaneously self-consciousness and as such absolute inwardness. It is for this reason that Sartre concludes that it is not the I that makes possible the unity and individuality of consciousness, but rather the reverse in that this unity and individuality cause the personal I to become manifest under specific circumstances. What are these circumstances?

In order to obtain a view of these it will first be necessary to describe the condition of consciousness before they appear. What, in Sartre's view, is the appearance of a consciousness, still lacking in any I-structure whatsoever? As a consequence of the thesis of intentionality, it is consciousness *of* a transcendent object. As such, however, it is simultaneously *self*-consciousness, because human consciousness cannot "exist" other than as consciousness of itself.

However, such consciousness is not conscious of itself in the same way as it is of an object. As consciousness of an object, it is a *positional* consciousness, while as consciousness of itself it is *nonpositional.*

As an *intentional being directed at* it posits the transcendent object, whereas as *inwardness*, though conscious of its positing activity, it does *not* posit *this* activity as a transcendent object. For example, when Peter sees a tree, he is *positionally* conscious of the consciousness-transcendent object "tree."[11] As such, he is at the same time *non*positionally conscious of himself, insofar as he is that positing activity. However, the term "himself" does not in this instance denote a mysterious selfhood lying hidden *within* Peter's consciousness, but only his consciousness insofar as this is a tree-positing activity. This consciousness is still entirely impersonal or, if preferred, prepersonal in nature. Sartre indicates it with the phrase "consciousness of the first degree." A consciousness of this type is applicable to Roquentin in the novel *La Nausée*, who perceives the roots of a chestnut tree in the park and interprets his experience in terms that strongly call to mind the description of the first-degree consciousness in *The Transcendence of the Ego:* "I *was* the root of the chestnut tree. Or rather I was all consciousness of its existence. Still detached from it – since I was conscious of it – and yet lost in it, nothing but it."[12]

The distinction between an *impersonal, first-degree* consciousness and a *personal, second-degree* consciousness is worked out by Sartre in the second section of the first part. Here he explains why the *cogito* of Descartes and Husserl essentially differs from first-degree consciousness. With respect to that *cogito* it is stated that it is a reflexive operation in which consciousness curves back on itself. It is not just consciousness, but rather consciousness *of* consciousness; it is a consciousness that reflects on first-degree consciousness, which in fact it also is.

Thus, first-degree consciousness is always a *positional* consciousness of a transcendent object and as such a nonpositional self-consciousness at the same time. Second-degree consciousness is a *nonpositional* consciousness of this nonpositional self-consciousness of the *first degree*, which signifies that the latter is more or less objectified but not yet explicitly posited by the former. The I emerges from this objectivation. The I is nothing but the reflected *self*-consciousness of the *first degree*.

As distinct from first-degree consciousness, which is of a totally prereflective nature, second-degree consciousness needs to be characterized as a *reflective* consciousness, to the extent that first-degree consciousness is being posited by it. This does not, however, imply that this second-degree consciousness is also a reflective *self-*consciousness. On the contrary, as self-consciousness it is at the same time of a *prereflective* nature for the reason that it does *not* posit explicitly the self-consciousness of the first degree. Therefore, second-degree consciousness has an extremely problematic status, since – depending on the perspective from which it is perceived – it is both prereflective as well as reflective in nature.

Before investigating if and to what extent second-degree consciousness can in its turn be made an object of reflection, first a few words concerning the evidence of the Ego that appears simultaneously with the emergence of this consciousness. It is Sartre's opinion that the Ego that emerges as a result of the Cartesian *cogito* does not possess the same degree of evidence inherent in the *cogito* as the activity of consciousness.

The argumentation with respect to this proposition proceeds in an extremely astute manner. On the basis of two forms of memory: the reflective (consciousness of the second degree) and the so-called nonreflective (consciousness of the first degree) it is demonstrated that the Ego does not possess the irrefutable evidence inherent in both forms of memory.

What precisely is the difference between a reflective and a nonreflective memory? This distinction may best be illustrated with the aid of Sartre's own example. Suppose yesterday I perceived (on a first-degree level) a landscape. Today this experience may be recalled to memory in two different ways: (a) I may remember that *I* perceived the landscape (the reflective memory, a consciousness of the second degree) or (b) I may remember only the landscape. In this case, the first-degree experience of yesterday is "revived" in a manner of speaking, which signifies that the I is absent, as was similarly the case yesterday. If we now inquire into the degree of evidence of both forms of memory, it becomes apparent that both are apodictically evident. *The fact that* memory occurs cannot be refuted in either case. However, the I only emerges insofar as the reflective memory as a second-degree consciousness is a consciousness with respect to the *perception* of the landscape (the first-degree consciousness).

Not that memory itself – the second-degree consciousness – is the object of reflection, but rather the perception of the landscape yesterday (the first-degree consciousness). The *perception* of yesterday is objectified to an "I perceived." It is true that the I emerges; however, it does so only insofar as it is objectified as *perception* and it is therefore just as subject to doubt as any other objects that are being posited by consciousness.

Whatever holds valid for the reflective memory holds equally valid with respect to Descartes's *cogito*. As a second-degree consciousness, this is, as previously indicated, a double consciousness, in the sense that it is consciousness *of* the first-degree consciousness that in fact it also is. The I emerges only insofar as the latter is posited as *object,* and is for this reason as subject to doubt as the I that emerges in consequence of reflective memory.

After this excursion into the evidence – or, more correctly, the nonevidence – for the Ego, which is the result of its transcendent character, we finally return to the question of whether or not consciousness of the second degree may, in its turn, be again made the object of reflection. Sartre's reply to this question is unequivocal: "All reflecting consciousness is, indeed, in itself unreflected, and a new act of the third degree is necessary in order to posit it. Moreover, there is no infinite regress here, since a consciousness has no need at all of a reflecting consciousness in order to be consciousness of itself. It simply does not posit itself as an object."[13]

On the basis of this quotation one cannot avoid the conclusion that in *The Transcendence of the Ego, three* levels of consciousness can ultimately be distinguished. For the sake of clarity these, in conclusion, are summarized and in each instance provided with a concrete example:

1. *First-degree consciousness:* Nonpositional consciousness of itself. The term "itself" in this instance indicates the positional consciousness of a transcendent object. *Example:* I perceive a tree and am conscious of "myself." Here the term "myself" refers only to the "perception of the tree."

2. *Second-degree consciousness:* Nonpositional consciousness of itself. In this instance, the term "itself" signifies the nonpositional consciousness of itself, as formulated under (1). *Example:* I perceive

a tree and am conscious of "myself." The term "myself" here does not denote the "perception of the tree," but the nonpositional consciousness of this "perception of the tree."

3. *Third-degree consciousness:* Positional consciousness of itself. In this instance also, the term "itself" again indicates the nonpositional consciousness of itself, as described under (2). *Example:* I perceive a tree and am conscious of "myself." Even though in this instance the term "myself" again denotes the nonpositional consciousness of the "perception of the tree," now this nonpositional consciousness – as distinct from that described under (2) – is explicitly posited. Thus, in summary we may state that the first-degree consciousness is an entirely impersonal self-consciousness, containing no I-structure whatsoever; the second-degree consciousness is a personal self-consciousness underlying the formation of the I. The third-degree consciousness is also a personal self-consciousness, in which now the I is explicitly thematized and posited as an object, as a Me.

All three of these instances concern individual consciousness, for the reason that consciousness in each instance is being limited by itself and its unity is being effected by the consciousness-transcendent object. The *impersonal* individual first-degree consciousness is the transcendental condition basic to the emergence of the *personal* second- and third-degree consciousness.

INTERMEZZO: THE TURNAROUND OF 1940

In the entry of Sartre's diary dated "Monday, March 11, 1940" in the *Carnets de la drôle de guerre,* we come upon a fascinating introspection.[14] Sartre states that he and Gide have a tendency in common to negate reality. Where he himself is concerned, he establishes that his own consciousness has served him as a refuge, from which he – in a contemplative state of mind – could cause the world to vanish. By assuming such an attitude, even his own person became something quite unreal. Literally he states: "[M]y person was no more than a transitory incarnation of that consciousness, or, better, a certain link that attached it to the world, like a captive balloon." A littler further on he remarks that flight behavior also forms the basis for his article *The Transcendence of the Ego:* "It was this [escapism] also which inspired a little earlier my article on the transcendence of the Ego, where I frankly put the I at the door of consciousness, like an indiscreet visitor."

He states that this was also the attitude that he assumed against the threat of war. Now, however – that is to say in 1940 – under the influence of Heidegger and as a result of the war, this attitude has changed: "It is the war and Heidegger who have put me on the right path; Heidegger by showing me that there was nothing beyond the project through which human reality realized itself."

These influences have far-reaching consequences with respect to Sartre's epistemological position. He now distances himself in lucid terms from the proposition pertaining to the impersonality of transcendental consciousness, developed in the *The Transcendence.* Though he is still of the view that the Ego is transcendent to consciousness, he says nevertheless that: "The selfness or totality of the for-itself is not the I yet it is the person – I am in the process of learning, basically, to be a person." The latter quotation provides us with an autobiographical argument to support the conviction that we are involved with a epistemological break between *The Transcendence* on the one side and *Being and Nothingness* on the other. Elsewhere an attempt has been made to demonstrate and locate this break systematically. (See some of my publications mentioned in the Notes.) Here however we are solely concerned with the fact that this break – or, if preferred, this change of epistemological position – has occurred under Heidegger's influence. It is known (see for example *Questions de méthode*) that already in 1933 Sartre read Heidegger in Berlin; apparently however, only toward the end of the thirties was he induced to alter his philosophic intuitions by the writings of Heidegger. For, so far as is known, Sartre never expressed himself in such clear terms with respect to the role that Heidegger played in the transition from *The Transcendence of the Ego* to *Being and Nothingness.*

Like Heidegger, Sartre, in *The Transcendence*, also radicalizes Husserl's philosophy (see the preceding section). However, in contrast to his German colleague, this radicalization does not imply that he is leaving the Cartesian way. Heidegger, in *Sein und Zeit*, attempts to conquer the dualism between being and consciousness by means of *"Dasein,"* while Sartre remains true to the Cartesian tradition of the *cogito.*

After the characterization of transcendental consciousness in *The Transcendence* in terms of an impersonal consciousness without Ego (see the preceding section), the metaphor in the quotation from the *Carnets* may be more readily understood. This consciousness is a "balloon," not however a balloon entirely free in its movements, but rather one that is tied to the world – a "captive balloon." The intentionality of consciousness, the line connecting consciousness to the world, is the person. This person is not located *within* consciousness, it does not "inhabit" consciousness. It is only a "transitory incarnation of that consciousness."

It is this conception of the person that changes under the influence of Heidegger. Heidegger's *Dasein* is by no means situated beyond the world; quite the contrary: it is precisely located *in* that world (*in der Welt*). Even though Sartre maintains the *cogito*, he nevertheless now assigns it – in rather curious adjustment to Heidegger – a different ontological status by relocating it. The empty consciousness is no longer suspended *above* the world, but is now situated *in* the world or, expressed with the aid of a metaphor adopted from *Being and Nothingness* – empty consciousness now becomes a "hole" (*trou*) in being.

This relocation of consciousness means that the "line" between consciousness and the world is also transposed and now, similarly, is located in the world. The intentionality of consciousness can no longer be understood as a vertical "line," since it has changed its position and now finds itself on a horizontal plane. The consequence of this change of position with respect to the conception of the person is self-evident. While in *The Transcendence* the person was still a line *between* consciousness and the world, after their blending it becomes impossible to avoid an entwining of consciousness and person. The *impersonal* consciousness now becomes a consciousness endowed with selfness (*ipséité*),[15] it becomes a *pour-soi*, it becomes a *person*.

Before entering into the radical consequences of this change, it would be opportune first to consider whether or not Sartre's attempt to integrate his own ontological conceptions with those of Heidegger was successful. It is well known that Heidegger, in his *Brief über den Humanismus*, criticized Sartre's attempt to draw him into the argument for his own purposes and, from the Heideggerian viewpoint, this criticism can be easily understood. It is possible for one to disagree fundamentally with Heidegger's enterprise in *Sein und Zeit*, yet if one accepts his criticism of Western metaphysics since Plato, it is difficult not to conclude that Sartre attempted to realize the impossible. A choice has to be made whether to remain within the Cartesian tradition and attempt to conquer the dualism between consciousness and being by means of a creative revisionism (Sartre himself chooses this method in *The Transcendence* as well as in – as will become evident later – the *Critique of Dialectical Reason*) or to break radically with this tradition to return to the pre-Socratic roots of Western philosophy. A combination of these two alternatives, already present in the *Carnets* and further developed in *Being and Nothingness* cannot avoid shipwreck. In support of this view, pertinent arguments will be put forward in the following section.[16]

BEING AND NOTHINGNESS

In the second "conclusion" to *The Transcendence of the Ego* it is claimed that the thesis defended in the article offers the only possible way to refute solipsism, which becomes inconceivable when the I loses its privileged status.[17] In *Being and Nothingness* Sartre rejects this conclusion. Even though he vindicates the viewpoint that the Ego is transcendent to consciousness, he nevertheless rejects his 1936 solution to the problem of solipsism. He states: "Even if outside the empirical Ego there is *nothing* other than the consciousness *of* that Ego – that is, a transcendental field without a subject – the fact remains that my affirmation of the Other demands and requires the existence beyond the world of a similar transcendental field."[18] By means of the theory of the look a further attempt is made to come to terms with solipsism. This will be discussed later. For the moment it will suffice to note that Sartre, in a subsequent phase of his development, was equally dissatisfied with the solution given in *Being and Nothingness* and even though he did not consider it to be incorrect, he nevertheless thought it too abstract, since it lacked the historical dimension.[19]

Finally, in the *Critique of Dialectic Reason*, comes the third and last attempt at refuting solipsism. In what may be called a historical-transcendental analysis (see the next section), the apodictic evidence of the *dialectic cogito* is generated in such a manner that *this cogito* implies the *cogito* of the other. In anticipation of the subsequent argument, we may note that the *"homme historique"* (this term denotes the dialectic *cogito* in the *Critique*) may be viewed as a historical-materialist version of the impersonal transcendental consciousness from the *The Transcendence*.

Why does Sartre repudiate outright the second conclusion of his 1936 article? Why is it that he now feels it necessary to demonstrate the existence of another, a "similar transcendental field"? The problem of the existence of the other — as was suggested in *The Transcendence* — simply does not apply on the level of an impersonal Ego-less transcendental consciousness. The only way to comprehend Sartre's renewed interest in the problem of solipsism, is to assume that the personification of transcendental consciousness, as stated in the *Carnets*, becomes formalized in *Being and Nothingness*; this implies that consciousness, though still "I-less," is simultaneously characterized as personal, as endowed with at least some form of "selfhood." Is this in fact the case? And if so, how precisely does this personification come into being?

At the beginning of the paragraph "The Self and the Circuit of Selfness," Sartre explicitly dissociates himself from the position taken up in his early article. Here again he sticks to his view that the Ego is transcendent to consciousness; however, he adds: "yet we need not conclude that the for-itself is a pure and simple (impersonal) contemplation. But the Ego is far from being the personalizing pole of a consciousness which without it would remain in the impersonal stage; on the contrary, it is consciousness in its fundamental selfness which under certain conditions allows the appearance of the Ego as the transcendent phenomenon of that selfness."[20]

From both the quotations cited it seems abundantly clear that personification of transcendental consciousness is indeed carried out in *Being and Nothingness* and that this is why the problem of solipsism once again appears in that work. It is far less clear, however, where precisely this personification should be located, since in the statements quoted, it is argued only *that* consciousness is personal in nature, but not *why* this is so.

In the relatively short Introduction to *Being and Nothingness* the ontological and epistemological basis is laid for the phenomenological descriptions of the concrete manifestations of human consciousness. Consequently, it is evident that the personification of transcendental consciousness is already carried out in that Introduction.

Indeed, a careful analysis of sections III and V of the *Introduction* indicates that the "pre-reflective *cogito*" (this term denotes transcendental consciousness in *Being and Nothingness*), contrary to what has been suggested by Sartre himself, should not be regarded as a consciousness of the *first* degree but as a *second*-degree consciousness. Within the framework of the present chapter it will not be possible to map out the complex argumentation concerning the second-degree character of the "pre-reflective *cogito*." The following summary must suffice: In *Being and Nothingness* Sartre no longer characterizes transcendental consciousness – as he did in *The Transcendence of the Ego* – as a mode of being, whose essence implies its existence, but as a consciousness whose existence implies its essence.[21]

A comparative analysis of these statements makes clear that "implies" has a different meaning each time, and that the inversion of the terms "existence" and "essence" in the second statement is not arbitrary, which means that the two statements contain two entirely different propositions. The first statement says only that consciousness of an object is at the same time always self-consciousness, while the second declares that consciousness of an object is always a form of *personal* self-consciousness.

An assertion in section V confirms the correctness of this analysis, in the sense that here the "pre-reflective *cogito*" is characterized explicitly in terms of a "consciousness of a being, whose essence implies its existence; . . ."[22] Since the characterization "a being, whose essence implies its existence" can only be applicable to a first-degree consciousness, as described in *The Transcendence,* it is therefore now asserted that the "pre-reflective *cogito*" is a consciousness of a first-degree consciousness, which consequently means that the "pre-reflective *cogito*" is a second-degree and, thus, a personal consciousness.

After this brief consideration of the Introduction to *Being and Nothingness,* we now return to the quotation given earlier in which the first "solution" for the problem of solipsism was refuted. Is transcendental consciousness also personified in this quotation? "Even if outside the empirical Ego there is *nothing* other than the consciousness *of* that Ego – that is, a transcendental field without a subject – the fact remains that my affirmation of the other demands and requires the existence beyond the world of a similar transcen-

dental field." Here we see undeniably how the phrases "consciousness *of* that Ego" and "a transcendental field without a subject" are
mutually identified. From the viewpoint of *The Transcendence,*
such an identification is not acceptable, since in that article we are
confronted on the one hand with a totally transparent, empty, prereflective and *impersonal* consciousness, and on the other hand
with a consciousness-transcendent I, situated in the world. To be
sure, transcendental consciousness was by its very nature a nonpositional consciousness of itself. However, the term "itself" in the
phrase "consciousness of itself" denoted only, as already seen, the
positional consciousness of an object. Once more translated into an
example: The impersonal consciousness of the tree was also a nonpositional consciousness of itself; however, in this instance the
term "itself" denoted only the impersonal consciousness of the tree,
neither more, nor less. In the quotation mentioned however, transcendental consciousness ("a transcendental field without a subject") is identified without further ado with "the consciousness of
that Ego," that is to say, with a self-consciousness that – from the
viewpoint of the 1936 article – is already far more reflective in nature than transcendental consciousness and that, for this reason,
must be considered as a personal consciousness in which the Ego
has already appeared.

Formulated in a different manner: The impersonal transcendental
consciousness of *The Transcendence of the Ego,* a consciousness
totally without *ipse,* suddenly, in the citation, becomes a transcendental consciousness endowed with an *ipse.* Or, formulated in yet
another way: The impersonal transcendental field suddenly becomes a personal *"pour-soi."*

Once it has become apparent that the transcendental consciousness in *Being and Nothingness* has been provided with a personal
structure and that the personification of this consciousness is in fact
the consequence of the telescoping of two levels of consciousness
(first- and second-degree consciousness), which in *The Transcendence* are still explicitly distinguished, it becomes gradually more
comprehensible why, in *Being and Nothingness,* the problem of solipsism was bound to emerge again with great intensity. From the
1936 viewpoint solipsism was "inconceivable." However, at the
very moment when transcendental consciousness is provided with a

"selfness," solipsism presents itself again with undiminished force. Has Sartre, in *Being and Nothingness* succeeded in refuting the solipsistic position?

In preparation for an adequate answer, first a few words concerning the phenomenon of "bad faith," the description of which took so many pages in *Being and Nothingness:* The fact that this phenomenon can emerge is rooted in the ambiguous ontological status of human existence. As Sartre puts it, every human being is both facticity as well as freedom; that is to say, he is facticity and at the same time he is endowed with the possibility of transcending this facticity. Precisely because each individual is *not* what he is – that is, precisely because he is free – he is prone to, and capable of, bad faith. Prone to, since he cannot endure the tension of an existence between the poles of facticity and freedom. Capable of, since he, by means of his freedom tries to reduce himself totally to either facticity or freedom.

Insofar as an individual shows evidence of bad faith toward himself, this implies a case of self-deceit. Self-deceit is distinct from a lie in that the individual does not deceive another but himself. It is a form of belief (*foi*) and as such an activity of consciousness that must be located between knowing and not-knowing. It is, expressed in terms of *The Transcendence*, a second-degree consciousness. Self-deceit is an activity in which one is *nonpositionally* conscious of the fact that one is reducing oneself to either facticity or freedom. However, this activity is not yet posited explicitly. Self-deceit is a semiknowing, a pseudoknowing.

The thief who identifies totally with his "thievishness" (facticity), and also the gambler who identifies completely with his decision (freedom) to gamble no longer, are both equally guilty of bad faith. Even though they may still be vaguely aware that they deceive themselves, they nevertheless do not yet know *explicitly* that they are doing so. As self-deceivers they are "believers."

Not only in his relation to himself, but equally in his relation to others, man – according to Sartre – is inclined to bad faith. When the reduction of himself to facticity, to an object, to an *"en-soi"* as it were, is accompanied by a total conversion of the other to subject or when the reduction of the other to object is attended by the conversion of himself exclusively to subject, this implies bad faith. In its most extreme consequence such a mutual reduction leads to masochism and sadism and even though this conversion can never be realized in "ideal" form, human relations in all their variations are nevertheless governed by this model.

It is plausible that the overstrained concept of freedom in *Being and Nothingness* was strongly influenced by Sartre's war experiences. With good reason this work might even be titled a *"philosophie de résistance"* and, in a certain sense, viewed therefore as somewhat dated. War experiences have no doubt also influenced the grim theories concerning bad faith and human relations as developed in *Being and Nothingness*.[23] Nevertheless, primary philosophical considerations have lent decisive form to the Sartrean model of bad faith and intersubjectivity. Reflection on these reasons leads back again to the question of whether or not the attempt to refute solipsism in *Being and Nothingness* is successful.

At the end of the section in which he criticizes the solutions to solipsism offered by Husserl, Hegel, and Heidegger, Sartre formulates four criteria that, in his opinion, must be satisfied for a refutation of solipsism to be valid. The second of these he defines as follows:

> The *cogito* examined once again, must throw me outside it and onto the Other, just as it threw me outside upon the In-itself; and this must be done not by revealing to me an a priori structure of myself which would point toward an equally a priori Other but by disclosing to me the concrete, indubitable presence of a particular concrete other, just as it has already revealed to me my own incomparable, contingent but necessary, and concrete existence.[24]

Does Sartre's own solution presented in the theory of the look conform to this criterion?

In the French edition the exposition of this theory occupies fifty-four pages. It would be quite impossible to reconstruct this theory adequately in a few sentences. Here light is thrown only on such elements as are of immediate relevance to the question posed. The examples used to illustrate the theory of the look are familiar: The man in the park confronted with his equal, and the person who, driven by jealousy, glues his ear to the door or looks through a keyhole. An extensive description will not be given here; only Sartre's conclusions will be recalled.

1. The other reveals himself – as is indeed also the case for Husserl

and Heidegger – through the objects in the world: "[I]t is *on* the table, *on* the wall that the Other is revealed to me. . . ."[25]

2. The other as subject is not only the one capable of perceiving the same objects as me, he is first and foremost the one capable of making me the object of a look: "[M]y fundamental connection with the Other-as-subject must be able to be referred back to my permanent possibility of *being seen* by the Other."[26]

3. The physical presence of an other is not prerequisite for a look. There is not only a look when the other perceives me in the literal sense. The contingent manifestation of a look is of secondary significance. A slight movement of the curtain or the creaking of a branch may create a situation in which I, for example, am left with an impression of being spied upon, and in which I feel I am the object of a look. There is preeminently a question of a look where its concrete manifestation is not explicitly thematized. I am under the impression of being looked at, particularly when I do not direct my attention at the eyes of the one looking at me. Sartre puts it this way: "The Other's look hides his eyes; he seems to go in front of them."[27] Briefly summarized: The less the other is physically present as an object, the more strongly I experience his subjectivity.

This thesis is given concrete expression in the description of what happens when I, compelled by, for example, jealousy, look through a keyhole. Sartre describes a consciousness-in-a-state-of-jealousy in terms reminiscent of the characterization of *impersonal* consciousness in *The Transcendence of the Ego:* "My attitude . . . is . . . a pure mode of losing myself in the world, of causing myself to be drunk in by things as ink is by a blotter. . . ."[28] I am totally absorbed by my spying activities. I am only a consciousness of the world. To be sure, I am also a nonpositional consciousness of myself, but this consciousness is still totally devoid of an I.

Suddenly, a change occurs in the situation. I hear footsteps in the hall. I realize that I may be seen by an other. At that moment my consciousness changes, the I makes its appearance. However, this consciousness ". . . does not apprehend the *person* directly or as *its* object, the person is presented to consciousness *insofar as the person is an object for the Other.*"[29] It is in shame that I experience that I am an object for the other. It is the assumed other that instills me with a sense of shame for my spying.

It may, of course, be objected that this experience of shame does

not furnish us with *proof* of the existence of the other as a subject
(since one cannot exclude the possibility of having made a mistake
and that, in fact, there was no one in the hall) and that the other
could be nothing more than the product of my imagination.[30] Consequently, the solipsistical position would not have been refuted, on
the contrary, it would have been strengthened. Sartre is not very
impressed by this counterargument. He replies that the experience
of shame itself cannot be denied, since this is *evident* and, furthermore, that awareness of my error does not thereafter prevent but, on
the contrary, further increases my experience of shame. Thus, Sartre's argument has the following structure:

1. The existence of the other is a necessary condition for my
   experience of shame.
2. In the example given, I may well be in error with respect to
   the physical presence of the other. However, the experience
   of shame itself is evident and admits of no doubt.
3. Consequently, the other exists.

Is this "refutation" of solipsism convincing? It would seem that it is
not. It has become apparent that the apodictical evidence for the
existence of the other is, in the last resort, based on the *absence* of
such an other. The "evident" other is, consequently, no concrete
subject, he is only an *abstraction.* Precisely because the fundamental *presence* is manifest as an *absence,* it reinforces the solipsistical
position. If physical presence is only a probability there is no reason
not to consider the other-subject (*l'autre-sujet*) as the product of my
consciousness. Indeed, this conclusion is unavoidable when I make
the "evident" other the object of reflection. As a third-degree consciousness I realize that the I that I just now encountered in the
experience of shame (*second*-degree consciousness) was not the product of a constituting deed on the part of a real other, but of myself, in
the sense that it was I that looked at me. As third-degree consciousness I realize that the virtual other is, in fact, nothing other than the
Freudian "Super-ego," which means that it is a censorious other, not
insofar as this exists in reality (for example as Father or Mother), but
insofar as it is integrated into my own I.[31] One might reply that this
thesis is correct and that precisely for that reason the Sartrean proof
holds valid, since the "Superego" *implies* the concrete subjectivity
of an other I. However, it would then be necessary to stress the

indefinite article in the phrase "an other I." The censorious activity, the normative activity, cannot be ascribed to a concrete person. In other words the virtual other cannot be identified by means of a proper name (such as Ann or Peter). Yet this was precisely what Sartre wanted to achieve, as was evident from the aforementioned second criterion.

It has been pointed out that, in all likelihood, Sartre's experiences during the German occupation influenced his theory of bad faith and intersubjectivity. To this, however, the remark was added that philosophical considerations were of decisive importance. To some extent this has now become clear. But even the brief, yet instructive, evaluation of the theory of the look readily reveals that Sartre has not succeeded in irrefutably demonstrating the existence of the other as flesh and blood, as a *concrete* subject. The other who reveals himself in the look is only a pale ghost of the concrete other whom I meet in every day life. He is a fleeting shadow, *present* only as a look, insofar as he is internalized by me.

Looking and being looked at are, according to Sartre, the two ways in which people relate to themselves and to one another. In self-deceit they become objects through their own look or lock themselves up in their own subjectivity. In social intercourse, they let themselves be sentenced to a loss of freedom by the look of the other or they raise themselves to the status of absolute subject and destroy by their look the freedom of the other. The theory of the look as a basis for Sartre's conception of human conduct leaves no room for social intercourse in which *equal* subjects respect the ambiguity of human existence (facticity *and* freedom), with regard to themselves as well as to one another. The antagonistic theory of the look is one in which looks really kill and ultimately destroy either one's own or the other's subjectivity. It comes as no surprise that such a grim theory of human existence as the one presented in *Being and Nothingness* makes the development of a philosophic ethic problematic at the very least. When morality has anything to do with solidarity, then a philosophical ethic that attempts to legitimatize such solidarity needs an ontological foundation that would show the necessity and inevitability of solidarity and leave no room for a solipsistical position.[32] It is this foundation that is laid down in the *Critique of Dialectical Reason*.

CRITIQUE OF DIALECTICAL REASON

The *Critique of Dialectical Reason* pursues the following two goals, among others. On the one hand Sartre attempts to furnish irrefutable proof for the existence of a dialectical rationality. On the other hand he aims to uncover both the ontological and the structural-anthropological bases of the phenomenon of alienation, described by Marx.

In order to realize these goals, Sartre follows a philosophical route that is both Cartesian and historical-materialistic in nature. It is Cartesian, insofar as there is a striving for apodictical evidence of a dialectical *cogito*; it is materialistic for the reason that in a dialectical *cogito* consciousness and materiality are, of course, indissolubly connected; and finally, it is historical, since the structural-anthropological (ontological) condition under which alienation may occur as a historical phenomenon is such that it does not explain a *possible* alienation in a *possible* world, but rather the alienation in *our* world with *our* history.

The originality of the attempt made in the *Critique* is due precisely to the fact that a Cartesian method is being combined with a historical-materalistic method. To denote this original approach, the phrase "historical-transcendental" is used in this chapter, since this seems to be a reasonably adequate description of the way in which Sartre attempts to reach his goal. The approach is of a *transcendental* nature, insofar as it seeks to establish apodictical evidence. Simultaneously, it is of a *historical* character, since the evidence holds valid for this world only, with its history as we know it. Hence this is also the reason that in the Introduction to the *Critique* we read that it is necessary "to explore the limits, the validity, and the extent of dialectical Reason."[33] Just as Kant in his *Kritik der reinen Vernunft* measured the limits and extent of analytical reason, so Sartre, in his *Critique*, seeks to delimit the domain of dialectical reason. This domain is not that of possible worlds; it covers only the concrete world we live in. The historical-transcendental analysis in the *Critique* is carried out in four stages. The titles of the four chapters in Book I of the first volume of this work indicate these four stages consecutively.

The object of the first step is to demonstrate the *evidence* of the dialectical *cogito*; that of the second step to reveal the *apodicticity* of this evidence. Also in this step, the evidence for the existence of another dialectical *cogito* is generated and the solipsistical position refuted.

The third step outlines the structural-anthropological (ontological) conditions for the phenomenon of alienation and defines these in terms of "Scarcity" and of "Counter-Finality." Finally, in the fourth step, the fundamental structure of "Reciprocity" is uncovered and unveiled as "seriality." Within the framework of this chapter, the third and fourth steps will not be discussed. Step 1 will be described only very briefly, while step 2 will be reconstructed in greater detail.

Step 1. Individual praxis as totalization. On page 80 of the *Critique* we read: "The entire historical dialectic *rests on an individual praxis insofar as it is already dialectical. . . .*" Sartre describes this individual dialectical praxis as evidence furnished in a spontaneous experience. To the extent that I, as organism, spontaneously experience the relation with materiality, it is a first form of dialectics furnished spontaneously. The most elementary relation between man and matter manifests itself as "Need" (*Besoin*). This is the first negation of a negation and the first form of totalization. In the human organism negation announces itself as "Lack" (*manque*): The organism experiences its existence as threatened by the surrounding materiality. This lack is ignored, because the organism works the surrounding materiality and consumes it as nourishment. In this manner, negation of negation results in an affirmation: the preservation of the organism.

At this point it would be justifiable to ask: What is the transcendental conclusive force of this experience? The fact is that the functioning of an animal organism may be described in a similar manner. Why does Sartre ascribe a transcendental status to this dialectical human experience, since one can speak of a transcendental experience only if it is lived not merely spontaneously but also self-consciously?

Sartre explains this in the following manner: Contrary to what applies in the case of animal functioning, the dialectical functioning of man is "action." Action differs from animal functioning in two ways: in the first place because action never involves total adjustment to the surrounding materiality, but always also goes beyond any given situation; in the second place because action is always *conscious* of its functioning as organism. Therefore, Sartre reserves the term "work" (*travail*) for the dialectical relation between man and matter and does not use the term to refer to animal functioning. This means that work implies not only a transformation of matter by man but also man's consciousness of this manipulation.

This brief characterization of the first step will suffice for this discussion. In conclusion we may note that even though the evidence of the dialectical *cogito* has been demonstrated, the apodicticity of this evidence has not as yet been established. It remains to be proven that work is also an *inevitable* relation between man and matter: that man can exist only as a working being, as a matter-manipulating being. The demonstration of this inevitability occurs in the second step and is accompanied by the demonstration of the evidence for the existence of an other dialectic *cogito* than I myself.

Step 2. Human relations as a mediation between different sectors of materiality. Sartre describes how, from the window of his hotel room, he looks down and sees a road-mender on the road and a gardener working in a garden. The workers are separated by a high wall. Neither can see the other and each may possibly not be aware of the other's existence. Nonetheless, there is in this instance a question of a reciprocal relation between these two men. The relation, however, is of a negative order: They do not know each other. This conclusion is possible because the philosopher at the window mediates between them. He concludes, from above, that, because of the wall, it is not possible for either of them to be aware of the other. But there also is a relation between the philosopher and the gardener, as well as between the philosopher and the road-mender: the philosopher at the window posits himself as a "petit bourgeois intellectual," seeking to relax in a hotel, following a period of strenuous work or in order to write a book. However, he posits himself as such insofar as he realizes that he is not *one* of those working men and that he himself would not be capable of carrying out the work that they are performing. At this point one could object that the philosopher nevertheless recognizes them as men, because he still posits himself as a man facing other men. However, "Man" does not exist because "the concept of man is an abstraction which never occurs in concrete intuition. It is, in fact, as 'a holiday maker' confronting a gardener and a road-mender, that I come to conceive myself; and in making myself what I am, I discover them as they make themselves, that is, as their work produces them; ..."34 The word "work" is of decisive significance in this quotation. The relation between people exists exclusively insofar as they work (manipulate) the materiality by which they are surrounded. In a diagram it is possible to illustrate the relations between G (gardener), R (road-mender), and Ph (philosopher) in the following manner (Diagram I):

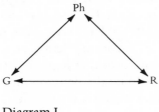

Diagram I

The relations between G and R on the one hand, and the relations between Ph and G and between Ph and R on the other are mutually dependent. There are not only relations among the individuals, Ph, G, and R, but at the same time there is a relation among those relations.

This point is of vital importance. Sartre warns us of the error in assuming that the relation between G and R is based exclusively on a subjective impression on the part of Ph. "It is important not to reduce this mediation to a subjective impression: We should not say that *for me* the two labourers are ignorant of one another. They are ignorant of one another *through me* to the extent that I become what I am through *them*."35 Ph's conclusion, I am a bourgeois intellectual on vacation, is made possible from reflection on the two laborers. Their presence is the necessary condition for the self-awareness of Ph, while this, conversely, is the necessary condition for the relation of negative reciprocity between G and R. So, the relation between G and R is no more independent from the relation between Ph and G, and between Ph and R, than both of the latter are independent from the relation between G and R. At this point however, the question may arise: What is the validity of these conclusions in the event that Ph does not perceive G *and* R, but only G for example? In that case, would not the reciprocal relation between Ph and G be realized independently of the relation between G and R? In order to answer this question, Diagram I is extended to Diagram II, as follows:

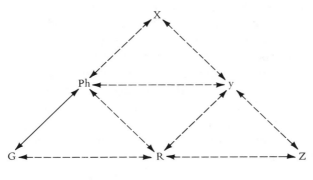

Diagram II

This diagram indicates that even in the instance where Ph perceives only G, in principle the pattern of Diagram I is repeated. Though Ph realizes that he is not G, he can do so only insofar as he is simultaneously aware that G performs only this particular type of labor. He can recognize the specificity of his work only insofar as he distinguishes it from other manual activities (for example: road repairs). In addition, Diagram II reveals that Ph is "any one" (*n'importe qui*). Any arbitrary laborer would be equally capable of making Ph the object of reflection and consequently realizing that he is not Ph, but only insofar as he is simultaneously aware of the specificity of his own manual labor.

It is clear that the relational Diagram II may be extended endlessly. All men are connected with one another, not because they participate in a Platonic idea of "Man," but because all of them participate in the dialectics of work.

At a first reading, the chosen example would seem trivial; however, after further consideration it reveals its deeper significance and its symbolic value. In a graphic manner a transcendental reflection is described in which fundamental reciprocity emerges as an apodictical evidence. The transcendental demonstrative force of Sartre's analysis is all the stronger because this evidence is not acquired through abstraction from the existing social order, but precisely by taking this as the point of departure. The point of departure is our capitalist society, in which, as a consequence of a rigid division of labor, interhuman relations are of a strongly atomistic structure, and private ownership occupies a central position. For this reason, the different elements Sartre's picture comprises have been selected with great care. The division of labor is symbolized by placing the intellectual at the window and the two workers down below (vertical division of labor). The reciprocity between the two is realized by an individual who, according to our current norm system, is valued at a higher level. Reflection (the looking down from above) is the prerogative of the intellectual. The wall (topped with bits of broken glass), by which the garden is separated from the street, is a symbol for a typical bourgeois form of private ownership and, at the same time, for the horizontal division of labor.

The example also demonstrates that the apodictical evidence of my own dialectical *cogito* implies the dialectical *cogito* of the other. In a *historical*-transcendental analysis it is evidently not only impossible to conceive of myself as nonworking and as nonexistent, but also, the nonexistence of the other is evidently unthinkable. In such an analysis, both my own existence as well as that of the other are given in one and the same experience. For the dialectical *cogito* it truly holds valid that this implies the *cogito* of the other; not however as the one *"for* whom" I am the object of a look, but as the one *"with* whom" I am allied fundamentally. This other is not given as a *"pour-autrui"* (for-the-Other), but as an *"avec-autrui"* (with-the-Other). In a historical-transcendental analysis, a not yet morally charged structural-anthropological solidarity emerges that may serve as the basis for solidarity on the moral level.

It is in this perspective that the term *"n'importe qui,"* denoting transcendental consciousness, is given greater relief. The historical-transcendental analysis is not the prerogative of a select few (philosophers for example); it is, on the contrary, accessible to all. Moreover, is also true that I conduct this analysis in the clear awareness of my absolute uniqueness (insofar as it is transcendental) as well as (insofar as it is of a historical nature) of my fundamental alliance with the surrounding materiality and with the others – in the past as well as in the present – who, like myself, work this materiality. Thus in the second step of the historical-transcendental analysis, important material is supplied for the structural-anthropological foundation of the methodology of the social sciences, unfolded in the *Questions de méthode* and applied on a large scale in *L'Idiot de la famille*.

CONCLUSIONS

The preceding, global reconstruction of the development of the concept of individuality in Sartre's work leads to the following conclusions:

1. If Sartre's philosophy implies a "*coupure épistemologique*" at all, then such a break should not in the first instance be located between *Being and Nothingness* and the *Critique of Dialectical Reason*, but between the *Transcendence of the Ego* and *Being and Nothingness*. However, it would seem to be more appropriate to avoid the term "break" in relation to Sartre's work and rather to describe his philosophical development as a dialectical process, in which there are certainly opposing viewpoints, but in which such viewpoints have ultimately been "*aufgehoben*" in the Hegelian sense of this word. In this way one may interpret the historical-transcendental consciousness that we meet with the *Critique of Dialectical Reason* as a synthesis of the two widely divergent types of transcendental consciousness described in *The Transcendence of the Ego* and in *Being and Nothingness*.

2. If one obtains the apodictical evidence of the *cogito* through the use of a classical Cartesian method, a confrontation with the problem of solipsism is unavoidable. By means of a radicalization à la Husserl of the "*doute méthodique*," one may possibly avoid an extreme form of ontological solipsism. If consciousness "exists" only as consciousness *of*, then one cannot exclude the possibility that the apodictical evidence of the *cogito* implies the existence of a nonconscious mode of reality. The intentionality of consciousness is decidedly not sufficient ground, however, for the assumption that the existence of the other-as-subject is fundamentally evident. Confronted with the problem of whether the other-as-subject exists, two alternatives are available. One either departs from the Cartesian framework – as did Heidegger – and places man as "*Dasein*" back in Being, or one revises this framework in a creative manner.

Both in *The Transcendence of the Ego* and in the *Critique of Dialectical Reason*, Sartre chooses the latter alternative. Neither the *impersonal* transcendental consciousness of the early article, nor the "*homme historique*" of the later work are concerned with the problem of the existence of an other I. In the first case because the existence of the other simply does not come up for discussion, and in the latter case because the dialectical nature of the *cogito* implies the existence of the other-as-subject.

Sartre's attempt in *Being and Nothingness* to synthesize a Cartesian and a Heideggerian method, which resulted in the personification of transcendental consciousness that finds itself *within* rather than *over against* the world, led to a renewed problematizing of the existence of the other-as-subject. His solution to this problem in the theory of the look failed and obstructed the way to a philosophical ethics.

3. In the third and last "conclusion" to *The Transcendence of the Ego* Sartre asserts that the conception of the Ego as a consciousness-transcendent object *in* the world makes possible the foundation of an ethic. The closing sentence of the article reads: "No more is needed in the way of a philosophical foundation of an ethics and a politics which are absolutely positive." Much has been written concerning the possibility of an ethic on the basis of the ontology developed in *Being and Nothingness*. Some are of the opinion that this work stands in the way of the construction of a normative ethic. Others take a somewhat more optimistic view. Whatever the case may be, one thing is certain: Sartre never *published* an ethic and, therefore, the question that remains open is why he never did so. The answers that he himself gave on various occasions seek for the cause of this lack in the grim situation persisting in Europe after the Second World War. And just as the war influenced the tone and content of *Being and Nothingness*, so postwar political relations most probably contributed to the ethical lacuna in Sartre's philosophical work. But one of the most important *philosophical* reasons for the lack of a full-fledged Sartrean ethics is without doubt the fact that the solipsistic position is not overcome until the *Critique of Dialectical Reason*. The "philosophical foundation" that Sartre mentions in the third conclusion to the early article is still rather frail. Despite the impersonal character of transcendental consciousness and its connection with the world, this consciousness is nevertheless imprisoned in ontological solitude, since it is neither historically nor materially moored in the world. In *Being and Nothingness* consciousness is *in* the world to be sure, but interhuman relations are blocked by the conception of intersubjectivity. Moreover, historical and material dimensions are almost totally lacking in that work. Finally, in the *Critique of Dialectical Reason* the *cogito* is for the

first time really connected with the other and with the surrounding materiality. Therefore in this work the foundation is laid for "an ethics and a politics which are absolutely positive." But both this ethics and this politics have yet to be constructed.

NOTES

1 Michel Contat and Michel Rybalka, *Les écrits de Sartre* (Paris: 1970), p. 339.
2 Leo Fretz, "An Interview with Jean-Paul Sartre" in Hugh J. Silvermann and Frederick A. Elliston, *Jean-Paul Sartre: Contemporary Approaches to His Philosophy* (Pittsburgh: Duquesne University Press, 1980), p. 225.
3 *TE*, pp. 103–4.
  In *The Encyclopedia of Philosophy* C. D. Rollins distinguishes three forms of solipsism: "egoism" (a moral and psychological form of solipsism), a "metaphysical solipsism," and an "epistemological solipsism." A metaphysical solipsist claims that "only I exist" or that the "Self is the whole of reality." (See Paul Edwards, ed., *The Encyclopedia of Philosophy*, Vol. VII [New York/London: 1967].)
4 *BN*, p. 628.
5 See my interview with Sartre in Silvermann and Elliston, *Sartre*, p. 239.
6 In this chapter Sartre's posthumously published works are left out of consideration. For a more substantiated opinion about the possibility or impossibility of a Sartrean ethics, consultation of these works, especially of *Cahiers pour une morale* (Paris: 1983) and of *Verité et existence* (Paris: 1989) is necessary. See also my "Humanistic Foundation of Sartrean Ethics" in Leo Fretz, *Het indivudualiteitsconcept in Sartres filosofie* (Delft: 1984), pp. 235–70.
7 *TE*, p. 32.
8 *TE*, p. 33.
9 *TE*, p. 41.
10 *TE*, p. 38. The plural "consciousnesses" does not denote the consciousnesses of different individuals, but the moments of consciousness of one and the same individual.
11 The examples, which illustrate in the present section the different levels of consciousness, are not always taken from Sartre's text.
12 *Nausea*, tr. Robert Baldick (Harmondsworth, U.K.: Penguin Books, 1965), p. 188.
13 *TE*, p. 45.
14 *Carnets de la drôle de guerre* (Paris: 1983), pp. 391ff. The English translations of the quotes are by Christina Howells.

15 "Selfness" has been chosen to translate *'ipséité"* following the transla-
    tion of Hazel Barnes in *Being and Nothingness*.
16 For a discussion of the influence of Heidegger on Sartre in the *Carnets de
    la drôle de guerre* and in *Being and Nothingness*, see Leo Fretz and
    Amparo Ariño Verdú, "Sartre entre Husserl et Heidegger" in *Forum des
    Halles*, Paris, June 23, 1990, forthcoming.
17 *TE*, p. 103.
18 *BN*, p. 235.
19 See my interview with Sartre in Silvermann and Elliston, *Sartre*, p. 232.
20 *BN*, p. 103.
21 Cf. *La Transcendance de l'ego* (ed. Vrin), p. 66, "la conscience est un être
    dont l'essence implique l'existence." This is translated by Williams and
    Kirkpatrick as "consciousness is a being whose essence involves its
    existence" (*TE*, p. 84). And cf. *L'Être et le néant*, pp. 21–2: "comme la
    conscience n'est pas possible avant d'être, mais que son être est la source
    et la condition de toute possibilité, c'est son existence qui implique son
    essence." This is translated by Hazel Barnes as "Since consciousness is
    not *possible* before being, but since its being is the source and condition
    of all possibility, its existence implies its essence" (*BN*, p. xxxi). For
    reasons of logical consistency I prefer "implies" (Hazel Barnes's transla-
    tion) to "involves" (Williams and Kirkpatrick's translation) as equiva-
    lent of the French *implique*.
22 *BN*, p. xxxviii.
23 See my interview with Sartre in Silvermann and Elliston, *Sartre*, p. 238,
    where Sartre says: "I did some work in the resistance like everyone else
    and *Being and Nothingness* was also a book against the Germans. It has
    an anti-German aspect and there is most certainly some violence in it
    and more generally some antipathy, which undoubtedly can be ex-
    plained in this way."
24 *BN*, p. 251.
25 *BN*, p. 233.
26 *BN*, p. 256.
27 *BN*, p. 258.
28 *BN*, p. 259.
29 *BN*, p. 260.
30 See A. J. Ayer's critique: "And how can it be certain that anyone is
    watching me? It may be certain that I have the feeling of being watched,
    and this may reasonably be taken to involve a belief on my part that
    other subjects exist. But what we require is a logical justification of this
    belief, and this, so far as I can see, Sartre makes no attempt to provide"
    (in "Novelist-Philosophers: Jean-Paul Sartre," *Horizon*, 12, no. 67, July
    1945, p. 106).

31 See my *Het individualiteitsconcept in Sartres filosofie*, pp. 77–82, and my "Sartre et Freud" in Claude Burgelin, ed. *Lectures de Sartre* (Lyon: 1986), pp. 241–51. See also Ivan Soll, "Sartre's Rejection of the Freudian Unconscious" in Paul A. Schilpp, ed., *The Philosophy of Jean-Paul Sartre*, Vol. XVI (La Salle, Ill.: The Library of Living Philosophers, 1981), pp. 582–604.
32 See the appendix titled "Humanistic Foundation of Sartrean Ethics," pp. 235–70 in my *Het individualiteitsconcept in Sartres filosofie*.
33 *CDR*, p. 21.
34 *CDR*, p. 101.
35 *CDR*, p. 103.

II Psychology and ethics

4 Sartre's moral psychology

Across its long history moral philosophy has been as concerned with the cultivation of certain moral dispositions, or traits of character, or moral psychologies, as it has been with establishing the validity and universality of moral rules and principles. Moral psychology begins with the inner person: not how we outwardly conform to external moral rules, but how we are in our hearts and souls and, particularly, how we are when we are truly flourishing as human beings. It is therefore concerned with the ethics of virtue, and a casual glance at the respective moral psychologies of Aristotle, Augustine, Spinoza, Hume, Kant, and the existentialists would reveal analyses of such virtues as integrity, justice, prudence, courage, magnanimity, sincerity, and authenticity. These are not innate dispositions, or inherited traits of personality like shyness or cheerfulness. They are acquired by teaching or practice or reflection, and to a certain extent reveal what we have made of ourselves; thus they express our moral way of being, and our fundamentl moral outlook, and not just something we happen to have.

Sartre's concern with the ethics of character, the conditions of self-determination and human agency, and the phenomenology of moral life, places him within this tradition of moral and philosophical psychology. This essay is concerned with elaborating and clarifying a number of interrelated aspects of Sartre's moral and philosophical psychology, particularly as they are developed in *Being and Nothingness*[1]: self-determination and agency, responsibility for self, the unity of a life, moral reasoning, and self-knowledge. Some of Sartre's responses to the shortcomings of his earlier views on these issues will also be studied, particularly as they are developed in *The Family Idiot*.[2] Before turning to Sartre's views, however, some of the territory characterizing moral and philosophical psychology will be mapped out.

Embedded in our folk psychology and in our Western conceptual framework for persons, as well as in our legal systems, is a model of rational moral autonomy that reflects some of our deepest beliefs about what human flourishing is, and what is most distinctive and morally important about persons. The moral autonomy it sets forth is the kind that we would ascribe to people who have not passively acquiesced to social expectations, roles, and values, but who have, by reasoning, choice, or moral reflection, arrived at their own moral outlook and view of the good life; who have achieved a level of personal and interpersonal integrity, by assuming a stance of self-criticism and self-questioning toward their desires, beliefs, volitions, actions, and habits; and who know with some acuity what they are doing with their lives, and what their true goals are. Obviously not everyone actually attains this level of moral autonomy and self-knowledge, but we hold it as an ideal to which we should aspire, and we evaluate ourselves and others in light of it.[3] We consider its achievement a virtue, just as we consider the lack of it (as manifested in self-deception or self-ignorance) a moral shortcoming.

However familiar and intuitively appealing this model may be, it still invites some important questions – particularly with the advance of a number of sciences that make the claim that we are not really masters of our own house:

1. To what extent can we really determine and control our way of life, our moral dispositions, and our fundamental moral outlook? How much of this process is rational?
2. On what grounds can we be held responsible for our way of life and our character?
3. Can we blame people who, because of environmental or hereditary factors over which they have had no control, end up with destructive character traits, or psychopathological attitudes?
4. How does a human life "hang together"? Does it add up to anything more than a complex flux of events and experiences?

Sartre's position on these issues changed importantly during his career. In *Being and Nothingness* (1943), he argued that the freedom we enjoy as moral agents consists in an autonomous and creative agency (and not, as many critics charge, in radical indeterminacy or causelessness). We are free, in a morally important sense, to be as we want to be. This means that we are free to choose who (but not what) we are, and to lay out the ground plan of our way of life, within a range of given determinants and situational constraints. We are also free, within certain bounds, to remake ourselves, and the assumption of alternative ways of life, life plans, and moral outlooks always remains a living option. To this Sartre adds that regardless of whether we actually remake ourselves, or achieve moral autonomy, we are always and already completely responsible for our actions and our way of life.

This view clearly has strong Kantian underpinnings in the way it conceives people as the source of their own moral authority and moral being ("Think for yourself" was one of Kant's favorite sayings), in its defense of freedom as the condition of possibility for moral responsibility, and in the way it elevates people (qua moral agents and persons) above the realm of nature and the empirically determined. The existentialist's emphasis on individual freedom, choice, and authenticity is prefigured in *Religion within the Limits of Reason Alone*, where Kant argues that "man *himself* must make or have made himself into whatever, in a moral sense, whether good or evil, he is or is to become. Either condition must be an effect on his free choice. . . ."[4]

In *The Family Idiot* (1971–2), his massive biography of Gustave Flaubert, Sartre continued to identify freedom with self-determination, and continued to defend the importance of moral autonomy; but he allowed comparatively little constructivity – and even less plasticity – in the given determinants. We are socially conditioned "all the way down," and we can make something of ourselves only within the narrow limits of what we have already been made into. Yet Sartre still retained his belief that we are totally responsible for ourselves.

The differences between the moral and philosophical psychology of these two stages of Sartre's career are significant. In the former work, the center of Sartre's concern is largely with the origin of our actions, insofar as these can be traced to a deep-lying source of creative agency by virtue of which we choose ourselves ab initio. The form his explanation takes is largely transcendental, and in the tradi-

tion of Kant and Husserl. In the latter work, he is concerned with
our assumption of responsibility for ourselves, by means of the activity of integrating and identifying with the many *antecedent* and
given psychological, biological, and historical influences that condition us. Moral agency is to be found *within* the limits of our given
psychological, cognitive, emotional, and motivational makeup, and
not in spite of them, or in some deeper source of agency that is (in a
transcendental sense) presupposed by them. Some of the differences
between these two concerns will be examined in the following
pages.

HARD DETERMINISM

One way to set the stage for an elucidation of Sartre's views on self-
determination and human agency is to begin by showing how the
hard determinist approach to moral psychology drastically decreases
the range of determinants of our actions over which we can exert
control. According to this approach, which Sartre accuses of bad
faith and "seriousness" (*BN*, p. 40), our personal identity is formed
for us, by circumstances and forces external and antecedent to our
purposes, choice, will, or understanding: it is not, in any significant
sense, formed *by* us. As the biochemical and neurosciences are showing, our cognitive, motivational, and psychological makeup stands
at the tip of a massive causal iceberg that extends far beyond our
awareness and control, and deep into our prehistories. We think
ourselves free (that is, faced with genuine possibilities, exercising
choices, and possessed of a certain creative agency) only to the extent that we are ignorant of the vast work network of natural causes
of our actions (neurophysiological, for example) and the lawful relations governing them. Although the reflexive power to alter certain
aspects of our inherited psychological and motivational makeup
may be granted as one of the intermediate factors in the formation of
this makeup, this power is itself formed by antecedent circumstances not subject to our control, will, or choice.

Hard determinists argue that these are sufficient grounds for considering that the kind of freedom and control that we would like to
have, and that is embodied in our folk model of moral autonomy, is
deeply incompatible with determinism and with the deterministic
picture yielded by the sciences. They argue that ascriptions of full

responsibility for actions cannot properly be made, since we cannot do otherwise than what the constraints of our given psychological and motivational makeup allow us to do.[5] More basically, we are unable to be different from what we are, and unable to do otherwise than what we in fact do – at least in the strong sense of being able to do otherwise than what we do that is required by those who defend human agency (that is, the freedom to assume alternative ways of life, life plans, and moral outlooks).

In addition to this, hard determinists argue that because our psychologies are the products of antecedent conditions and forms of conditioning in which our volition and choice played little or no part, it is as senseless to blame people if they are unable to change themselves as it is to praise them if they are successful.[6] This is because the very ability and motivation that is required to modify inherited character traits is itself a product of heredity or childhood conditioning, which are factors over which we initially have no control.[7]

SELF-DETERMINATION: A GENERAL FORMULATION

Defenders of human agency like Kant and Sartre are concerned to show that we are not helpless prisoners of our character, past, or biology, or vehicles of impersonal historical forces and that our reasons and choices are not mere rationalizations for behavior that we would nevertheless engage in. There are a number of ways to theorize this, but the general approach adopted by Kant and Sartre postulates that qua selves or persons, we are unique agents capable of determining ourselves by our own reasons, choices, and purposes. At least some of the determinants of action are internal to the self or agent in a way that physical causes and antecedent conditions are not. This means that we can, at a level we consider morally significant, determine ourselves "from the inside," without being fully influenced by alien forces (external or internal). We are, within bounds, authors of our own life histories and moral being, because we contribute through our own actions, choices, or intentions to the making of what, qua moral agents, we are.

The idea that we can determine ourselves from the inside supposes that a certain subset of our beliefs, emotions, and attitudes, as well as a certain subset of our emotional and motivational dispositions, are not given as unchangeable natural characteristics, like eye color or brain size or skeletal structure (what Sartre calls "facticity"). It supposes that we do not *have* these characteristics *simpliciter* (that is to say, that we are wholly one with them), but have a *relation* to them, by virtue of which reflexivity we are capable of being different from them.

The connection between reflexivity and action may be clarified by considering how certain objects are characterizable by reference to a core of determinate properties, which are more or less fixed and given to them. A bit of wood, for instance, can be adequately characterized by listing such properties as its genetic and biochemical composition. People, by contrast, are more than they appear to be, supposing that a similar inventory of de facto properties were to be attempted. They are not exhaustively characterized by fixed and given characteristics (that is, by their facticity), but are also constituted in some way by what Sartre calls their possibilities – by what they are aiming at, or beginning, or projecting themselves toward.

This is an important distinction for moral philosophy: If what we are is constituted to a certain extent by our projects and goals, then it is always open to us to consider who we are in light of who we might want to become, or who we should become. We are capable of raising morally evaluative questions like "What do I really want to do with my life?" – questions that, in Sartre's terminology, effect a "rupture" with the given. In doing this, we are exercising a capacity that may be unique to persons, namely the capacity to question,[8] to step back from and reflect upon many of our beliefs, desires, and emotions, and many of the traits, dispositions, and motivational patterns we find outselves with, and then to form higher order evaluations, preferences, or choices regarding which of them we want to be constitutive of our identity as persons and moral agents.[9]

Although the precise nature of this reflexive capacity is subject to dispute by a number of contemporary philosophers – who describe it variously as strong evaluation,[10] rational reflective self-evaluation,[11] second-order desire,[12] participatory reflection,[13] reflexive knowledge,[14] radical choice – it is generally agreed that it has the power to alter and reshape its objects. Fundamental changes in the way we evaluate, reflect upon, or understand such things as our way of life, our relations with others, our emotions, our final ends and our death necessarily occasion changes in who we are; that is, the object of evaluation or reflection, and the evaluating or reflecting subject, change and extend their range together. Because we are capable of thinking about who we are in light of certain de jure questions, and because we can shape ourselves on the basis of these thoughts and evaluations, we can be considered responsible for ourselves in a way that many other creatures cannot.

Obviously, this general formulation of the idea of self-determination leaves unanswered the question of the depth of interdependence between self-knowledge and self-formation. The weak view is that it extends only to some of our actions, beliefs, and desires. A stronger version holds that it covers certain aspects of the motivational and psychological makeup from which our actions and desires spring. A still stronger version holds that the control we can exert goes "all the way down": that is, that we are capable of making choices and initiating actions that involve the deepest levels of our being.

It is this latter view that is of interest to philosophers of existence like Sartre and Heidegger, who argue that it is entirely up to us to determine (in a moral and existential sense) what kind of being we are going to be. They claim that unlike many other creatures, we do not exist in a straightforward de facto sense. That is, it is not the case that we are, and can only be, what we are; it would be more accurate to say that we have ourselves *to be*, or that we have our own existence to *assume*. The unavoidable split or *décalage* between an existent and its existence means that it is entirely our own responsibility to work out what we are going to do with fundamental life possibilities confronting us, and what basic orientation we are going to take in the face of existence.[15]

Sartre therefore follows Kant in defending the general idea that qua selves or persons, we are unique agents capable of determining ourselves by our own choices, intentions, reasons, and purposes. Like Kant, he also addresses the problem of determinism, arguing that these identity-shaping choices are not themselves caused by previous events or antecedent conditions in accordance with the laws of nature.[16] This does not mean, however, that Sartre accepts the radical libertarian view that our choices are matters of mere chance, or random breaks in the causal network (cf. *BN*, p. 437) – a view that he emphatically denies. His argument, rather, is that the self or person enjoys a special kind of agency, wherein the ultimate

determinants of its actions are its own choices, intentions, and purpose. By postulating the existence of a special deep-lying or transcendental source of agency, Sartre, like Kant, believes that some of the
fears about diminished responsibility and agency can be allayed; for
then a distinction can be generated between actions that are ultimately determined by causal forces alien to ourselves (including
certain internal forces), and actions that are determined ultimately
by ourselves *for* ourselves – that is, by the real, or transcendental, or
existentially authentic, or self-determining agent.

Sartre's idea that the ultimate determinants of an agent's actions
are his or her own choices, intentions, and purposes can be spelled out
in a different way. At a certain depth, human agency is explained by
itself, and no further explanation is possible. The explanation of a
particular action, for example, will refer to an agent's desires in a
given situation, the explanation of which will refer to a larger frame of
attitudes, dispositions, and beliefs, which in turn will refer to a larger
framework of projects. Ultimately this chain of explanation will terminate, not in something external and antecedent to the agent (in
facticity, or in the causal iceberg), but in the agent itself. Whatever lies
at these depths, Sartre argues, it must be fundamental; that is, it must
represent the most basic set of terms by means of which we, qua
moral agents, define ourselves; and it must not be derived from or
conditioned by anything else. In Kantian terms – and Sartre's argument has a strong Kantian bearing here – it must represent the condition of possibility of personal experience.

Before continuing, it is worth pointing out two problems with the
Kantian and Sartrean idea of a special form of agency. The first is its
uncritical acceptance of the incompatibility of freedom and determinism, and its assumption that a kind of absolute Maginot line has
to be established to protect the realm of human agency from the
realm of the causally determined. The assumption here is that human agency cannot be built up from some initially unfree or nonagential material. The second is a problem of infinite regress: Even if
our actions are explained by some deeper agency, then what explains
this deeper agency? However many levels of agency are postulated,
there will still be a level inviting the question "What explains it?"
To be consistent, the source of agency must in turn be explained,
and ultimately this must be by something external and antecedent
to it – unless one holds the implausible thesis that self or agent, like

a god, is its *own* ground and source of being. Some of these problems are addressed in Sartre's later work.

RADICAL CHOICE AND THE FUNDAMENTAL PROJECT

What is the nature of the special deep source of agency that Sartre reserves only for the human agent? In virtue of what are we ultimately self-determining? Sartre's views on this source of agency are much less rationalistic than Kant's, for he emphasizes the deeply futural, prerational, existentially contingent, epistemically limited, and desire-based nature of our capacity for self-determination and autonomy, namely the radical choice of self and the fundamental project.

Sartre argues that our identities as persons and moral agents are not ready-made, imposed, or discovered; nor are they the product of conditioning, genetic inheritance, neurophysiology, or an economy of unconscious drives. Instead, they are chosen as a kind of ultimate end, and the way this choice of identity is realized across many years of experience is best characterized in teleological terms as a kind of project; that is, it is a long-term endeavor of making ourselves who we are.

Sartre likens our capacity to determine our personal identities by choice to the creation of an artwork (for example, the relation between a sculptor and his or her block of marble).[17] In both cases order must be created from a raw material that to a certain extent underdetermines the final form (but which does not afford complete arbitrariness); in both cases a certain constructive process is required of the sculptor-agent; in both cases he or she can evaluate, criticize, and deliberate about the ongoing process of the creation; and in both cases the sculptor alone can be considered responsible for the finished product. (The analogy would clearly be a misleading one if restrictions were not placed upon the plasticity of the raw material and upon the constructive powers of the sculptor.)

We make ourselves and define our way of life by projecting ourselves toward the future, and by constantly going beyond the given situation in which we find ourselves. The multifarious actions, desires, beliefs, and experiences our lives comprise must, in Sartre's words, "derive their meaning from an original projection" that we make of ourselves (*BN*, p. 39). Given this strong teleological organization, our life histories are best characterized as coherent long-term projects that exhibit an inner dynamic and intelligibility, rather than as a series of events strung loosely together, in blind or mechanical response to external events and antecedent conditions. Projection toward the future is the way in which order and meaning are created from the "raw" psychological, existential, and historical material of life; it is the way a future is fashioned. Merleau-Ponty captures a sense of this:

One day, once and for all, something was set in motion which, even during sleep, can no longer cease to see or not to see, to feel or not to feel, to suffer or be happy, to think or rest from thinking, in a word to "have it out" with the world. There then arose, not a new set of sensations or states of consciousness, not even a new monad or a new perspective . . . [but] a *fresh possibility of situations. . . .* There was henceforth a new "setting," the world received a fresh layer of meaning.[18]

The explanatory power Sartre attributes to the concepts of the choice of self and the fundamental project is vast, and the claims he makes about them have clearly transcendental import: The project is "the original relation which the for-itself chooses with its facticity and with the world" (*BN*, p. 457). It concerns "not my relations with this or that particular object in the world, but my total being-in-the-world" (p. 480). Again, it is the "primary project which is recognized as the project which can no longer be interpreted in terms of any other and which is total" (p. 479). Finally, in distinctly Kantian terms, he claims that "what makes all experience possible is . . . an original upsurge of the for-itself as presence to the object which is not" (p. 176).

To complicate matters, Sartre makes a number of puzzling claims about responsibility for self and moral desert, which reflect his conviction that since we choose ourselves absolutely, we must be responsible in an absolute sense. In making these claims, he widens the scope of moral responsibility far beyond what we normally consider tenable, and in apparent defiance of a large class of moral excusing and exempting conditions under which we view certain actions. We are, he claims, totally responsible for ourselves, including those things that befall us (cf. *BN*, pp. 553–6); we are responsible for all aspects of our situation; there are no accidents in life; and we always have the sort of lives we deserve. The assumption seems to be that unless we make ourselves absolutely, we could not be responsible at all.

To clarify some of these sweeping claims, the concepts of the choice of self and the project will be explored in greater detail, and then examined vis-à-vis the issues of moral reasoning and self-knowledge.

Sartre conceives the fundamental project in strong holistic terms as an interconnected system of relations. Every aspect of a person's life – profession, tastes, choice of friends, habits – expresses a "thematic organization and an inherent meaning in this totality" (*BN*, p. 468). With the right method, the structure of a person's whole way of life and way of being can be discerned in a single act. A particular case of jealousy, for instance, "signifies for the one who knows how to interpret it, the total relation to the world by which the subject constitutes himself as a self" (p. 563).

Despite his various descriptions of the project as the "transcendent meaning" of each concrete desire, and as the "center of reference for an infinity of polyvalent meanings," Sartre vigorously rejects the idea of a transcendental ego or essential self – some transcendent pole to which all experience must necessarily refer, or to which it must belong. The unity and interconnectedness of a person's way of being do not come from the top down, but are functions of the relations *between* the many different aspects of life experience. Even the psychophysical ego, which might be thought to serve as the naturally given anchor for character predicates, and as the seat of psychological unity, is merely a synthetic and ideal construct that appears only upon a constructive (and "impure") reflection. Sartre argues that the ego is an object of conscious experience, but not a real structure that is coextensive or autochthonous with it.[19]

Second, the project is actively constructed, and not given or fixed. The numerous antecedent conditions that are ordinarily construed as having a causal influence in the formation of our identity (such as genetic, environmental, and social factors) affect us not for what they are in themselves, but for what we make of them insofar as we project ourselves beyond them, confer meaning upon them, and construct from them a signifying situation. Sartre grants to causal forces only an attenuated role vis-à-vis the original and constructive powers that we bring to bear on them. The environment, for example, "can act on the subject only to the extent that he comprehends it; that is, transforms it into a situation" (p. 572).

The idea that we do not passively submit to an external schema of causation, but define ourselves by our project beyond it, does not mean that the choice we make of ourselves occurs in a causal vacuum. Obviously we do not choose our parents, or our biological and neurological makeup; we find ourselves "thrown into" a situation, and endowed with certain brute characteristics (that is, facticity). But factical characteristics to a certain extent underdetermine how we *assume* them, find meaning and moral significance in them, and take them up as part of a whole way of life. They do not come ready-made, or with labels on them. One of the illustrations Sartre provides is the case of physical disability:

Even this disability from which I suffer I have assumed by the very fact that I live; I surpass it toward my own projects, I make of it the necessary obstacle for my being, and I cannot be crippled without choosing myself as crippled. This means that I choose the way in which I constitute my disability (as "unbearable," "humiliating," "to be hidden," "to be revealed to all," "an object of pride," "the justification for my failures," etc.). (*BN*, p. 328)

We alone can create the *meaning* of the ensemble of factical conditions that root us in a particular situation: We are, in Sartre's words, the beings who transform our being into meaning, and through whom meaning comes into the world.[20] Sartre's indebtedness to the Kantian and Husserlian theory of *sinngebung* (meaning-giving) and transcendental constitution is plainly evident here: The creation of meaning is not itself something that can be adequately characterized in causal terms, as part of nature's causal network. It is an ontologically primitive and underived process. Strangely, we are also unaware of ourselves as being the deep source of meaning; our prereflective experience (as Nietzsche and Husserl also remarked) tends to dissimulate its own meaning-conferring and organizational activity. We tend to be naive realists, assuming uncritically that our thought pictures a world that is always and already divided up at its true joints, as if the meanings and distinctions we find in objects are there as brute, mind-independent givens.

Finally, Sartre is careful to divest his claims about the project from the foundationalist claims characteristic of certain traditional kinds of moral philosophy. The choice we make of ourselves, "that by which all foundations and all reasons come into being" (p. 479), is not itself founded, and is in no way a source of absolute epistemic or moral certainty. It is not made of the "purest crystal, the hardest thing there is" (Wittgenstein). As a kind of "groundless ground," or contingent foundation, it is fragile and ever-diremptable. Paradoxical as this may sound, it brings out the sense in which there is nothing deeper than radical choice that might in turn define it. Radical choice functions as the unsupported "bedrock" of a whole complexly interrelated way of being in the world. This explains Sartre's claim that the "absolute event or for-itself is contingent in its very being" (BN, p. 82), even if it is "its own foundation qua for-itself" (p. 84).[21] Sartre's rejection of all forms of essentialism and foundationalism means that the hold we have over our identity is much more tenuous than we like to think: Nothing concerning our identity as persons and moral agents is immune to change or radical revision.

FOUNDATIONALISM AND THE CHOICE OF SELF

Major life changes are common phenomena. People find themselves at crossroads in their lives, often not knowing what they really want or in what direction they should best go. Over time, they develop into better or worse persons, undergo conversions, adopt new religious or moral beliefs, slowly break free of negative emotional patterns, and make fresh starts. If, as Sartre argues, the fundamental projects that describe their life histories are not grounded, are the changes they undergo changes from one project to another, or changes *within* a single project? To what extent can people actually control these changes, through deliberation, moral reflection, and searching for rational justification? And to what extent are they responsible for what they become?

Some of these questions might be clarified by considering in greater detail Sartre's theory about the ultimate groundlessness of the roots of our way of being in the world. The metaphor of bedrock is a felicitous one here, for it evokes a suggestive image of autonomy: Bedrock is that upon which other things rest, without itself resting upon anything. The choice of self that serves as Sartre's model for self-determination is autonomous in roughly this sense; our basic way of being in the world, our very connection to existence, is constituted ultimately by the choice we make of ourselves, and this does not rest upon or refer to anything more fundamental. We apprehend this choice, Sartre claims, "as not deriving from any prior reality . . ." (*BN*, p. 464); it is so deep-rooted and autonomous ("*selbstandig*") that it "does not imply any other meaning, and . . . refers only to itself" (p. 457).

These are clearly transcendental claims. The idea that the most fundamental relation we have to existence is not cognitive or epistemic or rational, but one that these relations *themselves* rest upon and that makes them possible (namely choice and projection), is a transcendental claim in the sense that it is about what is basic to all human experience; it refers to the *whole* of our form or framework of personal experience, and not to any particular content within that experience. That is, the relation is not an empirical one because it is not built up from and gradually shaped by years and years of accumulated particular experiences. It is, rather, a constitutive feature of these empirical experiences, and so it is not something that from within experience, or on the basis of experience, can become grounded.

MORAL REASONING

One way to clarify these transcendental claims is to consider some of their practical consequences. The validity and efficacy of moral reasoning in ordinary decision making provides a good test case, for it involves such activities as deliberating about morally conflicting courses of action, engaging in moral argument and discussion with other people, weighing pros and cons, and searching for the moral and rational justification of our choices. Sartre argues that *within* a way of life, when means and not ultimate priorities are in question, choices about conflicting courses of action may be guided by deliberation, moral argument, or the search for rational justification.[22] The controversial point he makes, however, is that moral reasoning at this level has signficance only insofar as it *presupposes* a prior commitment to a whole way of life and way of being – a commitment that is not itself something at which we have arrived by moral reasoning or deliberating or searching for moral justification. This underlying and often implicit background commitment makes possible certain kinds of moral argument and justification about a number of normative issues that are internal to a way of life, but it is not itself an appropriate subject of argument and justification.[23]

Sartre's restriction of the scope of moral reasoning to local or internal issues reveals just how deep rooted and primary he considers the commitment to a way of life, and the choice of self, to be. His claim that the choice of self is a choice of what will actually *count* as reasons for us (*BN*, pp. 461–2) suggests that we alone choose what rules of argumentation, and what moral conflict-resolution procedures, we will agree to be bound by; and, more generally, that we alone choose what will count as a relevant moral concern among the vast spectrum of possible normative concerns. In his own words, the choice of self is "that by which all foundations and all reasons come into being" (p. 479). Such is its depth that it is "prior to logic"; it is a "prelogical synthesis" that "decides the attitude of the person when confronted with logic and principles." For this reason, "there can be no possibility of questioning it in conformance to logic" (p. 570).

These are strong claims and appear to lend to Sartre's account of self-determination an antirationalist air. They leave a noticeable gap, for instance, for the probing and fundamental "external" questions that we sometimes raise about our lives as a whole, questions like "What should I do with my life?" "Who am I in all of this?" and "Who should I be?" These questions are *about* our projects, or our ways of life, or our basic moral frameworks in their entirety; they are not meant to *presuppose* them. They express our desire to find lasting and independent (or noncircular) reasons and moral grounds for what we are doing with our lives; but Sartre's claim that the choice of self is a choice of the very forms of reasoning we will countenance seems to deny just this.

Sartre's point, however, is not that the attempt to work out these deep questions will turn out to be meaningless or wholly arbitrary; or that they are unanswerable, and that we are left in the dark. It is rather that in the process of working out these issues, the choices and actions we make that involve the deepest level of our being cannot be determined entirely on objective and rational grounds. Eventually, we will find that the search for justification, and the moral reasoning in which we engage, just comes to an end, and we are thrown upon our own finite and fallible resources; action begins where reflection leaves off.[24] It is at this stage, as Heidegger, Sartre, and others argue, that the basic questions of existence can be worked out *only* by existing.

Limitations like these are not only signs of our cognitive shortcomings, the poverty of our rationality, or (as Hume would argue) the preponderance of emotional, affective, and habitual factors in our makeup; nor are they only a function of our finite temporal perspective – that is, the fact that our lives are too short, and the future too pressing, to bother too much with reflection. They reveal the deep formal properties and inner structure of any individual's way of life: Questions of moral and rational justification are necessarily *internal* to a way of life (or to the project or basic moral framework), but as a whole, a way of life does not afford external rational justification.[25] This is another way of arriving at the idea that the radical choice is a groundless ground.

This view is not without problems. While Sartre clearly wishes to avoid underpinning his theory of self-determination with an unchecked subjectivism, it is still not entirely clear precisely where he allows moral reasoning and rational justification to leave off and choice to take over. The idea that there is both an objective and subjective side to self-determination is not deeply controversial; what is, however, is the question of the scope and force of the subjective and irreducibly decisionistic element that comes into play when we exercise a choice with regard to our fundamental life possibilities.

Part of Sartre's unclarity about the line between the objective and subjective in self-determination is a function of his peculiar choice of examples, many of which focus on the extremes of human behavior, or upon the lives of extraordinary individuals (mostly French male writers). To see this bias, one need only look at his account of situations of extreme moral conflict.

MORAL REASONING IN EXTREME SITUATIONS

If Sartre is right in arguing that the choice of self is that which makes possible moral reasoning about project-internal concerns but is not itself an appropriate subject of moral argument and justification, then it would allow that moral reasoning *across* different ways of life and moral frameworks is bound to incur question-begging and confusion (rather like scientists in different paradigms talking at cross-purposes). This is clearly illustrated in situations of extreme moral conflict, when ultimate priorities are called into question.

A well-known instance of this is Sartre's case of the young man in occupied France who finds himself at a critical turning point in his life: He is forced to choose between joining the Resistance and taking care of his aged mother.[26] Here, the conflict of duties, responsibilities, and moral intuitions is ultimately a conflict between two ways of life, and not a conflict between moral claims within a single way of life. The man is forced to choose between two different moral practices, and two different moral environments, and the virtues and vices that will come to characterize his future actions are correspondingly divergent: In the one case, courage, dedication, selflessness, and loyalty, as well as willingness to kill, deceive, and betray; in the other case, friendship, affection, and honesty.[27] The force of Sartre's example is clear: The choice between these different ways of life is ultimately a choice between two possible types of person, for which there is no conceivably common decision criterion. Commenting upon Sartre's example, Stuart Hampshire has noted that a choice of this depth leaves the young man feeling that he has denied or negated a part of himself.

A person hesitates between two contrasting ways of life, and sets of virtues, and he has to make a very definite, and even final, determination between them. The determination is a negation, and normally the agent will feel that the choice has killed, or repressed, some part of him.[28]

The decision is a particularly torturous one because the man's moral inquiry and reasoning about which of the two courses to follow inevitably comes to an unsatisfactory end. Sartre allows that he *could* guide his inquiry and eventual choice by relying upon Christian doctrine, Kantian ethics, or general principles of utility. But the abstractness of their principles in specific and highly complex historical situations unavoidably underdetermines his final choice, and requires an element of interpretation and decision on his own part. Again, a choice made on the basis of trusting his feelings will itself rest on a prior choice about what counts as a morally significant feeling. Careful, rational, intellectual deliberation is equally unhelpful, for if he engages in deliberation, it is simply a part of his original project to realize motives by means of deliberation rather than some other form of discovery (for example, by passion or action).[29] When a person deliberates, Sartre claims, the "chips are down" (*BN*, p. 451).

In the final instance, when he is faced with a choice of whether or not to accept a way of life, moral argument, deliberation, and searching for rational justification come to an end.[30] He finds himself at the very end point of a whole way of seeing and doing things, and he must choose from a perspective characterized by ignorance, epistemic finitude, existential contingency, and moral uncertainty. Accompanying this is the stark realization that however sure and well-made his choice may appear to be, it is neither self-justifying nor supported by an external foundation. There is no possibility of putting his choice of a way of life on a secure and rational foundation.

Who could help him choose? . . . Nobody. . . . I had only one answer to give: "You're free, choose, that is, invent." No general ethics can show you what is to be done; there are no omens in the world. The Catholics will reply, "But there are." Granted – but, in any case, I myself choose the meaning they have.[31]

SELF-KNOWLEDGE

One can't take a point of view on one's life without one's living it.
– Sartre

Sartre further develops his picture of persons as finite, deeply situated, prerational, and epistemically limited beings in his account of self-knowledge. A number of activities are involved in searching for self-knowledge, namely trying to identify and describe with some acuity what we are doing with our lives, what things we hold most valuable, what our deeper feelings are, where our moral and cognitive limits lie, and how we stand as moral agents in interpersonal and communal relations. These activities are intimately linked to self-determination and responsibility, and therefore to the attainment of moral virtue. Searching for self-knowledge is an essential component of moral reflection about our fundamental life possibilities, and is propaedeutic to the choices we make that involve the deepest level of our being; it is also essential to "owning up" and overcoming self-deception, and to facing death.

But self-knowledge is a notoriously difficult task, which most of us put off. Not only do we commonly lack the requisite investigative and moral resolve to follow through with these issues; we also face the problem of a kind of "reflexive feedback loop," for we are at once the knower and the known, and changes in the way we come to identify, discriminate, and describe our states of mind and our experiences often produce changes in those very states.[32] Our situation as self-inquirers resembles that of the traveler who pushes into a changing countryside that is altered by his or her very advance. Self-knowledge, in other words, is both discovery and creation.

Sartre's account of self-knowledge shows just how limited our attempts must be when we try to work out the fundamental "external" questions that we sometimes raise about the whole of our way of life, individual life history, or basic moral framework. He argues that the global architecture of our way of being is elusive and easily overlooked, not because it is hidden and recessed like some dark secret in the soul, but because it is so close to us: It is the always presupposed background or horizon of our life experience, but it cannot be fully spelled out and articulated insofar as it remains presupposed. To indicate this, Sartre calls the fundamental project a "mystery in broad daylight" (BN, p. 571), implying that its immanence and sheer proximity is the source of our constant epistemic oversight and undersight. But he also wishes to imply that we always already understand the project, even if not in a clear, explicit, or propositionalizable way.

There is certainly an element of truth here: With respect to knowing what we are really up to, and who we are in the midst of all the actions, interactions, and experiences that make up our lives, we often cannot see the forest for the trees. Because we are so immersed in day-to-day living, the broader picture, the deeper truths, and the important patterns in our lives often escape explicit notice and recognition. In some instances this is not without practical and psychological advantage: Certain kinds of self-ignorance and self-deception have a strong adaptive function, even in our endeavor to become more autonomous.[33] And yet, continuing the metaphor, it would clearly be counterintuitive to characterize ourselves as being entire strangers to the forest which we overlook. Somehow, in inexplicit, vague, and indirect ways, we sense or intuit or embody the broader picture and the deeper truths, while not knowing them as such or being able to put them into propositional form. In addition to this, we are at times granted flashing self-insights of unparalleled depth, which slip away even as we try to express and articulate them.[34]

Sartre preserves the intuition that we are somehow attuned to the deeper truths about ourselves. Such is the scope of his concept of consciousness that he can claim that the fundamental project is fully experienced by us. By this he means that we have a deep "lived" sense and tacit understanding (compréhension) of ourselves and our "ownmost possibility of being"; we do not have to search the depths "without ever having any presentiment of [their] location, as one can go to look for the source of the Nile or the Niger" (p. 569). But this self-experience tends to give us both too much and too little of what we need for a clear and accurate self-knowledge. On the one hand, it is tacit and undeveloped, and effaced by the objects of our awareness: Sartre calls it variously "pre-reflective," "non-thetic," "non-positional," and non-analytical, thereby linking it to his version of the Heideggerean concept of preontological comprehension.[35] On the other hand, our prereflective self-consciousness presents everything "all at once" (p. 571; cf. also p. 155), in a state of extreme indifferentiation, "without shading, without relief. . . . All is there" (p. 571).

To complicate measures, Sartre places tight restrictions on the scope of our reflexive knowledge, by drawing a sharp distinction between knowledge (connaissance) and consciousness (conscience). His aim in establishing the divergence between knowledge and consciousness in reflexive matters is to show that while the fundamental characteristics of our way of being in the world are fully experienced by us, and understood in a tacit and incipient way, we do not objectively know them as such. This is stronger than the empirical claim that we generally tend to avoid self-examination and "owning up," or that we often lack the tools necessary for identifying and conceptualizing the deeper choices we have made of ourselves. It is the claim that objective knowledge can only reveal the project from an external point of view – a view that of necessity fails to capture the full sense of our experience; it cannot reveal the project from the inside, as it is for itself.

[We] are always wholly present to ourselves; but precisely because we are wholly present, we cannot hope to have an analytical and detailed consciousness of what we are. Moreover this consciousness can be only non-thetic. (p. 463)

[If] the fundamental project is fully experienced by the subject and hence wholly conscious, that certainly does not mean that it must at the same time be known by him; quite the contrary. (p. 570)

The idea that the fundamental project is lived but not known does not entail the stronger skeptical conclusion that the project is unknowable. The fact that we cannot objectively *know* our project from the inside – that is, study it, analyze it, and conceptualize it insofar as we live it – is rather like the fact that the eye cannot simultaneously see itself seeing – which clearly does not imply that it is invisible.[36] In both cases, however, we can only know it from the outside and at a distance, as another person knows it; that is, as a kind of quasi-object. We cannot fully capture and explicate what is lived prereflectively, and understood tacitly, and this epistemic barrier includes those very truths and important patterns in virtue of which so much of our lives are prereflective. "What always escapes these methods of investigation is the project as it is for itself, the complex in its own being. This project-for-itself can be experienced only as a living possession . . ." (p. 571). Epistemically, we suffer a blind spot to the project: We are "able to apprehend it only by living it" (p. 463).[37]

This blind spot is found even in self-analysis, where we are both analyst and analysand. The process of articulating, deciphering, and conceptualizing our tacit preunderstanding and self-experience unavoidably leads us further away from the lived, immediate, first-person perspective, and forces us to take an external, mediated, and partially falsifying perspective on ourselves.

A good comparison for my efforts to apprehend myself and their futility might be found in that sphere described by Poincaré in which the temperature decreases as one goes from its center to its surface. Living beings attempt to arrive at the surface of this sphere by setting out from its center, but the lowering of the temperature produces in them a continually increasing contraction. They tend to become infinitely flat proportionately to their approaching their goal, and because of this fact they are separated by an infinite distance. (p. 286)

These epistemic restrictions may seem counterproductive, given that the central principle of Sartre's existential psychoanalysis is that everything about a person can be communicated, and given that a properly conducted "regressive analysis" will lead us back to the

"the original relation which the for-itself chooses with its facticity and with the world" (p. 457). They are not, however, inconsistent with Sartre's overall enterprise of establishing a philosophy of existence. For just as he is critical of the claim of reason, so he is critical of the claims made by epistemology, which, he argues, unjustifiably privileges knowledge over being ["the illusion of the primacy of knowledge" (p. xxviii)].

Perhaps aware of the epistemic restrictions placed on self-knowledge by the dichotomy between the project-as-lived and the project-as-known, and still wishing to allow room for a practical self-insight that would have far-reaching moral consequences, Sartre introduced the possibility of "purifying reflection." Possessing some of the characteristics of genuine existential psychoanalytical self-insight, when the analysand not only acknowledges the truth of the analyst's interpretation, but lives and embodies it, a purifying self-reflection would be a nonobjectifying and nondistancing "spelling-out" of our self-experience and our tacit, preontological self-understanding; it would be the moment when knowledge *becomes* decision, and when reflection coincides with action. Because the demands on the notion of purifying reflection were so high, and because the dichotomies between the reflective and the prereflective, and the lived and the known, were so sharply drawn, it remained an undeveloped but insinuating theme in *Being and Nothingness:* It was a kind of promissory note rather than a theory of self-knowledge.

It is important to note that the wide-ranging power Sartre attributes to the concept of consciousness, and to the irreducibility of subjective experience, is purchased at the expense of a narrow model of knowledge (*connaissance*). Knowledge as he conceives it is "thetic," "positional," and analytical. It is based on a subject–object dualism, and it presupposes "reliefs, levels, an order, hierarchy" (p. 155). Moreover, knowledge is so structured that it can apprehend its object only from the outside, at a distance. Sartre obviously derives this model of knowledge from the objective causal analysis that characterizes the natural scientific viewpoint; and, with other phenomenologists and antireductionists, he claims that causal analysis falsifies subjective experience, or fails to capture its real nature.[38] While his overriding intent is clear – to show that knowledge is only a "founded mode of being" (Heidegger) – his model unjustifiably ignores a number of different forms of knowledge, not all of which are analytical, dualistic, or abstract (such as tacit knowledge, knowledge how to do something, moral knowledge), and not all of which are reducible to preontological comprehension.

Furthermore, the idea that prereflective experience is sharply distinct from knowledge fails to account for the fact that certain kinds of experience are conceptually and theoretically mediated. As with scientific theories proper, observation is often shaped by conceptualization and theoretical construct. What we notice about our feelings, desires, beliefs, and other higher order intentional states, and how we interpret them, often involves a conceptual and theoretical element, which enables us inter alia to generalize beyond what is immediately given, to identify long-term patterns, and to sum up and simplify initially diverse events.[39] The theoretical element in turn shapes our experiences, which become integrated again into the repertoire of prereflective experience. Under certain conditions, changes in the way we conceptualize and theorize our experience are accompanied by changes in the nature of experience itself.

PROBLEMS WITH SARTRE'S EARLY MORAL PSYCHOLOGY

Sartre's denial of the efficacy of moral reasoning, his holist approach to life architecture, and the constraints he places upon self-knowledge, create serious problems for the explanatory scope of his moral psychology. Most notably, it has difficulty explaining the many different forms of psychological and moral development that occur across an individual's life history.

Rather like the theory of incommensurability and meaning-variance that is designed to account for large-scale changes in scientific paradigms,[40] Sartre's theory of the project commits him to holding that changes in the way we shape our lives are discontinuous and ultimately unjustifiable. New identities and ways of life do not grow or evolve from previous ones, as if they were articulations of an underlying and self-same reality.[41] Nor are they formed gradually as a result of prolonged moral reflection and attention.[42] The clearest example of life change on Sartre's model is the radical conversion, when a person adopts an entirely new way of life all at once (p. 464). This involves a total break with the past, a complete reinterpretation of the meaning of past events and present situations, and the adoption of an entirely new moral framework. A global flip-flop like this is liable to happen in an instant.

These extraordinary and marvelous instants when the prior project collapses into the past in the light of a new project which rises on its ruins and which as yet exists only in outline, in which humiliation, anguish, joy, hope, are delicately blended, in which we let go in order to grasp and grasp in order to let go – these have often appeared to furnish the clearest and most moving image of our freedom. (p. 476)

The problems with this view of life change, identity, and self-determination are obvious: It is too extreme – what Iris Murdoch has called "a grandiose leaping about unimpeded at important moments"[43] – and results in what Sartre later called a "revolutionary and discontinuous catastrophism."[44] The architecture of a life is at once too rigid and too fragile. With no middle ground between change and constancy, and no solid foundation, the integration of the project stands precariously balanced against its complete disintegration. Moreover, the "price" of changing the project is too high (p. 454): Given its interconnectedness, if anything is to change, everything must change. Problems like these are not unexpected consequences from a theory that refuses to give a balanced role to rationality and to the power of knowledge. Sartre was aware of some of these problems:

I was often told that the past drives us forward, but I was convinced that I was being drawn by the future. I would have hated to feel quiet forces at work within me, the slow development of my natural aptitudes. . . . I subordinated the past to the present and the present to the future; I transformed a quiet evolutionism into a revolutionary and discontinuous catastrophism. A few years ago, someone pointed out to me that the characters in my plays and novels make their decisions abruptly and in a state of crisis, that, for example, in The Flies, a moment is enough for Orestes to effect his conversion. Of course! Because I create them in my own image; not as I am, but as I wanted to be.[45]

In the end, the fact that the theory of the project can only allow changes that are global, and not gradual, piecemeal, self-willed, or rationally governed, is contrary to Sartre's stated aim of showing how we can be self-determining agents. First, it results in a kind of determinism by the fundamental project. Once it is chosen, we are virtually locked into our project, and our voluntary and rationally planned efforts to change its basic structures are futile. When we deliberate about alternative ways of life, the "chips are down." We can only hope for a radical conversion – but even this hoping involves circular reasoning, for it is an expression and realization of our current project.[46]

Second, Sartre's restrictions on rationality have the unwanted consequence of making self-determination an unintelligible and nonrational achievement. With no recourse to objective and noncircular evaluation, and the rationally guided formulation of choices between different ways of life, the question "What is best for me?" is not rationally decidable. The history of personal changes that we undergo across our lives is a history of brute facts. We cannot find any lasting and project-independent reason why our lives take the form that they do, and why certain life changes occur and others do not: Beyond the biased and revisable reasons we might formulate from within, and in terms of, our current project, we must accept these facts as ultimately inexplicable (or absurd). But this clearly runs contrary to the idea that we are self-determining, and the authors of our life histories.

It is also clearly counterintuitive, for it implies that there are no lasting and independent grounds to enable us to distinguish between the good and the better (if not best) choices that we make in determining the way of life we want. (The same holds, a fortiori, for the idea that we can distinguish between poor and poorer choices.) Nor does it allow us to say that a better choice would be evident to us in light of greater knowledge and moral understanding.[47] But this is precisely the point of postulating that we are capable of making choices that concern the deepest level of our being: For when we ask fundamental practical questions (such as "How am I going to live my life?" "What kind of life would be fulfilling, given my talents?"), we are fully aware that we can take a wrong turn and fail to lead a morally significant and morally flourishing life. And we are fully aware that in light of greater knowledge and maturity and wisdom, we actually could work out these fundamental questions with increasingly greater moral certainty and justification.

AGENCY AND SELF-DETERMINATION IN SARTRE'S
LATER WORK

Human history does not walk on its head.
                                        – Marx

Beginning with *Saint Genet* (1952), Sartre began to address some of
the problems of his earlier views on responsibility, agency, and self-
determination. *Saint Genet* introduced in largely untheorized form
the notion of the social conditioning of selfhood. It also took childhood seriously, thereby marking a clear improvement on *Being and
Nothingness*, where the role of ontogeny and childhood was so under-
emphasized that it seemed that the *pour-soi* emerged into the world
fully formed. It was with the *Critique of Dialectical Reason*,[48] however, that a theory of social conditioning was developed, even
though its central concern was not moral psychology.

In the *Critique* Sartre attaches a great deal of importance to the
social constitution of personal being, and to its susceptibility to
estrangement not by the complex psychological stratagems of self-
deception, but by uncontrollably powerful social forces. Moreover,
his interest is more with our practical freedom to change our situation than with our psychological or inner freedom to change ourselves. This shift in interest reflects a response to the criticism that
the earlier conception of freedom – freedom as the ability to choose
between a number of theoretically possible ways of life at any one
moment; or to confer on things their value as causes or motives – is
merely an abstract and nonsocial form of freedom. It is also a response to the criticism that his moral psychology failed to account
for the low probability that people actually do exercise this kind of
self-transformational freedom.

Sartre allows that individuals determine the existentially specific
character of their lives, within certain given material conditions;
but he adds that their actions, desires, and beliefs are deeply expressive of, and constituted by, their class background and historical
milieu. Many of their roles and attitudes bear no mark of their own
intentional or purposive activity (p. 232), but are the impositions of
their class and other material conditions. From early childhood onward people carve out their personal identities by means of and in
terms of the materials and instruments provided them by the social

environment; at the same time, they face obstacles and counterfinalities that steal their praxis and seriously thwart their efforts
to become autonomous and self-directing. Sartre claims, for example, that

> there can be no doubt that one *makes oneself* a bourgeois. In this case, every
> moment of activity is embourgeoisement. But in order to make oneself
> bourgeois, one must be bourgeois. . . . [I]ndividuals find an existence already
> sketched out for them at birth; they "have their position in life and their
> personal development assigned to them by their class" (Marx). What is
> assigned to them is . . . a fundamental *attitude*, as well as a determinate
> provision of material and intellectual tools. (p. 232, emphasis in original)

MORAL PSYCHOLOGY IN *THE FAMILY IDIOT*

The Family Idiot preserves and deepens the theory of the social
constitution of personal being, adding to its range the constitution
of the body, kinesthetic experience, and the ego construct. Sartre
shows a growing sensitivity to the brute materiality, inertia, and
opacity that affect historical reality and that deeply limit an individual's attempts to change it and win control.[49] Like large scale historical processes, a human life is not something that at any one
moment can be reshaped or authenticated by radical choice. Certain forms of social conditioning of personality are so deep-rooted
and extend so far back into childhood that their effects on all subsequent behavior remain insurpassable: No amount of praxis will
enable us to escape their grip. This means that the endeavor to
achieve a degree of moral autonomy and personal integrity is possible only within the limits set by these forms of conditioning. In
The Family Idiot it is clear that Sartre conceives self-determination
not as a function of a choice that is ultimately underived (cf. *BN*, p.
464), as if we are possessed of the power to sculpt ourselves from
the ground up; it is a function of reworking and integrating an
already sculpted material.

It is also clear in *The Family Idiot* that Sartre still holds that being
responsible presupposes the ability to determine the kinds of persons
we are; but with a Marxist theory of social conditioning, a theory of
childhood development and the ontogenesis of agency, and a theory of
social "predestination," the range of self-determination is heavily

restricted, and the kind of control that we can expect over our way of life and basic moral framework is not the kind achieved by radical choice. Gone are the claims about our sovereign power of choice and our virtually unlimited ability to confer new and different meanings upon situations. The notion of praxis, which replaces the notions of transcendence and choice, is a socially conditioned and wholly material process; it is no longer merely *at* the world, but *in* it.[50]

Two ideas stand out in *The Family Idiot:* first, that we are "totally conditioned" by our social existence; second, that we are free agents, and not merely vehicles for inhuman forces operating through us. Sartre wishes to show how our freedom resides not in the capacity to *transcend* our conditioning, but in our capacity to *assume* it and to make something of it. That is, he wants to show that agency is not an absolute and always presupposed given, but an achievement, a contribution that is built up in terms of our socially conditioned cognitive, emotional, motivational, and affective resources, and in terms of the practical constraints of a particular historical situation. This has important implications for moral agency and responsibility: Despite – or in virtue of – these limited resources and constraints, one is in the end "always responsible for what is made of one. Even if one can do nothing else beside assume this responsibility." To this Sartre adds:

I believe that a man can always make something out of what is made of him. This is the limit I would today accord to freedom: the small movement which makes of a totally conditioned social being someone who does not render back completely what his conditioning has given him. Which makes of Genet a poet when he had been rigorously conditioned to be a thief.[51]

This is a forceful statement, and it brings out the mistaken assumption of some forms of determinism that causal forces are purely external and mechanistic: that is, that we are the product of heredity and environment, receiving inputs but passing them on essentially unmodified by any distinctive contribution of our own. On the face of it, however, Sartre's theory of deep social conditioning is not unproblematically compatible with his theory of self-determination: for if social conditioning goes "all the way down," then the contributions we make to our identity and way of life (including our endeavors to achieve a degree of moral autonomy) must themselves be functions of prior conditioning and numerous other antecedent conditions for which we cannot reasonably be held responsible. Moreover, the deeply constituted cognitive and psychological characteristics that we find in ourselves – "fundamental attitudes" and limited intellectual tools – must restrict us to certain ways of viewing what we might become. If this is so, then why suppose that the contribution we make to our identity – what Sartre calls the "small movement" of freedom – is really the work of our own hand, and not causal forces acting through us?

Again, on what grounds can we be held responsible for ourselves, if the theory of total social conditioning is true? If we cannot be held responsible for the antecedents of those actions, desires, and beliefs that are expressions of a socially constituted character and psychology that is not initially subject to our will or choice, then how can we be responsible even for our most basic choices and contributions, if they too are the products of prior conditions and circumstances that are outside of our control?[52]

The skeptical answer is that in the very contribution we make to our identity we are realizing at a more reflective (and rationalized) level the same socially conditioned psychological makeup that we seek to change by means of evaluation, choice, or volition. Conditioned as deeply as we are during infancy and childhood, it is not really up to us to become the persons we want to become: We can only become *what* we already are, and so it is only in an otiose sense that we can be considered self-determining and responsible. To take a concrete example: While we may be able to "step back" from some of the values, beliefs, and attitudes we have acquired in our formative years, and ask whether these are the values we really want to be defined by, the very act of standing back will itself be a product of the inculcated values that are called into question. We think and act with and in terms of these values and beliefs, not from an external perspective and not confronted with the genuine possibilities that our folk model of moral autonomy demands.

Some of Sartre's claims certainly seem to support a skepticism like this. He comments in his autobiography: "One gets rid of a neurosis, one doesn't get cured of one's self. Though they are worn out, blurred, humiliated, thrust aside, ignored, all of the child's traits are still to be found in the quinquagenarian."[53] Elsewhere he says:

We are lost during childhood. Methods of education, the parent–child relationship, and so on, are what create the self, but it's a lost self. . . . I do not mean to say that this sort of predestination precludes all choice, but one knows that in choosing, one will not attain what one has chosen. It is what I call the necessity of freedom.[54]

In *The Family Idiot* Sartre goes to great lengths to show how Flaubert is unable to transcend the conditioning (namely his constitutional passivity) that makes him what he is. Flaubert will never transcend the "sentence" of passivity, his "deep, always hidden wound"; he is free only to assume it (*IF I:* pp. 8–9).

Flaubert's future is barred by an iron wall. . . . "You will be the family idiot." If the child wants one day to find a way out of this, he must accept the sentence. And whatever his chance of success, he has no hope of altering it. (*IF I*, p. 383)[55]

Once again there seems to be an impasse between human agency and determinism: If a special form of agency is not postulated (that is, the self as a unique agent that determines itself by its own choice and purposes), then we cannot "really" be considered self-determining. We are either free and not fully subject to deterministic forces, or we are determined and unfree; either the self is ultimately formed *by* us – that is, determined by the self for the self – or it is formed *for* us, by causal forces and prior conditions acting *through* us. In either case, human freedom is supposed incompatible with determinism.

This familiar impasse, and the Maginot line strategy it invites, embodies a number of conceptual prejudices and confusions. One of the most notable of these is the idea that agency must in some absolute or primitive or underived sense be the work of our own hand, lest it be corrupted by anything alien and nonagential. But whatever this absolute sense might be, it rests upon an untenable assumption, namely that genuine agenthood cannot be derived from some initially nonagential material.

This is based on a fallacy (a version of the sorites paradox), the argument for which runs as follows: However many contributions to our psychological and personal makeup we have made, there must have been a first or primitive contribution; if this was a decision or action over which we had no control (for instance, as a result of a completely socially constituted psychology), then its product cannot be anything we are responsible for. All subsequent contributions will therefore have the same properties as the first, and such a process will never yield an action or choice by us where we can be considered responsible agents. This argument is clearly wrong: By parity of reasoning, there could not by any *Homo sapiens*, since every *Homo sapiens* must have *Homo sapiens* parents, and if one traces the family tree back far enough there must be a non-*Homo sapiens* ancestor whose offspring could not themselves be *Homo sapiens*.[56] Obviously there are *Homo sapiens*, so there must be a flaw in the argument. The error lies in the premise that unless we were absolutely responsible for making ourselves what we are, we could not be responsible at all. But nothing is ever entirely of our making, unless we are gods, so the premise of the argument must be too strong.

Another notable prejudice generating the impasse, and inviting the Maginot line strategy, is the supposed incompatibility of freedom and determinism.[57] Sartre's later view postulates a much more dialectical relation between these two ways of conceiving human action, and is more closely aligned with what has traditionally been called compatibilism. This, roughly, is the view that determinism (broadly construed) is a necessary condition of freedom and human responsibility; and that it is neither necessary nor sufficient to postulate the existence of absolute or contracausal agency to explain the possibility of freedom. Versions of this view have been adopted by Hume, Marx, Engels, and Mill. Mill's compatibilist account of character clearly resembles Sartre's claims about our capacity for self-formation: A person

has, to a certain extent, a power to alter his character. Its being, in the ultimate resort, formed for him is not inconsistent with its being, in part, formed *by* him as one of the intermediate agents. His character is formed by his circumstances (including among these his particular organisation), but his own desire to mould it in a particular way is one of those circumstances, and by no means one of the least influential. . . . [If] we examine closely, we shall find that this feeling, of our being able to modify our own character *if we wish*, is itself the feeling of moral freedom which we are conscious of. A person feels morally free who feels that his habits or his temptations are not his masters but he theirs; who even in yielding to them knows that he could resist. . . .[58]

Sartre's claim that freedom is the small movement that makes of a totally conditioned social being someone who does not render back completely what their conditioning has given them does not imply that we have the godlike capacity to determine *which* characteristics of our makeup will be constitutive of ourselves. We cannot choose or rewrite our being. We do, however, have the capacity to determine *how* some of these characteristics are to be constitutive, and the domain marked out by this capacity is the domain of our moral agency and moral responsibility.

The contribution we make to what we are must be conceived as a contribution in an organizational and boot-strapping sense, rather than in the special transcendental sense of creative agency that Kant and the early Sartre postulated: It involves the reordering and transformation of an already given material with and by means of that very material. The result is a better unity and integration of already existing dispositions, character traits, emotional patterns, motivational structures, and cognitive abilities; they are preserved and reorganized, and their energies rechanneled, from the inside, and with those very energies.[59] The model of self-determination that Sartre uses here resembles in some ways Engels's (quasi-Spinozist) model:

Active social forces work exactly like natural forces: blindly, forcibly, destructively, so long as we do not understand, and reckon with them. But when once we understand them, when once we grasp their action, their direction, their effects, it depends only upon ourselves to subject them more and more to our own will, and by means of them to reach our own ends. . . . The difference is as that between the destructive force of electricity in the lightning of the storm, and the electricity under command in the telegraph and the voltaic arc. . . .[60]

The emphasis in Sartre's later moral psychology is not with the ultimate origin of our desires, acts, and mental states in a special and absolute source of agency; it is with the practical and material process of introducing order and integration into what otherwise might be "blind, forcible, and destructive." This means that the question of the responsibility that we have for our way of life and moral outlook, and the question of moral autonomy, is not answered by looking at whether it is our own ultimately self-caused or uncaused actions that lie at the source of our ways of feeling, acting, desiring, and thinking. Such a question targets only the issue of whether we are responsible for *having* these particular characteristics.[61]

The question of moral responsibility and autonomy turns on the question of whether we have *taken* responsibility for what has already been made of us: that is, whether the deep-seated psychological characteristics, motivational patterns, and emotional tendencies we find ourselves with are characteristics that we have organized and actively taken up as part of our identity. The difference between merely having these characteristics, and actually assuming them and incorporating them as constitutive of who we are, is rather like the difference between the destructive force of electricity in the lightning of the storm, and the electricity under command in the telegraph and the voltaic arc.

NOTES

1 Jean-Paul Sartre, *Being and Nothingness,* tr. Hazel E. Barnes (London: Methuen, 1969), hereafter abbreviated in text as *BN.*

2 J. P. Sartre, *L'Idiot de la famille* (Paris: Gallimard, Vols. I and II, 1971; Vol. III, 1972), hereafter abbreviated in text as *IF,* followed by volume and page number.

3 Philosophical variations of the ideal of rational moral autonomy are to be found in Lockeian, Kantian, existentialist, rationalist, and utilitarian moral thought.

4 I. Kant, *Religion within the Limits of Reason Alone,* tr. T. Greene and H. Hudson (London: Open Court, 1934), p. 40.

5 Cf. J. Hospers, "What Means This Freedom?" and P. Edwards, "Hard and Soft Determinism," in *Determinism and Freedom in the Age of Modern Science,* ed. S. Hook (New York: Macmillan, 1958).

6 Psychopathology lends some credence to this view. People suffering from severe personality disorders are often powerless to change themselves in any significant way. In the worst cases, their life histories are composed of the repetition of the same destructive behavior patterns that were first established in an unhappy childhood; however hard they try to change, their efforts do not enable them to escape unconsciously motivated behavior.

7 Reason, considered to be a transformational and liberating force – the "master of the passions" – is virtually powerless: So deeply rooted is our psychological makeup that reasoning and the exercise of the intelligence

only give us greater facility in rationalizing behavior that we would carry out anyway.

8 Sartre argues that "human reality can detach itself from the world – in questioning, in systematic doubt, in sceptical doubt, in the *epoche*, etc. – only if by nature it has the possibility of self-detachment" (*BN*, p. 25).

9 John Locke defended a version of this: The mind has "a power to suspend the execution and satisfaction of any of its desires," and so "is at liberty to consider the objects of them, examine them on all sides, and weigh them with others. In this lies the liberty man has" (*Essay on Human Understanding*, II, XXI, p. 48).

10 C. Taylor, "Responsibility for Self," in *The Identities of Persons*, ed. A. Rorty (Berkeley: University of California Press, 1976), and *Sources of the Self* (Cambridge, Mass.: Harvard University Press, 1989).

11 E. Tugenhat, *Self-Consciousness and Self-Determination*, tr. P. Stern (Cambridge, Mass.: MIT Press, 1986).

12 H. Frankfurt, "Freedom of the Will and the Concept of a Person," *Journal of Philosophy* 68 (1971).

13 D. W. Hamlyn, "Self-Knowledge," in *The Self*, ed. T. Mischel (Oxford: Blackwell, 1977); cf. also J. D. Velleman, *Practical Reflection* (Princeton, N.J.: Princeton University Press, 1989).

14 S. Hampshire, *Thought and Action* (London: Chatto and Windus, 1982).

15 This, roughly, is Heidegger's idea that Being is an issue for *Dasein*. Cf. *Being and Time*, tr. J. Macquarrie and E. Robinson (Oxford: Blackwell, 1962), pp. 67–8.

16 The general formulation of self-determination is neutral on the question of determinism: It states that insofar as they are determinants of our actions, such things as choices, intentions, reasons, and purposes have as much of a role to play as those determinants that are physical causes; and that they require a different form of explanation. But this says nothing about the ultimate causal status of these determinants, or their amenability to naturalization and physicalist reduction. Conceivably, determinists, libertarians, action theorists, and compatibilists could agree on this general model of self-determination without agreeing on the causal status of the determinants.

17 J. P. Sartre, "Existentialism Is a Humanism," in *Existentialism and Human Emotions*, tr. B. Frechtman (New York: Citadel, 1957), pp. 42–3.

18 M. Merleau-Ponty, *Phenomenology of Perception*, tr. C. Smith (London: Routledge and Kegan Paul, 1962), pp. 406–7.

19 Cf. J. P. Sartre, *The Transcendence of the Ego*, tr. F. Williams and R. Kirkpatrick (New York: Noonday, 1957).

20 J. P. Sartre, "Kierkegaard: The Singular Universal," in *Between Existentialism and Marxism*, tr. J. Matthews (London: Verso, 1983), p. 160.

21 Pascal also noted the difficulty of maintaining a coherent attitude to the curious fact that we exist at all. When viewed from afar, our lives appear to be events that lack intrinsic necessity; they are just there, as apparently gratuitous facts (*Pensées*, no. 208).

22 Cf. Aristotle, *Nichomachean Ethics*, Book 3, on deliberating about means but not ends.

23 This bears resemblances to Carnap's distinction between internal and external questions, and to Popper's claim that the decision that commits us to rationality cannot itself be fully rationally justified.

24 Similarly, R. M. Hare argues that justification comes to an end when we are confronted with a decision whether to accept a way of life; only once it is accepted can justification be based upon the way of life. Cf. *The Language of Morals* (New York: Oxford University Press, 1964), p. 69.

25 Cf. P. Strawson, "Freedom and Resentment," in *Proceedings of the British Academy* (London: 1962) for a criticism of the idea of the external rational justification of our moral framework.

26 Sartre, "Existentialism Is a Humanism," pp. 24–9. The case resembles Kierkegaard's account of the criterionless decision between the aesthetic and ethical way of life in *Either/Or*.

27 S. Hampshire, *Morality and Conflict* (Cambridge, Mass.: Harvard University Press, 1983), p. 33.

28 Ibid., p. 155. This is suggestive of the Spinozist maxim *Omnis determinatio est negatio*.

29 The etymology of the term deliberation reveals something about Sartre's belief in its futility: It is de-liberation.

30 Compare this with Wittgenstein's antifoundationalism: "Giving grounds, however, justifying the evidence, comes to an end; – but the end is not certain propositions' striking us immediately as true, i.e. it is not a kind of seeing on our part; it is our *acting* which lies at the bottom of the language-game." (*On Certainty*, tr. D. Paul and G. E. Anscombe [New York: Harper & Row, 1969], p. 204).

31 Sartre, "Existentialism Is a Humanism," p. 28.

32 Cf. Hampshire's *Thought and Action*; cf. also C. Taylor, "Responsibility for Self."

33 Cf. A. Rorty "The Deceptive Self: Liars, Layers, and Lairs," in *Perspectives on Self-Deception*, ed. B. P. McLaughlin and A. O. Rorty (Berkeley: University of California Press, 1988), pp. 11–28.

34 In *The Family Idiot* Sartre analyzes Flaubert's "fulgurating intuitions" – self-insights revealing everything and nothing.

35 Cf. M. Heidegger, *Being and Time*, pp. 32–5, 67, 317, and 414–15 for the concept of preunderstanding. Sartre construes preunderstanding in ontological rather than epistemological terms: It is not a form of knowledge,

but a way of being, of projecting ourselves into the world and toward our ends.

36 Using Ryle's term, one might say that the project is "systematically elusive."

37 On the issue of the blind spot in reflexive knowledge, cf. my paper "Kant and Sartre on Self-Knowledge," in *Man and World*, 19, no. 1 (1986): 73–93.

38 Cf. Merleau-Ponty, Preface to the *Phenomenology of Perception*. Cf. also T. Nagel "What Is It Like to Be a Bat?" in *Mortal Questions* (New York: Cambridge University Press, 1979).

39 On the idea that personal being is a product of theoretical activity, cf. R. Harre, *Personal Being* (Cambridge, Mass.: Harvard University Press, 1984).

40 As this is defended in the work of Kuhn and Feyerabend.

41 Cf. C. Taylor, "Responsibility for Self," and *Sources of the Self*, Part 1.

42 A notion developed in Iris Murdoch's *The Sovereignty of Good* (London: Routledge and Kegan Paul, 1970).

43 Ibid., p. 37.

44 J. P. Sartre, *The Words*, tr. B. Frechtman (New York: Braziller, 1964) p. 238.

45 Ibid.

46 This is also Merleau-Ponty's criticism: To say that we are our fundamental project amounts to saying that our life is already made, and that its development is nothing but a repetition of the primordial choice. It is impossible "to name a single gesture which is absolutely new in regard to that way of being in the world which, from the very beginning, is myself. There is no difference between saying that our life is completely constructed and that it is completely given" (*Sense and Nonsense*, trans. by H. and P. Dreyfus [Evanston, Ill.: Northwestern University Press, 1964], p. 21).

47 Cf. Tugendhat, *Self-Consciousness and Self-Determination*, p. 213.

48 J. P. Sartre, *Critique of Dialectical Reason*, tr. Alan Sheridan-Smith (London: New Left Books, 1976), hereafter abbreviated in text as *CDR*.

49 *The Family Idiot* reveals the importance of countenancing historical and contextual factors in discussions of moral psychology. Some philosophical analyses of agency, responsibility, and self-determination are unjustifiably abstract and unhistorical. By relying on simple analytical models of human experience (e.g., desire-belief matrices, first- and second-order desires), they neglect the phenomenology of moral life, and overlook its long-term temporal dimensions. While the method of analysis is neat, and puts the problems into manageable form, it is not always true to the context, and to the complexity of concrete moral-psychological experi-

ence. At its worst, the method tends to distort the very form of the problem. The strength of Sartre's approach is that it takes a life as a whole as the basic unit of empirical significance in moral psychology.

50 This is Merleau-Ponty's description of Sartre's view of consciousness.
51 Sartre, "Itinerary of a Thought," in *Between Existentialism and Marxism*, pp. 34–5.
52 Cf. also T. Nagel, "Moral Luck," in *Mortal Questions*. Nagel remarks that the area of genuine agency, and of legitimate moral judgment, seems to shrink under this kind of questioning to an extensionless point.
53 Sartre, *The Words*, p. 254.
54 J. P. Sartre, "On The Idiot of the Family," in *Life/Situations*, tr. P. Auster and L. Davis (New York: Pantheon, 1977), p. 116.
55 Cf. also *CDR* pp. 329–30 for a discussion of the case of an individual who wishes to transcend his "class being." However much intelligence, work, or patience he displays, "he has simply realized his being – the very thing he cannot change – in slightly different circumstances."
56 The example comes from D. Dennett, *Elbow Room: The Varieties of Free Will Worth Wanting* (Cambridge, Mass.: MIT Press, 1985), pp. 84–5.
57 For criticisms of incompatibilism, see the articles by Schlick, Hobart, and Foot in *Free Will and Determinism*, ed. B. Berofsky (New York: Harper & Row, 1966).
58 J. S. Mill, *On the Logic of the Moral Sciences*, from *A System of Logic*, Book VI (New York: Bobbs-Merrill, 1965), pp. 14–15.
59 Sartre's account of Flaubert's constitutional passivity bears out his claim that "no determination is imposed upon an existent which he does not surpass by his way of living it" (*IF I*: p. 653). During boyhood and adolescence Flaubert assumes the passivity that he lived on an elementary psychosomatic level as an infant "in order to make it a more developed behaviour and to assign it a new function – passive action becomes a tactical, flexible defense against a danger better understood, pure blind sentience becomes resentment. Preserved, overcome, traversed by new and complex meanings, its sense cannot fail to change" (*IF I*: p. 54).
60 F. Engels, *Socialism: Utopian and Scientific* (Moscow: Progress Publishers, 1954), p. 72.
61 Cf. H. Frankfurt, "Identification and Wholeheartedness," in F. Schoeman, ed., *Responsibility, Character and the Emotions* (New York: Cambridge University Press, 1987), pp. 27–45.

5 Understanding the committed writer

"A life develops in spirals: It always passes through the same points, but at different levels of integration and complexity" (*CRD* I, p. 71).[1] This observation, which underpins Sartre's synthesis of biographical and historical methods in studying the individual and society, might also apply to the preoccupation with committed writing that characterized his own life and work. The reader cannot fail to note the persistence and the far from linear development of the concepts and methods which articulate that preoccupation. The range of concepts itself promises complexity. Psychological, moral, social, political, historical, linguistic, literary, and aesthetic issues must all be integrated through a correspondingly intricate method that draws its inspiration, without lapsing into eclecticism, from a number of different intellectual traditions. The tracing of the spiral is fascinating, frustrating, and exemplary – fascinating because of the commitment and tenacity of Sartre's arguments, frustrating because those arguments reach no conclusion, exemplary because the inconclusiveness is itself inherent in the problem analyzed and in the method of analysis: Sartre's open-ended writing itself enacts an open dialectic.

Two of the major theoretical points through which Sartre's spiral passes are *Qu'est-ce que la littérature?* (1947), usually taken to offer the classic description of "committed" literature, and *"Questions de méthode"* (1960),[2] which presents a more complex view of the interaction of individual, society, and history, prescribes a method for revealing the dialectical relationship of social conditioning and individual project, and prepares the reader for the potentially surprising claim that a writer as apparently uncommitted as Flaubert may be considered to be *"engagé."* However, a number of Sartre's posthumously published works provide important supplementary material that should help us to qualify existing views of his priorities, his development, and his methods; this second group of texts includes *Les Carnets de la drôle de guerre* (written from 1939 to 1940 and published in 1983); *Cahiers pour une morale* (1947–8, 1983), and the second volume of the *Critique de la raison dialectique* (1958–62, 1985). A third group of texts may be said to apply or test Sartre's theories of committed literature and develop his method of interpretation. In this essay I consider first the significance of the texts mentioned here; the third group will be represented by "*Orphée noir*," (1948) in which Sartre discovers the possibility of "committed" poetry, and, finally, by a perforce highly selective view of *L'Idiot de la famille* (1971–2), in which theory and interpretation most strikingly converge.

Qu'est-ce que la littérature?, the apparent starting point, is already situated within Sartre's own history. Its arguments refer to Sartre's earlier phenomenological writing; consciousness is free but situated, consciousness "nihilates" what is, consciousness is capable of imagining what is not the case. It may be either unreflective or capable of reflecting upon its own activity. It is responsible for conferring an always provisional meaning upon, or creating a human world within, the undifferentiated, impassive plenitude of Being-in-itself. It therefore changes what is by revealing it and endowing it with meaning – or, according to *Qu'est-ce que la littérature?*, by naming it (*Sit* II: p. 72). Language is an extension of the revealing power of consciousness; hence, for Sartre, the privileged role of the writer as a committed agent: "The 'committed' writer knows that words are actions; he knows that to reveal is to change, and that one cannot reveal unless one has the project of changing" (p. 73). The writer invites the reader to reflect critically upon his situation, and to realize freely his responsibility for bringing about change. And the linguistic medium of revelation, reflection, and change can only be the transparency of prose, in which, Sartre maintains, words are referential and directly transitive bearers of meaning, of a *signification*. Poetry cannot serve the committed writer's project of "revealing": for poets, words have the opacity of objects rather than the transparency of signs. By functioning as the image or the symbol of an affective atmosphere – "anguish transformed into a thing" (p. 61) – they embody a *sens* rather than reveal a *signification*.[3] Poets deny the instrumentality of language that is necessary to the action that seeks to change the world, while the committed writer should, apparently, restrict himself to simple denotation; his function is to "call a spade a spade" (p. 304). The only *engagement* available to the poet is a seemingly negative form of "bearing witness," or *témoignage:*

> Poetry is a case of loser wins. And the authentic poet chooses to lose to the point of death in order to win. . . . So if we insist on talking of the *engagement* of the poet, let us say that he is the man who commits himself to losing. . . . He is sure of the total failure of the human enterprise, and contrives to fail in his own life in order to bear witness, through his particular defeat, to the defeat of humanity in general. (p. 87)

The positive implications of a willful failure and of a committed defeatism may seem tenuous, and yet, as we shall see, this tiny concession to poetic *témoignage* as a form of *engagement* will have a fruitful future in Sartre's work.

I have discussed more fully elsewhere some of the qualities and some of the theoretical shortcomings of Sartre's arguments in *Qu'est-ce que la littérature?*[4] – shortcomings that may often be ascribed to the formulaic character of polemical assertion. My present purpose is to indicate how those arguments may be more consciously elaborated or modified in other twists of Sartre's spiral. Some of his definitions are, of course, all the more suggestive for being summary. His distinction between involvement (*embarquement*) and *engagement* is one of them: "A writer is *engagé* when he tries to be as lucidly and as completely conscious of his involvement as possible; that is to say, when he raises *engagement*, for himself and others, from the level of immediate spontaneity to the level of reflection" (p. 24).

The distinction between the passive involvement of *embarquement* and a reflectively active awareness is clearly an essential one; it begs the question, nonetheless, of the extent to which the contemporary and, a fortiori, the historical situation may be intelligible to the *embarqué* individual, however enlightened. And yet that intelligibility must be crucial for effective action. Sartre rejects the claims of specific ideologies and their associated political parties – by implication, Marxism and the Communist party – to be the repositories of historical wisdom and the vehicles of effectively committed action. In another enlightening distinction he argues that *embrigadement* in – that is to say, commitment to – a specific political party, which has its own ways of denying freedom and stifling communication, should not be confused with *engagement*. And yet his own historical review of the relations between the writer and his public, and his description of the situation of the writer in 1947, offer no alternative method that might validate his intuitions. Nor is there a more effective consideration of the short-term context of events as they are immediately experienced. The *"pluridimensionnalité"* of the event or of the "historical fact" justifies the novelistic technique of multiple point of view, but Sartre does not explore the problems posed by the complexity of events for the process of reflection, interpretation, and action, whether for the writer or for the historical agent in general. Rather, reflection seems to lead to a confrontation of thesis and antithesis, in which the opacity of the situation is recognized on the one hand, and its intelligibility is simply asserted, against all the odds, on the other:

A lucid view of the darkest situation is already, in itself, an act of optimism. Indeed, it implies that this situation is *thinkable*; that is to say, we have not lost our way in it as though in a dark forest, and we can on the contrary detach ourselves from it, at least in mind, and keep it under observation; we can therefore go beyond it and resolve what to do against it, even if our decisions are desperate. (p. 289)

The words "go beyond" cannot be taken here as part of a dialectical movement toward synthesis: Sartre seems to be caught in an impasse in which the transition from reflective awareness to practical action eludes him. It is true that elsewhere in his argument both perception and language are seen to be forms of action,[5] but at what point does their action become committed and, more crucially, effective? Should the writer attempt to act directly upon the reader's thoughts and feelings, as Sartre at one point suggests, only to maintain elsewhere that literature can never be considered to be a form of action, even if it provides a necessary condition for action – that is, "the moment of reflective consciousness?" Authors do not *act upon* their readers; they simply appeal to their freedom (p. 197). It is true that he envisages a "praxis" that would involve action *within* history and an absolute perspective *upon* history, thereby synthesizing "historical relativity" (which can be none other than the situation) and "the moral and metaphysical absolute" (which can be none other than freedom) (p. 265). But his practical imperatives are imprecise, and his argument seems to be tautologous rather than dialectical: Action in and upon history, involving the interaction of freedom and situation, is the subject of the act of writing that, by implicating the situated freedom of the writer, is itself a form of action in and upon history. Furthermore, the relationship between metaphysical and sociopolitical freedom is not rigorously defined or clarified, with the result that at times committed action seems to presuppose a degree of the very freedom that it is its function to promote. Nor does Sartre adequately confront the problem of the different forms of alienation which may attenuate that freedom.

Many of the difficulties posed by the arguments of *Qu'est-ce que la littérature?* appear to arise from the lack of a systematic method, and it is therefore not surprising that in standard accounts of Sartre's development "*Questions de méthode*" is seen to be of crucial importance in its attempt to establish a more rigorous approach to the interaction of individual and society – an essential prerequisite for a view of commitment, whether of the historical agent in general or the writer in particular. In the latter case, its findings are supplemented concisely, in the first instance, by the arguments of *Plaidoyer pour les intellectuels* and eventually, at vastly greater length, in *L'Idiot de la famille.* In the former Sartre revises – though not, as we shall see, for the first time – the theory of language outlined in *Qu'est-ce que la littérature?*; in the latter he attempts to apply, massively but inconclusively, a "totalizing" method of investigating the interpenetration of individual and society. As we discover from "*Questions de méthode*," these approaches aim to reveal the dialectical relationship of social conditioning and the individual project (for instance, the project of writing) through which that conditioning is both "surpassed" and "preserved" (*CRD* I, p. 68). Sartre proposes a theory of mediation that would account for that relationship, a theory that presents the family as the crucial intermediary through which an individual internalizes, from his childhood, the pressures of his social context, whether of class, group structures, economic conditions, or ideology. This process is traced through a "progressive-regressive" method that, synthesizing Marxist and psychoanalytic approaches, takes a more complex view of time than was possible in *Qu'est-ce que la littérature?*. There Sartre seemed unable to resolve a number of conflicting views of time. He had attempted to combine a definition, proposed earlier in

L'Être et le néant, of individual consciousness as an absolute that creates its own temporality, with the vision of an extra-historical utopia postulated in *Qu'est-ce que la littérature?* as the ideal context of committed literature; the "moment" of reflective consciousness had also been implicated, as was the relativizing force of History. But the reader has little sense of a fruitful integration of these different elements. In "*Questions de méthode,*" however, the regressive phase of Sartre's method would move back to the formative historical and sociopolitical circumstances internalized by the individual in the opacity of childhood and would thus reveal both his "historical singularity" (*CRD* I, p. 89) and "the depth of the lived" (p. 92). It would investigate three levels of significance; that of the abstract "universal significations" of a given period (for instance, capitalism); of a specific social group within that period (for instance, the *petit bourgeois* family); and of the individual member of such a family (for instance, Flaubert) in his unique and subjective attitudes and behavior, revealing "the concrete reality as a lived totalization" (p. 88). The regressive stage would also involve a study of the processes whereby one level of significance is "differentiated" (pp. 88 and 92) at a higher level; how, for instance, capitalism is variously "lived" and objectified by different families of the intellectual *petite bourgeoisie* in the mid–nineteenth century. Within this stage there is therefore a constant "*va-et-vient,*" as Sartre calls it, a moving to-and-fro, between interpretations of the period's "universal" social structure, the immediate social context of the individual, and the "singularity" of his subjectively lived experience. It is then the task of the progressive phase of the method to reveal synthetic, goal-directed relationships between these levels. It would show how the individual, through his project, transcends and yet preserves his social conditioning in order to create his own *être-dans-le-monde* (being-in-the-world) as an objective but not definitive totality. Indeed, the notion of the "individual" should itself be superseded, Sartre suggests, by that of the "singular universal": Having been totalized, and thus universalized, by his epoch, the individual retotalizes it through the singularity of his own projects.

"*Questions de méthode*" confronts a number of the problems of definition, description, and analysis left unresolved in *Qu'est-ce que la littérature?* – the reconciling of the subjective and the objective in the concept of the "*universal singulier,*" the awareness of historical process, and of the dynamic complexity of the social context. It recognizes, too, the forces of alienation at work in that process and in that context: The individual's project, in tension with the pressure of conditioning, may become modified or distorted, leading to an alienated form of self-objectification in which "the final objectification may not correspond exactly to the original choice" (p. 93). These distortions may themselves become the subject of further interpretation, and may themselves be transcended. However, the method itself could be said to be subject to a form of alienation; it is "totalizing" in that it sees the object of its study – the integration of individual, society, and history – as a never fully accomplished process of unification that is constantly permeated and "detotalized" by the forces of negation and temporality, to which the interpreter is himself exposed. Complete (as distinct from totalizing) knowledge of the process of totalization from an external or absolute point of view is impossible: The knower is implicated in the known and is part of the very moment of totalization. Despite Sartre's acknowledgment of Marxism as the philosophy of his time, he still resists the view, as he did in *Qu'est-ce que la littérature?*, that a single conceptual system can claim to offer a definitive interpretation of history. His own approach is more pluralist. It acknowledges the relevance of Marxism in the analysis of socioeconomic factors, draws upon psychoanalytic method in investigating subjective attitudes and behavior, but emphasizes, particularly, the relevance of *compréhension* as a vital stage in the process of interpretation – an approach given even greater prominence in the second, posthumously published volume of the *Critique de la raison dialectique*.

This summary may indicate the development of a more sophisticated method, but it also suggests a limitation: It is an approach that concentrates particularly on the capacity of the interpreter to understand the situation and responses of the potential historical agent. It gives little indication of how the situated individual, that potential agent, may come to understand, express, or change the situation, for himself and for others – how, in fact, he would fulfill the vocation envisaged for the committed writer in *Qu'est-ce que la littérature?*: that of being "as lucidly and completely conscious of his involvement as possible" and of "[raising] *engagement*, for himself and others, from the level of immediate spontaneity to the level of reflection" (p. 24). The question of the intelligibility of the historical situation for the *embarqué* individual, the object of the interpreter's study, seems to have been begged again. And yet that intelligibility, as we saw in *Qu'est-ce que la littérature?*, seems to be a condition for the transformation of *embarquement* into effective *engagement*.

However, this conclusion is qualified by supplementary inferences that may be drawn from an increasing number of Sartre's other texts. Some, such as *"Orphée noir"* (1948) and *Plaidoyer pour les intellectuels* (1965, 1972), are already familiar to his readers but have tended to be undeservedly marginalized by his bulkier works, despite the fact that the former are undoubtedly helpful for the interpretation of the latter. Others, whose publication was either long postponed, in the case of *L'Engagement de Mallarmé* (1948–52, 1979), or posthumous, complement and qualify the insights of the works already discussed. The problem of the intelligibility of the situation, whether for the interpreter or the *embarqué* individual, stimulates repeated reflections on the nature of ignorance and on the difficulties involved in isolating and interpreting the historical event. The problem of the need to act in situations where the individual may appear to be impotent in the face of historical change raises the questions of passivity, of the means whereby the individual may transcend the "objective history" of his time, and of the relation of both to the notion of freedom. The degree of opacity that, in these reflections, Sartre recognizes as a fundamental aspect of "lived" experience leads both the reader and Sartre himself to ask whether the transparency of prose is the only adequate, or the most adequate, medium for the communication of that experience.

Given that these ideas and arguments are not systematically worked out, the interpreter of Sartre might be well advised to adopt – or, at least, to adapt – the procedure that he himself promotes in *"Questions de méthode"*: that of a *"va-et-vient,"* a moving to-and-fro, between different levels of significance, between earlier and later "interiorizations" and "exteriorizations," between published works and the more tentative, submerged explorations whose very tentativeness, undistorted by polemical or circumstantial constraints, sometimes has an air of greater authenticity. The method may allow us to pause to investigate different points on the Sartrean spiral without arresting the movement of the always provisional whole.

As we saw, *"Questions de méthode"* offers us another major link between those different points: the notion of *compréhension*. This is a technical term that Sartre derived from a long-standing intellectual tradition, which reappears insistently from his earliest to his latest writing, but which is absent from the vocabulary of *Qu'est-ce que la littérature?*. It refers to one of two apparently conflicting traditions in German thought of which Sartre was well aware: that of *Erklären* (explication) and that of *Verstehen* (comprehension). The former adopts methods of psychological or social analysis and explanation based on mechanistic or biological models; the latter seeks to understand social, psychological, and historical phenomena in terms of distinctly human intentions and meanings, grasped as synthetic wholes and apprehended either through empathy and intuition or by rational reconstruction. It draws a sharp distinction between methods appropriate to the natural sciences and those that should be applied in the human sciences. Its refusal to assimilate culture to nature would certainly have been congenial to Sartre. The *Verstehen* tradition is exemplified in social psychology by Max Scheler, to whose work Sartre often referred either explicitly or implicitly; in psychology by Karl Jaspers, whose *Allgemeine Psychopathologie* (1913) Sartre had helped to translate in 1928, and whose reflections on the experience of failure had also influenced him; in sociology by Max Weber; and in history by Wilhelm Dilthey, whose presence in Sartre's work, as we shall see, is diffuse and pervasive. The *Erklären* tradition in sociohistorical analysis could be said to be represented by classical (or what Sartre in *L'Idiot de la famille* disparagingly calls "scientific") Marxism, and in psychoanalysis by Freud, although here Sartre's own comments are pertinent. In his *Cahiers pour une morale*, in a sustained passage of reflection on *compréhension*, and in the context of an explicit reference to Jaspers, he observed that Freudian psychanalysis is "a study based on *compréhension* that is hidden beneath an analytic and explanatory myth" (*CM*, p. 287). Later, in the context of a discussion of determinism and freedom, he asserts that there is a "rigorous parallelism" between historical materialism and psychoanalysis: Both reduce the "superior" to the "inferior" (p. 449):

The mainspring of the class struggle is self-interest. In individual human activity it is sexuality or the will to power. In both cases the *method* is justified but the principles are arbitrary. There is nothing to validate the end point chosen for the process of psychoanalytic regression. At the level of social infrastructures there is no proof that the organization of production is the cause of, for instance, demographic variations, and not the reverse (see the economic revolution of the twelfth century). (p. 450)

It is true that there are hints in the *Cahiers* of Sartre's later more positive, although still ambivalent, view of both Marxism and Freudian psychoanalysis: Their virtue is that each involves a practical method that is "destined to change the world" (p. 450) – a primary goal, it will be remembered, of the activity of the committed writer as it is defined in *Qu'est-ce que la littérature?*. But it is noteworthy that when Sartre seeks to integrate Marxism and psychoanalysis into the arguments of the *Critique* and of *L'Idiot de la famille*, they will be substantially modified by his own "*méthode compréhensive.*" The motive for this modification may be found in the rider attached to Sartre's appreciation of the intention to "*changer le monde*": In both Marxism and psychoanalysis, he believes, this overrides the need to "know" the world. And for Sartre, as we have seen, knowledge is the essential prerequisite for change. We have been returned to the question of intelligibility, and to the question of the relationship between the interpreter and the object of his understanding. Hitherto, Sartre believes, the problem of *compréhension* has been badly formulated, and he suggests that it is "perfectly simple: to explain is to elucidate in terms of causes; to understand is to elucidate in terms of goals" (*CM*, p. 287). This somewhat summary way of dealing with a quite complex issue will need to be subsequently developed, notably in relation to the problem of ends, but in the meantime it may be noted that the term *compréhension* is invoked in the context of both the interpretation of history and the historical agent's often preconceptual grasp of his situation.

In relation to Sartre's practice of existential biography and to his view of historical interpretation, the method called *Verstehen* derives from Wilhelm Dilthey, whose approach became familiar to Sartre in 1938 through the work on the philosophy of history of his then close friend Raymond Aron (*CDG.*, p. 227). Aron himself maintained that Sartre also knew Dilthey's work directly, and there is certainly considerable internal evidence, throughout Sartre's œuvre, in support of this view.[6] It has become commonplace to suggest that Sartre awoke to the need for commitment during the Second World

War: it is certainly clear from what remains of his own diary for 1939 and 1940 that the need to comprehend his own historical situation had become a pressing one. Hence his interest in the causes of the First World War, and his desire to grasp the motives of Kaiser Wilhem II. Hence, too, Sartre's dissatisfaction with traditional modes of historical explanation, and his attempt to reinterpret the "causes" of the First World War in terms of an approach involving *compréhension*. Furthermore, Dilthey's presence in the subtext of Sartre's arguments is persistent: Dilthey's ambition, echoing Kant but diverging from him, and prefiguring Sartre's *Critique de la raison dialectique*, had been to formulate a "critique of historical reason." A brief consideration of Dilthey's position can undoubtedly help to clarify Sartre's own evolving views.

The first point that may be made is that Dilthey's work is not limited to a concern with historical reason. The method that he evolved was intended to apply to all knowledge of the human world. As with the *Verstehen* approach in general, his method draws a clear distinction between the natural and the cultural world, and between our means of knowing them. In the natural sciences, phenomena are explained by being subsumed under general laws that presuppose a form of necessity. In the interpretation of the cultural products of human action, such products are seen as suffused with meaning, as the signs of the "life-experience" of their creators, including the conative and affective, as well as the cognitive, aspects of mental life. They reveal our purposes and values, beyond those of which we may be explicitly aware. This life-experience is what Sartre later calls the "*vécu*" (the lived), but for the early Sartre, already, our most fundamental human projects are "lived," rather than "known."[7] For Dilthey, as later for Sartre, the interpretation of the "signs" of lived experience, which cannot be reduced to a logical form, takes the individual life as its starting point, and a descriptive rather than explanatory psychology as a crucial basis for that interpretation, before moving to more complex structures: Dilthey took works of literature (and, notably, poetry), autobiographies, diaries, and biographies to be crucial documents for the interpretation of the relationship between individual experience and historical meaning. Sartre, having reflected on the diaries of others, and particularly on the "confessional" diary of Gide, saw his own diary – even in its potential errors – as a source of future historical understanding. Moreover, anticipating the terminology of *Qu'est-ce que la littérature?*, in his *Carnets de la drôle de guerre* he saw his diary as a form of *témoignage*, a bearing witness that had given him a sense, not previously experienced, of his own historicity, and that might lead to moral change (*CDG*, pp. 90–2). (The developing relationship in his work between a psychology of the *vécu*, existential biography, and historical interpretation scarcely needs stressing.) But Dilthey, furthermore, thought it necessary to go beyond the individual life toward a grasp of the "objective mind," the *Esprit objectif*, which would, in turn, make possible a fuller understanding of the individual life. His use of the term was, like Sartre's, consciously different from that of Hegel, for whom it was a stage between the subjective and the absolute mind, a stage in a metaphysical "ideal construction," a process that, according to Dilthey, "leaves temporal, empirical, and historical relations behind," and in which "the world-spirit regains its pure ideality." For Dilthey the "objective mind" embraced institutions, customs, the state, the law, ideology, religion, language, literature, art, and philosophy; through it, history pervades the present, and the "inner" and "outer" worlds become interrelated. It is mediated to the individual from his childhood through his family; the individual is its bearer and representative. This is the sense in which Sartre uses the term *"l'Esprit objectif"* – first, and most allusively, in the *"Présentation des Temps modernes"* (1947); finally, and in a far more sustained description, in the third volume of *L'Idiot de la famille.*

Dilthey, then, brings both historical knowledge and a reformed psychology to bear on the understanding of goal-directed "life-expressions"; that, in turn, contributes to historical understanding. Such an understanding clearly transcends a narrow preoccupation with political issues, with the acts of "great men," or with what would now be called *l'histoire événementielle* (the chronicle of events) (and to which Sartre, in his diary, takes particular exception). The process of understanding involves a system of dynamic interactions and its method a "hermeneutic circle" that will constantly move between complex wholes and their parts, ultimately relating each element to the whole of the epoch in a way that has nothing to do with cause and effect.[8] This "totalizing" emphasis is familiar from Sartre's later work on the *engagement* of the writer as historical agent, but it is prefigured by his attempt to grasp the interrelatedness of the "layers of signification" involved in an understanding of the 1914–18 war, and which, in most methods of explanation, he claims, would be considered as parallel, juxtaposed "facts": the "fact" of Wilhelm II's withered arm, the "fact" of Anglo-German relations. Sartre's aim is to "discover a relationship of *compréhension* between that English policy and this withered arm" (*CDG*, p. 365). Such phenomena would be integrated by the historian's grasp of Wilhelm's "project" as a "situated totality" (p. 376) and of Wilhelm's own "preontological *compréhension*" of himself (p. 370), which coincides with that project; these are grasped, in practice, through Sartre's empathic "reliving" (in Dilthey's sense of *"nacherleben"*) of Wilhelm's aspirations and resentments. These "signifying relationships" would be integrated, in turn, with the internalized social, political, geographical, economic, but always human, context (pp. 367–8). (It is not surprising that expositors of Dilthey often resort to terms that anticipate or echo those of Sartre in the quotation that opens this essay, or in his characterizing of the progressive-regressive method as a *"va-et-vient"*; Dilthey's method involves a "spiral," or a movement "to and fro" between different levels of a dynamic system or structure). However, Sartre still returns to the material privileged by Dilthey – to the account of the single life, such as Ludwig's biography of Wilhelm II, or to his own integration of the *Esprit objectif* of Flaubert's epoch with the "lived experience" of Flaubert. Since a human project is the source of "signifying relationships," any description of "the concrete development of an ideology based upon political data should be accompanied by a monograph on one of the important individuals of the epoch, in order to reveal the ideology as a lived situation, constituted as a situation by a human project" (p. 401). Such monographs would be distinguished from a eulogy of "great men": Sartre's subjects are seen as representative "singular universals," and the "internalized" understanding of a situation and of an ideology, whether "lived" or more explicitly "known," is clearly essential both to the *engagement* of the historical agent and to that of the historian himself.

The fact that the term "hermeneutic" was transposed by Dilthey from textual to historical interpretation is not fortuitous. For him literary texts, and language itself, are paradigms of "life-expressions" and of our mode of understanding. Our understanding of a sentence enacts the relationship of parts to the whole, as does the coherence of a literary text, which embodies but transcends the author's conscious intentions, thus enabling the interpreter to know the author (Genet? Flaubert?) better than the author knows himself. For such literary expression creatively discloses something that is not available to immediate self-consciousness (again *"le vécu"* rather than *"le connu"*), nor to introspection: Dilthey believed that if we contemplate "inner states" they tend to disappear.[9] Understanding, he maintained, is itself a mode of action, rather than of contemplation, and there is a dialectic of creation and understanding via the created, objectified expression, which finds its place in a shared matrix of meaning (Ermarth, p. 282), and from which the original experience may be understood in "a regressive movement of thought" (the expression is Dilthey's: *GS* VII, p. 319). This emphasis on creative action and creative understanding also extends to the sphere of history: It is because we are historical beings that we inquire into history, and he who studies history himself makes history (*GS* VII, p. 278). But for this very reason it is difficult to isolate a starting point for the understanding of history; equally, despite the "totalizing" interrelationship of significant parts and wholes, the final meaning of history as a totality will never be fully known. Sartre, against Hegel and Marx, often, of course, expresses a similar view. As he puts it in *Vérité et existence* (1948, 1989), "What makes Truth impossible is that man makes history, and that he makes it anew through the act of knowing it" (p. 133).

These convergences help us to "situate" Sartre (or to resituate him: his methods have tended to be considered primarily in the context of the Marxist tradition). They also underline the importance of *compréhension* in his interpretation of social and historical action, and of literature as a mode of that action. But they have not yet enabled us to associate that understanding with commitment. In what way, for instance, does *compréhension* refer us to freedom as a value? In what way does its emphasis upon action, and even upon the transformative action implied in Dilthey's view of "life-expressions," entail a commitment to change and to the promotion of freedom? For Dilthey, the human agent is free within certain limitations, and free to choose between them; they "express themselves externally as the pressure of the world on the subject," and it is his goal to transcend them; the "tragic" experience of finitude is itself an impulse to action and to understanding, and a "will to inner freedom . . . results from inner limitations" (Rickman, p. 245; *GS* VII, p. 244). (For the Sartre of the

Cahiers the tragic involves the discovery that our finitude and our failure are conditions of our freedom [*CM*, p. 340].) It is these tensions that, for Dilthey, "promote the restless progress of change." Within this "system of interaction" other more concrete tensions operate. The "great changes of the world" originate in a dialectical movement of "negative emotions of rejection" – the sense of "urgent, unfulfilled needs" and the desires that they prompt, dissatisfaction with the existing state of affairs – and of more dynamic energies, which include "positive will, potency and faith." The "real agents" are themselves both positive, in that their impulses find expression in "value, good and purpose," and negative, in that the desire to subjugate others is also an active force (Rickman, pp. 206–7; *GS* VII, pp. 164–5). Historical action and historical understanding both arise from and reveal these tensions.

Sartre, too, argues that *compréhension* operates on two levels. It may result in solidarity with the oppressed, but it is also implicated in the struggle between enemies (*CRD* I, p. 746): both involve the recognition of the freedom of the other. However, in the *Cahiers* Sartre chooses to emphasize the more positively reciprocal aspects of *compréhension*. It does not involve an adoption of the goals of the other, which would result in joint action with him; it is rather a "sketch" of that adoption, a grasp of the freedom of the other in relation to his goals "because I have a preontological *compréhension* of the original structure of any goal" (*CM* p. 288). This grasp is not the simple intuitive contemplation of a system of means directed toward an end; it is rather "an original active intention" which "engages" me in the action of the other and gives it meaning: My grasp of it itself involves a project. This *compréhension* is, in what appears to be a renunciation of the position of *L'Être et le néant*, a form of "sympathy," and this sympathy is now an original structure of my perception of the other (ibid.).[10] Indeed, the whole sequence that develops this description of *compréhension* seems to resolve in part, at least, the "untheorized" tension between the conflictual relations of consciousness and other in *L'Être et le néant*, and the imperative that impels consciousness to will the freedom of the other in *Qu'est-ce que la littérature?*. Space does not allow us to follow here all the twists and turns of this development in the *Cahiers*. It is inherently far from clearcut, and it takes us beyond that relatively simplistic imperative, since *compréhension* itself involves an awareness of the ambiguity of the other's situation: the conditioned nature of his goals and his unconditional freedom. At this stage Sartre differentiates among three possible attitudes toward this ambiguity. The first two are inauthentic. I may either transcend the goal of the other, going beyond it toward my own, thereby seeing it as a limit of his freedom and taking the whole structure to be a given fact. In this case I no longer understand ("*je ne* comprends plus" [p. 290, Sartre's emphasis]). Or I can appropriate the goal of the other (Sartre takes the example of an adviser who gives gratuitous advice about how the other may achieve his goal, thereby making the other simply the instrument of achieving his own). The "authentic" alternative is to will that the other attain his goal, and to "engage" oneself in that goal, not by attempting to accomplish it oneself, but by changing the situation in such a way that the other may act effectively to realize it. In this way the autonomy of the other is respected; my awareness of his freedom as being "in difficulty" is implicated (*CM*, p. 295), as are the other's nonalienating recognition of my will, and my recognition of his appeal to me as a gift of his confidence. *Compréhension* becomes reciprocity and assistance, while both appeal and response are a form of mutual generosity. This apparently utopian scenario is not without its "incomprehensible" situations, its refusals, its obstacles, its risks, and its limits. However, authenticity involves taking risks (p. 306), and, as in Dilthey's theory, limitations may be dialectically turned to positive account. Differences of class, nationality, and condition limit the power of the appeal, but since those limits themselves have their origin in freedom, an authentic appeal will be aware of postulating, as a kind of "categorical imperative," a world in which such inequalities would no longer exist.

The move from conflict with others to the possibility of reciprocity is, however, only one aspect, although the major one, of a more wide-ranging "conversion." In his *Carnets de la drôle de guerre* Sartre had noted his earlier intention to confront the problem of passivity, which was "so essential in modern philosophy" (p. 226). Apparently elided in the emphasis on the lucidity of consciousness that seems to pervade the arguments of *L'Être et le néant*, it nonetheless still haunts the descriptions of the body, of affectivity, and of facticity that develop, in the treatise, the philosophical intuitions of *La Nausée*, where Roquentin so often seems at the mercy of his physical sensations. Earlier still, even in *La Transcendance de l'ego*, the work in which the thesis of the transparency of consciousness seems to be most unambiguously sustained, passivity mysteriously shadows spontaneity: "Consciousness takes fright at its own spontaneity" (p. 80). When the power of passivity is recognized, it is often seen as negative, as is the embodiment of consciousness when our physical existence ceases to be the active but unnoticed instrument of a project. However, the dialectic of appeal and response that is implicated in the committed *compréhension* of the *Cahiers* creates a synthesis of action and passivity in which the latter is quite markedly rehabilitated. At the moment when my active help is accepted, I freely become the passive medium of the other's achievement of his goal, and my body, rehabilitated too, becomes his instrument. My assistance is now *"passion, incarnation"* (*CM*, p. 297, Sartre's emphasis). Freedom is expressed in an "active *compréhension*" which is gradually transformed into passivity: the greater the freedom, the greater the "passion" (p. 298).

In the *Cahiers* Sartre's example of the appeal/response dialectic is the characteristically homely one of helping a would be passenger to catch an already moving bus. The consideration of more complex social situations, and ones in which problems of conflicting interests are both more pressing and more oppressive, will be developed primarily in the *Critique de la raison dialectique*. But in the meantime it is clear that, in the act of committed writing and its modes of *compréhension*, the medium of poetry, hitherto associated with passivity and affectivity, with the opacity of the material world, with "embodied" words that have a "face of flesh" (*Sit* II, p. 66), is also rehabilitated. *"Orphée noir"* (1948), and *L'Engagement de Mallarmé* (1948–52, 1979) effect this further conversion. The former, while evoking the situation of francophone Black African poets, often echoes the concepts of the *Cahiers* but develops them in relation to a specific collectivity; the latter, like *Saint Genet*, concentrates on a single subject, but more fully anticipates the concept of the "universal singular," and the interaction of *compréhension* with modified versions of Marxism and psychoanalysis that is characteristic of *L'Idiot de la famille*; both contribute to the attenuation of the prose/poetry distinction essential to the revaluation of committed writing set out in *Plaidoyer pour les intellectuels* and help to expose the weaknesses of *Qu'est-ce que la littérature?*.

"*Orphée noir,*" in particular, allows us to see why the notion of *compréhension* is absent from the earlier essay. Sartre argues that the oppressed white European worker must adopt technical, scientific, practical weapons to combat the alienation and oppression of the technical world in which he has to work, and he must define his condition as an "objective situation" if he is to confront it effectively. For him, language itself is technical and pragmatic. Such constraints tend toward "the more and more rigorous elimination of the subject," and we already know that *compréhension* is *par excellence* the method of grasping the subjective experience of others. "*Orphée noir*" underlines this: The "universal and abstract" concept of class is best approached through "intellection," while the "concrete and particular" experience of race may be grasped through "*ce que Jaspers nomme compréhension*" (*Sit* III, p. 280). This perhaps dubious characterization of class will later be modified, and in the sociopolitical theory of the *Critique* "intellection" will be seen to have its place; in retrospect, however, it also seems, rather than *compréhension,* to be implicit in the emphasis of *Qu'est-ce que la littérature?* upon the pragmatic medium of prose. Now, in "*Orphée noir,*" we may infer that committed white workers are, by virtue of that technical pragmatism, almost inevitably vulnerable to the alienating effects of *embrigadement,* and it is no longer the case that poetry is inadequate to the expression of commitment. Rather, the specific situation of the European worker is inimical to the convergence of the "social" and the "subjective" in poetry. The limitations of poetry as a vehicle of social action and expression are not absolute, but relative to a certain moment in the class struggle. Indeed, the sacrifice of subjectivity, the source of poetry, which the white worker must undergo in the interests of efficacy, is seen as a "mutilation" (p. 239).

It is, of course, *compréhension* that allows us to grasp the other as subject rather than as object, and Sartre by implication justifies its application to a social situation by defining "*négritude*" initially as a collective subjectivity. Indeed, this mode of understanding is all the more relevant since the relation of the black to his original situation is itself one of *compréhension.* The technical, utilitarian, instrumental attitude of the white worker to the natural world reflects that of his culture; what Sartre takes to be the black's proud rejection of technology expresses a "*compréhension* through sympathy" of nature (*Sit* III, pp. 263 and 265) which resolves the dichotomy between nature and culture itself. (We recall that the distinction between two modes of knowledge, that of analytic explanation, and that of sympathetic comprehension, is based on that dichotomy.) We already know that for the interpreter *compréhension* involves an imaginative re-creation, through empathy, of the subject's situation and response. The black poet's "sympathetic" understanding of his world is more fundamentally still an affective rather than cognitive apprehension of his "lived" situation. And here it is also worth recalling that in Sartre's thought the former definition of understanding predates, as, indeed, it outlives, his concern with the more cognitive functions of consciousness. As early as 1932, alongside his earliest notes for *La Nausée*, he already refers to "*compréhension*" (his italics) as a preconceptual faculty for grasping objects and relations between objects as synthetic wholes. At this level the object and thought are one, and the implication is that the subject/object dichotomy is thereby resolved.[11]

Sartre's own empathy with the black peoples' *compréhension* of nature is perhaps authenticated by the repression in "*Orphée noir*" of his own frequently expressed antipathy for the natural world – surpassed only by his even greater antipathy for a technical and scientific approach to it. Be that as it may, he is now able to show how, in the experience of *négritude*, the interrelationship of the subjective and the objective is radically modified, moving from a sense of their original synthesis in "*compréhension* through sympathy" to an experience of separation and tension, and thence to the possibility of a new synthesis in poetic expression. The terms "subject" and "object" cannot, even so, be eliminated from Sartre's discourse, although their import may change. The fact that the distinction between subject and object is inscribed in our analytic language (specifically, Sartre takes French to be such a language [p. 244]) compromises his attempt to express their synthesis; hence, perhaps, his own adoption, in "*Orphée noir*," of a hyperbolic, fervent, would-be poetic prose.

Yet the tracing of the dialectical journey to a new synthesis is, as Sartre sees it, essential to our understanding of the experience of the black poets, and to the sense that poetry is not only a possible, but a necessary medium for the expression of a commitment to change. It may therefore seem strange that at a crucial juncture Sartre appears to deny the possibility, for the white man, of "comprehending" the lived experience of *négritude*. He himself can only aspire, he believes, to examine their poems objectively (p. 261), and his superficial tactic in "*Orphée noir*" is to allow the poetry to make its own appeal to the freedom of the reader. However, he unmistakably continues to act as the empathetic mediator, and the reciprocity involved in the act of reading, a reciprocity already more than adumbrated in *Qu'est-ce que la littérature?*, is enacted in the fact that his reading changes him. Apart from the fact that he now takes a far more positive view of affectivity and passivity, the notions of *témoignage* and *engagement*, still distinguished, as we saw, in *Qu'est-ce que la littérature?*, begin to converge. They do so precisely because the act of *témoignage*, of "bearing witness" through writing, itself becomes still more closely associated with the apparent passivity of suffering, and with a rehabilitated affectivity. (We shall see that both are essential to the *engagement* of Flaubert in *L'Idiot de la famille*.) Emotion is no longer, as it was in Sartre's earlier writing, a self-deceiving way of evading the difficulty of practical action.[12] It is now a positive project, "a clearly defined way of living our relation to the world, and which involves a certain comprehension of the universe. It is a tension of the soul, a choice of oneself and of others, a way of transcending the raw data of experience, in short, it is as much of a project as any voluntary act" (p. 262). The *témoignage* of suffering and sacrifice is still, as it was in *Qu'est-ce que la littérature?*, a secularized reenactment of Christ's Passion: In his self-awareness the black poet sees himself as "the man who has taken upon himself all the sorrows of humanity, who suffers for us all, even for the white man" (p. 270). But his *témoignage* is no longer associated with the passive defeatism attributed to the poet in *Qu'est-ce que la littérature?*, and it goes beyond the authenticity claimed in the *Cahiers* for the poetic commitment to failure. However, a prerequisite for reconciling a metaphysical and negative *engagement* with sociopolitical action must be the discovery of history. Nature, and the original participation of the black peoples in nature, have no history, even if the passivity that Sartre tends to associate with that participation has become, in *négritude* (and in one of the least convincing passages of his argument), a "patience," "an active imitation of passivity" (p. 264). It is through the discovery of exile, colonization, slavery, and suffering (with the more negative, but paradoxically energizing, passivity that they involve), and, above all, through the imposition of an alien language, that the black peoples experience a rift between themselves and the world, and a reflective awareness of their own race and of the force of history. Such an awareness must, however, compound the loss of the ancestral spirit that they had originally "lived" in the "indivisible simplicity of nature" (p. 241): their sense of race, itself a fusion of subjectivity and collectivity, will now have been objectified. Their writing will both manifest that loss and actively seek to repair it, attempting to reintegrate reflection and the "lived." But it will go further. For the refusal of a defeatist complicity with suffering creates a more urgent possibility of revolt and freedom: "The black man enters into history in that the intuition of suffering confers upon him a collective past and a future goal" (p. 276). The poetry of *négritude* is therefore implicated in a dialectical process: It is the moment of negation that moves toward the synthesis in which a nonracial society would be realized. *Négritude* bears the seed of its own destruction; it is a transition and a means to an end, rather than the ultimate goal itself (p. 280). Therein lies its commitment.

But why poetry? Sartre now seems to recognize that certain themes, in their synthesis of reflection and imagination, mind and body, find their necessary expression in poetry. The experience of exile, at once individual, collective, and historical, itself creates the *dédoublement,* the lack of self-coincidence, that is essential to the reflective awareness of oppression, while the exile of the body acts as the "magnificent symbol" both of the exile of the spirit, and of exile from the spirit of Africa. Africa itself becomes the imaginary continent of a "mystical geography," both present and absent, eclipsing by its presence the reality of Europe, yet intangible and evanescent, out of reach beyond the frontiers of white culture – of that alienating *Esprit objectif,* as we might call it. However, from image and symbol to myth and, specifically, to the Orphic myth of poetry, is a short step that enables Sartre to associate the black quest for reintegration with one of the archetypal themes of Western culture. It is this syncretism that may allow his readers both to recognize and, in simultaneous *compréhension* and reflective awareness, to move beyond the black–white schism toward participation in the lived experience and the aspirations of another race. Hence, they may reach a common humanity. For the black, we infer, the loss, the schism, the quest that is akin to the descent of Orpheus to Hades, are the source of poetry and of potential recovery; for both black and white, that poetry may be the source of understanding and change.

The first strength of that poetry lies in its effort to make present what had been lost in absence: self-coincidence in the "original simplicity" of existence. One source of that recovery lies in the *Esprit objectif* of the blacks' own culture: the rhythms, the ancestral myths and incantations, the oral traditions that embodied their "objective negritude" (p. 253). Another source lies in a subjective descent into the self, to reveal the desires that, according to Sartre, are at one with an explosive cosmic energy. Eventually, man and Nature converge in the "objective-subjectivity" of the poem, which exists like an object in the world. It is a synthesis of contraries, "unstable repose, explosive fixity, self-renouncing pride, an absolute that knows to be transient" (pp. 283–4), and it is this which finds its most intense expression in the "committed" automatic writing of Césaire. We remember that in *Qu'est-ce que la littérature?* aesthetic value is already seen to have its origin in the recognition of "a rigorous harmony between subjectivity and objectivity" (p. 108). However, that synthesis has new significance in *"Orphée noir."* For it also brings together destruction and creativity, and dramatizes, within its very means of creation, not harmony but disjunction. It energizes, indeed, those creative tensions that Dilthey saw as the motor of change in history. Its destructiveness goes beyond the gratuitous negativity of the surrealist movement whose method the black poets superficially adopt, and which Sartre had already castigated in *Qu'est-ce que la littérature?*. For they seek to destroy, even as they are forced to speak and write it, the pallid language imposed upon them by an alien *Esprit objectif.* From its failure to signify their deepest experience directly they create a new subversive, indirect, language, a language that Mallarmé, and Sartre after him, saw as the essence of poetry, and which has as its aim "to evoke, in deliberate shadow, the silenced object through allusive, never direct, words that are reduced to an equal silence" (*Sit* III, p. 246).[13] The poem now exemplifies the attributes earlier ascribed to the "literary object" in *Qu'est-ce que la littérature?*, despite the essay's general emphasis on direct expression: "The literary object, although it comes into being *through* language, is never given *in* language; on the contrary, it is by nature silence, and a challenge to words" (*Sit* II, p. 94).

In the poetry of *négritude*, then, "for once, at least, the most authentic revolutionary project and the purest poetry flow from the same source" (*Sit* III, p. 285). "For once" might suggest that the potential for *engagement* is not inherent in poetry itself, and that their conjunction in the highly specific political, cultural, and linguistic situation of the black poets is not only unique but contingent. In order to validate the claim that pure art is more generally capable of commitment, a more extreme test case is necessary. Flaubert, superficially the most *désengagé* of writers, whose work seems devoid of any overtly committed content, and who himself seemed hostile to sociopolitical action and change, provides it. And given Sartre's long-standing antipathy to Flaubert, he might also be thought to provide a greater challenge to the method of *compréhension; L'Idiot de la famille* demonstrates, however, that empathy need not entail sympathy.

At first sight it might appear that the challenge of "committing" Flaubert is more a question of intention – and of somewhat inconsistent intention – than of achievement. In the first volume of the *Critique de la raison dialectique* Flaubert's project of writing is referred to as a form of "literary" commitment; in an interview published during the same year, in 1960, Sartre maintains that Flaubert's "pure art" conceals the strongly held views on social and political matters of a committed author (*Sit* IX, p. 14). However, the question of the positive or negative implications of this *engagment* is not directly posed. When speaking eleven years later of *L'Idiot de la famille* itself, and pressed to indicate the possible relationship between Flaubert's "total noncommitment" and "literary" commitment, Sartre recognized that Flaubert's apparent position might have been that of a reactionary property owner, but postulated a more profound *engagement* "through which he attempts to save his life" (*Sit* X, p. 112). "Literary" commitment is presumably the means of that salvation, but the imagery of circularity so prevalent in Flaubert suggests to Sartre that it may also embrace the notion of "totalization" and of a more radical redemption: "This circularity is totalization. To take the universe as a whole, and man within it, to give account of it from the point of view of nothingness, is a profound commitment. It is not a literary commitment in the sense that one 'commits oneself to writing books'." Flaubert's *engagement* is, like Mallarmé's, a "true passion, in the biblical sense" (*Sit* X, pp. 112–13). We recall that in *Qu'est-ce que la littérature?* the Passion was already the exemplary enactment of *témoignage*, and, indirectly, through its association with loss, failure, and the "loser wins" reversal, of that negative form of *engagement* alone open to the poet; we also know that in *"Orphée noir" témoignage* and *engagement* had converged in the suffering of the black poets and in the poetry of *négritude*. Our more recent knowledge of the *Cahiers pour une morale* may help us to clarify further Sartre's later allusion to Flaubert's "passion." In the *Cahiers "la Passion du Christ" forms the climax of a sustained meditation, partly inspired by Jaspers, on the experience of failure. The likelihood of failure, Sartre argues, is implicit in all human action, for there is an inevitable discrepancy between the goal projected and the goal achieved. In the first place, it is impossible fully to define my goal at the outset, for it is "a complex that expresses my whole personality" (CM, p. 451)*; furthermore, the consequences of my attempting to achieve it cannot be effectively limited, as they potentially involve "the whole world"; my goal is unstable in that action and project dialectically modify one another; it is alienated from me and distorted by the free judgment of others. The agent is nonetheless free to decide whether his action has met with failure or success; however, the option for success has its own negative consequences, in that the full realization of the goal would suppress any further possibility of transcendence. Further, even in success the "particularity" of the achieved goal frustrates the more fundamental impulse to "fulfill the human condition, that is to say, myself as universal and as absolute" (p. 453). But Christ's Passion effects what appears to be the final reversal:

And, in the end, failure becomes a *Passion*. In Christ's Passion, indeed, the individual and particular body attests to the Universal which is in Heaven and which is made flesh. The failure of Christ is the incarnation of the Universal in the Particular, the destruction of the Particular, and thus the pure affirmation of the Universal. Absolute failure becomes the sign of the absolute impossibility for man of being-in-the-world and hence the destruction of the world in behalf of man's aspirations. (p. 454)

And yet ambivalence persists. For while failure "is the revelation of freedom and even of Transcendence," its culmination in a denial of the world and in a "substantializing" of the negative (ibid.) would seem to be incompatible with *engagement*. If Flaubert's "true passion" has both to implicate and to redeem his nihilism and his commitment to failure, we suspect that its enactment of the "loser wins" reversal must involve a return to the real world, and that the Universal and the absolute must in turn be sacrificed to the "universal singular" and to the relative.

We shall consider later whether one of the more positive sequences of *L'Idiot de la famille* helps to resolve ambivalence and effect the convergence of *témoignage* and *engagement*. But in the meantime it should be noted that Sartre's own development since "*Orphée noir*" may help him to meet the challenge of "committing" Flaubert, and that he is unequivocally affirmative in his adoption of *compréhension* as the essential method of approaching Flaubert's life and work. Indeed, this approach may lead us to ask whether *L'Idiot de la famille* is itself an example of *écriture engagée*.

Saint Genet (1952) fails to integrate adequately Genet's individual experience and his historical context, but it is significant that even the negative and perverted power of an apparently sterile beauty may produce a positively demoralizing response in his bourgeois readers. According to Sartre, Flaubert's readers, too, will be exposed to a similar subversion. In *L'Engagement de Mallarmé* the nihilism of the pure poet, itself akin to Flaubert's, is transcended by a critical consciousness that transforms art, language, and, hence, history itself: Mallarmé is the battleground and ultimate reconciliation "on behalf of all," of "the Singular and the Universal." The poet has become the exemplary writer. The creative allusiveness of Mallarmé's poetic language had already energized, as we saw earlier, Sartre's reflections on committed poetry in "*Orphée noir*"; it inspires, too, the further attenuation in *Plaidoyer pour les intellectuels* (1965) of the distinction between prose and poetry set out in *Qu'est-ce que la littérature?*. Unambiguous clarity is now reserved for the purely technical language of the *écrivant*, for the practical and conceptual communication of specialist information. The mission of the *écrivain* is, on the other hand, a "totalizing" one: to bear witness to "the whole" in a synthesis of the subjective and the objective, the individual and the sociohistorical. But the *écrivain* will not experience or convey this synthesis in the mode of explicit knowledge: In a distinction now familiar from earlier definitions of *compréhension*, it is "lived," rather than "known." Furthermore, this "unsayable" experience, this "silent nonknowledge" (*Sit* VIII, p. 437), can be communicated only through "an ambiguous object that presents it allusively" (p. 444) and through a style that exploits and transforms the materiality of language, its ambiguities and its potential distortions of experience – the language, one might say, that is already part of the *esprit objectif* and that must be internalized again: "style is at the level where the external is internalized, in the individual attempt to move toward meaning it is what one might call the *flavor* of the epoch, the *taste* of the historical moment as they appear to a person individually shaped by that same history" (p. 450). It is through the power of style, in a definition still further elaborated and refined, that the Flaubert of *L'Idiot de la famille* will internalize the "historical moment" and seek to communicate the "unsayable."

The crucial role of the historical and sociopolitical context, absent from *Saint Genet*, and its dialectical relationship with the "singularity" of subjective attitudes and behavior and with the project of writing, had already been adumbrated then, in *L'Engagement de Mallarmé* and developed in *Plaidoyer*. The emphasis on *compréhension* is itself consolidated in the posthumously published second volume of the *Critique de la raison dialectique* (1958, 1961–2), which explores the interrelationship between *compréhension*, praxis, progress, and the intelligibility of history. "Dialectical" *compréhension* is seen to transcend the limitations of both "positive Reason" and "analytic Reason." Analytic reason cannot "understand" progress. Progress, and the praxis that is implied in it (and the praxis of writing would be no exception), is an "object of *compréhension*" (*CRD* II, p. 413); it is a "fundamental *notion*" that is also a "knowable, comprehensible and lived reality" (p. 412).[14] Apart from its involvement in the very enterprise and experience of progress, *compréhension* is further implicated, too, in "the practical field": indeed, *compréhension is* a form of praxis. Here Sartre seems to develop his concern with two modes of *compréhension:* the historian's understanding of the agent's praxis, and the agent's understanding of the situation in which he acts. Both modes of understanding-as-praxis interact dialectically with their objects, transforming them and being in turn transformed. Further, "progress," as distinct from "process," is seen to be a goal-directed "oriented change" (p. 417), and the recognition and understanding of that orientation are seen to be necessary to the intelligibility of history. (It need scarcely be added that both the recognition, however implicit, of our goals, and our understanding, albeit never complete, of history, are essential to the possibility of *engagement*.)

The interrelationship of situation and change postulated in *Qu'est-ce que la littérature?* has, then, become more complex. Furthermore, the goal-directed praxis of the artist is given striking, though brief, attention; "the progress of an artist is absolute," although it takes place within history (*CRD* II, p. 411). This apparently optimistic assertion is borne out a little later by the example of none other than Flaubert. For Sartre argues that the goal achieved in the completion of *Madame Bovary* far exceeds the original intention: "The achieving of the goal [the completion of *Madame Bovary*] is in no way the pure and simple accomplishing of the projected end. It is its totalization *together with* all the totalizations of totalizations which were moments of it" (p. 416). In the *Cahiers pour une morale*, we recall, the discrepancy between project and achievement exposed the threat of failure inherent in every human endeavor. Now it appears to carry a more optimistic message. However, in this second volume of the *Critique* a degree of ambivalence remains. Negatively, praxis is still at the mercy – as it was in the first volume – of "counterfinality," of facticity, and of the "noncomprehensible," antidialectical, and alienating practico-inert. Nonetheless, such elements of "violent negativity" themselves become dialectically integrated, as necessary moments of contradiction, into the movement of transcendence (*"dépassement"*) and progress. Flaubert's inability, unlike his elder brother, to identify with his father, is, according to Sartre, an example of that transcended negativity that will eventually help to integrate, and be integrated in, both individual and social progress (pp. 422–3). It remains to be seen whether, and how, the dialectic of contradiction and transcendence, and the complementary "loser wins" reversal, operate in Flaubert's experience as it is "understood" in *L'Idiot de la famille*, and whether the "absolute progress" of the artist will also involve a more relative, but nonetheless crucial, form of social progress. If so, Flaubert may prove, indeed, to have been an *"écrivain engagé."*

Flaubert's complex integration into the society of his day is a far cry from the *embarquement* of the individual in *Qu'est-ce que la littérature?*, and his project of writing is clearly subject to conditioning constraints from which the "committed writer" of the earlier essay was relatively immune. That complexity is strikingly exemplified in Sartre's interpretation of Flaubert's "fall" at Pont-l'Évêque in 1844, a fall that is usually diagnosed as epileptic, but which Sartre also attributes to a form of hysteria. (Flaubert, who was driving his

elder brother home from Deauville, collapsed in the carriage at his
brother's feet.[15]) On the one hand this can be "understood" to be
Flaubert's escape (and Flaubert's illness "understands itself" in ways
that are beyond the contemporary medical knowledge represented
by his father), an escape, "chosen" and intentional despite his loss of
consciousness, from an impossible family situation. The passivity
induced by his subjection in infancy to his mother's efficient but
unloving care had inhibited the action that would be necessary if he
were to try to obey the imperatives of his father's bourgeois expectations of him. (After this "*crise,*" Flaubert was allowed to give up his
law studies and remain at home to write. It was a catastrophe that
made salvation through writing possible.) But that family situation,
fraught with its own contradictions and tensions, had also mediated
to him the tensions of the reign of Louis-Philippe, and through a
series of dialectical twists that it would take too long to follow here,
Sartre argues that Flaubert's "*crise*" *prophesies* the fall of the Bourgeois Monarchy in 1848, and anticipates the rule of Louis Napoleon,
with its eventual failure and defeat (*IF* III, pp. 430–1). The Romantic
notion of the "poet as prophet" is transformed. Flaubert's own neurosis is a "totalizing" of the subjective and the objective; it is the
"lived" experience of what one might call an accelerated historical
comprehension which, although not accompanied by an explicit
prise de conscience, authenticates Flaubert's own later representations of the period as a form of *témoignage* and commands the as-
sent of his readers. Despite, and because of, their misreading of his
work, they recognize that it expresses "organically" (p. 430), rather
than contingently, their own point of view and their own historical
situation (the Bourgeois Monarchy, the Second Republic, the advent
of the Second Empire). Again, this recognition does not involve an
explicit *prise de conscience;* together, Flaubert and his public "have
lived their action as though it were a passion" (ibid.). Nonetheless,
Flaubert's experience of his illness is, according to Sartre, a "full
expression of his freedom" (*IF* II, p. 2136). Together with a spiraling
synthesis that transcends the contradictory tensions of passivity and
creativity, through the interaction of a personal and a collective
"neurosis," Flaubert's illness enables him to achieve, for and with
his readers, the "historialization" and the communication that are
the prerequisites of committed literature. His writing enacts a dialectical *process;* if this also constitutes *progress* in the sense of the

"goal-directed" change described in the second volume of the *Critique*, it does so in part through his renewal of a specialized form of praxis. For Flaubert's literary style involves the project of refining and transforming language itself. Furthermore, although he at first seems to reinforce, through the doctrine of Art for Art's sake, the gulf between the imaginary and the real, his writing eventually reconciles them, as we shall see, in a form of *"l'imaginaire social."* It also reveals, questions, and changes the *sens* (understood to be both the "direction" and the "meaning") of history. Ultimately, through the reversal of the "loser wins" mechanism, his experience and his praxis substitute the positive for the negatively corrosive as he moves beyond suffering, failure, and impotence in an eventual conversion to creative optimism.

Sartre's surviving notes for his study of *Madame Bovary* indicate his frustration at the difficulty he experienced in linking theory and "practical" criticism: *"Why write the first three volumes if they cannot be found on every page of the fourth?"* (*IF* III, 2nd ed., p. 783, Sartre's emphasis).[16] (The reader is even more frustrated by the impossibility of reconstructing, from Sartre's fascinating but fragmentary thoughts, the specific ways in which *Madame Bovary* might have exemplified the Flaubertian committed novel.) And it is intriguing to find that in the "completed" sections of *L'Idiot* the work that elicits Sartre's most positive interpretation is one of the least conventionally *engagé*. His response to *Saint Julien l'Hospitalier*, the second of Flaubert's *Trois contes*, may help us to reach a tentative conclusion concerning Sartre's evolving view of committed writing.

Despite its late date – it was written from 1875 to 1876 – *Saint Julien*, according to Sartre, takes us back yet again to Flaubert's fall or "conversion" at Pont-L'Évêque, adding the final twist to the spiral that had its source in 1844. We already know that the spiral "totalizes" the personal and the historical; if we disentangle the details of Sartre's interpretation we find that in its "tactical" and "strategic" intentions (*IF* II, p. 1919) the fall also implicates the emotional, the moral, the socioeconomic, a more long-term historical perspective, the linguistic, the aesthetic, the ontological, and the metaphysical.[17] It "embodies," in a strong sense, Flaubert's desire for his father's tenderness, hitherto denied; it emancipates him from ordinary human goals and therefore delivers him, provisionally, from the shame of failure (pp. 1915, 1931); it allows him to enjoy in advance the inheritance that will enable him to live, in his seclusion at Croisset, a life of feudal parasitism within the framework of bourgeois property ownership. (Flaubert's rejection of his bourgeois destiny is an illusion, but it implicates a return to medieval values [p. 1878].) The fall also "embodies" language. Tactically, the body says the unsayable (p. 1920), and in so doing it calls into question the practical functions of language; strategically, the *signification* of words gives way to a *sens*, to an "immanent and indecipherable unity" (p. 1978). Flaubert, already alienated from language in his early childhood, adopts an astonished distance from language that leads him to abandon his earlier would be expressive eloquence – an aesthetic distance that allows him to see language as a totality and to exploit both its materiality and its direct "signifying" function in order to make present the unsayable.[18] Aesthetic distance, too, implies the preeminence of the imaginary as Flaubert's crisis radically detaches him from the real, while imagination itself reinforces the aesthetic goal: Far from being gratuitous, the imagination becomes a "rigorous technique" for the transmutation of the sensible and tangible world into its unreal but precise counterpart (p. 1936). This "aesthetic attitude" may have positive or negative ontological implications, and in the years following his crisis Flaubert oscillates between them (p. 1950). It may on the one hand effect the "derealization" of the artist in his contestation of the real, but at the same time Flaubert's "imaginarizing observation" may yield a more detailed view of the object than would "practical" observation, and may integrate it into an imaginary totality. Or, on the other hand, the artist may discover a pervasive "non-being" at the heart of reality that no image can represent. This impotence will exacerbate the internalized "art-as-neurosis" common to the writers of Flaubert's generation; deriving from the tension between an inherited antibourgeois attitude and their bourgeois status, it finds expression in the cultivated "non-humanity" of Art for Art's sake.

As we shall see, these implications do not exhaust the significance of Flaubert's fall, but Sartre can provisionally conclude that in its "teleological unity" it is the "discovery of a totality." We may infer that, as such, it transcends the "singularity" of Flaubert's experience, transforming it into an *universel singulier*. Sartre also provisionally concludes that the experience finds its *témoignage* in Flaubert's completion in 1845 of the first *Éducation sentimentale*, and, notably, in the figure of Jules, whose discovery of his vocation as an artist dramatizes the "loser wins" reversal apparently effected by Flaubert's illness. Yet Jules's conversion falls short even of a full commitment to art: It represents a "rationalized" version of that reversal. As such, it has its value: It leads Flaubert to "understand" his own art. However, there is also a "profound and original" version (p. 2135) of "loser wins." It is essential to Flaubert's *engagement*, it is dramatized in *Saint Julien l'Hospitalier*, and it can be understood only in the light of the *symbolic* significance of the crisis of Pont-L'Évèque.

For Flaubert's fall is not only a "mimed" suicide. It is also a parricide, the murder of the resented and diabolical "symbolic" father. But the death of the "empirical" father in 1846 compounds the imaginary guilt of the son and, although in reality it brings about his deliverance (Flaubert begins to recover), it fails to assuage his abjection and despair. Sartre claims that all Flaubert's works will henceforth reenact the original crisis: the Passion of the son and the murder of the father (p. 1909).

Saint Julien, however, does more, with an intensity and a resonance that go far beyond Flaubert's self-deprecating assessment of it. Sartre makes much of the fact that Flaubert was first attracted in 1845 to the tale told in the stained-glass window, and to the possibility of retelling it. For Julien, the murder of his father leads to sainthood, hence the fascination of the legend for Flaubert. (Sartre brushes aside the fact that Julien also kills his mother.) Julien's early passion for slaying animals symbolizes Flaubert's youthful misanthropy and his conviction that life itself is a malediction; Julien's ambivalent struggle against the prophecy that he will murder his parents enacts Flaubert's own horror of his unbearable resentments. Why, then, did it take Flaubert thirty years to create his version of the legend? The reasons are complex – apart from the fact that the long penitence that precedes Julien's apotheosis dramatizes the patience and suffering that, Flaubert believed, are the lot of the genius. In the early 1870s Flaubert's pessimism, and his obsession with failure, are intensified by the Prussian victory, by the fall of the Empire, and by the Commune. In 1875 he is prey, again, to family troubles, and threatened by the loss of his refuge at Croisset, an experience scarcely less traumatic than the fall itself. Vulnerability and anguish revive the need to express both his rediscovered guilt and his now idealized recollections of childhood: In Flaubert's tale

Julien's parents are remarkable for their tenderness, as are his memories of them. Both sons are now, Sartre claims, identified with the slaughtered father, and through Julien Flaubert weeps the tears that he wishes his father had, in reality, wept for him (p. 1902). Earlier, Flaubert's "mimed suicide" was provoked by his resentment of his father; Julien's recognition of his father's image in his own reflection prevents his suicide.

Sartre, in evoking the significance of sadism, sensuality, ambivalence, tenderness, remorse, of solitude and abjection, descent and ascension, offers a powerful reading of Flaubert's story. It might seem, however, to place an emphasis only on the purely personal significance of a tale of compensation, and to lack any collective resonance. The metaphysical dimension that Sartre explores would seem at first to support this view. Julien's penitence involves the sin of despair and a form of self-inflicted suffering that, according to Sartre, leads him further away from God (that increasing distance is part of his punishment); his embracing of the leper is a sign of abjection rather than of hope for salvation. Here, the "loser wins" mechanism must be seen to operate against *all* the odds. Sartre's interpretation presumes the total malediction of God the Father upon humanity, and the discovery of human "authenticity" in self-hatred; yet, it also implies the transformation of God (and, Sartre suggests, of Flaubert's father), into the hidden but benign instrument of a miraculous salvation. On one reading, Sartre argues, the tale indirectly expresses Flaubert's conviction that the real, that impoverishment of infinite possibility, exists only to inspire the need for an impossible transcendence, a transcendence in the imaginary (p. 2116). On another reading, the very structure of the tale, the double level of the lived (Julien's experience) and the told (the narrator's perspective, the "God's eye" view), dramatizes the possibility of such a transcendence. It is that structure, too, which enables the narrative to go beyond a purely personal symbolism and endow it with moral and historical significance – if we are able to accept Sartre's account of Flaubert's fall as a "lived" prophecy of the advent and the defeat of the Second Empire.

It also allows Sartre to move from a *compréhension* based on empathy and imaginative reconstruction to an unexpected sympathy. For at the level of the "lived," he argues, we experience the series of catastrophes that befall a monstrous and sadistic hero; at the level of the "told," we share the point of view of the Artist, or of

God, the source of that absolute love that leads Julien to sainthood. It is Flaubert's ability to convince us of that love which leads us in turn, Sartre believes, to love an abject parricide. It also suggests to Sartre that Flaubert's self-hatred has been transformed into the possibility of a positive and fruitful self-love.

For the agnostic Flaubert and the atheist Sartre such an interpretation surprisingly implies a radical, if fictional, "suspension of disbelief." However, it may seem more surprising still that Sartre's own suspension of disbelief is not contingent upon the art of Flaubert alone. For Sartre, the humble country priest of his contemporary Bernanos inspires a love so great that even the skeptical reader raises God from the tomb in order to save him.[19] It would seem that despite the possibility, for the committed writer, of "changing the world" by ridding it of its mystifying beliefs, Sartre prefers to show that the Christian, whether medieval or modern, and the atheist, whether of the nineteenth or the twentieth century, may communicate through what appears to be a version of the *Esprit objectif* described in Sartre's third volume. It is pervaded by a "Christian atheism" in which ancient beliefs still feed the imagination and the sensibility of the most hardened skeptic. But Flaubert's revelation of love is more universal still, and thus transcends even the potentially mystifying power of lingering religious belief: What *Saint Julien* enacts is "the great ontological law, the law of love which rules us all" (p. 2133).

In much of this sequence it is difficult to distinguish between the voice of Sartre and the voice of an imagined Flaubert: Sympathy has led to projection and identification. And yet we recall that in Sartre's *Cahiers* love, sustained by *compréhension*, had already become the mainspring of a nonalienating reciprocity: It is this "conversion," perhaps, that inspires his interpretation of *Saint Julien*, and the sense that both love and freedom are the means and the goal of *engagement*.[20] We remember, too, that the symbolism of a secularized Passion, so fundamental to Sartre's discussion of Flaubert, had already acted, both in *"Orphée noir"* and in the *Cahiers*, as the paradigm for a form of *engagement*. In the *Cahiers*, however, its Christian significance was judged to imply too radical a transcending of the real. But the symbolism of *Saint Julien* in turn transcends the "derealizing" function of the imaginary, and demonstrates that art, as Sartre argues at greater length in the third volume of *L'Idiot de la famille,* may institute a dialectic of the imaginary and the real. The *"real* structuration" of the legend and of the medieval work of art, itself a product of what he calls the "social imagination," is not only the vehicle of Flaubert's conversion from horror to optimism, but the mediation between the "singularity" of his lived experience and its creative objectification in a "singular universal."

Despite the fact that *L'Idiot de la famille* continues for a third volume, Sartre's discussion of *Saint Julien* at the end of the second creates a strong sense of culmination and of (in Sartre's case always provisional) closure. We infer that the *Esprit objectif,* which Sartre associates with the practico-inert, is internalized, modified, and externalized by Flaubert, like the language that is, in its materiality, one of its primary elements. The *Esprit objectif,* itself changed by the "praxis" of writing, becomes the locus of an indirect communication: it may mediate as well as alienate. Sartre, therefore, does not neglect the act of reading. Its negative aspect may, he argues, imply an atomized series of purely external relationships, of separate individual "totalizations." Or a given work may be read within the perspective of a "pledged group" that provides the "normative determination" of the reading. Such would be the reading of Marx's manifesto of 1848 for a young member of the Communist party. (Sartre's argument here reminds us forcefully of the shortcomings of *embrigadement* as they were discussed in *Qu'est-ce que la littérature?*) In either case the work itself is subject to a form of inertia, and its mediation is disabling rather than enabling: it destroys the possibility of reciprocity (*IF* III, p. 55). But Sartre also postulates a more dynamic form of reading, one in which the reader's subjectivity reveals and heightens the contradictory imperatives of the *Esprit objectif* in order to transcend them toward a synthesis "in the unity of a 'constantly developing totalization' " (p. 56).

The *Esprit objectif* of an epoch is at one and the same time the sum of the works published at the date under consideration, together with the multiplicity of totalizations effected by contemporary readers. As we know, thoughts are living things. They are born of the original thought, which is nothing other than practical activity insofar as it reveals the environment in the totalizing perspective of its reorganization. . . . Knowledge and ideas are – more or less directly – practical; thus it is through our personal *praxis* (techniques, ethical systems, religions, etc.) that we should try to accomplish the thoroughgoing totalization that books require of us. Thus action, as it totalizes doctrine, transforms us: We become the representatives of a group, either past or future – either the group whose presence we sensed behind the currently dominant practico-inert idea, or the group that we will bring to birth as we win it over to our practical totalization. For the *Esprit objectif* tells us in contradictory but imperative ways, who we are: in other words, what we must do. (pp. 57–8)

For Sartre, then, Flaubert's writing is at once a revelation and a contestation of his own and his reader's situation. His work implements, transforms, and transcends the contradictory imperatives of the *Esprit objectif*. In doing so, it not only demoralizes but may also energize the readers who, with him, both passively suffer and actively create that objective mind. Flaubert also, according to Sartre, contests in the name of love the self-hatred that is part of that shared suffering: Individual progress and social progress go hand in hand. Flaubert's "conversion to optimism" dramatizes Sartre's: his sense of the possibility, despite the inauspicious context of both subjective and objective neurosis, of committed writing and committed reading; his vision of the *Esprit objectif* itself, no longer inert, as a dynamic, spiraling movement that implicates both. Further, from Sartre's understanding of Flaubert's comprehension of his time we may conclude that the process and the progress of writing and reading are as open-ended as *L'Idiot de la famille* itself.

NOTES

1 Page references to Sartre's work are given in the text, with the following abbreviated titles: *Cahiers pour une morale, CM; Les Carnets de la drôle de guerre, CDG; Critique de la raison dialectique* (the 1960 edition of Vol. I), *CRD; L'Idiot de la famille* (the 1971–2 edition), *IF; Situations,* Vols. II–X, *Sit* II–X.
2 "*Questions de méthode*," which forms the introductory section of the first volume of *Critique de la raison dialectique,* first appeared separately, but without its concluding pages, in *Les Temps modernes,* no. 139 (September 1957), and no. 140 (October 1957).
3 I shall continue to use the French words *sens* and *signification*, which, as defined above, have specific connotations in Sartre's writing. In addition, since the terms *engagement* (which implies active involvement in a situation as well as commitment to a cause), *témoignage* (bearing witness, testimony), and *embarquement* (passive involvement) appear as technical terms in Sartre's analyses, they will usually be given in French. For an

illuminating account of these terms, and of *embrigadement* (militant membership of a specific political party) in relation to "committed" intellectuals writing before Sartre, see David S. Schalk, *The Spectrum of Political Engagement* (Princeton, N.J.: Princeton University Press, 1979).

4 See Rhiannon Goldthorpe, *Sartre, Literature, and Theory* (Cambridge: Cambridge University Press, 1984), ch. 6, in which I also consider "*Orphée noir*" in a different context, discuss *L'Engagement de Mallarmé*, and analyze Sartre's thought on the ambiguity of the historical event and of historical action in *Cahiers pour une morale*. *L'Engagement de Mallarmé* first appeared in *Obliques*, ed. Michel Sicard, no. 18–19 (May 1979): 164–94. It was subsequently republished, in an edition by Arlette Elkaïm-Sartre, under the title *Mallarmé: La lucidité et sa face d'ombre* (Paris: Gallimard, 1986).

5 See "speech is a specific moment of action and cannot be understood apart from it" (*Sit* II, p. 71), or "to speak is to act: once named, nothing is quite the same. It has lost its innocence" (p. 72).

6 The relevant works of Raymond Aron are *La Philosophie critique de l'histoire. Essai sur une théorie allemande de l'histoire* (Paris: Vrin, 1938), reprinted 1969, and *Introduction à la philosophie de l'histoire* (Paris: Gallimard, 1938). The seventh volume, edited by Bernard Grœthuysen, of Dilthey's *Gesammelte Schriften* (Stuttgart, Teubner; Göttingen, Vandenhoeck & Rurecht, 1914–77), contained, among other texts likely to interest Sartre, Dilthey's notes for a *Critique of Historical Reason* and reflections on the "objective mind." The volume was published in 1927, and would therefore have been available during Sartre's stay at the French Institute in Berlin, as Aron's successor, from 1933 to 1934. (By 1938 Grœthuysen had become the philosophy editor at Gallimard, and expressed his enthusiasm for the publication of Sartre's *La Nausée* in that year.) References to the work of Dilthey will be given in the text; they will include, apart from the *Gesammelte Schriften* (*GS*), the selections edited by H. P. Rickman, *Dilthey, Selected Writings* (Cambridge: Cambridge University Press, 1976), and Michael Ermarth's study, *Wilhelm Dilthey: The Critique of Historical Reason* (Chicago: University of Chicago Press, 1978).

7 See *L'Être et le néant* (Paris: Gallimard, 1943), p. 658.

8 Both Dilthey and Sartre use the term "epoch" in a specialized sense, seeing it as a center of concrete purposes and values, in terms of "lived" emotions and impulses, and as a whole but finite system of dynamic connections discovered through intersubjectivity. See, for Dilthey, *GS* VII, p. 155, and Rickman, p. 198; for Sartre, "*Écrire pour son époque*" (1946), in *Les Écrits de Sartre*, ed. Michel Contat and Michel Rybalka (Paris: Gallimard, 1970), pp. 670–6, and *IF* III, p. 440ff. Dilthey also modi-

fied Hegel and anticipated Sartre in considering, against the Idealist tradition, that history had its basis in the "facticity" of "concrete physical and social conditions" (GS VII, pp. 287–8); the function of the historian was to reveal the "Realdialektik" of the oppositions (among them, reason and contingency) which impel the dynamic interaction between the human mind and those conditions. Sartre distinguishes between the truly dialectical and "totalizing" relationships, the "living conflict" between individual and epoch revealed through the progressive-regressive method, and the "simple inert juxtaposition" that satisfies Marxist historians (CRD I, p. 94). A further convergence between Dilthey and Sartre is anticipated in Dilthey's review of Das Kapital; Michael Ermarth draws attention to Dilthey's criticism of Marx's theory of labor as the source of value. It relapsed, according to Dilthey, into an "unhistorical way of thinking," and tended to overlook "the real needs of individuals and the relation of these needs to scarcity" (Ermarth, p. 293; GS XVII, pp. 186–7). Sartre's concern with need and scarcity is, of course, fundamental to the argument of Critique de la raison dialectique.

9 Similarly, Sartre, in La Transcendance de l'ego (1936–7), took the Ego, as an "ideal unity of 'states'," to be an object for consciousness that vanishes when I attempt to grasp it directly.

10 At times Dilthey and, as we shall see later, Sartre, both associate compréhension not only with sympathy but with love. Among proponents of the Verstehen method such a view is controversial, as Dilthey himself realized, and both he and Sartre elsewhere gave greater priority to the cognitive aspects of compréhension, emphasizing interpretative reconstruction rather than a less corrigible empathetic or sympathetic projection.

11 See "Le Carnet 'Dupuis'," in Jean-Paul Sartre, Œuvres romanesques, edited by Michel Contat and Michel Rybalka with the collaboration of Geneviève Idt and George H. Bauer (Paris: Gallimard, Bibliothèque de la Pléiade, 1981), p. 1685.

12 See Esquisse d'une théorie des émotions (1939; Paris: Hermann, 1965), p. 41.

13 Sartre quotes from Mallarmé's prose work, "Magie." See Stéphane Mallarmé, Œuvres complètes (Paris: Gallimard, Bibliothèque de la Pléiade, 1951), p. 400.

14 Sartre differentiates sharply between the "notion," which is the result of compréhension, and the more analytic "concept": "A scientific approach implies the rigor of concepts. As a philosopher, I try to achieve rigor through notions, and I make the following distinction between the concept and the notion: A concept is an externally constructed and, at the same time, atemporal definition; . . . a notion is a definition from within, and which comprehends within itself not only the time of the

object envisaged, but the time of its own act of cognition. . . . So, when you study a man and his history, you can proceed only through notions. . . . The distinctions that I make between concept and notion, and between knowledge and *compréhension*, coincide ("*Sur 'L'Idiot de la famille'*," *Sit* X, pp. 95–6). It may also be noted that in the first volume of the *Critique* Sartre had criticized Marxism for its insufficiently dialectical view of "*real* temporality" (Sartre's emphasis) and of progress (*CRD* I, p. 63, n. 2).

15 For full accounts of *L'Idiot de la famille* see Christina Howells, *Sartre: The Necessity of Freedom* (Cambridge: Cambridge University Press, 1988), and Hazel E. Barnes, *Sartre and Flaubert* (Chicago: University of Chicago Press, 1981).

16 For Sartre's notes on *Madame Bovary* see the third volume of the revised edition of *L'Idiot de la famille* (Paris: Gallimard, 1988).

17 Sartre interprets Flaubert's emotional response alone in terms of six different levels. See *IF* II, pp. 1825–6.

18 For a sustained interpretation of the linguistic and stylistic "conversion" that follows the crisis of Pont l'Évêque see *IF* II, pp. 1972–89. In defining Flaubert's style as "a constant dialectic of *sens* and *signification*" (*IF* II, p. 1982) Sartre has consciously moved away from the opposition he had set up between them in *Qu'est-ce que la littérature?*. Referring to (and misquoting) his earlier essay, he now maintains that, in a painting, the *sens* of the yellow sky above Golgotha ("anguish transformed into a thing") would be lost, were it not for the *signification* of the Crucifixion. His position in *L'Idiot de la famille* is much closer to that of *Plaidoyer pour les intellectuels*.

19 *IF* II, p. 2124. In the last words of his diary Bernanos's young priest concludes that the greatest grace of all would be to love oneself, in humility, as one would love any other of God's creatures (*Diary of a Country Priest*). This context suggests that Sartre's attribution of a newly discovered "self-love" to Flaubert has a positive connotation.

20 In Hoederer, one of the protagonists of *Les Mains sales* (1948) and one of Sartre's few convincingly "committed" characters, political insight and action are motivated by a loving concern for others. Hoederer makes clear to the young intellectual Hugo, whose motives are confused both by class guilt and by egoism, that to love people for what they are, or despite what they are, is of greater value than a commitment to abstract principles and ideologies.

6 Sartrean ethics

The title of the present study represents a philosophical wager. After all, Sartre never produced a completed ethical system even though his entire work is shot through with the ethical problematic. It will consequently be necessary for this study to account for the insistent recurrence of the moral question in Sartre's works as well as for the reasons why he was never willing to answer this question in any definitive manner.

To be sure, Sartre did, in fact, write on ethical questions. His *Notebooks for an Ethic* (1947) are subsequent to *Being and Nothingness* (1943); two other texts (1964 and 1965) are subsequent to the *Critique of Dialectical Reason* (1960). The first of these are notes for lectures given by Sartre at the Gramsci Institute in Rome (1964); the second (1965) are notes intended for a lecture at Cornell University canceled at the last moment by Sartre in protest against American bombings in Vietnam. The *Notebooks for an Ethic*, published posthumously in 1983, are a collection of fragmentary comments or aphorisms without any single emphasis. The two other texts (1964 and 1965) remain unpublished. I shall refer to these latter works as *The Rome Lectures* and *The Cornell Notes*. These are coherent texts that set forth fully developed lines of reasoning. Moreover all three of these texts have in common the fact that they were never published by Sartre and consequently, in Sartre's eyes, offered no satisfactory philosophical solution to the ethical question.

However, we shall not be able to limit ourselves to those three texts. If Sartre left them unfinished, it was because the ethical question had not as yet found a fixed and well-defined place within his

Translator: Oreste F. Pucciani.

work. Inversely, if the two major stages in his philosophical work, *Being and Nothingness* and the *Critique of Dialectical Reason*, both are accompanied by an attempt at a Sartrean ethic, the *Notebooks* in the first instance, *The Rome Lectures* and *The Cornell Notes* in the second, we must conclude that the two major works gave rise in and of themselves to the ethical question that motivated those attempts. We shall be obliged, therefore, to reexamine Sartre's work in an attempt to locate the significant points of tension where the ethical and philosophical questions arise as well as the articulation of these questions. If ethics exist for Sartre, it is as an ethic of freedom and liberation. In the articulation proposed here it will always be a question of the alienation of freedom as well as of the possibility that freedom may discover itself to be free.

BEING AND NOTHINGNESS: LACK, VALUE, "MORAL PERSPECTIVES"

The "for-itself" is lack of being: It fails to be the being within which no negation has any place; it fails to be the "in-itself." This is the point of departure for Sartre's analysis of "lack" in the passage titled "The for-itself and the being of value," where we find the first significant articulation of a philosophical problematic with the moral question. It is this ontological lack of being that, pointing the for-itself in the direction of a totality of itself, can alone make intelligible any given concrete ontic lack. It is only by starting from the aim of a preexisting totality that a lacuna can be detected: a lack of food, for example, in the case of hunger. Without this totalizing aim, and assuming hypothetically a purely external lack as assailing the for-itself, hunger would be blind, inexpressible panic. If, on the contrary, hunger is organized behavior, it is because hunger is the lack that it is only in the light of what lies beyond it – that is, its projected satisfaction. But this aimed at totality, which contains the meaning of our most insignificant concrete behavioral acts, is unattainable. It is an impossible synthesis. Indeed, as Sartre says, it is "the lacked of all lacks" (*BN*, p. 69): This intended coincidence of the in-itself–for-itself is something that the for-itself will never achieve because, if it did – that is, if it realized the possible or the lacking "whose synthetic assimilation would transform the for-itself into *itself*" (p. 71), it would already be beyond this achievement "with another horizon of possibilities" (p. 77), hence launched into a new quest for the in-itself–for-itself.

Specific "lackeds" ("*manqués*") have their source in the "lacked" of the for-itself as such which Sartre calls the "self – or itself as in-itself" (p. 65). And he adds that "the being of the self is value" (p. 68). With the concept of value the ethical problematic comes into rela-tionship with the ontological structure of the for-itself. To be sure, all value is not ethical. For value to be ethical it must be thetic; it must become the object of a reflexive position. In the nonthetic translucidity of the for-itself, value haunts every concrete lack; but inversely every ethical value can be understood only in terms of the "supreme value," that is, the quest by the for-itself for its *self* or for its self-coincidence.

This ontological structure, in which moral value is rooted, can alone make intelligible the duality of moral value, that is, "to be unconditionally and not to be" (p. 68). This duality of being and having-to-be may well prove to be a stumbling block in the elucida-tion of value. If one takes it for a fact, equivalent to other facts, as sociologists do, then its specificity as moral value will vanish and it will no longer be a free appeal to human freedom; on the other hand if one takes it as pure ideality, "then it will collapse for lack of being" (p. 69). Value is paradoxical and can be grasped only if one holds together the two poles of its duality: It has a being; it is neither simulacrum nor illusion; it has sufficient weight in order to require freedom to take its direction from it. All the same, the being of value is only to be beyond being, hence to be a nonbeing; the constraint that it exercises is not that of a road sign directing the flow of traffic; it does not require positive disciplinary conformism but calls upon the free invention of the behavior it prescribes. Whence the ambigu-ity of ethics: Its free unconditionality – nothing imposes values on liberty from without; here freedom meets up with its own "self"; and because it is impossible to found this self (since the for-itself can found itself as nothingness but not as being) there results its perpet-ual falling back into the "concrete facticity" of prescriptive con-tents, all of which implies "a total contingency of being-for-value (which will come up again in connection with morality to paralyze and relativize it) and at the same time a free and absolute necessity" (p. 70).

It is not the work of ontology to make pronouncements about this ambiguity. However, in the last pages of *Being and Nothingness* Sartre did open up "moral perspectives." The principal result of the intelligibility of value in terms of "lacked" (*manqué*) is to exclude the possibility of considering it as something "lacking": as an external object which, were it accessible, would bring about a fulfillment but which, because it is inaccessible, becomes transcendent ideality. This double objectification, which is a flight before what is intrinsically elusive in value, is stigmatized by Sartre as the "spirit of seriousness":

The spirit of seriousness has two characteristics: It considers values as transcendent givens independent of human subjectivity, and it transfers the quality of "desirable" from the ontological structure of things to their simple material constitution. For the spirit of seriousness, for example, *bread* is desirable because it is *necessary* to live (a value written in an intelligible heaven) and because bread *is* nourishing. (p. 544)

It is not difficult to guess what this reification of value produces on the strictly moral plane:

bad faith, for it is an ethics which is ashamed of itself and does not dare speak its name. It has obscured all its goals in order to free itself from anguish. (p. 544)

This is the stuffy ethic of the righteous, the just, the bastards, the notables of the Bouville museum.

Does an ethic exist that is not alienated or alienating? If one were to look this mutual relationship of freedom and value in the face, could this bring forth a pure and authentic ethic? What would happen if freedom, instead of fleeing itself, should turn back upon itself and take itself as value? Is freedom as value or a value of freedom conceivable? Or would freedom run off with everything, rendering henceforth irrelevant any plea in terms of value? Or would freedom become alienated by its own value? Sartre reserves the answers to these questions for a subsequent work. The problem is not solved: It is certain that value and alienation go together, but does the alienation come from value as such or only from an inauthentic understanding of it?

NOTEBOOKS FOR AN ETHIC: TOWARD THE
BEWITCHMENT OF FREEDOM

The *Notebooks for an Ethic* seem in a sense to deepen rather that to remove this uncertainty: "Values reveal freedom and at the same time alienate it," (*CM*, p. 16). But in another sense Sartre now grants a definitive positive importance to value. "A classification of values must lead to freedom: Classification in such an order as to make freedom more and more apparent. At the top: generosity" (ibid.).[1]

There is now a hierarchy of values and there is at least one good moral value: generosity. Value as such is not alienating. It is the driving force and the responsibility of the free project, the constantly renewed mobility of the relationship of freedom to the world. In value "there is not the slightest trace of compulsion since compulsion possesses the double character of enslaving me (I am the means for the required end) and of saving me from dereliction" by persuading me of the self-sufficiency of the end and of my own irresponsibility (CM p. 261) whereas the "having-to-be" constitutive of value, on the contrary, "means that everything depends on me and that I am alone in my practical activity, delivered over to myself" (p. 259). Alienating compulsion is an aspect not of value but of its conversion into "obligation." Sartre thus distinguishes between value and obligation (or compulsion), the latter constituting an alienated destiny of the former while the former retains an opening onto freedom.

But where does obligation as alienated reversal of value come from? Not from the project itself: "The structures of the end, of the operation and of the project are such as to exclude the possibility of such a reversal" (p. 263).

Alienation comes to freedom from the fact that it arises in a world already permeated by the values of other people, hence in a world of competition among many freedoms. "Obligation comes to the for-itself through the Other. It is not a dimension of the for-itself as such, but a category of the for-the-Other" (p. 269).

One might well say at this point that very little seems to have changed since *Being and Nothingness*. Was it not there also that the for-the-Other, without being implied necessarily in the ontological structures of the for-itself, modified and alienated the for-itself in its most intimate being as the objectifying look turned intersubjectivity into a merciless jungle of conflict? In the *Notebooks* Sartre recalls these analyses of the for-the-Other, thus seeming to assume that he has nothing more to propose:

> I explained in *Being and Nothingness* how a look literally emptied before my eyes a tree of its substance. . . . The will of the Other steals away my universe, my person, and the result of my deeds; in reality, if my deeds, the world which I see, the result which I create in it have some secret meaning which escapes me. . . . it is because I operate completely in the dimension of the other; my initiatives, my deeds, my ascertainments are *objects* for him; I exist and act *as watched.* (p. 270, emphasis in original)

The example now put forward by Sartre is already present in *Being and Nothingness* (p. 234): It is the soldier advancing into enemy territory in a universe mined with dangers "who knows that what he sees will be interpreted, reclassified into a broader picture in some unforeseeable way" (*CM*, p. 271). Thus "obligation," the alienating reversal of value, would simply be the ineluctable internalization of my being-for-the-Other, the objectifying hold on my freedom by the other on my free project.

But there is more. Following up the military parallel, Sartre develops in a direction characteristic of the contribution of the *Notebooks* with respect to his earlier work and which prefigures the *Critique de la raison dialectique*:

> We all know the stories involving a colonel who has forgotten the password which he had given out in the morning and whose way is obstinately barred by a sentry who notwithstanding recognizes him. In these stories the sentry is always congratulated. But the real meaning is to show the master in his facticity and in the reality of his living flesh running up against his own will which has become an essential structure of the universe. This is also the meaning of the sorcerer's apprentice. (p. 273)

Here, if the colonel finds himself alienated, it is not because the sentry returns his look and transcends his transcendency – according to the infernal reciprocal nonreciprocity of *Being and Nothingness* – it is because, on the contrary, the sentry, far from being an active freedom, has become an inert receptacle of order, a functional part of the universe on which the active project of the colonel has been engraved and where it lies deposited. The sentry is *matter*, a medium for the conduct of the operation and has become such. The "will" of the colonel has not been distorted by some human antagonism nor in a reversible altercation of "looks," but in an impersonal petrification of freedoms by virtue of the material field of their inscription. "This is the meaning of the sorcerer's apprentice": His creature or creation has escaped him not as a riposte to his creative freedom but through an equivocal autonomy that no one intended. This "bewitchment" of freedom by the matter that it fashions will become, as we know, a major theme of the *Critique*, the "practico-inert" with the "counterfinalities" that go along with it.

If the sentry is to be congratulated, it will be in the name of moral "values": intransigence, courage, discipline, and so on. Sartre does not spell out this aspect of the question in the *Notebooks for an Ethic*, but it is obvious that these so-called values are none other than "obligations" – that is, alienated or "reversed" values. The sentry's inertia in which the military instruction is engraved and which is returned in nonhuman form endowed with all of the absurd indifference of matter is upheld by the inert "moral" discourse that obliged the sentry to respect this "obligation." This petrification of value is what Sartre called in *Being and Nothingness* "the spirit of seriousness." As to its origin, we now know this: It arises from the alienation attendant upon the fact that freedom becomes "other" when it is engraved into a thing. The exploitation of this material depth of alienation is what characterizes the *Notebooks* in contrast to *Being and Nothingness* and to the relatively formal or abstract design of the dialectic of objectifying "looks."

One can understand the difference of emphasis between the two texts in light of the internal duality of value. As we have seen, value is both ideal and factual, free transcendency and facticity – and this because it is the mobilization of the relationship between the for-itself and the in-itself even though this relationship *can never become the object of a synthesis and always leads back to the antagonism of its two terms*. In *Being and Nothingness* the interpretation of this relationship stresses the active transcendence of the for-itself. Value, the "lacked," the in-itself–for-itself, is the *ideal* of the for-itself whose irrealizable character propels freedom "beyond being." The spirit of seriousness, "bad faith," which petrifies value into being, is the activity of the for-itself turning against itself, freedom's refusal of self (the self-alienation of freedom); and further it is by *the other for-itself*, by *autrui*, that alienation comes to the for-itself (conflictual alienation). In the *Notebooks*, everything comes about as if the emphasis had been placed on the in-itself side of the relation-

ship; as if the "lacked," the in-itself–for-itself, were less the ideal
driving force, the creative breakthrough of freedom but rather a passive residue composed of a monstrous mix of the for-itself and the
in-itself from out of the depths of their material mediations. There is
no question here of suggesting that *Being and Nothingness* sins
through subjective idealism, a tendency corrected in the *Notebooks*
and, more decisively, in the *Critique*. From the outset, without ambiguity, the in-itself *is* and *is there* and it is as borne by it that the for-
itself makes itself not to be it; if the for-itself tears itself away, it is
because it is caught up in the in-itself and it is precisely this monism
of the relationship whose terms are not *positively separate beings*,
but *dialectically distinct types of being*, which justifies our exploring its two faces without separating them.

THE REAL ROADS TO FREEDOM AND THE FORCE OF
THINGS: THE ENGINEER, THE PRIMITIVE, THE
ARTIST

Freedom in the *Notebooks* will be considered less in the ontological
purity of the question posed by its quest than in the concrete and
diversified content of its real itineraries. Sartre deals mainly with
three types of relationship of man to the world as they are mobilized
respectively by the "engineer," the "primitive," and the "artist."

The "self" or technical value, the in-itself–for-itself of the engineer consists in transforming the contingency of the external world
to the point where it becomes only "pure mediation between myself
and myself" (*CM*, p. 554) to overcome its externality by making it
into an "instrumental reservoir" completely subordinated to productive freedom; it is the "project to the nth degree . . . to create an ever
more intensive instrumental field . . . to remove from the universe
the last square inch of uselessness. . . . At the end of the infinite
series of my efforts, the world will have become necessary because
of me and for me and I shall have created myself by means of the
world, hence I shall have given myself a necessary existence" (p.
555). This materialization of the ideal or idealization of matter will
always fall short; however, it will have real effects and they will be
truly alienating.

"I have created a *machine*" (*CM*, p. 556). This invented being is
real. Its reality consists in this: If ideally speaking the machine is, to

the point of infinity, the transparent means to my end, totally invested in the future of my freedom, completely finalized, a pure copy of my project without any autonomy of its own, then truly, it inverts my end and dominates it:

the connecting-rod ... must be set in a certain position *in order to* ... However, concerning this same object, we read that it has taken a certain position *because* it has just taken a different one. Thus its finality in time constantly disappears into causality, the future into the present; future time as sufficient reason gives way to the past as explanation. (p. 557, emphasis in original)

This conversion of finalizing freedom into causal determinism comes from the materiality of matter, from its proper regimen of externality. *Thereupon technical freedom becomes other than itself in its product:* Its future is alienated and made subject to the past and to the present – the machine, which was the "value" of freedom, is now what "obliges freedom" to use it only according to instructions established with a view to a "future" that is nothing more than the sempiternal repetition of the present understood as a profitable return and good working order. Sartre concludes: "By attempting to found things in terms of freedom, one succeeds only in turning freedom into a thing" (p. 562).

And still freedom is *not* a thing and does not comes to an end in it. What is created by the engineer is an unstable mix "which is no longer a thing and which is not existence, a fluttering of being between the mechanical and the spiritual, between the subjective and the objective, between the dialectical and the causal, between action and inertia" (p. 562). By a kind of forward flight into activism the engineer overlooks this muddled mix. But it is also the matrix for another attitude, another relation of the for-itself to the in-itself: the passive and magical attitude.

Sartre describes at length what he calls "the universe of desire" (p. 364 et seq.); this is the "primitive" universe in which the interpenetration of human freedom and matter is not "lived" as the technical and productive phantasm of subordinating matter to human freedom but as fascination with the inherent powers of this interpenetration, that is, as a feeling of the sacred and the magical. Lack, which Sartre here calls "desire," aims at fulfillment not through changing the world but through incantatory passivity; the work required for the satisfaction of desire is considered to be nonessential and the objective and static world to be essential. The material bogging down that happens to the engineer in his personal experience, a kind of blind spot perhaps never consciously perceived by him in his work, this the man of desire makes the object of his quest. He expects the universe to submerge and outdistance him, to give lavishly of itself according to its own rules and without any human intervention, to produce of itself the luxuriant blossomings and births of satisfaction – fruits, fish, flesh; "Nature is for him a perpetual *gift* which comes or does not come. There is or there is not fish in the river, game in the forest. Rain falls or it doesn't. Work and will are mediations but desire is desire for the immediate" (pp. 364–5); the only "activity" to which desire will consent is the empty deepening of its own hollowness to the extent that, making the object present by means of the imagination, the man of desire acquires the *imaginary* right to obtain it. If all of a sudden a fruit or a root takes shape, this will not be a matter of contingency; this appearance, "homogeneous with desire" (p. 365) will constitute a *proof* of the essential and eternal mutual belonging of desire and the world as well as the consecration of the legitimacy and efficacy of empty incantation. This desire in the final analysis is only alienated freedom and desire for justification. "*Desire is an Other*" (p. 366)

Sartre speaks of the so-called primitive populations but not without making it clear that there is no sharp distinction between civilizations without history and technical civilizations. No difference in nature: In both cases, under different regimes, what is involved is freedom alienating itself to things, passively or actively.

One can see in the artist, who can be called a kind of frontiersman, the proof of the joint belonging of the two worlds. "The world of desire" is characterized, as mentioned, by the magical bond of imaginary satisfaction and the real satisfaction of desire. It is in the inflation of the imaginary that the artist is related to the primitive. To be sure, the moment of imagination is equally present in the technical sphere but "in a secondary instance . . . (and) absorbed in the unity of the whole" (pp. 565–6): invention is subordinated to the efficacy with which it is brought into relationship with the world. Art, on the contrary, is the imaginary taking itself as its own end, the choice of "making new being spring up out of Nothingness" (p. 566) rather than, like the technician, using Nothingness as a means of transition toward Being. If the artist is related to the "primitive" by his choice of the imaginary, he differs from him in that art, by detaching itself from its sacred and magical origins, acquires its own techniques and operations: "he is more interested in the creative power of desire than in the means for satisfying it. . . . His problem is: How can one push the power of desire to its limits in such a way that the imaginary being that springs up can have a *real* presence" (p. 566). In other words, the artist, like the primitive, seeks to trap the real by means of the imaginary but not through incantatory passivity; the artist shares with the engineer the consciousness of his operation. However, his operation is of a singular nature: He creates an object that is just as real as the machine, but this reality is not the work of art itself; it is only the *analogon* on the basis of which the work appears.

The freedom of the engineer, like that of the man of desire or the primitive, is alienated. Of the freedom of the artist Sartre says, with more ambiguity, that it is "mystification" (p. 567): mystification coming from the fact that it makes being appear "as if being were produced in the dimension of finality, as if being-in-itself were a being-for" (p. 566). The engineer sought the transparency of the *reality* of the machine as the expression of his free finality and saw the latter truly "turned inside out" by the irreducible inertia of matter. The artist, more devious, disguises matter in an illusory dress of finality, for nothing can "turn inside out" nor confute an illusion since, from the start and intrinsically, it has been created in a radical contestation of being by nothingness and of nothingness by being so that henceforth "turning inside out" and inversion are constitutive of its proper nature rather than a perversion of it. Is the artist then alone in remaining free in the material incarnation of his freedom? We shall see.

At all events, with these two figures, the engineer and the primitive, two extremes between which one can conceive of a vast array of other materializations of freedom, Sartre has progressed with respect to *Being and Nothingness*, in the elucidation of the "quasi-nature" that inclines freedom toward alienated complicity rather than authenticity. Why is man infernally "other" for himself and for "others"? How is it possible for a freedom to oppress another freedom? Sartre's answer: Fundamental alienation – prior to all conflict – comes from the upsurge of freedom in a material world that distorts it while being its only possibility. It is a "preoppressive" situation impossible to get

around but which renders intelligible all actual oppressions: It is
because freedom is already other than itself that it can treat another
freedom inhumanely.

If this very pessimistic analysis of the ethical problem can be accepted as true, then a legion of questions arise: In view of so much
negativity, in what would positive moral engagement consist? How
would one go about creating an ethic of freedom? In what sense is
the struggle against alienation to be understood? How are we to
understand the meaning of freedom that the *Notebooks* retain for
value? What is to become of the supreme moral value of generosity,
which, according to Sartre, lies closest to freedom? It would seem,
indeed, that if original alienation is the alienation caused by the
simple materialization of freedom, then there is no way out; as in *No
Exit*, the last word would be *"continuons"* and now even more desperate because this would be a cosmic *No Exit*, extending out to the
whole of the relation of man to the world since this relation can
never dispense with matter.

   In fact the *Notebooks* are very pessimistic with respect to the
sociohistorical liberation of freedom. For example, Sartre discourses
at length on the Hegelian conception of the master–slave relationship (pp. 397 et seq.) in which he refutes Hegel's optimism concerning the dialectically liberating factors internal to slavery. Hegel overlooks, writes Sartre, the significance of the *constituted* texture of
the world of slavery. The slave possesses an "intrasubjective freedom" (p. 400). Indeed! Nothing is less disturbing to the master than
this stoical inner consciousness of someone who, regardless of what
he thinks, continues to obey. Stoicism cannot lead to revolt; on the
contrary, it is an instrument for perpetuating an oppressive system.
Shall we then say with Hegel that work and activity, the effective
transformations of the world accomplished by the slave, are liberating factors? For Hegel they are liberating for two reasons. The first is
their reality: It is the slave who holds the concrete mastery over
things, while the master, who does nothing, is in fact confined to a
narcissistic impotence. The second is that these factors reactivate in
the slave, with the passing of time, the anguish before which he

recoiled at the moment of struggle. Work is the repression of immediate desire, the negation of the body. The slave, by forcing himself to this, comes to realize progressively what he had been incapable of doing during the struggle: to prefer his annihilation to his life. For Sartre this is mere abstraction that does not take into account slavery as the weight of an enduring institution. How could a slave of the second generation, when oppression had become "natural," reexperience the anguish of the original struggle? At this point work would not favor a reconquest of freedom as negation; it would only be acquiescence to the plunge into submission. As to the "reality" of the product of work, it is for the slave absolutely unreal. The enjoyment of the manufactured object is so radically forbidden to him that he does not even understand its meaning. "This tunic he is weaving will take on its meaning and value only when worn by the master. . . . The object to which he is giving form escapes him; he forms it for the Other and in the dimension of the Other" (p. 403). And so one can come to conceive, writes Sartre, of a third motive for revolt: The slave is mistreated, he is hungry, poor; "these are the true elements of his liberation" (p. 404). And for two reasons. First, the slave's hunger is "absolute subjectivity"; it escapes the power of the master who cannot have wished it so since it contradicts the harmony of slavery. Hence it belongs to properly to the slave. Further, it is the revelation of a world where master and slave are in a "position of equality": the world of food:

[If] perfumes, rituals, art objects "are incomprehensible to the slave," the master's food is forbidden without mystery. . . . Hunger is illimitable transcendence toward food that it reveals as forbidden; and it is the refusal of hunger and consequently the refusal of the interdict. It implies a project of freedom from hunger, hence from slavery. (p. 404)

The liberating force of hunger will later be developed in the *Critique* as "need": need as free action and imprescriptible right to satisfaction, a radical force in the transformation of the world. But here Sartre immediately steps back from the potentially revolutionary significance that he has now granted to hunger:

However, the conditions of a slave revolt are not present. What remains is the possibility of theft, which is always easy. The slave "makes out." But theft and "making out," far from overturning the rule of the master, confirm it. Hidden theft is recognition of the property of the master. The stolen object retains in itself, like the host, the presence of the Other. (p. 405).

Sartre concludes darkly: "Everything turns against the slave" (p. 405). And this is because of the original alienation described throughout all of the *Notebooks*

which is not a result of violence – this is very secondary – but rather the result of the fact that man is from the beginning present to himself as Other. The upsurge of man in the world is a sin against freedom by alienation. And so long as man does not get out of this phase of alienation, all of his attempts to assert his freedom will be caught from behind, alienated, and will end up in oppression. But this is a vicious circle that does not invite one to optimism since alienation perpetuates oppression and oppression perpetuates alienation (p. 398).

GENEROSITY

If, on the historical level, Sartre's ethical attitude can be characterized as relatively pessimistic, on the contrary, in the individual and interindividual area, in the area on which *Being and Nothingness* touched in terms of the darkest pessimism, the value of "generosity" becomes the conceptual instrument of a new and fresh optimism. Generosity in its individual dimension allows the acceptance of the in-itself and even its active disclosure, and an assumption of the deperdition of freedom in its incarnation.

In relation to the Other, generosity consists in grasping his "being-in-the-midst-of-the-world," that is, his share of finitude and facticity, his "fragility" or his essential "exposedness" with respect to the in-itself, which falls, unbeknownst to him, as his lot to the extent that the active transcendence of his "being-in-the-world" is his perpetual surpassing of it as well as offering to him this dimension of himself of which he was unaware. Here, the in-itself, revealed by generosity, becomes positive mediation (qua opacity overcome) between myself and the Other and, as such, is even the possibility of authentic love. "We can understand what it means to love in an authentic sense: I love if I *create* the contingent finitude of the Other as being-in-the-midst of the world by assuming my own subjective finitude. . . . This vulnerability, this finitude, *is the body*" (pp. 516–17). Here Sartre is referring to the least significant aspect of the body, the body as flesh. What is given to me first of the Other, according to my most discerning comprehension, are his ends, his freedom, his existence. But if I love the Other,

I catch glimpses constantly of the *being* of this existent beneath his existence itself, like a sunken city beneath the water. I see dimly the perpetual relationship between the soles of the feet and earth, of body to weight; I see dimly *through* the physiognomy that masks the *features of the face.* This dancer is first of all *dance.* But the trembling of her breasts is not dance; it is inertia. This runner *is sweating.* Beneath the project I see dimly the order of life and beneath the order of life I catch a glimpse of the order of Being. (p. 518, emphasis in original)

To be sure, in some cases to perceive the being-in-the-midst-of-the-world of the Other can be useful with respect to the safety of the person: I see a man from the back, that is, from a dimension of his body that he cannot know and through which he is exposed to the in-itself in a certain way: A stone is falling from a slope behind him; it will hit him; I can prevent this, there is still time. But this useful information is only a specification of what is at stake in the relation: There is love because I save someone not just ontically, from some particular danger, but ontologically, in and by my freedom. If left to the Other, this would be opacity and loss of his being-in-the-midst-of-the-world. There is love because I save him for himself or, more simply, *in order that this in-itself may become a being-for.* The fragility and the facticity of the Other, reclaimed by my freedom, is henceforth there *in order that* I may protect it and find wonder in it.

With respect to *Being and Nothingness*, where the destructive limpidity of the for-the-Other was carefully worked out, the reversal seems to be complete. There my only attitude before the freedom of the Other, was to objectify him, to transcend his transcendence, to rob it of its possibilities, to imprison it in an in-itself haunted by threats kept secret from him. "Through the Other's look I *live* myself as fixed in the midst of the world, as in danger, as irremediable" (*BN*, p. 244). The Other plunges me into the anguishing dimension of the "nonrevealed" with which he affects my freedom by his objectifying manipulations. In the "Concrete Relations with the Other" every attempt to escape from this infernal pattern – notably in the case of love – only made matters worse. In the *Notebooks*, on the contrary, objectivity, the nonrevealed, which happen to the Other in spite of himself and in spite of me by virtue of his rootedness in being, I reveal and permeate with freedom; I bring them to transparency and reciprocity.

The fact remains that we can question intrinsically the meaning of "generosity": It reveals "being-in-the-midst-of-the-world"; it "creates" contingent facticity. This is to say that it reveals and creates what did not wait for it to be: It transforms being which is what it is into being-for and affixes to the indifference of the in-itself a kind of finality in the second degree. We should recall here the operation of the artist, "mystification": giving form to being in such a way as to make it point to an absent finality. In the *Notebooks* Sartre creates an explicit bond between generosity and the work of art: "The true relationship to the Other [is] never direct: [it must pass through] the intermediary of the work" (p. 487). "We rediscover here [in the generous relationship to the finitude of the Other] the characteristics of the work of art since in the latter *also* there is need for a 'matter to be formed' which will lend its being" (p. 514). In other words, authentic love for the Other, with its own proper matter, the vulnerability of the body, taken over by and for freedom, but without suppressing the reality of its contingency, is related to an aesthetic creation of the interhuman relationship; like aesthetic creation properly speaking, it confers upon materiality or the in-itself an *imaginary* finality: It realizes an irreal – everything comes to pass *as if* henceforward the fragility of the Other existed *in order that* I should protect it whereas it *is* its insertion in the pure indifference of the in-itself; it irrealizes the brutality of the real since this indifference is the support or the incarnation of the imaginary finality that it uncovers.

Generosity, love, in the positivity which the *Notebooks* grant them, would thus become an "aesthetic" attitude; if they escape alienation, it would be perhaps at the price of the "mystification" inherent in the artistic position. And it will be on the basis of the aestheticism of this ethic that Sartre will find his justification for abandoning it; it was, he will say, "a writer's ethic for writers" (*Sit* IX, p. 33).

SAINT GENET, ACTOR AND MARTYR

Any imaginary position has, qua imaginary, its own reality. However, even if ultimately Sartre came to think that there is not in the concept of "generosity" the substance for creating an "ethic," he did not abandon the notion itself. He returned repeatedly, without changing it, to the positive idea of love as total acceptance of the person even in the most opaque dimensions of his body: sweat, bouncing breasts, drooling snot described in the *Notebooks* correspond to the description by Genet of the blue chemistry of the entrails of Decarnin upon which Sartre comments as follows: "With what admirable rigor" Genet loves Jean even in his viscera or even in a body louse that comes from him for "one loves nothing if one does not love everything. True love is salvation and protection of the whole of man in the person of one man by a human creature" (*SG*, p. 532). In an interview with Francis Jeanson in 1965 Sartre expressed again the full force of this concept of love, which he contrasts with the concept of intersubjectivity developed in *Being and Nothingness* while at the same time in no way denying the reality of either side as if, finally, it were a question of two possible roads to freedom, one negative, the other positive:

In the Hell described in *Being and Nothingness* love was only the desire to be loved. . . . But I have never had the occasion to describe positive love . . . except in the *Saint Genet* where, on the contrary, I explained that it was not at all a fact of death, but a fact of life and that love was the acceptance of the total person – including his viscera.[2]

But in all of this there is nothing with which to create an Ethic. To claim the opposite would be tantamount to falling into the trap of the alienating *faribole*, which every ethic becomes if it is not "concrete totality" that has surpassed and synthesized Good and Evil (cf. *SG*, p. 186). For ethics, as Sartre says of freedom in the *Critique of Dialectical Reason*, will be "total or totally alienated" (CRD, p. 420) and the cleavage between Good and Evil is alienation itself, the cutting in two of freedom through separation from self. Evil, in fact, is what men of substance, that is, those who have the oppressive-repressive means to enforce their "order," cast out from their freedom: Its negative portion. Freedom, cut in two, subjected to the separation of its positive and negative sides, is thus made a stranger to itself. "Le mal, *c'est l'Autre,*" is as much for the Just who cut themselves off from their own freedom as for the Wicked upon whom a being is imposed from without.

This situation is our situation: That of a Manichaean struggle at the heart of which "ethics" can never be anything more than a combat weapon in the hands of the strong or an ideology of justification: "Any ethic which does not explicitly consider itself to be impossible *today* contributes to the alienation and the mystification of man" (*SG*, p. 186). In this struggle there is not, without bad faith, any other possible choice than struggle itself according to practical priorities and with full knowledge that a true ethic is only a horizon as yet inaccessible. It is only from within this struggle that in the long run the ethical "synthesis" will emerge. Sartre goes on to refine his argument: There is no "beyondness of Good and Evil," no ideal point from which to avoid confrontation. Whether it is a question of telling edifying stories of military heroism between opposing forces – two enemies grappling with each other in mutual respect, the common stuff of valor – or of the indifference of the prostitute listening to the tall tales that the Communists as well as the Nazis were full of – men, all the same, always running after the moon – whether it is a question of reconciliation from above or confusion from below, the result is identical: "an instant betrayal" (*SG*, p. 215) – once again a manner of taking sides in the struggle.

Sartre concludes: "We are not angels and we do not have the right to understand our enemies, we do not yet have the right to love all men" (*SG*, p. 215). But love, in its true and effective positivity, however, involves a certain "whole" – as we have seen, "salvation and protection of the whole man in the person of *one* man by a human creature." What is the relationship of these two "totalities" to one of which love is forbidden whereas it constitutes the true nature of the other?

The whole of man, which in reality is grasped through love, is a "whole" that one could call ontological; what can be grasped of the whole of man through *one* man loved totally is finally the human condition or the meaning of the being of a being that is "in a state of fragility" in the in-itself, and that, as for-itself, is the surpassing of this fragility. In other words, what is revealed through love is in the *indicative mode* of ontology. The *imperative mode* of ethics aim at a different totality; extensive rather than comprehensive, "all men" rather than "the whole of man." These two totalities do not overlap. If the intensive or comprehensive totality is ontological, the extensive totality can obviously be decoded from within a social and historical problematic: It is *today* that ethics are mystification and alienation in the insurmountable framework of Manichaeism. We do not *as yet* have the right to love all men. Here a circumstantial factor is introduced or added to the ontological: The particular figure that the relationship of man to the world takes on in *our* world, a figure that implies a disintegration and a quantification of the human. If the expression "all men" – as an impossible totality – is spoken in the *quantitative* mode, this is because it is quantity that makes humanity impossible today.

THE CRITIQUE OF DIALECTICAL REASON

The quantitative factor of alienation will not be theorized by Sartre until sometime later in the *Critique of Dialectical Reason.* It will become *scarcity:* There is not enough for everybody.

Originally and ontologically the Other is the Same. There is a comprehensive reciprocity of freedoms; but when scarcity comes to define human relationships, this reciprocity, without disappearing, is changed into antagonistic reciprocity. The Same becomes the absolute Other, the counter-man in that the existence of each one is potentially a mortal danger for all others. To this struggle unto death which *Being and Nothingness* presented as the fate of all human consciousness, the Manichaeism which in *Saint Genet* made all ethics both impossible and necessary, Sartre now assigns a material origin: "Scarcity is lived in practical terms through Manichaean action. . . . It is at this level that we must define *violence* as a structure of human action under the reign of Manichaeism and in the framework of scarcity" (*CRD*, p. 244).

Scarcity, however, is not the only alienation conceived in the *Critique:* Even in a hypothetical reign of abundance, it would be necessary, writes Sartre, to extract from the universe by means of work the products necessary for the organism and, by the mere fact of the confrontation of praxes with matter, "the unity of human multiplicities overturned by material counterfinalities would necessarily continue to exist" (*CRD*, I, p. 235). Counterfinality or the overturning of praxes through the materialization in which they interpenetrate each other and become unified passively is thus a form of alienation independent of scarcity. Alienation through scarcity is conflictual and antagonistic; alienation through counterfinality is bewitched and disfiguring.

We must at this point recapitulate if we are to grasp the central message of the *Critique*. As to the intelligibility of alienation, the development was schematically as follows: In *Being and Nothingness* the two faces of alienation – the spirit of seriousness or reification of the quest of the in-itself–for-itself and the theory of the for-others, or the mortification of individual consciousness via the Other – appeared to be a kind of fate of enigmatic origin.

In the *Notebooks* Sartre discovered, as he entered into the elucidation of alienation, the secondary and derived character of the conflict of consciousnesses with respect to fundamental alienation: the conversion of freedom by virtue of its material inscription in being. The in-itself–for-itself thus becomes the real mix of these two types of being, the for-itself and the in-itself, an unstable mix in which the two terms become distorted.

The *Saint Genet* again places emphasis on the dimension of conflict, of Manichaeism, on the alienating force of the "Look" of the Other – Genet made into a "thief" by watching eyes that catch him red-handed.

The *Critique* picks up and modifies the previous results. There are two faces to alienation. The one explored in the *Notebooks*, the bewitched inversion of praxis by matter, Sartre now calls the "practico-inert," which creates among men relationships of "seriality." The other, the alienation emphasized in the *Saint Genet*, the Manichaean conflict, now finds its explanation not in the ontological structure of matter, but in the circumstantial state of distribution: scarcity.

The last word in the *Saint Genet* with reference to ethics was a word of heart-wrenching lucidity: Though ethics are impossible in the present state of reality, they are necessary as a horizon or a regulatory idea. If one can denounce the *"fariboles"* of Manichaeism, it is only in the light of an ultimate and at least possible reconciliation of all men. The *Critique* abandons this distraught lucidity; the double and inseparable modality, the impossible-and-necessary, are now split in two: Either the liberation is effective but then it is not moral, or there is morality but then it is alienating. As if the hope of creating theoretically an ethic of freedom, a hope announced in *Being and Nothingness*, preserved in the *Notebooks* through the value of "generosity" and maintained in the *Saint Genet* as a regulatory horizon, had now lost all relevancy.

With reference to alienation as it is understood in the *Critique* in its double sense of scarcity and seriality or the entanglement of freedom in the practico-inert, how is the liberation of freedom conceived? The group-in-fusion or the Apocalypse, the proper revolutionary moment of freedom is involved here. The dialectic mobilized by Sartre in order to account for the formation of the group-in-fusion is complex and cannot be reproduced here. There is mortal danger: It is consequently against a background of scarcity and against scarcity itself that fusion takes place. There is also production of the totalizing dimension of the freedom of each person that dissolves all serial or practico-inert separations among people. At this point a new form of human "totality" springs up, intensive rather than extensive and modifying the sense of "quantity" to the point where it is no longer alienating. The fusional liquidation of "seriality" in the face of mortal danger or of scarcity is a signal for the transformation of the status of number and multiplicity. Each one feels himself called to the group because he is the *same* as the other and it is this "sameness" in the heart of action that changes the group into a *ubiquitous power*, a *demultiplied force*, a flight of a hundred pairs of legs, a vigilance where a hundred pairs of eyes watch out for danger, an attack where a hundred fists are raised. Here quantity, far from expressing separation and the aggregate, serial alienation, melts into a communal flux where the whole always precedes the part in a synthetic force transparent to action.

What can one say about this insurrectional figure of the group-in-fusion with respect to the "extensive" regulatory idea in the *Saint Genet* of "all men" lovable perhaps on the day of the overcoming of Manichaeism? The Apocalypse as the maximal reciprocity of freedoms is violent and short – short both in its extent and in its duration. "All men" are not involved under the sign of a global reconciliation but, since the relation of the "whole" of the group to its parts is intensive and not extensive, the Apocalypse is total even in its partiality. The whole of human freedom is expressed in it and recognizes itself there even if only a handful of insurgents is involved, even if the fusion is itself precarious and liable to fall back into inertia. It is a question of a different figure of totality: no longer global and consequently inaccessible, but partial and effective. So what now is the meaning of fusional revolutionary intensity (*the whole* of human liberty in *one* insurrection) with respect to the fusional intensity of love as outlined in the *Saint Genet* (*the whole* of humanity in *one* person)? As between the two intensities it is doubtless impossible to decide. It is as if we had here two sides of Sartre's thought or two major aspects of the investment of freedom, whose the synthesis is not certain: on the one hand the taking up of militancy, of fraternal and activist engagement; on the other a much more individualistic sequestration in the profound incarnation of the relationship of freedom and the in-itself (of which generous love would be the "successful" modality).

At all events the appearance of this new relationship within a human multiplicity is, contrary to the hypothetical perspective adumbrated in the *Saint Genet* ("all men lovable on the day of the advent of authentic morality"), no longer the correlative of a moral horizon. On this Sartre is clear: In fusion there is neither utilitarian selfishness *nor moralism* nor "altruism." There is no utilitarianism: It is not because of some calculation of personal interest (effectiveness in resisting danger) that each person comes to the group; the calculation of human relations and their external manipulation are much more an integral part of serial juxtaposition than an explanation of radical reshuffling. Nor moralism either, the idealistic aspiration to be united in transparency with the Other, since the radical nature of fusion is such – in its *"mêmeté"* – that when I enter the group, the Other has already disappeared; I can consequently no longer relate to the Other as Other, not even under the moral modality of "altruism" that postulates the alterity of the Other in order to overcome it.

The movement that produces fusion is simply an upsurge of freedom that *cannot be seen as a contradiction* (it totalizes itself as being in danger in the "series") *without thereby already being occupied with resolving it,* that is, with liquidating the series by this totalization itself.

The group-in-fusion has its source in what Sartre calls the "constituted" dialectic. The "constituting" wellspring of this upsurge of freedom, which in the Apocalypse and only there is valid for a human multiplicity, is to be found in individual praxis in its most elementary form: need.

Need arises in the organism only when the latter is already engaged in resolving the tension that it is experiencing and is living its present disorder only through a projection of the possibility of its being satisfied. This upward surge, which is already the process of resolving the contradiction that motivates it, is comparable to the group's coming into fusion. But the movement of need is also comparable to that of "lack" in *Being and Nothingness*, which, as we recall, was already lack *refused* from the point of view of a totality that would fulfill it and that, since it is always "lacked," calls up value as an authentic moral appeal at least hypothetically possible. We can now ask if the dialectic of lack and value and that of need can come together?

To be sure, they have in common the fact that here negation must be negation of negation, internal negativity, and that being, which is thus its own nothingness, must be a project or a projection of self onto that which it is not. Furthermore, in concrete terms, lack and need are the same thing; in both cases Sartre has in mind such simple behaviors as hunger and thirst. But there is a difference. Lack cannot be fulfilled by what was "lacking" without this fulfillment's implying a further "lacked" that will preclude this fulfillment or launch it again on its impossible quest for being. Need, however, can and, better, *must* be satisfied: It is the imprescriptible right to satisfaction. And this "right" is not of the nature of a moral right – that is, an infinite requirement whose fulfillment becomes increasingly elusive in proportion to the sublimity of the spheres of high ideality that it implies. It is, rather, a vital effective urgency of the sort that in certain cases motivates "fusion": The possibility of death is not given with life. "Lack" and "need" both express the relationship of the for-itself or of praxis to the in-itself, but each in different ways.

"Lack" is pierced through with the throbbing pain of a destiny of incompletion; this is its obsession with value, its quest for the in-itself–for-itself, which certainly presents a face of alienation but which perhaps also has a face of authenticity that could well be that of the free ethic of liberty whose possibility opens up at the end of *Being and Nothingness*, whereas "need" is plenitude and dialectical affirmation that renders vain any ethical beyondness. Lack is an occasion for an ontological drama permeated by a poetics of transcendency and failure: Man is more than man; he is basically a metaphysical being, outstripping his empirical insertion and yet, as always, driven back into it even though, simultaneously, in the remarkable impossibility of finding satisfaction there; in short, man is a "useless passion."

"Need," on the other hand, is the irrepressible dialectical efficacy of man's relationship to the world. Can we say in order to explain

this difference that it is motivated by the "realism" achieved by
Sartre in the *Critique?* Yes, but on condition of not taking this
realism in any positivistic sense. As a matter of fact we must not
say that need is a lack that can be fulfilled merely by providing
what is objectively "lacking" and that the nostalgic insistence of
the "lacked" (*"manqué"*) will have been reduced to nothing by the
indubitable positivity of the object of satisfaction. We should say,
rather, the contrary: That it is in *Being and Nothingness* that the
relationship of lack to its object is understood in a trivially positivistic or prosaic sense such that consequently it becomes necessary for
the full extent of the philosophical investment granted to freedom
to be located somewhere else . . . in the indefinite elsewhere of
value. And that in a very Kantian hiatus, after all, between the
onticoempirical achievements of freedom on the one hand (the satisfaction of lack) and on the other the limitless stake that measures
them and gives them meaning, we should say that lack is only a
pretext for an ontologico-metaphysical or transcendental question
which is *that of the possibility of the relationship of the for-itself to
the in-itself:* an impossible possibility. This relative inconsistency
of the relationship of lack to its object, whence Sartre infers its
intrinsic and ontological lack of being, could well be merely, genea-
logically speaking, the result of an unconscious class-position: Is it
not the bourgeois who thinks that eating, drinking, sleeping, breathing, are "natural" functions whose nonconflictual nature prevents
them from bearing the full existential weight of the question of
freedom?

It is this self-evident quality, this serene lack of awareness, that
makes it permissible to philosophize about a glass of beer but only
insofar as the latter has no other philosophical meaning than not to
constitute a question *in itself* or to be eminently overwhelmed by
any question that it might raise. It is this quality that will disappear
in the *Critique:* Here need becomes question, tension, problem. *It is
what is at stake in freedom,* the crucial locus of articulation of its
relationship to the world. "Everything is revealed in need," writes
Sartre from the first pages. In other words the whole is no longer to
be sought *elsewhere;* it is no longer draped in the chicanery of
sleight of hand; it is no longer quest and obsession. All of dialectical
tension is contained in need. Henceforth Sartre will take into full
account the cultural and conflicting dimension with which the

slightest of our physiological behaviors is permeated, shot through as they are with the complexity of the world not only in its material curvatures but also in its sociohistorical relationships of force. Everything is revealed there, need reveals everything precisely because it is not purely biological, because there is no virgin state of reproduction, because the organism is henceforth always an option or a decision regarding the threshold of its satisfaction or, on the contrary, the level of intolerability at which revolt can be justified.

If need is thus from the start a *totalizing* response to a total configuration of the material and social world into which it is inserted, what then happens in the *Critique* to value or the in-itself–for-itself, whose mission in *Being and Nothingness* was to bear the burden of totality? How are we now to understand the earlier ontologicopoetic "drama"?

In this connection Sartre specifies explicitly the relationship of the two works: If man is "as Heidegger says 'a being from afar'," "if he *projects himself* into the milieu of the in-itself–for-itself," this does not come "from some prenatal choice, as *Being and Nothingness* might lead one to believe erroneously," but "from the univocal internal relationship which joins man as practical organism to his environment" (*CRD*, pp. 337–8). This relationship is such that there is an obligation for the organism to pass through the inert or the in-itself in order to reproduce itself; praxis cannot learn itself by itself except in this "dimension of alterity"; this is the "fundamental relationship" of the project to the world, the relationship that comes from the structure of being of the relationship of the in-itself and the for-itself, the relationship that could continue to induce alienation even in a hypothetical reign of abundance: not the dream of being God (as was value in *Being and Nothingness*), but the obligatory interpenetration of free transparency and of the inertia of the in-itself. It is from this interpenetration that the alienating configurations of the practico-inert arise. This fundamental relationship of the project to its alienation can become a fundamental project of alienation – precisely in the case where the taut relation of the practical and of the inert is no longer lived as tension and attempts to become absorbed into the ideality of matter.

There is no longer any escape here as far as value is concerned. It becomes deception, a copy of inert constraints that it disguises by conferring on them the translucidity of *praxis*. In value freedom has supposedly only to do with freedom; but there is no better means than this supposed ideality for reproducing submission to an established state of things. This is the practico-inert itself, an index of double alienation, alienation through idealization. Just as highly qualified work is intended to become "human value" in "anarcho-unionism" (CRD, p. 355), idealization gives assurances that the worker will not become aware of the exploitation to which he is subjected: He achieves his "freedom" in his work. Here Sartre makes a distinction between "imperative" and "value." The worker might work not because he places value on highly qualified work but in the awareness that there is no other solution for him in the world as it exists, if he wants to survive, except to submit to the imperative of work since this is his prefabricated destiny, given his place in the heart of the practico-inert.

An analogous distinction between "obligation" and "value" was already present in the *Notebook for an Ethic.* In a sense it is an identical distinction in the two works. In both cases value derives from the internality of freedom whereas obligation and the imperative are forces of external constraint weighing on freedom by virtue of worked matter. But the meaning of the distinction changes radically from one work to the other. In the *Notebooks* the internality of value was proof of its intrinsic freedom, whereas obligation, the sedimentation of value in the inertia of things, was the source of all alienation. The intent of the distinction was to preserve value. In the *Critique* it is the opposite: If value is lived internally whereas the imperative is lived externally, this is because value is a more profound and deceptive internalization of the practico-inert, in fact so thoroughly internalized that it is no longer felt as constraint. The imperative, on the other hand, because of its relative externality, is conflictual; to obey it is subjectively problematical since not to obey it is an ever present possibility. Hence, the imperative is closer to liberty than is value; at least there is greater chance of its exacerbating its machinations than in the case of serene legitimation of value.

In one of the unpublished texts subsequent to the *Critique* Sartre states clearly:

By and large we can put on one side: 1) imperative – radicalism – revolt – refusal of destiny and of seriality – group-in-fusion; on the other 2) values – evolution – acceptance of Destiny as made and endured at the same time – dominant classes. . . . The ethic of values poses freedom as *power* and, in fact, alienates it whereas the ethics of the imperative subjects freedom to interdiction but in reality calls it forth.[3]

The same thought was expressed succinctly in the *Critique* as follows: "Value is not the alienation of the ends nor of the achieved objective; it is the alienation of *praxis* itself" (p. 356, n. 1).

This criticism of value, writes Sartre, is not to be taken in a strictly Marxist sense and as claiming that what is involved is a pure and simple superstructure generated by an economic infrastructure. Such a conception underestimates the power of value and forgets that the idealistic transposition of the practico-inert that it brings about is an alchemy possessing its own effects: Value is not a mechanical copy but a false transparency in which is invested and perverted the whole force of freedom with the result that although a ferocious conditioning is involved, this conditioning is nonetheless experienced from within as absolute and unconditional freedom. If one misunderstands the intrinsic reality of free ideality that value mobilizes and that carries with it the adherence of the one who adopts it, one falls a prey to it; proof of this is "the profound moralism of Russian society," which presents as values "certain notions common to all (particularly that of *life*...)" (p. 356, n. 1).

To free oneself from the practico-inert is doubtless a dream; thus it happens that the group in fusion, as the only moment of intense and intensive liberation, is destined to fall back into the practico-inert when the urgency of the struggle has passed, when it organizes and by becoming the matter of its own operation, loses its ubiquitous transparency. But the dream remains: a dream of "immaterial matter." "Those who would overcome this regime of alienation" must "diminish the hold of materiality by replacing opacity with tenuity, heaviness with lightness, in other words, they must create an immaterial materiality" (p. 293).

However this may be and without going that far concretely, the possibility remains to be rid of value as a facsimile of the practico-inert or, at least, to be on guard against it. This does not mean that we should deny the structural necessity of which the relationship of the for-itself to the in-itself is the bearer nor the relationship of need to the inert, but rather that we should be on guard with respect to this necessity by refusing to solidify it by valorizing as necessary any particular concrete content, and thus we should preserve the possibility of a flexible reinterpretation of this relationship.

THE *ROME LECTURES,* THE *CORNELL NOTES:*
ETHICAL RADICALISM

In his unpublished manuscripts of 1964–5 Sartre delves more deeply into the perspectives that he had outlined only briefly in the *Critique* in the two notes dealing with value and ethics. How does value give rise to alienation if an explanation via economics does not suffice? Sartre bases his argument on the concept of desire. Desire is *need lived in impotence by the "son of man":* Satisfaction comes to him through the Other and it is dependency that determines in him an "alienation and a fundamental culpability"; this alienation – presence of the Other in the free practical organism – reproduces itself at the same time as the organism and by the very force of the latter, by the affirming force of need, reversed by the fact of its impotence. Here satisfaction brings back nonsatisfaction, increases impotence and failure, confirms the gap that separates freedom from itself: It is precisely the sort of fresh impetus in and through the impossibility of attaining one's goal that characterized in *Being and Nothingness* the ontological dramaturgy of value but reduced here to its protohistorical foundations, the primary relationship of the child to the world and to the Other.

The ideality of value as moral value springs from the same impotence. It is not only in his organic life that the son of man is subjected to the Other: It is in his entire *cultural* life. Just as in his early childhood he received the food for his subsistence in his helplessness to procure it for himself, he now receives – and this is the very essence of educational training – everything over which he has no *real* power in the form of *ideal* values. To the son of man, who cannot own property, for example, property will be transmitted as a value. What will later become of his moral life will be his manner of integrating into reality, as the man he will have become, the idealities that, as a son, he received in impotence: In conflict and contestation, in casuistical bad faith or in the pursuit of idealizing self-training.

Over and against Marxist explanations what is gained is the intelligibility of the individual nature of ethics, its effective rooting in the heart of freedom, where freedom itself will be vampirized. Understood in this sense, ethics becomes a poisonous emanation of impotence, or of what Sartre called elsewhere the rottenness of the parental bond.[4]

Must we then, if we despair of value, also despair of ethics? And if all criteria are lost, does only a jungle of competing interests remain: the greater or lesser success in the tactical and opportunistic adaptation of means to the concrete end pursued? In a sense, yes: in the same sense in which above all it is essential not to hide from oneself real antagonisms beneath idealistic bombast. But in another sense, no: because fierce opportunism, the fetishism of interest are precisely the first to require in order to function behind their blinkers, the protection of value systems. Sartre, in his unpublished manuscripts of 1964–5, calls for an "ethical radicalism" that might serve as the "moral" sense of the *Critique*. In what must this consist if it is to escape all the denunciations with which Sartre charged value? This ethical radicalism, tangent to amorality by virtue of the ontological fact of freedom, is anything but a normative ethic of radicalism or a system that would prescribe appropriate behaviors under all circumstances for the safeguarding of the purity of freedom. It is nothing else but the refusal of all preestablished, normatively privileged, and inertly valorized patterns for the exercise of freedom. It is not that freedom will have been magically released from the constraints of the practico-inert, but it will become defined within a given configuration of constraint *by the intensity of its power of invention to alter the parameters of facticity.*

Sartre uses in both texts the example of followers of the Resistance subjected to torture.

Given the end: not to speak (posed under certain circumstances and never in and of itself: If the end is unavoidable, it must be within a choice of a concrete complex of an entire universe – my comrades, history, and the past which have brought me into this cause, the image of myself that I wish to preserve and so on). Given also the situation of crisis (with the exacerbating constraint represented by torture): For some to alter the habitual order of facticity will amount to diminishing the importance of suffering, to turning it into "an inevitable fact of no significance"; for others who feel themselves incapable of this, it will be a choice of death; others again will seize a contingent opportunity for bringing about their end. One such person tells how, subject to the torture of the bathtub, it was torture itself that saved him. He was able to take advantage of a moment of suffocation that seized him at the very instant when he had decided to speak and so recovered possession of himself. Another told how he spent the night before his arrest with his mistress and, weakened by his amorous exertions, would certainly have given in if he had been questioned at once but, questioned some three weeks later, he had had time to take himself in hand.

What is significant about the radicality of freedom is not its worthy alignment with respect to the end that it has chosen, preferably at the cost of its life, which would carry it beyond all suspicion, but rather its capacity to leave no stone unturned for its own sake in the reordering of the practical field despite every hierarchy. If it happens that value systems can also come into the picture, it is also as tactical procedures enabling the reordering of the field on an equal footing with any other tactical procedure.

Thus "ethical radicalism" is not the unconditional conditioning of freedom by value or by some inert and stationary end, but it is the unconditional deconditioning of those conditions that are obstacles to the reproduction of the end – that is, of the relation to the world in which freedom has been freely engaged. A minimal ethic, synonymous with the fact of freedom to the extent that this fact, since it is the fact of a being lacking being, hence projected beyond itself, is simultaneously the position de jure and de facto of this being, a being that is no longer haunted by the question of its impossible superior legitimacy. Right without any ideal wrong side of obligation or of duty, a right for freedom to be the irrepressible upsurge that it is if it has chosen not to allow itself to be repressed. Here Sartre waivers on the one hand between the "amoral" formulation of this right of fact: "There is no ethic of need: Its absolute urgency is enough. . . . To breathe for a buried miner is a practical necessity, never a duty" and on the other hand a "moral" function by the fact of this right: "On this postulate (of need) we shall build a humanism" (CRD, p. 351). This formulation recurs in L'Idiot de la famille: "Out of need a humanism is being born" (IF, p. 433).

The fact is that one and the same thing is involved rather than two divergent interpretations of the same phenomenon. The humanism in question cannot be compared to that of the Autodidact in Nausea nor to that of the expert workman taking pride in his work nor to any humanism founded on values: It is, simply, in relation to need – in which "all is revealed" – the index of a lucidity about this revelation itself in the refusal, henceforth, of all value ideologies that, in their different ways, bring about an intensification of alienation to the practico-inert.

The fact remains that the practico-inert does not dissolve, except momentarily, in the "ethical radicalism" of its modifications. We have learned this from the group-in-fusion delivered over to the unwieldiness of "organization." We have learned this also from *The Wall* concerning the "successful" ruses of those who resist interrogation and whose bewitched successes turn into the cruelest defeats. We have learned this even from the Resistance movement as a collective organization. Even if it had not existed in all its radicalism, the Allies would still have won the war and it is far from certain that its existence had any weight at all in their victory (cf. *Sit.* III, p. 30).

Shall we conclude from these pitiless reconditionings of unconditional modifications, from the precariousness of the upsurgings of "ethical radicalism," that their radicality is only an appearance, a false absolute, a dead body carried away in the raging din of History? Sartre maintains, on the contrary, that radicality exists only as detotalized, absolute as singular, lucidity as opacity. At the end of the second volume of the *Critique,* there is no longer any question of saying that "we are not *yet* angels." Rather that we shall never be angels or Martians or any other kind of creature specializing in the overview. And this for all the best dialectical reasons in the world, for the correct rational functioning of negativity, namely because there is no total rationality in the world that is not a part of the world, hence that does not fall short of its own totality. But also without reason or, more positively, for the enjoyment of that unreason that God would unfailingly lack if He were possible in spite of every dialectical law: "To experience oneself, to take risks, to discover oneself by discovering things, to change while changing the world: This is to live. What better is there? I would refuse to be a God if it were offered to me. Down to the simple fact of being permanently in danger, there is nothing that cannot be a source of enjoyment."[5]

And so, moral or not, if only because of this enjoyment, man is not such a useless passion after all.

NOTES

For the works of Sartre the following abbreviations will be used: *BN* for *Being and Nothingness*, tr. Hazel E. Barnes, 7th paperbound ed. (New York: The Citadel Press, 1971); *CM* for the *Cahiers pour une morale* (Paris: Gallimard, 1983); *Sit* X for *Situations*, Vol. X; *SG* for *Saint Genet, Actor and Martyr*, tr. Bernard Frechtman (New York: George Braziller, 1963); *CRD* for *Critique de la raison dialectique* (Paris: Gallimard, 1985).

1 Sartre returns here to generosity as "free passion," which, in "La liberté cartésienne" (*Sit* I, p. 329), he had criticized as an instrument for crushing the self of freedom in systems of preestablished values. Phenomenological studies of generosity as a perfected form of the philosophical *cogito* have appeared subsequently; cf. J.-L. Marion, *Généalogie de la psychanalyse* (Paris: 1985), p. 39.

2 F. Jeanson, *Sartre dan sa vie* (Paris: Seuil, 1974), p. 232. Sartre still maintained ten years later, in 1975, in an interview that he granted to M. Rybalka, O. Pucciani, and S. Gruenheck that he had presented a positive conception of love in the *Saint Genet*: "Pucciani— One often has great difficulty with your analyses of love, of the 'for-others.' You yourself have said that in *Being and Nothingness* you depicted above all negative love. Sartre— Yes, certainly. Beginning with *Saint Genet* I changed my position a bit, and I now see more positivity in love" (interview with Jean-Paul Sartre, in *The Philosophy of Jean-Paul Sartre*, ed. Paul A. Schilpp (La Salle, Ill.: Library of the Living Philosophers, 1981). For more concerning the positive and total "incarnation" of love, cf. Sartre, *Intimité*, in: *Œuvres romanesques* (Paris: Gallimard, Bibliothèque de la Pléiade, 1981), edited by Michel Contat and Michel Rybalka, p. 281; also *Le Diable et le Bon Dieu* (Paris: Gallimard, p. 209).

3 The references for these unpublished texts can be found in the following articles: Pierre Verstraeten, "*Impératif et Valeur*," R. Stone and E. Bowman, "*Un premier regard aux notes de la conférence de Sartre à l'Institut Gramsci*, Juliette Simont, "*Autour des conférences de Sartre à Cornell*," in *Écrits posthumes de Sartre*, Annales de l'Institut de Philosophie et de Sciences morales (Bruxelles: 1987); cf. also Juliette Simont, "*Morale esthétique, morale militante: au-delà de la 'faribole'*," in *Revue philosophique de Louvain*, no. 73 (1989).

4 Sartre, *Les Mots*, p. 11. Cf. the description of "the universe of desire" in the *Cahiers pour une morale* and the alienation attached to it. One of Sartre's ways for affirming the mutual belonging of the two worlds, the primitive world (of desire) and the blank world (technical) was through childhood: If the primitive is "all of man," it is especially to the extent

that every person, as a child, is a primitive made passive by his need which inverts itself into desire. The primitive "is with respect to nature like the child with respect to his parents" (*CM*, p. 366). As to the extensions of the thematic of the difference between desire and need, the latter being the free right to its satisfaction, the former being on the contrary theoretically impossible to satisfy since its satisfaction itself would reactivate its internal impotence, cf. *L'Idiot de la famille*, I, p. 433: "*Flaubert dès l'origine vit son désir comme un besoin*. . . ."

5 Sartre, "*L'Engagement de Mallarmé*," *Obliques*, no. 18–19, p. 187.

III History and structure

7   Sartre and the poetics of history

The purpose of this essay is to reflect on Sartre as a philosopher of the imagination in order better to describe and assess his approach to the philosophy of history. Sartre was, of course, an existentialist and we shall consider what it means to formulate an "existentialist" philosophy of history. But his was equally a philosophy of consciousness and the paradigm of consciousness for him was imaginative consciousness. Realizing this fact will open the door to a more adequate comprehension of his work as a whole, but especially his social thought, including his theory of history. For a basic thesis I wish to defend is that Sartre likens the intelligibility of history to that of an artwork because he considers the former as much the product of creative freedom as he does the latter. So we shall begin with a reading of major theses from his *Psychology of Imagination* and move through his posthumously published works, *The War Diaries* and the *Cahiers pour une morale,* in order to observe their expansion and application in both volumes of the *Critique of Dialectical Reason* and *The Family Idiot.* In so doing, we shall try to make sense of Sartre's claim that history in general and his Flaubert study in particular constitute "a novel that is true" (*un roman vrai*).

THE IMAGE AND THE WORK OF ART

Given the way Sartre's philosophy of history will end, with the centrality of the concept of struggle and the impossible reconciliation of the unavoidable notions of fraternity and violence, it may seem odd to begin our reconstruction of his theory with an examination of philosophical psychology and especially his philosophy of art. But one will overlook a core dimension of Sartre's reading of

213

history if one ignores its psychological and aesthetic nature. More-over, the implicit concept of "committed" history will make little sense if not placed in the context of Sartre's well-known theory of committed literature.

Since others in this collection have treated these topics at length, I need only sketch the elements of Sartre's theory of the imaging consciousness relevant to his subsequent reflections on the meaning of history. As he argues in *Psychology of Imagination*, the image is not a "thing," not even a mental thing, but a form of consciousness, a way of being present to the world. This way is called "inten-tionality" by Husserl and his followers in the phenomenological movement. Sartre never questioned the claim that consciousness is characteristically other-referring, that it "intends" an object in its every act. Where he augmented the Husserlian thesis was in his account of the way consciousness "intends" its objects imagina-tively (as distinct from perceptively or emotively).

Sartre offers us the following definition: "The image is an act that intends [literally "aims at" (*vise*)] an absent or nonexistent object in its corporality by means of a physical or psychical content that is given not for its own sake but only as an 'analogical representative' of the intended object."[1] Unlike perception, imaging intends its ob-ject "as a nothingness"; that is, it affirms or believes its object to be nonexistent, absent, existing elsewhere or in some neutral mode that prescinds from existence entirely. Moreover, the spontaneity of imaging consciousness is contrasted with the passive syntheses of perception; and the unblinking eye of Sartrean consciousness is aware of having adopted the imaging mode of being "present–absent" to the world by "derealizing" what would be the perceptual object, were such available for perceiving. In other words, I can imag-ine my friend in certain circumstances while knowing that they do not in fact obtain, yet be aware too that it is my friend "in flesh and blood" and not some simulacrum that I have in mind.

Perhaps the most distinctive feature of Sartre's theory and one that figures in his understanding of history is his concept of the "analogical representative" or *analogon* in imaging consciousness. This may be a physical thing, like a carving or the printed letters on a page, or physiological changes, like the eye movements that serve as content for hypnagogic images. The analogon is synthesized with cognitive, emotive and, often, kinesthetic elements to yield the intended object. Indeed, we have an analogon only as long as we have the imaged object. The carving, for example, is simply a piece of polished wood until it is "derealized" into the analogue for the aesthetic object.[2]

It is not my purpose to enter further the disputed territory of aesthetic theory but only to underscore that the early Sartre in particular will understand the historical event as an analogon for what we commonly call history. In other words, history, for him, is no more a concatenation of brute facts or simple events than the aesthetic object is a mere linkage of perceptual items. There is a synthesizing activity of consciousness at work in both cases and, most important of all, there is a correspondingly *moral* dimension to each. This is the root of Sartrean "commitment" in both history and art and the basis for his "existentialist" theory of each.

THE CHALLENGE OF HISTORY: *THE WAR DIARIES*

It is common to divide Sartre's public life into two periods, before and after his discovery of "History, Marxism, and the collective dimension" during the Second World War.[3] Indeed, Sartre originated that interpretation himself.[4] But as his posthumously published *War Diaries* indicates, his interest in the nature and meaning of historical events dates at least from the late 1930s. In the notebooks that Private Sartre carried with him during the "Phony War," interspersed among the observations of a conscript near the front we discover reflections that will find their way into *Being and Nothingness* as well as the seeds of a philosophy of history: "[H]istory was all around me. First of all philosophically: Aron had just written his *Introduction to the Philosophy of History* and I read it. Then it surrounded me and found its way into me as into all my contemporaries; it made me feel its presence."[5]

To a large extent Sartre's early observations on the nature of history are in response to the important work of his friend and former schoolmate, Raymond Aron. Sartre's criticism focused on Aron's "skeptical moderation" regarding the *unity* of history, namely his claim that "the complexity of the historical world responds to a pluralist anthropology."[6] Aron will allow a multiplicity of interpretations of an historical event in accord with the interests of the individual historian. While admitting the possibility of such a plurality of interpretations, Sartre is distressed by their lack of *convergence* in Aron's thought. In these early reflections we already glimpse indicators of Sartre's mature emphasis on individual consciousness or praxis as well as his sense of the political-moral implications of a philosophical anthropology and the theory of history one builds upon it. At this stage he has only the core concepts of *Being and Nothingness* to express the ontological basis of his response to Aron. Let us survey that ontology briefly as he employs it in the *War Diaries*.

Sartre acknowledges three distinct, irreducible dimensions of being, which, inspired by Hegel, he terms being-in-itself or the nonconscious, being-for-itself or consciousness, and being-for-others or the interpersonal, the public. He employs powerful metaphors to capture the difference between these three realms. The in-itself is inert, opaque, "sticky," and so forth. It is the sphere of brute fact, of chance, and of our facticity. The for-itself is spontaneous, translucent, the internal negation ("nihilation") of the in-itself, a "hole" in being. Finally, the for-others is the domain of other for-itselfs as other; correlative to our embodiedness, it is our liability to have the meaning of our projects "stolen" from us by the look (*le regard*) of the Other. Although he does not develop these categories here as he will in *Being and Nothingness*, they are sufficiently well formulated in his mind so that he can employ them with ease, as we shall now observe.

When two or more for-itselfs enter into relationship, Sartre argues, there is a reciprocity that is an *existential modification* of each. Exhibiting the kind of thinking that will remain through the *Critique*, Sartre urges that such reciprocity, even if taken to be a mere nominalist sum of constitutive consciousnesses, *presumes a prior unity*. He does not think this unity need be based on transcendental consciousness and ultimately on God as does Aron, who, rejecting the God hypothesis, dissolves the prior unity as well. Instead, Sartre asks whether there is not "an existence proper to the reciprocal existential modification, an existence that would pose itself in terms neither of the for-itself nor of the for-others" (*CDG*, p. 252). The answer, he implies, lies in *that special in-itself of the for-others*, which he will soon call the "event" (p. 363). This would be the locus of historical facticality. Sartre's only example confirms this view.

Consider a conversation between two people. Besides the respective facts that each happens to be talking, there is the mutuality that we call the *conversation itself* that exists beyond the being-for-itself of each participant, though not independent of the individuals involved. To borrow Sartre's metaphorical mode, "The in-itself recoups what escapes it in the nihilation [of the in-itself by consciousness] by giving this same nihilation the value of a *fact* having appeared in the very bosom of the in-itself" (p. 252). "This fact exists-for no one," he insists against the idealists, "it simply *is*" (p. 253, emphasis his).

Sartre agrees with Aron that, whether it is a question of explanation or of understanding, the same historical event can carry different layers of meaning (*signification*). The First World War, for example, can be judged from a variety of perspectives. But he questions the *irreducible parallelism* of these "systems of interpretation" that Aron adopts from Weber, the belief that each account is true of the event under a different description. For, Sartre objects, these descriptions and explanations *never converge*.

Sartre has always been a realist in epistemology and an individualist in metaphysics.[7] His response to Aron builds on this foundation by insisting that these different levels of signification are *human* and that their *unity* depends on that of the primitive pro-ject of human reality.[8] The rivalries in Europe on the eve of the Great War, for example, are human choices. Sounding like a full-blown existentialist, Sartre explains it is human agents who decide the meaning (*sens*) of any given situation and "man is a unitary totality" (p. 361).

But the First World War is what Durkheim calls a "social fact." How can even a plurality of individuals account for its unity, if such there be? Sartre has not yet developed the social ontology that in the *Critique* will enable him to address this issue adequately.[9] In the meantime, he has at his disposal only the ontological triad of being-in-itself, -for-itself, and -for-others. Every fact is a fact-for-others.

That Molière presented a particular play at the Hotel de Bourgogne on the sixth of May, 1680, though the product of a plurality of consciousnesses (*Mitsein*), *as a fact* confers a kind of synthetic unity on these consciousnesses "in the mode of in-itself." "And that unity," he adds, "is opaque and inexhaustible; it is a veritable absolute. . . . Its content is entirely human, but the unity itself insofar as it is existence *in-itself* is radically nonhuman [*inhumain*]" (p. 363). This is the facticity of the for-others discussed earlier. Sartre now identifies it as the event (*l'événement*). The major role of the event surfaces as he explains: "For it is this event in its absolute existence that the historian intends." This is the absolute reality Sartre believes will save him from the ravages of historical relativism. But it will not do so easily. As he admits, "the profound ambiguity of historical research lies in the need *to date* this absolute event, that is to say, to place it in human perspectives" (p. 363). So the possibility of multiple interpretations arises from the "for-others" character of the event, from its availability to and assumption by consciousness. But its status as in-itself accounts for its factical condition. The event joins that line of ambiguous phenomena and "metastable" conditions that populate Sartrean thought, symptomizing a basic tension in his own work and perhaps in the human condition.[10] In the present case, because there is an event in-itself (the "absolute event" to borrow his locution), one can distinguish the interpreted and the interpretation. In other words, one is not left with a Nietzschean eternity of interpretations of interpretations. There are "absolutes" in Sartre's thought. One such is the historical event; another is individual choice.

His reflections on the nature of the event lead him to conclude that the historian must move on *three planes:*

> that of the for-itself, where he tries to show how the decision appears to itself for the historical personage; that of the in-itself, where that decision is an absolute fact, temporal but not dated; finally, that of the for-others, where the pure event is grasped, dated, and surpassed by other consciousnesses as being "of the world." (p. 364)

By discounting the "absolute event," Aron has had to accept the parallelism that leads to relativism. But as a result and more seriously, in Sartre's eyes, he has neglected the role of the individual agent in historical causality. By focusing on the situation acting on the individual, such a philosophy of history leaves us with a disjunction of equally significant levels. Proposing the counterhypothesis, Sartre would have us consider "the man projecting himself [*se jetant*] across situations and living them in the unity of human reality" (p. 365). In other words, he is sketching the core of an "existentialist" theory of history. So in March of 1940 Sartre enunciates the strategy he will pursue for the next thirty years in his attempt to elucidate at one and the same time the epoch and the individual agent.

Having established provisionally three levels of historical investigation, Sartre turns to the one that will hold his lifelong interest, that of the individual project as historical cause and of the agent as instantiation of a social whole. The actuality of the German threat directed him to its analogy with the First World War. In the intellectual framework we have just described, his reading of Emil Ludwig's biography of Wilhelm II suggests the first statement of a theme to be repeated with variations throughout his career: Can we find an "internal relation of comprehension" (p. 365) between Germany's English policy and the Kaiser's withered arm? Let us summarize Sartre's early thought on the meaning of history with a survey of his answer to this question, fully aware that he intends it as "an example of method and not . . . a factual historical truth," a working hypothesis, "a metaphysics of historicity [historialité]" to show "how historical man freely historicizes himself [s'historialise] in the context of certain situations" (p. 366).

Sartre begins this hypothetical analysis with a warning against a simple psychoanalytic answer that, by its implicit naturalism, is antihistorical. In words that reverse in advance a famous phrase of Foucault's, he insists: "History is understood only by *the recuperation and the assumption of monuments*" (p. 365, emphasis his) – in other words, only by turning monuments into documents.[11] Without such assumption of the past, one may have causal sequence but not history properly speaking. The challenge Sartre sets himself is to determine "whether the different historical levels (including the social and geographic) are not unified in the midst of *the same project* and [hence] to determine to what degree Wilhelm II is a cause of the War of 1914" (p. 366). From what follows, it is clear that Sartre's principal concern is the Kaiser, not the war.[12]

So Sartre sets out on the first of his "existential psychoanalyses." As he will do with increasing thoroughness in the cases of Baudelaire, Tintoretto, Genet, himself, and especially Flaubert, he marshals the facts to be interpreted: facts of empire, of inter- and intrafamilial relationships (Sartre has always been at his best in psychological descriptions), of the personnel serving the Crown, of Bismarck's political legacy, of social, economic, and geographic circumstances, and, above all, the fact of the Emperor's congenitally disfigured left arm.[13] He makes much of the fact that Wilhelm as Crown Prince succeeded his grandfather, that a marked generation gap intervened between the ruling groups and that the young emperor, choosing to live with his infirmity by demonstrations of autonomy from the liberalizing influence of his English mother, became the person he was, a "human totality," precisely in the way he appropriated the aforementioned facts. In other words, the parallel levels of explanation-comprehension *converge* when we treat the historical personage in terms of the unity of his "historicization" (p. 386).

Although scarcely organized into a coherent theory of history, these reflections in the *War Diaries* certainly evidence Sartre's early interest in the subject and exhibit features that will characterize his mature theory in the *Critique* such as the epistemic and moral primacy of the individual's "historicization" (later called "totalization" and more properly "personalization"), the recalcitrance of the historical event, and the unity that results from the "datable" nature of the event.

THE DAWNING OF A THEORY OF HISTORY: *CAHIERS POUR UNE MORALE*

Though Sartre's masterwork, *Being and Nothingness,* contains valuable thoughts on temporality, facticity, and the human project, its looking/looked-at model for interpersonal relations leaves us at best with a philosophical anthropology, not a social philosophy properly speaking. Indeed, the individualist spirit conveyed by that work left many in doubt that an existentialist philosophy of history was possible.[14] In his *Cahiers pour une morale,* notebooks for the ethics of authenticity he had promised in *Being and Nothingness* but never published, he seems to sanction this view with a Nietzsche-like aphorism: "Existentialism against History by affirming the irreducible individuality of the person."[15] Yet these same *Cahiers* contain some of Sartre's most sustained reflections on the nature and scope of historical thought. Let us gather his somewhat scattered remarks under three headings, namely the historical event, the conditions of historical activity, and the dialectic of historical understanding, the better to observe the seeds of a theory that will come to flower in the *Critique* and *The Family Idiot.*

The historical event

As we have just seen, this topic captured Sartre's attention from the start. What he underlines here is the *ambiguity* of the historical event, arising from three sources.

First of all, as a human, not a natural phenomenon, the historical event shares the ambiguity of the human condition. Human reality, as we know from *Being and Nothingness*, is a "detotalized totality,"[16] it can never be fully identical with any whole in which it attempts to integrate itself. But this is seen to be true of the historical collectivity as well,[17] and for the same reason: Because of the "inner distance" proper to consciousness, which Sartre terms "presence-to-self," the ontological ground of Sartrean freedom and the reason why human reality is always more or other than its predicates (it "is what it is not and is not what it is," in Sartre's famous formula). Races, nations, classes, sexes as well as social predicates such as exigency, obligation, and duty (*CM*, p. 269) – all are shot through with that otherness, that lack of self-coincidence, which characterize their component human realities. They will never be entirely what we say they are – another lesson from *Being and Nothingness*. "In History too existence precedes essence [that is, representation]," he now writes. "The *separation* in History brings it about that it is never totally what one thinks it to be" (p. 38).

The second reason for the ambiguity of the historical event is its ontological position "intermediary between physical fact and free *Erlebnis*" (p. 42). The event is subject to the laws of the physical universe (for example, I can send a message via carrier pigeon) and to its hazards (the bird may be killed by a predator). Yet that same event is the product of purposeful human action, limited by the detotalizing activity that is human freedom, but allowing a grasp of the agent's intention. It is this ambiguity that enables Sartre to employ two types of account in his historical explanations, namely what we have elsewhere termed the "Marxist-determinist" and the "existentialist-moral."[18] The former addresses those impersonal occurrences often attributed to the "system" or to "force of circumstance"; the latter ferrets out those individuals whose actions or omissions leave them responsible in a moral sense, that is, accountable, for the resultant situation. It is an essential feature of Sartre's theory of history that responsibility can be ascribed to such agents in most any case. The social ontology of the *Critique* is fashioned to warrant such ascriptions of responsibility for properly "social" phenomena.

From this bifocal nature of the event follows the further ambiguity of the necessity–contingency relationship. Thus a given undertaking can be said to have succeeded both because of human initiative in overcoming obstacles and because these obstacles were not greater. If my enemy had not had the sun in his eyes as I passed by, I should not have achieved my mission. Yet it is up to me to preclude foreseeable dangers. "The possibles," Sartre writes, "are realized in probability." "Freedom," he adds, "moves in the sphere of the probable, between total ignorance and certitude" (p. 348). He sees this ambiguity as the basis for statistical reasoning in the social sciences.

Where the *Diaries* spoke of the historical fact as being-for-others recouped by being-in-itself, the *Cahiers* refers to "necessity in the heart of contingency but recouped by contingency" (p. 65). The reversal is instructive. Earlier Sartre was struck by the brute recalcitrance of the historical fact as having occurred. Now it is its lack of necessity that interests him. He discovers a "threefold historical contingency" in the historical event based on "the instrument, the body and the other" (p. 59). The unpredictability of technological advances, the liability of our bodies to the vicissitudes of physical and biological nature and, above all, the sheer multiplicity of the other as interpreter of our actions (for he now admits that "the manner of living the event is part of the event itself" [p. 40]) – these confer a radical contingency on the historical enterprise.

These contingencies and the ambiguity of the historical event are synthesized in a distinction Sartre introduces between the "material event" such as the fall of cannon balls, the loss of caloric energy, and death as a biological phenomenon (what we might term the material "analogon"), on the one hand, and the historical object, the battle of Waterloo, for example, on the other. The latter is the concern of the historian and requires that in studying the behavior of a specific regiment, for example, one consider its institutional form as something that antedates its members as well as respect the "subjective unity" of camaraderie and loyalty among its members, its esprit de corps, leader, symbols, and the like. And each of these items in turn offers a multifaceted visage to the prospective inquirer. In sum, the historical object is "at one and the same time material, organic, and spiritual" (p. 35).

Conditions of historical activity

Early in the *Cahiers* Sartre notes that "a philosophy of history ought to inquire in the first place about the nature of action" (p. 56). The most important thesis about human action for his subsequent theory that we find in these notebooks is that action is the "interiorization of exteriority and exteriorization of interiority" (p. 56).[19] As interiorization, action is both an interpretation and an appropriation of the past as facticity; as exteriorization it is the transcendence of this facticity and the casting of one's lot with the uncertainties and vulnerabilities of the world, with what we shall discuss shortly as the realm of "inertia." This exteriorized action Sartre terms the "work" (*l'œuvre*).

The work: Sartre is sensitive to the specifically historical problems of the common effect (*l'œuvre commune*) of such collective enterprises as the legal code, the conquest of Algeria, or the triumph of a temperance league (Durkheim's "social facts," the proper object of the historian's craft). Although he speaks of a concrete "we" (*nous*) in such cases, this collective subject has "a density of being that saves me the agony of being responsible for my Ego" (*CM*, p. 138). This kind of "responsibility" for a common effect, which is a way of avoiding individual responsibility, can easily slide into the anonymity of the "they" (*l'on*), precursor of serial being in the *Critique*. Although sensitive to the need for a collective or social subject, he is far from resolving its nature in such a way as to preserve the freedom and responsibility of its individual members. This awaits the concept of the mediating Third in the *Critique*.

Given that exteriorization is an act of freedom, how am I to grasp the freedom implicit in the other's *œuvre* and thereby gain access to truly human history? This is the standard question for any theory of historical action that distinguishes action from conditioned behavior and seeks to interpret the former. One way, of course, is the *Verstehen* of Aron and the German social theorists, which Sartre will adopt fully in the *Critique*. But he suggests a variation on this method taken from his aesthetic theory, which indicates that the artistic model is never far from his mind. The problem is to grasp another's objective or goal. The artwork, he argues, "presents itself to me as an absolute end, [as] exigence and appeal. It addresses itself to my pure freedom and thereby reveals to me the pure freedom of the Other." But Sartre extends this experience: "If then I grasp the other's work [*l'œuvre*] (it matters little that it be an artwork) as absolute exigence requiring my approval and my concurrence, I grasp the man in process of acting freely [*de faire comme liberté*]" (p. 516). He admits this is an optimal case, that there are other ways to grasp the freedom of one who denies his freedom – the more common situation. In the present case, I grasp the other in terms of his future, which appears as an unconditioned end for my freedom.

Significantly, my grasp of the other's freedom in such a case has an evaluative and reciprocal character. Separating himself from the notorious "looking/looked-at" model of interpersonal relations employed in *Being and Nothingness*, Sartre takes a notable step toward social consciousness and collective identity when he speaks of the "comprehension" that accompanies my appeal (*la demande*) that another freedom recognize my own, as giving birth to "a certain type of interpenetration of freedoms that could well be the human reign [his version of Kant's kingdom of ends subsumed into Marx's reign of freedom]" (p. 302). Unlike his earlier model, Sartre assures us that "this [mutual] recognition is in no way [an] alienation" (pp. 291–2). "Comprehension," which he sees as "an original, active intention" and "an original structure of the perception of the Other" (p. 288), is distinct from "the look" not only in its specificity (that is, it reveals the *sens-fin* of *this* action) but in its *nonobjectifying* (nonalienating) character. It is to this last feature that Sartre will later appeal in discussing his sociohistorical ideal. Although he mentions "comprehension" (*Verstehen*) in the context of grasping another's freedom, its function in the *Cahiers*, unlike in the *Critique*, is less epistemic than moral.

The Other: We have seen that from the beginning Sartre's reflections locate the historical event in the realm of being-for-others. If the other consciousness invests that event with ambiguity, it alienates it in the basic sense of "objectifying" it as well. Sartre at this stage believes that "History will *always* be alienated" (*CM*, p. 54).

He explains, "History is the *Other:* it is the history of men insofar as they are others – all for each and each for all." And he adds in criticism of Hegel and of Marx that "it is also the history of Spirit perpetually seeking to escape alterity and never succeeding" (pp. 51 and 53). This escape from alterity will be a major theme of the *Critique.*

Although it is inaccurate to say Sartre equates alienation with objectification *simpliciter,* it is clear that for him one cannot live history as we know it without becoming alienated. As he observes: "To act in History is to accept that the act become *other* than one's conception [of it]. That is the true synthesis of unity and duality: to recoup the act *having become other* and to penetrate it with subjectivity once more (synthesis of the same and the other), to reappropriate it for oneself" (p. 53). One's very thoughts, the apparent core of subjectivity, once expressed assume a life and weight of their own (the "inertia" others confer upon them). The challenge of an existentialist theory of history as Sartre is formulating it at this point is to achieve that (impossible?) synthesis of same and other that would be "disalienated" history, a history that is truly "ours," not just "theirs," and yet no less "mine." Is such a "reappropriation" of the past possible at least as an ideal? Herein may lie the major function of the imagination for Sartre's theory: to establish such an ideal synthesis as the condition for appropriating history as a whole. The matter is broached for the first time, cryptically, in these notebooks. It will be worked out in the *Critique.*

Inertia (matter): Sartre's ontology throughout its entire evolution can be read as a dialectic of spontaneity and inertia. In the case of historical action that duality surfaces not only in the ambiguity of the fact, which we have just considered, but in the agent–inertia relationship as well. As Sartre avows: "We are in this untenable situation that nothing comes *from outside* to undermine our efforts insofar as they are lived in freedom [his principle of historicity][20] and yet these efforts have their destiny outside themselves" (*CM,* p. 89). Sartre is alive to the phenomenon of historical consequences extending far beyond and often contrary to our intentions. In this regard, he cites an example close to the plot of *Dirty Hands:* I kill my wife's lover and discover that I have deprived of its leader a party about to seize power. What we may call the interest–destiny dyad becomes paramount in the *Critique* where "interest" for the exploiting race or class becomes "destiny" for the exploited.[21] But by then he has at his disposal the concept of the practico-inert, as we shall see.

Temporality: From the temporal point of view, inertia marks the heaviness of the past, what Sartre calls "time-object," as a kind of in-itself. It absorbs my past (the facticity that I have "to have been") into the past in-itself of humanity that shades into the limiting case of physical time which we retroject on the world before the advent of humans (see *CM*, p. 97).

Being and Nothingness argues that human reality "temporalizes" itself and the world according to the threefold "ekstatic temporality" of facticity, existence, and presence-to, which Sartre adapts from Heidegger (see *BN*, pp. 107–29).[22] Without this temporality and its concomitant ontological freedom, there might well be a sequence of natural occurrences, but there would be no history. In the *Cahiers* Sartre distinguishes historical from the merely biographical temporality described in *Being and Nothingness*: "Historical time is at once thing and spirit (following upon its radical ruptures) while the time of the individual is entirely consciousness" (*CM*, p. 115). By "thing" Sartre is referring to the in-itself of the for-others, which, as we saw, gives the historical event an "absolute" dimension. By "spirit" he is alluding to his version of Hegel's "objective spirit" that we shall discuss in the context of his Flaubert study, *The Family Idiot.*

Sartre elaborates this distinction between historical and biographical time in terms of the triple dimension of historical time. First, there is the time that "temporalizes itself with each absolute For-itself," in effect, individual temporality as necessary condition for historical time. Next there is "the time of intersubjectivities," namely the temporal unity of the mutual looks [*regards*], that is both time-subject and time-object since each consciousness is both looking and looked-at. Finally, we have what may simply be called "the Past," that melting of my time-subject into a prior series of time-objects for both myself and others, and that series' dissolution into the past in-itself of all humanity and thence into prehistoric, physical time, as noted previously.

This last, complex "definition" of the Past is meant to underline its nature as in-itself, as facticity and, above all, as a *one-way* relationship with the present and the future. As he observes: "Hence my time is always dated in the past by universal time, whereas the present and the future share an unjustifiable, nondated time, as absolute time." And he concludes: "In historical time there is a double tear: that of the Other (which is reciprocal) and that of the Past (which lacks reciprocity)" (*CM*, p. 97). So the Greek circle of time that Nietzsche tried to revive is broken on the rocks of the Sartrean Other and the object-time of the Past. Scarcely transcending the categories of *Being and Nothingness*, Sartre has undertaken an account of historical time that distinguishes it both from physical chronology and from individual time, while defending its directionality and the recalcitrance of the past. "Absolute" or "undated" time is confined to the ekstatic present and future, unlike in the *War Diaries*, but Sartre continues to be concerned with the same problem of unifying and "ordering" the past.

Dialectic and history

If Sartre's reflections on history in the *Carnets* were in dialogue with Raymond Aron, those in the *Cahiers* can be read as a conversation with the French Hegelians, specifically, with Kojève and Hyppolite (see *CM*, pp. 64 and 68ff.). But if Sartre views history in a dialectical light, his is a peculiarly existentialist "dialectic": It generates otherness and resists synthesis. In fact, Sartre has misgivings about a dialectic of History in the Hegelian (and Marxian) sense because otherness or alterity, "the true moving principle of History, . . . is larger than dialectic and englobes it" (p. 61). Again, the challenge faced in the *Critique* is to discover a dialectical relation that does not of itself generate alterity or that yields a nonalienating form.

By "dialectic" Sartre understands the "synthetic unity of a totality spread out in time" (*CM*, p. 472). It is a part–whole relationship, where each element gains its meaning in reference to the whole that it constitutes but which reciprocally establishes it as a part. But it is a temporalized totality; the reciprocal signification of part and whole depends on what each was and/or will be (see p. 472). In fact, it is the future that counts most in Sartrean dialectic. Of course, the existentialist project is essentially forward looking. But Sartre will subsequently refer to "a certain action of the future [on the present]" as the touchstone of any dialectic (*SM*, p. 92 n). At this stage of his thought, however, the nature of that future and the totality it forms at the level of historical dialectic are undetermined.

Sartre's assessment of totalities and with it his understanding of a dialectic in history can be summarizd in four theses. First, there are totalities, not a totality, in history. Since *Being and Nothingness*, he has insisted that any totality of which the for-itself is a part must always be a "detotalized" totality. Now he adds that "no interior attitude can synthesize . . . the dimension of the For-itself and the For-others, which are existential categories and incommunicable dimensions" (*CM*, p. 485).

As there are totalities, secondly, so are there dialectics in history, each related negatively to the others. These dialectics are coterminous with existentialist projects understood as transcendings of situations, negations that conserve as they surpass (see p. 478).

Third, though Sartre's "dialectic" resembles Hegel's in being a relation of same and other, it differs from the classical, Hegelian version in the following ways:

1. In the *contingency* that pervades it. This stems from the "spontaneous upsurge" of consciousness and from the hazards of the in-itself to which all action is liable.
2. In the irreducible *heterogeneity* of its basic components, notably, the in-itself and the for-itself. This does not prevent classical dialectical relationships at another level, for example, among situation, choice, and goal (*but*), but it does preclude ultimate synthesis; the for-itself (or *praxis* in his subsequent work) is never fully integrated into an organic whole.
3. In the role of the *imaginary* both in projecting a totalizing goal and in the creative moment that Sartre attributes to fundamental choice.
4. In the specific Sartrean understanding of *creative freedom*. He dismisses Hegelian freedom as "Spinozistic necessity transferred into temporal succession" (p. 480). Yet he agrees that "thus far, the dialectic is the only method conceived to explicate freedom, render it intelligible and at the same time preserve its character of creation" (p. 482). Still, he distrusts the Marxist version as he then understands it: "The link between structures of the historical fact is much more *loose* than Marx wanted. That has to be the case because man is not reflection [of his circumstances] but transcendence and invention. . . . Each of his works reflects and expresses [his] situation . . . *by surpassing it*" (p. 80).

5. Perhaps above all, Sartrean dialectic differs from the classical form by its insistence against Hegel that if History is not finished, the dialectic becomes a *hypothesis* and human existence an absolute (see *CM*, p. 482).

It is in pressing these differences over the next decade that Sartre fashions his theory of history.

Sartre's fourth claim regarding totalities concerns the possibility of *a* totality and hence *a* dialectic of History. Could such a reality be achieved? This is the final question of the first volume of the *Critique*. In the *Cahiers*, despite the misgivings just discussed, it receives a tentative, positive answer:

If we admit that a man can conceive the whole (the final state of humanity), this presumes that the whole is always given — which I believe. It is always given as the whole of freedom (freedom as comprehension of the human condition and [as] implying the freedom of all). Except that there is no longer a dialectic. In other words, either History is finished or we can grasp the dialectic only partially, in the past and by prolonging it (a bit) through extrapolation. (*CM*, p. 483)

It is at this point that history crosses over into moral philosophy and the dialectic assumes an evaluative stance. The style of life Sartre terms "authentic" enters his theory of historical dialectic here. Without elaborating this ethical dimension, let us note Sartre's picture of "the human condition" as it emerges from this dialectical vision of the end-goal of History:

If the dialectic is not a closed system, one must live the present moment in uncertainty. And this life in uncertainty becomes an absolute, no longer the Hegelian absolute but the absolute of the lived (*le vécu*). . . . Expectation, decision taken in uncertainty, oscillation, choice — precisely the features of the human condition — these cannot be integrated in any synthesis because they are exactly what are eliminated from a synthesis.

From this he draws the conclusion and the moral, "if each human is a risk, so too is humankind in its entirety" (p. 483). His philosophy never lost this sense of risk or of hope as its response. There is no guarantee that History will finally issue in lasting freedom, harmony, and peace. The "absolute" consciousness may choose unfreedom, discord, and violence instead. So *a* dialectic of History as a given in the nature of things is ruled out of court, as we have seen. Still, the possibility, the image, the ideal that can retrospectively turn histories into History is beginning to take shape.

The glimmer of hope that breaks forth from these texts comes chiefly from Sartre's existentialist thesis that meaning (*sens*) is created, not discovered. Whatever meaning in the sense of "synthesis" or "unity-totality" History bears will result either from our attitudes or our *œuvres*, the subjective and objective views respectively. We have discussed the "work" as revelatory of another's freedom and as invitation to one's free response. The "attitude" he has in mind is the project of living this impossible synthesis of the for-itself and the for-others in creative tension.[23] Failure to do so is what Sartre means by "inauthenticity." Since it is developed at length in his later works, we need merely note that this sustained tension that perpetuates without resolving the "dialectic" of my personal project becomes the suggested form of interpersonal relations as well as the (ideal) end goal of History, what Sartre calls "the whole of freedom" (p. 483) and whose foretaste, as later in the *Critique*, is the combat group. Thus he extends this "authentic" mode of acting to one's historical existence when he writes:

> The virtue of the historical agent is generosity. But true friendship intervenes here: the friend, he for whom the other is the same. Combatants who create together a milieu of intersubjectivity for the idea [which is always other]. This time, instead of the same being in the other, it is the other who is in the same. A nuance of quasi-objectivity in common subjectivity. (p. 54)

This extension of an existentialist "virtue" to the social realm prepares us for the positive values of mutuality and "free (nonalienating) alterity" among group members in the *Critique*. It also reflects Sartre's growing sense of "History" as a *value* to be fostered rather than simply to be recorded, not unlike Marx's distinction between History and prehistory.[24] Finally, it contributes to that mosaic of "committed" history that Sartre is relentlessly forming.

THE *SENS* OF HISTORY: DISCOVERY AND DECISION

Sartre's first systematic treatment of the issue of historical understanding is *Search for a Method*, published subsequently as a kind of preface to the *Critique*. His then unpublished reflections on history are fortified by open involvement with the political Left, but he is not sanguine about advancing the conditions for the "city of ends," as he has come to describe his sociopolitical ideal. "Do we have today the means to constitute a structural, historical anthropology?" he asks at the outset. And he answers with the conditional, "If such a thing as a Truth can exist in anthropology, it must be a truth that has *become*, and it must make itself a *totalization*." He adds that such a becoming, totalizing truth that refers both to being and to knowing is what Hegel meant by "dialectic." He takes it as a basic *postulate* of the book that "such a totalization is perpetually in process as History and as philosophical Truth" (*SM*, p. xxxiv).

He admits that his postulate, which is incompatible with the "positivists'" claims that "there are *several* Histories and several Truths," must in some sense be defended. He describes his task in *Search for a Method* as answering the question "whether there is any such thing as a Truth for humanity."[25] This translates into the challenge to show a relation (*rapport*) between historical totalization and *totalizing Truth*. That relation he calls *dialectical Reason* and he devotes the formidable *Critique of Dialectical Reason* published three years later to its defense.

Unlike Kant's *Critique of Pure Reason*, Sartre's *Critique* must answer not only the *quaestio juris* (How does one justify the claims of dialectical Reason?) but also the *quaestio facti* (Is there such a thing as dialectical Reason at all?). In this he joins the post-Kantian philosophers of history such as Dilthey, Rickert, Simmel, and Weber, who likewise seek to establish the *quid facti*. Yet it is not a matter of "discovering" a dialectic the way one discovers a planet or even a mathematical proof, for dialectical reason by definition encompasses the inquirer. Rather, the dialectic must emerge, must come to consciousness in such revelatory moments as the experiences of negation, necessity, counterfinality, and *dépassement* (translated as "transcending" or "overcoming"). But these moments, like the dialectic of which they form a part, demand the counterposition that Sartre calls "positivist, analytical Reason" (*CDR*, p. 823). The negative side of Sartre's justification of the dialectic is his argument that analytic Reason fails to render human reality comprehensible.

Search for a Method

In his Introduction to the *Critique*, Sartre warns that Volume I will comprise a theory of practical ensembles "as moments of totalization," whereas Volume II, the notes for which were published posthumously in 1985, will consider "the problem of totalization itself; that is to say, of History in its development and of Truth in its becoming" (CDR, p. 824). But in Search he lays out the method and principal concepts for this theoretical undertaking, namely comprehension, totalization, and the progressive-regressive method. As we should now expect, these are to be understood dialectically, that is, with a certain spiraling reciprocity, though the dialectic as such is treated only in the Critique. Let us examine each more closely.

Comprehension: Raymond Aron has remarked that "understanding [la compréhension] is fundamentally the decisive problem, one could almost say the sole [unique] problem, of the logic of history."[26] Though we have noted Sartre's not uncritical acceptance of this concept since the Diaries, only here does he examine it closely. He now sees comprehension (Verstehen) as the prereflective "translucidity of praxis to itself" (CDR, p. 74), heir to the "self-transparency" of the for-itself in Being and Nothingness. The same lingering Cartesian ideal of unqualified self-awareness permeates Search and the Critique. But since this clarity is not theoretical but practical, being a feature of praxis, it is now vulnerable to a very un-Cartesian mystification.[27] Because the historical agent understands what he is about, we have the possibility of comprehending him as well. But what we comprehend ideally is his own comprehension of his project, the "inside" of the action, if you will, and the first of the three "planes" on which the historian moves, according to the Diaries. Since this self-comprehension is prereflective (and in several ways functionally equivalent to Freud's unconscious), it is conceivable that we may (reflectively) know an agent better than he (reflectively) knows himself, the ideal of historical hermeneutics since Dilthey.

The door is open for such a hermeneutic of another's action because, as Sartre puts it, "Man is for himself and for others a signifying being . . . a creator of signs" (SM, p. 152). He cites as examples of such interpretation the participants in a boxing match (a case pursued at length in Critique II) and the people in a stuffy room observing someone walking toward the closed window (see pp. 157 and 153 respectively). We understand the other's project in a practical way. Neither a special faculty nor an arcane talent, "comprehension" is described by Sartre as "the dialectical movement that explains the act by its terminal signification in terms of its starting conditions" (p. 153). We must note this reference to the end and the conditions because comprehension, though originally progressive (focusing on the end), may be entirely regressive (condition centered) or both at once. In fact, what Sartre calls the "progressive-regressive" method comprises just such comprehension of a concrete historical action.

At this juncture and in the context of comprehension we must distinguish *sens* from *signification* in Sartre's works. Though both words can be translated as "meaning," *signification* refers to conceptual, static meaning whereas *sens* denotes the ongoing unity of a lived process. As such, the terms seem consonant with what Sartre calls "analytic" and "dialectical" reason respectively. Sartre first employed the distinction in aesthetics where he differentiated between images, which "presentify" *sens* and signs, which communicate *signification*. As he insists:

I shall say that an [aesthetic] object has *sens* when it is the incarnation of a reality that surpasses it but which cannot be grasped aside from it and whose infinity does not allow adequate expression in any system of signs; it is always a case of totality: totality of a person, a milieu, an epoch, or the human condition.[28]

Thus the paintings of Paul Rebeyrolle, for example, are said to present the *sens* of the Cold War (see *Sit* IX, pp. 316–25). The terminological bridge to Sartre's subsequent dialectic of history consists in the equivalence he sees between *sens* and what he calls the "singular universal."[29] The latter expression, of Hegelian inspiration, appears more frequently in the later Sartre. Just as life is in every part of the body but is identical with none, and the soul, in medieval parlance, "is where it acts," so Sartre argues, is the entire Renaissance present in Michelangelo's "David" or in the Mona Lisa's smile (see *Sit* IV, p. 31). What makes the "incarnation" aesthetic, we may assume, is, among other things, its realization in an image and not a "system of signs." Now this reference to the *sens* of an epoch like the Renaissance suggests that "history," not as an analytic system of signs but as a dialectical totalization, might *incarnate* the "spirit" of a person, a people, or an age. This would presume a "poetic" use of the language of history that Sartre has not yet acknowledged. But his aesthetic theory is ready to accommodate the *sens-totalization* relationship that he now discerns in historical events. Moreover, this equivalence of *sens* with singular universal will lend a key to understanding the crucial term "totalization" to be considered next.

Once more the similarity between history and art comes into view when the aesthetic object is deemed capable of *incarnating* an infinite reality that is nonetheless a totality, such as a milieu or an epoch. "Incarnation" will reappear in the second volume of the *Critique*, where it is argued that Stalin "incarnates" the socialist bureaucracy for a quarter of a century of Russian history.[30]

Totalization: "Totalization" denotes the unifying function of "praxis" once this has replaced "consciousness–project" in the Sartrean vocabulary. We noted Sartre's early criticism of Aron's failure to correlate or unify the plurality of significations to which the action/event was subject. He now warns that "we lose sight of human reality if we do not consider [these] significations as synthetic, multidimensional, indissoluble objects, which hold individual places in a space-time with multiple dimensions." As he explains, "the mistake here is to reduce the lived signification to the simple linear statement which language gives it" (*SM*, pp. 108–9). In other words, we must adopt a dialectical discourse in order to respect human reality and its lived meaning (which, were he observing his own distinction at this point, he would call *sens*). Totalization "as a movement of History and as a theoretical and practical attempt to 'situate' an event, a group, or a man" seeks to capture this unity: "What totalization must discover is the multidimensional unity of the act" (*SM*, p. 111).

Sartre formulates what we may call the *principle of totalization* in his philosophy of history when he claims that "a man . . . totalizes his age to the precise degree that he is totalized by it" (*IF* III, p. 426). Sartre was groping for such a principle as early as the *Diaries* when he spoke of the Kaiser's withered arm. He approached significantly closer when he related Michelangelo's *David* to the *sens* of the Renaissance. But despite the distinction between *sens* and signification, one could dismiss these "totalizations" as merely symbolic. More difficult to dismiss (or to account for adequately otherwise) is the totalizing reciprocity that directs Sartre's massive study of Flaubert, *The Family Idiot*.

Sartre offers some indication of this reciprocity when in *Search* he recommends that the progressive-regressive method be fortified by "cross-references between the *object* [*Madame Bovary*, for example] (which contains the whole period as hierarchized significations) and the *period* (which contains the object in its totalization)" (*SM*, p. 148). Thus, Leconte de Lisle, as both signifying and signified (*signifiant-signifié*), "signifies the unsayable and lived *sens* of the epoch by his singular appropriation of the sign," for example, by wearing a monocle (*IF* III, p. 432). In the case of Flaubert, he explains, "the man and his time will be integrated into the dialectical totalization when we have shown how History surpasses this contradiction" between how Flaubert was and how his age took him to be (*SM*, p. 150). The point is not simply to note these facts, nor merely to connect them chronologically, causally, or even narratively. Totalization requires that we grasp the dialectical "necessity" of the contradiction, for example, between these two views of Flaubert, in terms of the praxis of the agent and the inertia and contrary praxes of his society. In other words, the historian's task is to bring to light the "synthetic bonds of History," its bonds of interiority. Sartre's dialectical investigation aims to determine what, in the process of human history "is the respective role of relations of interiority and exteriority" (*CDR*, pp. 56–7).

Reflecting on culture as a "temporalizing totalization" in the *Critique*, Sartre points out that each of us qua cultured, totalizes himself by "disappearing as a cultivated individual and emerging as the synthetic bond between everyone and what might be called the *cultural field*" (p. 54). What he means is that we are dialectically conditioned by the totalized and totalizing past and future of the process of human development. A cultural object, as it were, wears its history, and we are internally related to the field of cultural objects in which we act. Sartre admits that talk of an individual is merely a methodological point of departure, that one's short life soon becomes diluted in the "pluridimensional human ensemble that temporalizes its totalization and totalizes its temporality." Anticipating the theory behind his Flaubert study, he adds:

To the extent that its individual universals are perpetually aroused, in my immediate as well as my reflective life, and, from the depth of the past in which they were born, provide the keys and the rules of my actions, we must be able, in our regressive investigation, to make use of *the whole of contemporary knowledge* (at least in principle) to elucidate a given undertaking or social ensemble, a particular avatar of praxis. (p. 55)

Totalization can be either synchronic (structural) or diachronic (historical). The former is the terminus of a "regressive" argument in Sartre's vaguely Kantian sense of reasoning from the fact to the formal conditions of its possibility. Thus the first volume of the *Critique* employs a mainly regressive method to arrive at "the elementary formal structures" of sociohistorical development, namely, the series, the group, the institution, and their dialectical interrelation (p. 818).

Diachronic totalization, also called "temporalization," is an essential feature of individual praxis. Since organic praxis alone is constitutive of social wholes (group praxis is constituted by organic praxes), so its diachronic totalizations constitute History. Indeed, Sartre claims that "History is a totalization that temporalizes itself" (p. 54). In other words, history is to be grasped by a "progressive" movement, one that comprehends its "end" and its means. The second volume of the *Critique* was to pursue this method. Sartre's Flaubert study, in many ways the culmination of his theoretical work, employs both synchronic and diachronic totalizations.

Finally and in a way that invites consideration of the Flaubert case, Sartre distinguishes *micro-* and *macro*totalization. While related respectively as part to whole, the former refers to the concrete totalizing praxis of the organic individual whereas the latter denotes the social, cultural world as a network of significations occupying the space between the individual agent and physical nature, that conditions individual praxis and connects it with a web of meanings it may not have chosen. The conjunction of these totalizations, their ongoing *mediation,* is the *concrete universal.* Viewed as an event conjoining individual praxis and social possibility, the concrete universal is the "incarnation" of this web of meanings in both its temporal (diachronic) and its structural (synchronic) dimensions.

What enables Sartre to take this semantic turn while retaining the primacy of individual praxis that constitutes the existentialist core of his theory is again the claim that the individual is a *signified-signifier.* He has long accepted the Husserlian notion of consciousness as meaning-bestowing. He now conjoins this with the semiotic concept of the human as sign-giving, in a sense, the social side of Husserl's position. The individual finds himself amid a network of signs that designate him as a class member, a professional, and the like, but also as a man of his times (or a misfit). These are *macro*totalizations and their meaning, like the praxis that sustains them, is practical.

But unlike the structuralists, Sartre sees this signifying web both as itself historical (the "sedimentation," in Husserl's term, of prior totalizations) and as *dialectically* related to the micrototalizations of organic individuals. What counts in this respect, Sartre writes, is the "action of the *future* as such" (*SM*, p. 94). We must consider society as penetrating each action-motivation from the "perspective of the future" (p. 96). In fact, micrototalization emerges as the proper way to "appropriate" historical meaning as called for by the *Diaries* and the *Cahiers*. In pursuing his own end, the agent "interiorizes" his social world, using it as an instrument in his totalizing project. But he thereby concretizes that social world, advances it in time and changes it the way a colonist, for example, brings his culture to another people while distancing himself in several senses from that same culture to which he can never quite fully return.

The relation between micro- and macrototalization is dialectical and the dialectic again is mediated by the *concrete universal* (*IF* III, p. 432 n.), for example, the monocle *as* worn by Leconte de Lisle, which, as we saw, signified "the unsayable and lived *sens* of the epoch," or the practice of bourgeois "respectability" *as* maintained in late nineteenth-century France (*CDR*, p. 774). The paradigm, of course, is *Madame Bovary*, which is not a type but a "singular universal" (*IF* II, p. 1503). But again, it is the novel *as* written by Gustave Flaubert. The concrete universal "incarnates," in Sartre's term, the objective spirit of an age, but it does so as more than a symbolic form.[31] It mediates praxis enabling the generation of *sens* (meaning-direction) out of the interrelation of individuals with each other and with their cultural environment. In this sense the "Victorian" practice of respectability both signified and effected a certain oppressive relation between the bourgeoisie and the working class.

The progressive-regressive method: "I have a passion for understanding men," writes Sartre in the course of his extended "introduction" to Jean Genet's collected works.[32] His three-volume study of Flaubert confirms that claim. His interest in history is the expression of this passion as well. He approaches history via the singularity of an individual existence (the principle of totalization as exemplified by the Kaiser's withered arm or Leconte's monocle) in order to clarify the one by illuminating the other. Brought to reflective awareness in *Search*, the approach is christened the progressive-regressive method. It consists of three stages.[33]

Sartre recommends we begin with a rigorous phenomenological description of the object as the general level of *eidos* (Husserl's term for the intelligible contour or essence of the phenomenon described). This resembles the method employed in *Being and Nothingness* to reveal the essential structure of "human reality." Though he continues to employ arresting descriptions of paradigmatic cases in his later work, Sartre no longer calls his method "phenomenological."

The regressive stage, like its Kantian counterpart, moves from facts to the conditions of their possibility. Sartre sometimes calls these conditions "formal" (see, for example, *CDR*, p. 671). But other times they are clearly material or existential, for example, Flaubert's early childhood milieu.

The agent's progressive advance through a dialectical spiral of totalization and retotalization, Sartre believes, will account for the *inner necessity* of the historical phenomenon, for why Flaubert could say profoundly: "*Madame Bovary, c'est moi.*" A more complete comprehension of the agent-event is achieved when it is linked with the macrototalization of social ensembles.

The last two movements in the method constitute a kind of synthesis of existential psychoanalysis and historical materialism. Without an existentialist hermeneutic of the signs of an original choice, we would have to be satisfied with such "general particularities" as "the Soviet bureaucracy" or "the petite bourgeoisie" – terms from Marxist "economism," Sartre thinks, that masquerade as concrete individuals (see *SM*, pp. 24 and 43). But without the dialectical interplay of micro- and macrototalization, history would dissolve into biography.

Concluding this discussion of the key concepts of Sartre's philosophy of history introduced in *Search for a Method*, we should note that *Search* takes for granted what the *Critique* aims to establish: "whether there is such a thing as a Truth of humanity"; indeed, it assumes that this truth is totalizing, that a dialectical movement characterizes both being and knowledge. As observed earlier, the *Critique* must establish both the existence of and the warrant for dialectical reason. And yet, Sartre admits that the method of the *Critique* "must also be dialectical" (*CDR*, p. 823). So we should not

be amazed to find him shifting from regressive to progressive movements in the course of his argument throughout the *Critique*, even
though the general direction of the two volumes is regressive and
progressive respectively. Such circularity in methodological questions is inevitable; as dialectical, it need not be vicious. Like a good
novelist, the historian must convey the inevitability of events (the
cult of personality under Stalinism, for example) without compro-
mising the free choices of the agents involved.

We live in a "polyvalent world," Sartre argues, with a plurality of
meanings. "Our historical task . . . is to bring closer the moment
when History will have *only one meaning*, when it will tend to be
dissolved in the concrete men who will make it in common." He
repeats a claim from the *Cahiers*, namely that these plural meanings can be dissolved "only on the ground of a future totalization"
(*SM*, p. 90).

"Totalization" thus assumes both a moral and an epistemic task
in *Search* that links it with the earlier works and with the *Critique*.
It is the leading instrument of the committed historian. "The real
problem of History," as Sartre surveys it at the close of the *Critique*
Volume I, is whether we can *totalize* the vast plurality of totalizations with their partly erased, partly transformed meanings
"by an intelligible totalization from which there is no appeal." This
in effect is the problem of "totalization without a totalizer," he
explains, and we must seek "its motive forces and non-circular direction" (*CDR*, p. 817).

Critique of Dialectical Reason I

This prolix and repetitive volume is an attempt to lay the ontological and epistemic foundations for an existentialist theory of history.
As a theory of history, not psychology or biography, it must account
for the specificity of the social, of what Durkheim has called "social
facts" like battles or treaties as distinct from psychological phenomena like perceptions or beliefs. As "existentialist," it must preserve
the locus of individual praxis-responsibility amid impersonal social
relations and events. Beginning from the "facts" of class identity and
struggle, Sartre argues regressively to the formal conditions of their
possibility, namely the concepts of practico-inert, praxis, and mediating third, as well as the "transcendental fact" of material scarcity.

Although the argument of the text is directed at establishing both the fact and the warrant for dialectical, as distinct from analytical, reason, it is worked out with the help of these concepts and this fact, on which his mature theory hangs.

Just as his first reflections on the philosophy of history were in reaction to the published work of Aron and his subsequent thoughts in dialogue with the French Hegelians, the theory elaborated in the *Critique* can be read in large measure as a response to the criticism Merleau-Ponty had launched against Sartre's social thought in *Adventures of the Dialectic*.[34] "Praxis," for example, counters Merleau-Ponty's claim that Sartre's is still a philosophy of consciousness, "practico-inert," the notion that Sartre lacks a concept of objective possibility, and the "mediating third," the claim that Sartre cannot justify appeal to social wholes in any but a psychological sense.

Praxis: Although Sartre offers a complex definition (see *CDR*, p. 734), "praxis," as noted earlier, is fundamentally purposive human activity in its material environment. Like consciousness, whose function it assumes in the later works, praxis is ontologically free, for it is the unifying and reorganizing transcendence (*dépassement*) of existing circumstances in the practical field (see p. 310 n). But he has come to see that this transcendence is dialectical; that is, that it is simultaneously negation, conservation, and spiraling advance. In other words, it is totalizing. Moreover, if imaging is the paradigm of consciousness, for Sartre, physical labor is his model of praxis. "Insofar as body is function, function need, and need praxis," he argues, "one can say that *human labor*, the original praxis by which man produces and reproduces his life, is *entirely* dialectical" (p. 90).

The practico-inert: Functional heir to "being-in-itself" of the earlier Sartre, this concept is "antidialectical" in the sense that it negates the constitutive dialectics (praxes), "not by destruction or dissolution, but by deviation and inversion" (*CDR*, p. 340). Sartre's now classic examples are Chinese deforestation and Spanish hoarding of New World gold (see pp. 161ff.). In both cases the achievement of certain intended results entailed unintended consequences that undermined the end in view. The Chinese peasants lost land to flooding and the Spanish lost the buying power of gold to inflation. Thus Sartre points out that "within praxis . . . there is a dialectical movement and a dialectical relation between action as the negation of matter . . . , and matter . . . as the negation of action" (p. 159).

"Practico-inert" denotes the realm of sedimented praxis, of passivity and of counterfinality. It extends and refines the notions of otherness and recalcitrance that Sartre, since the *Diaries*, has attributed to the historical event as in-itself. It applies these notions to the social field of "collective objects" like the newspaper or a Gothic cathedral, to practico-inert ideas and systems like racism and colonialism and to institutions like an army or the state bureaucracy.[35]

But he refines these earlier notions of the in-itself and so of the historical event when he describes the practico-inert as "simply the activity of others insofar as it is sustained and diverted by inorganic inertia" (p. 556). The "sustaining" function of the practico-inert accounts for what philosophers of history have called the "trace,"[36] which for Sartre is "worked matter" that mediates our social and historical relations. It is this "dialectical," that is, mediating, role that distinguishes the practico-inert from other, "analytical" uses. Unlike the analytical "trace," the practico-inert is intrinsically subject-referring; it obtains *as* practico-inert only while interiorized-totalized by the historical agent.

Moreover, despite its "antidialectical" character (Sartre limits his dialectic to the interpersonal realm, joining other revisionist Marxists in questioning a dialectic of nature), the practico-inert does exert a kind of negative, deforming influence on individual and collective projects. Sometimes Sartre refers to this as a *"force* of inertia" (p. 278) that reveals itself, for example, in the "objective, negative exigencies" (p. 159) made by the colonialist or the capitalist "systems" on their practitioners,[37] in the "logic" of a series of human decisions that entail unintended, contrary consequences such as the inflation and concomitant devaluation that followed upon Spanish gold policy under Philip II (see pp. 165ff.), or in the "serial rationality" of the Great Fear of 1789 (see p. 295). In effect, the practico-inert serves to connect a class of automatic and impersonal processes with underlying praxes while retaining a certain rationality of its own: "There is a *rationality* of the theoretical and practical behavior of an agent as a member of a series [a social whole mediated by the practico-inert]" (p. 266). It is the "logic" of otherness, of exteriority, of passivity, of alienation, of social impotence, and "flight." Indeed, Sartre refers to "serial Reason" as "a special case of dialectical Reason" (p. 642).

"Social objects," that is, what since Durkheim has constituted the subject matter of sociology, Sartre observes, "are at least in their basic structure, beings of the practico-inert field" (p. 253). Indeed, the practico-inert constitutes "fundamental sociality" for Sartre (p. 318). Those objects, divided into *collectives* (series and institutions) and *groups*,[38] are the concern of the historian as well, first because, in Marxist terms, they constitute the object and the subject of History respectively (see p. 255), and, second, because as *practico*-inert they transmit sedimented past praxis into the present field of action. No doubt, these are ideal types since concrete reality is an admixture of both in various degrees. Still, Sartre admits, "we can identify, at the extremes, groups in which passivity tends to disappear entirely . . . , and collectives that have almost entirely reabsorbed their group" (p. 254).

A social object of major importance for Sartre's theory of history is the socioeconomic class. He claims that "on the ontological plane . . . class-being is practico-inert" (p. 686). Yet its relation to the practico-inert holds at the level of meaning as well. Recall that the human is a signified-signifier. Regarding the practico-inert, he notes that each agent's actions are situated "within a framework of exigencies that cannot be transcended; they simply realize everyone's class-being. Everyone makes himself signifying by interiorizing, by a free choice, the signification with which material exigencies have produced him as a *signified being*. Class-being, as practico-inert being mediated by passive syntheses of worked matter, comes to men through men" (p. 238). In fact, he defines "objective class spirit" as "milieu for the circulation of significations" (p. 776). As the young person in the *Diaries* inherited a facticity that included the Great War, so the working class youth of the *Critique* discovers herself "signified" by her class status and her possibilities limited by this same class-being. The vehicle for such significations and objective possibilities is the practico-inert.

The second major instance of practico-inert mediation in Sartre's theory of history is his concept of *objective spirit* or "culture as practico-inert" (*IF* III, p. 44). It is introduced in the *Critique* mainly to account for that "circulation of significations" which enables the members of a class to interpret the meaning of a particular event, practice, or institution in light of class struggle. Thus the Parisian

Commune of 1871, the bourgeois practice of "respectability" (exchanging calling cards, social and economic malthusianism, personal abstemiousness, and the like), the great governmental bureaucracy as well as the aesthetic and religious norms of an epoch are all aspects of "objective spirit." In the context of material scarcity, that is, in Western history with its haves and have-nots, these forms of practico-inert mediation constitute a kind of violence, namely "the sentence of things upon persons" (*IF* III, p. 632).

Finally and perhaps most important, as modified by the brute fact of material scarcity (*la rareté*), the practico-inert marks human history as a continuous *violent* interchange. Assessing the human enterprise thus far, Sartre concludes: "Man lives in a universe where the future is a thing, where the idea is an object and where the violence of matter is the 'midwife of History' " (*CDR*, p. 181). One can scarcely exaggerate the role of violence, which Sartre describes as "interiorized scarcity," in his theory and his philosophy of history. Lest we link Sartre with irrationalism in history, it is important to note that for him "human violence is meaningful." Not only does it render intelligible the tragic course of class conflict in the Western world, including recent conflict within socialist states, but it emerges as itself something more than "the contingent ferocity of man," namely "everyone's intelligible reinteriorization of the contingent fact of scarcity" (*CDR*, p. 815). If the fact that scarcity renders practico-inert mediation violent gives a tragic tone to the voice of history, the contingency of scarcity, its superability, offers hope that Sartre's reign of freedom might be realized in a true "socialism of abundance" (*IF* III, p. 189).

Still, in his drive for dialectical intelligibility, Sartre has not claimed complete historical rationality. First among the limits to such intelligibility is the surd of material scarcity itself. There is a sense in which even this can be subsumed in a society of abundance that technology may usher in. But, of course, the "ontological" scarcities of time and space remain, not to mention that ultimate facticity which hovers over Sartre's existentialist universe.

A limiting form of facticity that directly implies temporality is what Sartre calls "the depth of the world" (*CDR*, p. 541). By this he means those serialities of the society out of which the group is engendered. Just as the for-itself relies on the in-itself of which it is the internal negation, so the group carries with it those practico-inert serialities that it is overcoming. They cloud its intelligibility even as they condition its being.

Besides the limits established by scarcity and facticity, complete historical (dialectical) intelligibility comes to grief on three other obstacles. First, the antidialectic of practico-inert *process*, like the capitalist or colonialist "systems" mentioned earlier, supports a "serial rationality" of its own. Second, totalization, as we have seen, cannot include the totalizer himself. The agent-historian is always "situated." Finally, the impossibility of free organic praxis being completely integrated into the group leaves the social dialectic of the group (the "constituted dialectic") ever short of full organic unity except as a kind of Kantian ideal (see *CDR*, p. 708).

Praxis and the mediating third: The two most significant conceptual innovations in the *Critique* are the practico-inert and the mediating third. The former accounts for the otherness and, modified by scarcity, the violence that colors human history. The latter carries the intelligibility of organic praxis to the interiority of the group. According to Sartre, each organic individual *is* a third, but this feature is submerged in seriality. "Nevertheless," he insists, "it *does* exist in each of us as alienated freedom" (*CDR*, p. 366).

The true "subject" of history is the close-knit group, in the sense that it overcomes the passiveness and exteriority of the practico-inert and achieves a degree of mutual recognition among freedoms that Sartre visualizes as the "reign of man." He has in mind those combat groups he experienced, if only vicariously, during the Resistance as well as those spontaneously formed bands of revolutionaries that sprang up during the French Revolution. "Our History is intelligible to us," he writes, "because it is dialectical, and it is dialectical because the class struggle produces us as transcending the inertia of the collective towards dialectical combat-groups" (*CDR*, p. 805). Notwithstanding his abiding interest in biography and his commitment to the ontological primacy of individual organic praxis, Sartre has admitted that historically the solitary individual is impotent.[39]

We needn't pursue the revolving set of practical relations that constitutes the inner life of the group. The "mediating third" is a functional concept denoting the praxis of the organic individual *as* group member, that is, as communicating identity of interest and purpose (each member is "the same" for the others in that regard and each action occurs "here" in terms of common concern) without claiming an impossible unity within some superorganism. This allows for a true "synthetic enrichment" of individual praxis, justifying such social predicates as "power," "function," "right/duty," and "fraternity-terror," while eschewing the collective consciousness of Durkheim or the organic theories of idealist social philosophers generally.

Above all, the function of the mediating third is to foster the fullest possible mutual understanding among the members of the group. This is the Sartrean ideal of positive *reciprocity* that forms the counter value to "alienation" in his writings after *Being and Nothingness*. Indeed, his discussions of "good faith" and "authentic love" in the *Cahiers* reveal him prizing positive reciprocity already in his vintage existentialist days (see *CM*, pp. 434 and 497). In the *Critique* he explains: "In reciprocity, my partner's praxis is, as it were, at root *my praxis*, which has broken in two by accident and whose pieces, each of which is a complete praxis on its own, both retain from their original unity a profound affinity and an immediate understanding" (*CDR*, p. 131). Again, the affinity is evaluative and the understanding practical. The partners have cast their lots together.

By calling the group's life and action "constituted dialectic" and that of the organic individual "constitutive," Sartre again underscores what we may term his *principle of the primacy of individual praxis*. He claims that the impossibility for a union of individuals to transcend organic action as a strictly individual model is *the basic condition of historical rationality*; in other words, "constituted dialectical Reason (as the living intelligibility of all common praxis) must always be related to its ever present but always veiled foundation, constituent rationality" (*CDR*, p. 678). In fact, early in the *Critique* he redescribes his project: "When our whole investigation is complete, we shall see that individual praxis . . . is at the same time constituting Reason itself, operating within History seen as constituted Reason" (p. 96). The master key to the logic of History, therefore, is that sequence of *mediations* which enables organic praxis to effect group activities or which deviate and maintain praxes in serial impotence as passive, manipulated "objects" of history. As Louis Althusser once remarked, Sartre is "the philosopher of mediations par excellence."[40]

Generically, Sartre's synchronic analysis has yielded praxis, the third, and the practico-inert as those crucial mediating factors. He further elaborates praxis and the practico-inert (the third is a specification of praxis), but he leaves us to establish empirically how they operate in historical fact. That is why he claims to deliver in the first volume of the *Critique*, "not the real concrete, which can only be historical, but the set of formal contexts, curves, structures, and conditionings that constitute the formal milieu in which the historical concrete must necessarily occur" (p. 671). It is the *double circularity* of the constituted dialectic, namely *static* (horizontal and vertical) and *dynamic* (perpetual movement that sooner or later degrades groups into collectives), "that constitutes the final moment of the dialectical investigation and, therefore, the concrete reality of sociality" (p. 671). More specifically, his intent is to demonstrate that "*if* classes do exist," then one is forced to choose either to grasp them by static, analytic reason that allows them "no more unity than the compact inertia revealed by geological sections" or to understand that "their moving, changing, fleeting, ungraspable yet *real* unity" comes to them from a "practical reciprocity of either a positive [cooperation] or a negative [violence] kind" (p. 794). Comprehension will terminate in discovering "a real project of violence [or counterviolence]" between members of opposing classes (p. 794). Situated in the "formal milieu" just analyzed, this is the understanding that dialectical Reason accords to history as we know it.

Critique of Dialectical Reason II

The unfinished and posthumously published second volume of the *Critique*, subtitled by its editor, "The Intelligibility of History," undertakes the progressive reconstruction of the Stalinist project of "socialism in one country" in order to understand the totalization of a "dictatorial" (as opposed to a bourgeois or "disunited") society. Part of a larger undertaking that would have comprised a study of bourgeois democracies before examining world history itself, these notes begin with the analysis of interpersonal struggles, on the assumption that, given the transcendental fact of material scarcity that colors all our historical relations, the intelligibility of history at the macro level will depend upon that of struggle on the micro plane. Moreover, if violence as "interiorized scarcity" turns history into a tale of conflicts, the *unity* of "History" will depend on discovering that struggle need not be dispersive, that it can be "enveloped" in a larger totalization. Volume II is Sartre's response to this challenge. So he moves progressively from the simple but abstract (two boxers fighting) to the complex but "concrete" in the Hegelian sense of "with its relationships fully determined" (class conflict in post-revolutionary Soviet society).

Since this work is the immediate continuation of the first volume, all of the foregoing concepts are operative here as well. There are, however, two interrelated terms, namely "enveloping totalization" and "incarnation," that play a role proper to this work. Because the latter, as we have seen, was originally introduced in an aesthetic context, it merits our attention in view of Sartre's "poetics" of history. The former is the key notion to the second volume of the *Critique*.

Incarnation: As the boxing match is the "incarnation" of the lived violence that permeates an exploitative society (Sartre cites the example of a black colonial fighting a proletarian from the provinces), so Stalin is the "incarnation" of Soviet bureaucracy in the 1930s. Like his earlier examples of Michelangelo's "David" and Rebeyorole's paintings, these are totalizations that constitute the *sens* of a society at a particular period of its development. But the examples from the *Critique* share the social ontology made possible by the introduction of praxis and the practico-inert in that work. So Sartre can now speak of every incarnation's being linked with the historical ensemble in two ways: first as a "condensation" of that ensemble and, second, as referring us to the "ensemble of practical significations" that relate it to the social, historical field (*CRD* II, p. 199). Though metaphorical and vague, these dimensions of the term gain meaning from his examples. Let us consider the boxing match.

Recall that the methodological context is one of dialectical reason. Sartre argues that any match is the public incarnation of *every* conflict and that such violent sports incarnate the fundamental violence of every society based on scarcity. "To the very extent that in a synthetic unification the part is totalization of the whole . . . ," he writes, "incarnation is a singular form of totalization. And by this we do not mean that it is its symbol or expression, but that it is realized really and practically as the totality producing itself here and now. Every boxing match incarnates all of boxing as incarnation of all fundamental violence" (p. 36). Sartre's point is that the reality of a network of institutions, practices, practical significations, and sedimented praxes from the viewpoint of dialectical reason (that does not subscribe to the "hyperorganicism" of Hegelian or Durkheimian social wholes) – this reality simply *is* the negative reciprocity of the boxers as it brings to concretion here and now the complex of relations that the progressive-regressive method lays bare. The boxing enterprise as a social object – that is, as an ensemble of significations and possible (and prohibited) practices – makes objectively possible the phenomenon called the boxer (see p. 30). This particular pugilist training for that specific match "incarnates" the boxing enterprise as a social whole. This is what is meant by incarnation as "condensation."

We recognize once more Hegel's "concrete universal" minus the organic social wholes: "Incarnation is precisely that: the concrete universal producing itself without cease as animation and temporalization of individual contingency. So it is that *a* punch like *a* dance is indissolubly singular and universal" (p. 50). Given the primacy of individual praxis, what results is "dialectical nominalism," as Sartre calls it. It is essential to his social ontology as to his mature theory of history in general that "there are only men and real relations between men" (*SM*, p. 76). Though the *sens* of the Renaissance that Michaelangelo's "David" incarnated in Sartre's earlier use of the term was closer to the emblematic, the relational, and temporalizing nature of dialectical reason in his subsequent works gives incarnation a greater ontological status and epistemological significance. Just as he recommended we grasp the abstract significance of the First World War through a comprehension of the Kaiser's individual project of living it, so he can urge that we understand the violence that permeates an exploitive society by looking closely at the life projects of individuals who choose to make their livings as pugilists. "Incarnation" is the intersection of what we have called the principles of the primacy of praxis and of totalization in Sartre's theory of history.

Enveloping totalization: A refinement of the term "macrototalization" introduced in the first volume, it is the central concept of Volume II and yet, as the editor of that volume admits, remains rather fluid and incomplete (p. 462). What it adds to the earlier term is reference to praxis-process as the higher level unities that embrace the totalizing praxes of individual and collective agents. When that reference is clear, it harkens back to the fundamental question of Volume I and of Sartre's theory of history generally, Can there be totalization without a totalizer? But sometimes throughout the notes that constitute the posthumously published second volume, Sartre employs the term as synonymous with totalization *tout court*.

Thus he writes that "each singular totalization is enveloping as totalization as well as enveloped as singularity" (p. 59). Accordingly, one and the same social reality, the dictatorship of Joseph Stalin, for example, can be examined in two distinct directions: the path of "decompressive expansion" preferred by Marxist historians, who focus on large, impersonal socioeconomic forces, and that of "totalizing compression" such as Sartre pursues in describing the incarnational moment of the boxing enterprise. The latter way of proceeding is in Sartre's view "the only one susceptible of grasping the dialectical intelligibility of an event" because it alone reveals at the heart of the event itself those interactions between praxis and mediating circumstances by which the *lived project* "condenses" these mediating factors, granting them concrete efficacy (p. 59). It is not difficult to recognize the progressive-regressive method mirrored in enveloping totalization as method to object of investigation. Sartre summarizes this relationship in terms of the *sens* a dialectical historian seeks via this method, when he writes: "The same reality will be enveloping totalization insofar as it is produced by the temporalization of historical agents and *sens* to the extent that it is reactualized by the work of the situated historian." But he reaffirms his early distrust of historical relativism when he adds that "*sens* is not relative to the historian who knows it" (p. 308).

Sartre's entire project of constructing a theory of history could be described as the search for historical unity. As we saw, it distinguished him from Raymond Aron at the outset and it continues to separate him from both "positivist" historians, who are "pluralistic" in their account of historical understanding, and orthodox Marxists, who purchase unity at the price of abstraction, discounting such mediating factors as intrafamilial relationships. In a famous remark, Sartre castigated Marxist "economists" for overlooking the

simple truth that although Paul Valéry was a petit bourgeois intellectual, not every petit bourgeois intellectual was Valéry (*SM*, p. 56). He
devotes the major portion of Volume II of the *Critique* to demonstrating a similar claim of Stalin. Though the dictator was no doubt the
product of the confluence of social forces that eased his ascent to
power, the particular manner in which this occurred (as well as its
actual occurrence) is attributable to the life project of this former
seminarian from Soviet Georgia who interacted with the agents of
the October Revolution to fortify the bureaucratic "pyramid" that in
turn strengthened him. If the October Revolution was the incarnation of the workers' struggle, Stalin was the incarnation of that
Revolution during the period of his rule (see *CRD* II, p. 238). Thus
the history of the Soviet state is realized in the person and behavior
of its leader, including his unique temporalization of "socialism in
one country" in accord with his biography. The historian must respect the unique internalization-externalization of Stalin's biography in order to grasp the *sens* of the sociohistorical whole that the
dictator incarnates.

The details of this proposal for historical comprehension were
never worked out. Indeed, Sartre came to realize that it would constitute a gigantic undertaking, too great for a single scholar. To the
extent that he did attempt such a dialectical investigation of an
agent and his era, it was with regard to a literary artist and issued in
that curious masterpiece, his three-volume work on Flaubert.

The Family Idiot

This detailed study of Flaubert and his age moves beyond *Critique I*,
the concepts of which it combines with those of existential psychoanalysis introduced in *Being and Nothingness* and employed in
Saint Genet, to yield a synthesis of Sartre's various works, focused
appropriately on the concrete way a gifted writer "chooses" the
world of imagination. The parallels with Sartre's earlier "biographies" are many, but what concerns us here is this work as the
culmination of Sartre's early plan to study history by uncovering an
"internal relation of comprehension" between the agent and his
time. What can we learn about the Second Empire and the decades
immediately preceding it from Flaubert's decision to follow a liter-

ary rather than a legal career, to write novels rather than poetry, and, above all, to produce *Madame Bovary?* In proposing his answer, Sartre makes far greater use of the concepts of objective spirit and totalization than previously and introduces the dialectical notion of a spiral of "personalization" as the vehicle for the progressive moment of his progressive-regressive method.

What Sartre terms the "objective spirit" of French society at the midpoint of the nineteenth century ("culture as practico-inert" [*IF* III, p. 44]) left the would-be writer little choice but what he calls "neurotic art" (*l'Art-Nevrose*). This term denotes a complex of attitudes that valued detachment, solitude, derealization, failure (*l'échec*), misanthropy, and nihilism. The impossible demands of society on contemporary artists, Sartre believed, made it necessary for them to become, or at least to act like, neurotics (imaginary men) in order to write (see pp. 65–6). The French under Louis-Philoppe were developing a self-image that was positivist and utilitarian, as personified by Flaubert's father, a leading physician in Rouen. Sartre sees the son's "choice" of neurotic art in his personal crisis of 1844 as both an antiutilitarian reaction and a prophetic anticipation of France's own option for the unreal in the person of Napoleon III, the nation in flight from the dark side of its image as revealed by the massacres of 1848. For Sartre, this is the deep reason for Flaubert's popularity in the Second Empire: The unreal was addressing the unreal. The phenomenon of *Madame Bovary*, its composition, the scandal at its publication, its reception by the upper classes – these "incarnate" Second Empire France (in the language of *Critique II*) and instantiate what we have termed Sartre's principle of totalization: "A man . . . totalizes his age to the precise degree that he is totalized by it" (*IF* III, p. 426).

A new term enters Sartre's lexicon, *personalization*, meaning "the surpassing and conserving (inner assumption and negation) at the heart of a totalizing project of what the world has made – and continues to make – of [the individual]" (*IF* I, p. 657). After uncovering the societal and familial conditions for Flaubert's "choice" of the imaginary (the regressive moment), Sartre traces four turns in the spirit of Flaubert's personalization: the imaginary child, the actor, the poet, and finally the novelist (the progressive move) – all forms of self-derealization wherein his ego remains an alter-ego, mirrored off family, friends, and public. Sartre interprets the final turn from poet to novelist as follows: "The *poetic* attitude was only the flight from the real to the imaginary; *artistic* activity consists in devaluing the real by realizing the imaginary" (*IF* II, p. 1488). At last his self-hatred and resentment converge with his project of personalization: In derealizing himself as artist, he will derealize the world. His vocation crystallizes on that traumatic night in late January 1844 near Pont-l'Évêque, when Gustave falls at his brother's feet in symbolic death to rise as artist, *l'homme imaginaire*. Such, in brief, is Sartre's reading of the events in Flaubert's personalization.[41]

The effect of over three thousand pages of description and analysis is to reveal how one unusually gifted person totalized his age in dialectical reciprocity with his society, which enrolled him in its list of elite (conferring on him the rosette of the Legion of Honor, which after Sedan he refused to wear). The work is not merely biography or simply cultural history. Its amalgam of existential psychoanalysis and historical materialism (lightly but unmistakably present in references to class struggle and the bourgeoisie), affords us simultaneously an enriched understanding of the society that nurtured Flaubert and a deep comprehension of Flaubert's grasp of himself in relation to his times. It was Sartre's expectation that the "dialectical" historian would do something similar for Joseph Stalin and Soviet society in the 1930s.

AN EXISTENTIALIST THEORY OF HISTORY

With the *Critique* and *The Family Idiot* we witness a truly "existentialist" approach to history. What makes it so are the following features. First, the preservation of existentialist-*moral* responsibility throughout the most tortuous workings of impersonal processes and collective endeavors. What we have called the "principle of the primacy of (individual) praxis" is the reason why Sartre is able to ascribe responsibility to individuals for the exploitive relations that seem to make such behavior necessary and hence inculpable. Sartre has always sought the oppressive action behind impersonal, exploitive relations. His theory of the *practico*-inert preserves the influence of previous praxes, and the genius of the "mediating third" is precisely to guard the responsibility of the group member in the midst of historically efficacious group activity. It is the primacy of praxis that attempts to carry into history the existentialist-moral claim from his vintage existentialism that "we are without excuse."

This same praxis as "self-translucid," second, grounds the dialectical intelligibility of concrete history. No doubt, practico-inert structures, essences, and the like, are intelligible without immediate reference to praxis. But they yield the abstract, conceptual knowledge proper to analytical reason. In the concrete social realm, that of series, groups, and institutions in interaction, the intelligibility is *dialectical* and the dialectic is constituted by individual, totalizing praxes.

The third feature of an existentialist theory is its respect for the specificity of the social, in opposition to methodological individualism, which tends to reduce the social to the psychological. It is precisely the function of the mediating third to steer a middle course between methodological holism and individualism in social theory. Although the group is a "synthetic enrichment" of individual action and irreducible to it, the collective subject of history is nothing more than praxes in practical relation; in no way is it a superorganism (as Sartre takes Durkheim's collective subject to be). Again, the point of this "dialectical nominalism" is to preserve the primacy of an (admittedly socially "enriched") organic praxis in historical understanding.

It is not surprising, fourth, to find a concept of collective bad faith operative in Sartre's historical analyses. This extrapolation of the dividedness of human reality to the collective domain is based on the concept of "objective spirit," which, in the case of the French industrial bourgeoisie in the late 1800s, for example, masked oppressive action under the ideology of the rights of man. It is the primacy of praxis once more that enables Sartre to apply categories from his existentialist classic to the analysis of nineteenth-century French social history.

Finally, the existentialist concept of committed literature is extended to *committed* history. Sartre's theory not merely analyzes but advocates a certain totalizing view. Indeed, his continued writing of the Flaubert study in the midst of the student uprising of 1968 was justified in part by the fact that this was a "socialist" theory of biography.[42] If, indeed, the historical "facts" are ambiguous, allowing for a multiplicity of readings, then the interpretation that emerges as "true" for our times is the one that gives hope and purpose to the oppressed of the world. That, in effect, is Sartre's guide for the writing of histories and biographies that totalize one another. The ideal that inspires these efforts is called variously the "city of ends," a "socialism of abundance," or simply "freedom."

The sustaining question of Sartre's theory of history, Can there be totalization without a totalizer?, must find its response in the features just listed. The *sens* that the dialectical historian discovers is the actualization of an enveloping totalization, which in turn reflects the dialectical interplay of organic praxis and its practico-inert conditions. But the primacy of organic praxis, which dialectical nominalism demands, seems to exclude any larger historical unity that is neither praxis nor a relation between praxes. The experience of dialectical necessity where the "exigencies" and counterfinalities of the practico-inert reveal their positive force, might be taken to support the claim that some larger logic is directing the unintended results of individual actions. Sartre's growing sense of objective possibility in his later works attests to the power of the practico-inert and the force of circumstances.[43] But he has neither the conceptual equipment nor, arguably, the need to interpret these necessities as anything more than the force of inertia (facticity) that praxis actualizes. Whether this force is unifying or disruptive, whether it furthers History or retards it, though dialectically dependent on the inertial force itself (the exercise of freedom is fostered by some conditions and thwarted by others), is, in the final analysis, up to the use or abuse of individual freedoms.

But so sweeping a theory is not without its difficulties, as the preceding paragraph suggests. No doubt the root problem is the ambiguity of the spontaneity–inertia duality that has permeated Sartre's ontology from the outset. The precise measure of the contribution of freedom and facticity, of praxis and the practico-inert to any situation is impossible to determine. But Sartre could reply that this is a problem only for analytical reason that seeks such "measures" in the first place.

More difficult to counter is the criticism that dialectical "nominalism" (there are only individuals and real relations between them) is not as nominalistic as Sartre claims; indeed, that if it denied the existence of "real" relations as nominalism should do, it would be incapable of accounting for the social causality of the practico-inert the way it does. Failure to work out a metaphysics of relations leaves Sartre vulnerable to the criticism of Merleau-Ponty and others that he ignores truly social causality.

A third problem concerns the absence of independent criteria by which to assess the "truth" of Sartre's historical accounts. Of course, the nature of historical truth is at issue in the *Critique*, and again, Sartre would dismiss the demand for such criteria as "analytic" in inspiration. But he typically employs a mixture of coherence and adequacy to (dialectical) experience as his warrants for the plausibility of his constructions. And their resonance with the demands of social equality confirms their truth in the moral sense.

Finally, the project of a "committed" history is more problematic than its equivalent in literature. Even granted the close relation between fictional and historical narrative that Ricoeur and others have defended recently, Sartre's enterprise comes perilously close to blurring the distinction entirely.

A POETICS OF HISTORY

In the course of my analysis of Sartre's theory of history from its inception in the *War Diaries* to *The Family Idiot*, I have stressed how his understanding of imaging consciousness and his aesthetics were ingredients in his approach. In fact, the raw material of history, the facts, events, institutions, and the like, serve only as an *analogon* for the history of the historians. They craft their product by a totalizing praxis that yields the configuration that respects individual freedom and responsibility while allowing for the deviations and counterfinalities of social causality. Moreover, just as the creative artist by an "act of generosity" communicates with another freedom via the artwork that invites that freedom's recreative response through reading, viewing, listening, and the like, so too the historian "creates" a narrative, not out of whole cloth, to be sure, but neither *"wie es eigentlich gewesen ist."* The successful historian *re*presents as *sens* the enveloping totalization under investigation. The point of "committed" history as of committed art is to lend a voice to the exploited and oppressed even as it unmasks the bad faith of individuals and societies, holding up a critical mirror to those (usually bourgeois) who accept the author's invitation.

Sartre's "existentialist" project of interrelating history and biography was set from the time he first recorded his reflections on Ernst Ludwig's biography of Wilhelm II in *The War Diaries*. Though he subsequently conceptualized that relationship by his notions of totalization and incarnating a *sens*, his existentialist psychoanalyses of various figures, including himself, were implicit "histories" of the times in which these figures worked out their life projects. In the case of Flaubert, this history became explicit. But "incarnation" and "totalization" remain essentially *aesthetic* categories for Sartre. They entail an imaginative appeal to a part–whole relationship in which the "singular universal" is constituted as such by our comprehensive grasp of the individual qua mediated by an indefinite network of conditions. As "existentialist," this account will always focus on the free, responsible organic praxis (the primacy of individual praxis), but as "history," it must incorporate those agents into social wholes, whether series, group, or institution. Still, the constitution is imaginative: "That was how it happened," he writes of Genet's having been surprised as a thief, "in that or some other way. . . . It does not matter. The important thing is that Genet lived and has not stopped reliving this period of his life *as if* it had lasted only an instant."[44] The "as if" is significant. It carries over to Sartre's reconstruction of that fateful night on the road to Pont l'Évêque when Gustave Flaubert had the (epileptic?) seizure that constituted his "choice" of a literary career that it likewise made possible. The Flaubert study, Sartre claims, is "a concrete application of the abstract principles that I gave in the *Critique of Dialectical Reason* to ground the intelligibility of History" (*ORR*, p. 77). That same work he characterizes as "a novel that is true" (*un roman vrai*).[45]

In a way not unlike that of pre-"scientific" historians, Sartre's concerns with theoretical history are political and moral. But this too is in full accord with his existentialist aesthetic. The reciprocity between an individual life and its collective context not only lends mutual intelligibility but moral and political hope as well: "You can always make something out of what had been made of you"[46] – the maxim of Sartrean humanism and the existentialist history it inspires.

NOTES

1 Jean-Paul Sartre, *L'Imaginaire* (Paris, 1940), p. 45. References are to the N.R.F. edition, *Collection Idées*. All translations throughout this essay, unless otherwise noted, are my own.

2 I have developed these points in my "The Role of the Image in Sartre's Aesthetic," *The Journal of Aesthetics and Art Criticism*, 33, no. 4 (Summer 1975): 431–42.

3 Etienne Barilier, *Les Petits camarades* (Paris: Julliard / L'Age d'Homme, 1987), p. 35.

4 See, for example, "The Itinerary of a Thought," reprinted in Jean-Paul Sartre, *Between Existentialism and Marxism*, tr. John Mathews (New York: William Morrow and Company, 1974), pp. 34–5.

5 Jean-Paul Sartre, *Les Carnets de la drôle de guerre* [*The War Diaries*] (Paris: Gallimard, 1983), p. 227, hereafter cited as *CDG*.

6 Raymond Aron, *Introduction à la philosophie de l'histoire* (Paris: Gallimard, Collection TEL, 1981), p. 349.

7 His dialectical nominalism, however, does allow for a kind of collective, that is, social, subject as we shall see in our analysis of the *Critique*.

8 "Human reality," Sartre's translation of Heidegger's *Dasein*, becomes the "everyman" of existentialist philosophy.

9 I trace the genesis and nature of this social ontology in my *Sartre and Marxist Existentialism* (Chicago: University of Chicago Press, 1984; paper, 1986), chs. 5 and 6.

10 "So the event is ambiguous: nonhuman insofar as it encloses and surpasses all human reality, insofar as the in-itself regrasps the for-itself that escapes it by nihilating itself; human in that, as soon as it appears, it becomes 'of the world' (*du monde*) for other human realities who make it 'blossom' (*éclore à soi*), who transcend it and for whom it becomes *situation*" (*CDG*, p. 364). The ambiguity of the historical event will be a major theme of the *Cahiers*.

11 Foucault's directive was to change documents into monuments. See *The Archaeology of Knowledge*, tr. Alan M. Sheridan-Smith (New York: Harper & Row, 1972), p. 7.

12 Although lacking Sartre's powers of psychological description, much less his philosophical theory, Ludwig supports Sartre's approach when he writes in his Preface: "In short, this is an attempt to trace from the idiosyncrasies of a monarch the direct evolution of international political events – from his essential nature, the course of his country's destiny" (Emil Ludwig, *Wilhelm Hohenzollern*, tr. Ethel Colburn Mayne [New York: G. P. Putnam's Sons, 1927], p. x).

13 With characteristic honesty he admits: "My own way of being my [bad] eye is certainly my way of wishing to be loved by seduction of the spirit" (CDG, p. 371).

14 I develop these matters in the first two chapters of my Sartre and Marxist Existentialism.

15 Jean-Paul Sartre, Cahiers pour une morale (Paris: Gallimard, 1983), p. 31, hereafter cited as CM.

16 See Jean-Paul Sartre, Being and Nothingness, tr. Hazel E. Barnes (New York: Philosophical Library, 1956), p. 165, hereafter cited as BN; "There must be duality at the heart of freedom, and this duality is precisely what we call detotalized totality" (CM, p. 345).

17 See Search for a Method, tr. Hazel E. Barnes (New York: Random House, Vintage Books, 1968), pp. 26 and 124, hereafter cited as SM.

18 See Sartre and Marxist Existentialism, pp. 59 et passim.

19 We should note that this is how he describes "freedom" as well (see CM, p. 339).

20 "Nothing can act on History without being in History and in question in History" (CM, p. 50). This principle, which parallels his understanding of consciousness and his resultant opposition to psychological determinism in Being and Nothingness, constitutes his chief objection to historical materialism. By insisting on a one-way influence between economics and the superstructure, he argues, this theory places economics in effect outside history, despite its reference to the history of tools and technology. On the contrary, Sartre argues, if religion and ethics, for example, are affected by economics, the converse is equally true: "the economic is afloat in religion and ethics" (CM, p. 50).

21 See Jean-Paul Sartre, Critique of Dialectical Reason, tr. Alan Sheridan-Smith (London: New Left Books, 1976), p. 206, hereafter cited as CDR.

22 Sartre takes the term ekstasis from Heidegger and defines it as "distance à soi" (distance from itself) (EN, p. 183); that is, internal distance or non-self-identity. I am not what I am in the past, the present, or the future (Editor's note).

23 This is the moral of his Genet study four years later: "This game of hide-and-seek will end only when we have the courage to go to the limits of ourselves in both directions at once," Jean-Paul Sartre, Saint Genet, Actor and Martyr, tr. Bernard Frechtman (New York: George Braziller, 1963), p. 599.

24 See my "History as Fact and as Value: The Posthumous Sartre," in Sander H. Lee, ed., Inquiries into Values (Lewiston, N.Y.: Edwin Mellen Press, 1988), pp. 375–90.

25 Jean-Paul Sartre, Critique of Dialectical Reason, Vol. I, Theory of Practical Ensembles, tr. Alan Sheridan-Smith (London: New Left Books, 1976),

p. 822, hereafter cited as CDR. The quotation is taken from the Preface to the combined edition of *Search* and the *Critique*, partially omitted in the English translation of *Search*.

26 Raymond Aron, *La Philosophie critique de l'histoire* (Paris: Vrin, Collection Points, 1969), p. 175.

27 Thus in the later Sartre, even that sanctuary of infallible self-awareness, the preflective *cogito*, seems liable to external influence. Speaking of Flaubert's "truth-sickness," for example, he observes: "Presence to self for each of us possesses a rudimentary structure of praxis. . . . At the very level of nonthetic consciousness, intuition is conditioned by individual history" (*L'Idiot de la famille*, 3 vols. [Paris: Gallimard, 1971–2]), Vol. I, p. 148, hereafter cited as *IF*. See my "Praxis and Vision: Elements of a Sartrean Epistemology," *The Philosophical Forum*, 8 (Fall 1976): 30–1.

28 Jean-Paul Sartre, *Situations*, 10 vols. (Paris: Gallimard, 1947–76), Vol. IV, p. 30, hereafter cited as *Sit*. This parallels roughly his distinction made in *What Is Literature?* between "poetry" and "prose" respectively.

29 For such identification see *Sit* VIII, pp. 445–6, 449–50, and IX, p. 178.

30 See Jean-Paul Sartre, *Critique de la raison dialectique*, Vol. II, ed. Arlette Elkaïm-Sartre (Paris: Gallimard, 1985), pp. 207ff, hereafter cited as *CRD* II.

31 Still, Sartre does speak of Flaubert's "realism" as a "reciprocal symbolization" with regard to the social and political evolution of the petite bourgeoisie in the Second Empire (see *SM*, p. 57f.).

32 Jean-Paul Sartre, *Saint Genet: Actor and Martyr*, tr. Bernard Frechtman (New York: The New American Library, Mentor Books, 1963), p. 137, hereafter cited as *SG*.

33 Though he attributes this threefold method to the Marxist sociologist Henri Lefebvre (see *SM*, p. 52 n.), Sartre had employed the term and a form of the method before Lefebvre's work appeared. See, for example, *L'Imaginaire*, p. 435, and *BN*, p. 460. He insists it is a valid method "in all the domains of anthropology" (*SM*, p. 52 n.).

34 I have argued this point in some detail in "Merleau-Ponty and the *Critique of Dialectical Reason*" in *Hypatia*, ed. William M. Calder III, Ulrich K. Goldsmith, and Phyllis B. Kenevan (Boulder: Colorado Associated University Press, 1985), pp. 241–50. It should be noted that Ronald Aronson has developed the thesis at length in his *Sartre's Second Critique* (Chicago: University of Chicago Press, 1987).

35 I discuss these matters in detail in *Sartre and Marxist Existentialism*, ch. 6.

36 See, for example, Paul Ricoeur, *Time and Narrative*, tr. Kathleen Balmey and David Pellauer, 3 vols. (Chicago: University of Chicago Press, 1984–8), Vol. 3, pp. 119ff.

37 "Exigency is *always* both man as a practical agent and matter as a worked product in an indivisible symbiosis" (*CDR*, p. 191).

38 The practico-inert ensemble (series or institution) is "the matrix of groups and their grave" (*CDR*, p. 635). One dimension of the dynamic unity of the group is its ongoing resistance to the serial dispersion from which it arose and to the institutional alienation toward which it tends.

39 Jean-Paul Sartre, Philippe Gavi, and Pierre Victor, *On a Raison de se revolter* (Paris: Gallimard, 1974), p. 171, hereafter cited as *ORR*.

40 Louis Althusser et al., *Lire le capital*, 2 vols. (Paris: Maspero, 1965), Vol. 2, p. 98.

41 The two preceding paragraphs are taken from my essay, "Sartre-Flaubert and the Real/Unreal," in Hugh J. Silverman and Frederick A. Elliston, eds., *Jean-Paul Sartre, Contemporary Approaches to His Philosophy* (Pittsburgh: Duquesne University Press, 1980), pp. 108–9, used with permission.

42 See *ORR*, pp. 73–4.

43 See my *Sartre and Marxist Existentialism*, pp. 72–84, as well as Thomas W. Busch, *The Power of Consciousness and the Force of Circumstances in Sartre's Philosophy* (Bloomington: Indiana University Press, 1990).

44 *SG*, p. 17, italics mine.

45 *Sit* IX, p. 123.

46 *Sit* IX, p. 101.

8   Sartre on progress

How does one of the twentieth century's great thinkers help us illuminate one of its great paradoxes? What does Sartre contribute toward clarifying the problem of thinking about history as it has emerged in the late twentieth century? After a century and a half of celebrating and living by the idea of progress, amidst staggering scientific-technological progress, almost no one in the West continues to believe in progress. In the current climate of intellectual disillusionment no serious thinker is willing to defend Bury's formulation that the world is slowly advancing in "a definite and desirable direction" leading to a "condition of general happiness" that will "justify the whole process of civilization."[1] On the one hand, the postmodernist temper shows, as Lyotard says, "incredulity toward metanarratives" such as the idea of progress.[2] On the other, the current mood seems sympathetic toward *negative* metanarratives – those that suggest that things are getting worse. Witness, for example, the remarkable success of Allan Bloom's *The Closing of the American Mind*, or the works of Christopher Lasch – which suggest that as time goes by, we are losing the most vital of values, attitudes, and skills. The negative mood is starkly captured in Theodor Adorno's claim: "No universal history leads from savagery to humanitarianism, but there is one that leads from the slingshot to the megaton bomb."[3]

Still, genuine beneficial progress is all around us: scientific advancement, technological development, the incredible increase of human powers. Postmodernism notwithstanding, can we avoid noticing all the ways in which, over generations, human betterment has indeed occurred? Fashionable as statements such as Adorno's have become, they ignore the evidence that the last two centuries have seen enormously favorable cumulative changes, not only tech-

261

nological, but also economic, social, and political. Certainly we have not witnessed the interlinked advance of education, science, industry, democratic politics, social and political equality, and consequent general human happiness forecast, for example, by Condorcet's *Sketch for a Historical Picture of the Progress of the Human Mind* (1794). But in spite of all qualifications, one can point to genuine historical improvement in a number of vitally important realms, from science and technology to medicine and hygiene, industrial and agricultural productivity to the democratization of culture, education, and opportunity. And one can argue a more controversial point, namely that over time there have also been definite kinds of progress in social morality. Human beings have insisted through struggle, often successfully, that other human beings treat them better: In the past two hundred years a much fuller sense of human dignity has become widespread, and social systems have become more and more universal, more committed to granting, expanding, and protecting the rights of their members.

SARTRE AND PROGRESS?

How do we make sense of both the negative and positive trends? What is their relationship? It would seem at first that Sartre is not the thinker to help us. First, his reflections on the issue are few and far between: throughout the equivalent of dozens of volumes of published works, only a mention in his famous 1945 lecture, a note in *Search for a Method* (1957), and one serious reflection in *The Family Idiot* (1972). In addition, the posthumously published *Cahiers pour une morale* (1947–8) contains several brief reflections on the question, and an appendix to the second volume of *Critique of Dialectical Reason* contains twenty pages of notes written in 1961–2.

But more important, he never believed in, and he seems to have dismissed, the notion of progress. Consider his statement on progress in the notorious lecture, *Existentialism Is a Humanism*, explaining why "we do not believe in progress":

Progress is betterment. Man is always the same. The situation confronting him varies. Choice always remains a choice in a situation. The problem has not changed since the time one could choose between those for and those against slavery, for example, at the time of the Civil War, and the present

time, when one can side with the [*Mouvement Républicain Populaire*], or
with the Communists.[4]

Dismissive of claims of improvement, oblivious to positive historical trends since the middle of the nineteenth century, Sartre would
seem an unlikely candidate to help us think our way through the
intellectual and historical contradictions of this idea and reality today. Such a discussion, about long-term and contemporary historical
tendencies and how to theorize them, falls outside Sartre's purview.
Wasn't he, after all, in so many ways a premature postmodernist?
Not only did he seem oblivious to specific forms of progress, but he
also rejected the prevailing faith in, and fascination with, science
and technology. And from the beginning he rejected transcendent
ethical norms just as he rejected universal ideas. Indeed, he theoretically rejected all such totalizing concepts as forcefully as he rejected
the notion of society or any other "hyperorganism" – as not stem-
ming from and reducible to individual praxis.

PROGRESS MADE AND UNMADE

It is perhaps appropriate, then, that Sartre's first mention of progress
in the *Cahiers* skeptically connects the question of progress with the
meaning of history, raising themes that will later become important
in the *Critique*. In a sense, Sartre is working out the implications of
his philosophy for an understanding of history. He contrasts "Hegel's myth" that history is a totalized totality animated by, and
cohering in, a single Mind, thus revealing "direction, therefore progress," with the equally correct attitude that, "alienated from itself
by the nothingness that traverses it," history shows neither progress
nor direction. In the one view Mind creates, indeed is, the totality of
a single history; in the other, contingency and detotalization reign,
and the very reality of a single history is not progress but marking
time. Sartre seems to be suggesting that even if it may be argued that
a single monodirectional Hegelian History with a capital H is operative, also operative are the (much more important) pluralistic fractur-
ing, splintering, and detotalizing revealed by an existentialist perspective based on the "irreducible individuality of the person."[5]

We can thus point to the persistence of oppression, he suggests,
and even its worsening over time. Today sees proletarian and capital-

ist as the past saw slave and master, and we can even point to the *loss* of the former domestic intimacy and the *rise* in the number of suicides. On the other hand, the slave was a thing; "modern man is only alienated" (p. 31), meaning that his freedom, if mystified, has been recognized. Both the detotalizing and the totalizing, by which he seems to mean regression and progress, must be taken into account without hierarchizing these opposing aspects as philosophy has traditionally done (for example, by speaking of the appearance of disorder and the reality of order, or of contingency in details and necessity in the whole).

What then is progress? The reference to slave and worker suggests a kind of amelioration of social relations. How is this related to Sartre's concern for the tension between unity and plurality, a single History and irreducible individuality, totalization and detotalization? Clearly these dimensions are related, but how is not yet clarified or distinguished. Sartre suggests only a common view of "the philosophers," which he first rejects but will later discuss as his own, namely that "progress is the development of order" (p. 31). To the already noted oppositions Sartre adds another related one, deeply rooted in his basic concepts, which eventually will help clarify the others: between the given and the transcending of the given. Time consists of an endless number of autonomous moments and also consists of a series of synthetic transcendings of what has been given. "The transcendence of the moment is in spite of everything, because of the totalizing link, a means of progressing" (p. 32). In this sense progress can be seen as a going beyond the given (toward its fuller integration, its greater order?) that is built into the very nature of human experience. But as soon as Sartre seems to be suggesting that there is a tendency toward unity, toward a single ever-more-integrated History carried out by an ever-more-integrated humanity, he balks and instead asserts his other irreducible themes: individuality and plurality. Consciousness, always individual, is always an autonomous upsurge in an absolutely new situation and indeed itself defines that situation's meaning – which leads, inevitably, to breaks of continuity.

Even if the previous generation bequeaths its discoveries and inventions, these only form part of the new situation faced by individuals of the current generation. Firearms, for example, are a decisive advantage against wild animals, but they also intensify human strug-

gles. "The given is always problematic. Nothing is learned from it
[*On ne capitalise pas*], precisely because there is no single *one* being
who can capitalize on it (recognized in the commonsense saying:
Others' experience never helps us)" (p. 32). History is thus an "ideal
continuity perpetually broken by real discontinuity" (p. 33). Sartre
stenographically sums up the key ideas so far:

Impossible synthesis of the continuous and the discontinuous. Made and
unmade like Penelope's tapestry. Constant progress from M to M (1) insofar
as the generation M leaves from M and progresses as far as M (1). Movement
broken by nothingness: death and birth. At the distance of a birth and a
death, what was progress becomes proposed situation, that is, closed in on
itself and problematic. However it remains a fact that a return is impossible.
(p. 33)

PROGRESS LIVED OR IMPOSED FROM THE OUTSIDE

So far Sartre has attacked the notion of a single, continuous historical process. There is no subject to this process, and each generation
begins over again. In Sartre's next reflection in the *Cahiers* we can
see emerge a second inevitable conflict between his major philosophical premises and the historical idea of progress. He attacks one
of the key implications of virtually all notions of progress: that one
can decipher a pattern of advancement not recognized by the actors
themselves, a "cunning of history." Events that the participants experience negatively may actually have a positive historical effect.
Sartre sides with the way historical actors see themselves against
the way they may be seen by subsequent generations. Those living
in the ancient and medieval worlds did not see the passage from
Greek cities to Roman state unification as progress; nor from poly-
theism to monotheism; nor from "immediate man to reflected subjectivity." Indeed, "Christianity is not progress for the last pagans, it
is decadence . . ." (p. 47). What does it mean to distinguish objective
progress from the way history is lived and felt? It is indeed a "retro-
spective illusion" to give the

lived history of preceding generations an unconsciously lived meaning that
in fact cannot be lodged anywhere and which is only our way of living prior
history. If moreover we admit the existence of a *law of progress*, this law of
progress, not being lived by men, becomes an obligation-object [*consigne-*

chose], it is extrahistorical and is defined in the eternal. It therefore kills History. In a world for progress to be able to be one of the meanings of History, it must descend into History as lived, willed, and suffered progress. (p. 47)

When we proclaim that progress takes place *without its agents knowing about it*, we are operating a kind of "dupery, an essential mystification that steals their lived temporality from them" (p. 47). Does this mean that we must limit ourselves to the past's comprehension of itself? Are we restricted, by their blinkers, to their narrow lucidity? In other words, we may ask, is a given period's subjective consciousness an absolute? Sartre doesn't address this beyond minimal acknowledgment that, after all, those who made the history don't "know all the elements of their history and therefore take risks" (p. 47). By imposing an external law on it which acts on it from the outside, any law of progress destroys history – which is, after all, a "taking of risks." Moreover, all human beings act to improve their condition: We see in their lived immediacy millions of steps of a "*natural* progress." But this is local and immediate, and does not unite or refer to "future humanity."

In short, Sartre lays absolute stress on the consciousness of the actors themselves: "for the totality of events to be interpreted as progress, it must be judged and lived as such by a present society" (p. 48). This means either that we experience a happy and just society – an absolute end – being attained or, which is rather the case, that the given society sees *itself as producing* a better world. In other words, progress would become a "conscious factor of the historical project." History cannot be seen as progress when it is passively contemplated from the outside, but only as a mode of action that is lived as progress. The past, to address the most perplexing problem, can be viewed through the lenses of progress, but not, one might suppose, as an absolute truth developed in contemplation from our superior perspective. Rather, Sartre stresses, we can regard the past through the perspective of progress insofar as we use it as an instrument from which we draw "the necessary elements of future progress (for example, the spirituality of Christianity). Thus the past becomes progressive by the hypothesis-project of present progress, which is by a decision to orient history and which interprets prior history as its own antecedent" (p. 48).

Indeed, the project of progress cannot avoid seeing *itself* as "progressively prepared" by the past.[6]

There is, however, one "partial case" of progress, which has been "lived as real," namely science.[7] Through it, *Homo sapiens* has actually been able "to know more and to adapt his techniques of knowing to reality" (p. 49). It is taken as a model for the modern conception of progress as well as a source of social progress. For example, its principle of equality before the truth "prepares the democratic ideal." In fact, human subjectivity transcends science toward *its own* ends, and may even force its democratic appeal to deviate into antidemocratic directions. For example, ever more costly weapons can be possessed only by modern states, which consequently gain increased ability to hold their people at bay. In any event, we are now in a *progressive* period of history when the vast majority acts according to "the myth of a certain kind of progress." While not an objective reality, progress has become a "factor transformed by history itself" (p. 48). From this point on, progress becomes a goal of human action and struggle. Thus whether or not history has really been the unfolding of Mind, attaining this "single-Consciousness that is the ideal subject of history" (p. 49) can actually become a collective human project.

Yet, by being placed at the center of our self-understanding and our understanding of the past, progress "becomes inert thing for one group, while being lived as oriented activity for another" (p. 49). Conservatives respond by denying progress and taking it as an illusion; its proponents take it as an omnipresent law of all change. Third, seen as a means (which it is "by nature"), progress can be seen as leading to a variety of ends. Because man acts as he sees himself, and because action produces new situations, Sartre concedes that the "syncretic organization of the whole is real but indeterminate progress" (p. 50). Moreover, inasmuch as progress is not a law of history but a "secondary structure" seeking to be history's total structure, Sartre concludes that there is "a deprogressive progress."

PROGRESS AS OTHER

Real but indeterminate, *de*progressive: Sartre does not immediately explain what he means by these terms. They suggest that progress is more than a subjective project, but just what is never made clear. Sartre's next remarks on progress turn on the idea that "history is always *other* than itself" (p. 52). Whatever we create always becomes *other* than what we intended: History is "infinite alterity." Indeed, this seems to be the primary result of acting in history, "that the act always becomes *other* than its conception" (p. 53). Of course, we never return to our starting point because we make "material progress toward unity." But beyond the new, more structured unification that we effect lies "the same diversity, the same alterity" – therefore, "there is no progress" (p. 55).[8]

Sartre develops this in terms that foreshadow the *Critique of Dialectical Reason:*

> History is the *Other.* Whatever one does, whatever one makes, the enterprise becomes other, it is by its alterity that it acts and its results are *other* than those that have been hoped for. It has the unity of the other which contains in itself infinite alterity and it is always *other* than that which it is said to be, whatever one says. This is logical since History is the history of men insofar as they are all for each, each for the *others.* (p. 51, emphasis in original)

The irony of progress and indeed, the only possible attitude toward history, is that we can never recognize the world we have constructed, can never know what we have done. We must accept, in the words of an unnamed source, "that we will lead men to the threshold of the promised land and that we will stay on the threshold watching them go off into the distance" (p. 51). History always escapes its makers.

PROGRESS AS THE DEVELOPMENT OF ORDER

Earlier Sartre mentioned, then returned to, the notion of progress as development of order. The order was originally regarded as only partial, however, because it seemed to be braked by a certain passivity that cannot be touched by our action, a configuration of past being, gathered in what we know as an *essence.* "There *are* essences," Sartre said; "the novel becomes what it was" (p. 51). When he returns to this idea, *essence* is the very meaning of order. The *"real* and oriented evolution of certain realities toward their essences" may indeed lead to a final uniting of object and essence, followed by their mutual death. Sartre's examples are cultural – Greek, French, and Roman tragedy – but he generalizes to what appears to be any "perfecting of an object or tool" (p. 80).[9]

Progress as order seems to mean two things: first, as suggested, an object achieving its potentiality or essence; second, a better, tighter organization of the object and, indeed, the entire practical field. The goal seems to be to suppress the disorder with which we began. The notion of progress thus affirms "the ontological priority of order over disorder, since it is by order that disorder is constituted as such, and the ontic priority of disorder that *is* while order is not (is in potentiality)" (p. 445). Sartre would escape from the circularity of Hegel, Comte, and Engels regarding this question (that is, order is the meaning of disorder and disorder is the first state of order) by referring to human reality. It is humans who distinguish between the *given* (disorder) and its *projected* secret (order). "Thus *a* consciousness projecting order as end and as beyond disorder can consider its operation, which consists of ordering this disorder, as *progress*. In this sense action and progress are one and the same" (p. 445).

In this discussion of order it seems first as if Sartre is developing a way of talking about progress as development without talking about amelioration. But, to return to an earlier issue, to think a single meaningful path of progress, it is still necessary to see a *single* consciousness or Mind lying behind it, that of God. If we are talking about human progress, "it is necessary to assimilate humanity to *one* consciousness to conceive progress as one" (p. 446). Who then is the subject of progress? Progress is "logically possible only if we conceive *one* human nature that develops itself according to a plan established through a plurality of individuals, the external universe remaining constant – or if we conceive a series of generations whose goal and own possibility are unchanging and each one of whom picks up the functional work where the other left it off" (p. 446). The root problem is that in reality there is a plurality of individuals. Each person's order is not everyone else's. Each person begins in a different situation and makes a different choice.

At the end of his reflections in the *Cahiers* Sartre anticipates the concept of the "practico-inert" that will be so central in the *Critique*. Each generation's result, he says, "instead of magically leading the next generation to pursue the effort, falls outside the subjective into the objective Mind and gives itself without defense to a

new transcendence" (p. 446). In other words, rather than one generation's intentions and projects straightforwardly becoming the next's,
they become the given, the starting point, the situation from which
the next generation develops *its* intentions and projects. Sartre's
discussion on this point is especially illuminating, and, inasmuch as
it bears on the very possibility of social progress, I will quote it at
length.

What happens from generation to generation (and also in space) is the perpetual fall and transformation of subject into object. What was goal becomes
starting point. But as a result, *disorder*. Instead of the unity of a single
consciousness the intermediate result is both disorder and preparation for
order: it is a mediation. But if one must start all over from the beginning,
the mediation is lost, it remains obstacle. What was the Same becomes the
Other. Christianity as subjective operation of liberation becomes, for the
next generation, crystallized given and the principle of human government.
Perpetual opposition between the *given* order which is disorder for the new-
comers (the *established* order) and the living disorder (negation of order)
which is subjective order. Everyone returns to the other the characterization
of "disorder." Thus the situation always remains the same: a disorder
(which is subjective order of the living operation transformed into object)
starting from which consciousness exercises its negativity. (p. 446)

The next generation always begins anew, and the previous generation's achievements always become the next one's situation. For
these reasons – and because each individual's project differs from
everyone else's – human beings, we might say, are forever barred
from becoming humanity, from attaining the single consciousness of
a single project unfolding over history.[10]

But, it might be objected by proponents of progress, each generation's project begins from the specific place where the previous generation's left off, and takes those results as its given. Moreover,
moving from ancient society to Marxism, ideologies can be seen as
being more and more inclusive – another form of progress. Sartre's
reply is that each ideology itself becomes other – that is, when it
ceases to be active consciousness of a project and instead becomes
established as a given. In so doing, it inevitably *imprisons* more and
more people. What seems to be progress, then, is rather progress and
marking time (*piétinement*) (p. 32).

If, in spite of all possible objections, it is still possible to conceive
of progress, this is because, beyond the plurality of individual con-

sciousnesses, we claim to discover a unity, such as Mind. Hegel sees Mind as a substance that stands behind, and is realized by, individual consciousnesses. In other words, progress would be constructed "on the ruins of the *cogito*. One must choose: either progress is necessary or it is not – either one starts from the Other and progress is the order of the Other to which consciousnesses are submitted, subordination of the subject to Mind – or indeed progress is perpetually contested, lost, aberrant" (p. 447).

And so, by the end of Sartre's last reflections on the question in his 1947–8 notebooks, it would seem that the structure of being and of human action rule out the expectation of steady progress from one generation to the next or over generations. History seems a perpetual making and unmaking, whose results always become other than we anticipate. Progress is always in question. No single mind unites our actions into a single direction and meaning. Science alone suggests the steady accumulation of positive results, without deflections or undoings, that we regard as progress. We may still read a pattern of progressive development into the past, against the consciousness of those who lived in earlier times, but this reflects our own project rather than any steady improvement unnoticed by contemporaries. When history does seem to evolve in the direction of something we might call progress, it is progress in the development of order, which Sartre leaves unexplored. His characteristic stress on the specificity, plurality, and separation of consciousnesses seems to undermine belief in any kind of transcendent force or law of progress.

PROGRESS, TEMPORALITY, AND HUMAN PRAXIS

Ten years after these notes, in his second published comment on progress, Sartre adds another skeptical element. It follows a discussion of how the correct understanding of the dialectical temporality of history entails seeing humans as not being *in* time but rather as seeing time created *by* them.

Marxism caught a glimpse of true temporality when it criticized and destroyed the bourgeois notion of "progress" – which necessarily implies a homogeneous milieu and coordinates which would allow us to situate the point of departure and the point of arrival. But – without ever having said so – Marxism has renounced these studies and preferred to make use of "progress" again for its own ends.[11]

In other words the idea of progress as it has become dominant in modern life – the notion that human history is guided by a force of continuous, steady improvement, which is at root scientific and technical – distorts the proper understanding of temporality. It does so by claiming that humans are subject to forces beyond our control, which act *upon* us. Just as we are not subject to a single Mind, neither are we subject to History. Humans themselves act – separately and from generation to generation – and that is all.

CHANGING TO STAY THE SAME

Is progress thus unlikely, ruled out as a long-term trend by the very structure of human reality? Other dimensions of human reality – freedom and constant transcendence – suggest a very different way of looking at the question. In fact, Sartre has more to say on the issue of progress and will return to rethink it, more than a dozen years after putting aside the *Cahiers*. In 1961–2, Sartre returns to the question of progress in notes that have been appended to the posthumously published Volume II of *Critique of Dialectical Reason*. These twenty-three pages under his own title of *Progress* are the only sustained exploration of the topic in the entire Sartrean corpus.

At the outset, Sartre turns from considering progress in history, the theme of the reflections in the *Cahiers* and his note in *Search for a Method*, to exploring progress in relation to concrete human praxis. Here Sartre is less concerned than he was earlier about social progress in historical time and now seems to focus on a very local and specific kind of progress as a necessary aspect of human praxis as such.

Returning to the *Cahiers'* attack on the "cunning of history" but now using the language of the *Critique*, Sartre asserts that progress has meaning only as "*lived* in interiority, as practical organization of totalization." And then he presents his new emphasis: "It is an *act* – meaning above all the act of an individual."[12] Whether or not progress exists in history, Sartre says, our effort to use the term to describe the total meaning of history is only an extrapolation of a more basic meaning of progress, which he will now explore. Any individual, as free practical organism seeking simply to reproduce his life, must needs create something new. And this *new* is always problematic: It is never as originally envisioned, always imposes changed conditions, including the creation of counterfinalities and changed consciousness on the part of the acting subjects. In the *Cahiers* we saw Sartre speak of the alterity or otherness of our actions in history; now, having moved to the individual level, he explores this theme using the tools of the *Critique*, especially *praxis* and *practico-inertia*.[13]

The free practical organism, acting only to survive, will posit, grasp, or recognize its goal as a transcendent end it will "throw ahead" (*pro-jete*) of it. In this sense, "only a praxis can recognize progress. In other words, progress is a *practical structure* in its dialectical completion" (p. 413). The simplest and perhaps most striking way to put this is to say that progress is nothing more and nothing less than *labor*. Even at this rudimentary level, praxis as progress implies, among other things, the practical comprehension of a developing praxis and its transcendent goal. "Progress = a contradiction between permanence and change. In fact in this contradiction one term always escapes man as *agent*" (p. 413) – its result always remains external to action even if it was its goal. Every action, even one achieving a "positive counterfinality," has its practico-inert consequences: "a positive transcendence of the practical field by me, of me by my totalizing effort, of me by the practical field" (p. 418), leading to a *new* being and a *new* field. And so the paradox that "identity is singled out against change but is obtained by change and, as a result, is changed in its very reality. Changing to stay the same" (p. 412).

Is it possible to foresee the changes and control them? Sartre had discussed this issue in a different tonality near the end of the second *Critique*.[14] No, he now insists, because time cannot be reversed, change cannot be undone: since circularity is impossible the new situation can never fully be foreseen. A new situation itself retotalizes the practical field that projected it, including the agents who carried it out. Sartre summarizes:

the contradiction of progress
is that
    foresight is necessary: the end is pro-jected in order to be attained, and, in a certain way, something is known, something is pro-jected; but, on the

other hand, foresight, the original pro-ject or end, is itself retotalized by the attained goal and cannot in any way foresee its own concrete retotalization. It foresees that it will be retotalized but not how.

Thus *in progress* we go towards what we want (goal) and what we would not be able to want nor to foresee (totalizing end).

Besides work transforms us and we arrive *other* at the pursued end. (pp. 416–17)

Sartre comes to the first conclusion of these notes: "progress is *never restitution*. If it exists, it does so as oriented change" (p. 417) toward results that we can only partially know. The results may realize the original intention, but it "envelops and transcends it in *totalizing* it" with all its subsequent moments and results. Progress, as oriented change, seems to be a law of praxis. But we always wind up elsewhere and other than we expected.

We found no hint anywhere in the *Cahiers* of Sartre thinking about a tendency toward improving human life. And where progress appears throughout *Critique* II, Sartre seems to rush to deny that he means improvement. The *Critique*, for example, is concerned with understanding totalization, and this very theme makes the issue of progress inevitable. To what extent does totalization involve not only moving toward a single interrelated world but in a direction we might regard as progress? "A priori," Sartre says in referring to the logic of conflict between subgroups and its resolution, "we can decide nothing. The circumstances of praxis and the material givens alone can inform us" (p. 97). Throughout both volumes *progress* seems only to mean the fuller unification of the practical field achieved by praxis – perhaps better, tighter organization, mentioned in the *Cahiers*, but not an improved world.

But now, in these notes appended to *Critique* II, Sartre touches on the question of improvement. Progress, the intended results of a given praxis, may indeed have taken place, but, as in the case of introducing slavery, the internal family structure may have been transformed. Similarly, the European entry into Eskimo life may have introduced progress but also destruction. Can progress be evaluated by examining whether needs are more easily satisfied under a new arrangement? Progress can indeed become *improvement*.

In this sense progress becomes, for he who possesses at the start a historical consciousness, not any more the maintenance of the act but a positive
transcendence of the practical field by me, of me by the totalizing effort and
of me by the practical field, entailing the transformation of myself and of the
field in such a way that between this new being and this new field are better
relationships than between myself and my [original] field. (p. 418)

But the issue of improvement becomes inconclusive as Sartre continues to explore the question of counterfinality. What, he asks, will
be the relations between this new me and my new field, "which is
still *me and my field*" (p. 419)? He indicates that the question has
two aspects, the most frequent, changing to stay the same, and
changing to improve. Under the first he mentions two cases based
on need: The practical field increases in resources but also in counterfinalities, such as machines; it diminishes in resources and I *regress* by changing and limiting my needs in order to survive. Under
the second he talks of changing to improve my powers, effectiveness, knowledge. The negative version of this might be the case
when I emigrate because the immediate situation has become unacceptable, for example leaving southern Italy and going to Milan (as
in *Rocco and His Brothers*) in order to find work: "uprooting. Unfore-
seen transformation. The one who ends up there *is going to make
me into an other* at the same time that he realizes the possible that I
am" (p. 419). In the positive version, I profit from the situation in
order to increase my power: "*Change to become other*" (p. 419). At
times new circumstances themselves keep me from staying the
same: "One must disappear or become much more effective, much
more powerful, in the new society, than in the previous one" (p.
420). For example, "I buy one machine, but because of competitive
pressures, that may not suffice. If I buy several, I beat my competi-
tors but I find myself owning a large business. In order to protect my
interests I become wholly other, with other interests, another fragility" (p. 420).

REPETITION AND CHANGE

A certain kind of progress, I indicated, seems inherent in the very
structure of being. Looking more closely at individual action as progress, Sartre stresses the internal contradiction between repetition

and change. Integration of humans into a given society imposes certain rites of passage that are also forms of repetition: initiation, marriage, promotion. If I am educated by it, my society wishes to integrate me into it. Thus, for example, as did my father before me, in a process of repetition I enter an apprenticeship to learn the (relatively stable) skills I need in order to assume my role as producer. However, in repeating, I am *changing*. I take up my future role as essence, handed down from the past. And yet it is "a less determined future whose origin comes from (interiorized) contradictions between the teaching of science and the novel techniques" (p. 420). Inevitably, it would seem, any individual will be "beyond the past essence" he is supposed to assume.[15]

Which is why, after all, change is inevitable. In changing to remain just like his father, the child "will affirm his possibility of *being other* insofar as he is beyond his father, just as the emerging techniques are beyond the old ones" (pp. 420–1). Is such indetermination inherent in the very processes of socialization? In a situation where the young worker cannot become revolutionary and which is characterized by technical stagnation, he may find himself saddled with a destiny that is his father's past.[16] Breaking with this, or any version of one's essence, is catastrophic in comparison with the apparently continuous process of transcendence in which one accepts a waiting essence. But transcendence is in fact always a contradiction, and even in breaking, one in fact always preserves. Discontinuity contains its opposite and vice versa.[17] Repetition always seems to involve progress. Progress always seems to involve repetition.

Undeveloped thoughts follow: about the organism's organic development being, as we have seen, progressive, but then also regressive as it declines into old age; about the child orienting its progress through sighting an alienated way of being, an in-itself–for-itself ("I will be admiral, boxer, pilot"). The latter can entail the "profound negativity of socialized facticity" (p. 420). This concept, socialized facticity, means that I am not only *not* the basis of my existence (as Sartre had said in *Being and Nothingness*) "but not even of its social predeterminations" (p. 422). My essence, to be assumed by my project, is handed down to me. What does this have to do with progress? Sartre further clarifies this theme by focusing on how, after the massacre of Constantine following a nationalist uprising in May

1945, young Algerians were no longer able to pursue the goal of integration with France and the French that had been their parents' project, and the one they themselves were raised to pursue. "Therefore, catastrophic progress [was] entailed by the consequences" (p. 422). Progress here seems to continue to mean, simply, going beyond the given whether in seeking to realize one's essence or in breaking with it. The impossibility of young Algerians being who they were raised to be casts light on how progress appears:

> Progress consists . . . of the totality of this catastrophic side (negation of socialized facticity) and this repetitive but in fact changing side (realization of socialized facticity by the apprenticeship and inequality of the situation anticipated by the fathers and lived by the child), as march toward the *being* of everyone (both determined and undetermined). (p. 422)

How does one make progress toward *oneself* in relation to socialized facticity? Biological change, maturation, makes the organism's identity the reason for change. "This is the very structure of progress. *Nature*. . . . All *culture* is built on this fundamental [biological] structure" (p. 422). The various rituals of repetition socialize this temporal biological structure. "Result: progress = *movement toward self* but an endlessly receding self" (p. 422). Trying to realize one's socialized facticity means making a project for the future out of the essence of past adults. These givens become negated insofar as the self is affirmed: Both identification and rejection take place. Moreover, new techniques are used as ways of transcending socialized facticity toward one's own being.

What is Sartre's point in this difficult discussion? He is demonstrating that progress, in the sense of going beyond the previous generation, is built into the act of creating/assuming one's self, even where this act takes place strictly under repetitive forms. And now Sartre reintroduces issues of historical progress. He says that technical progress, as a means for going beyond the previous generation, only becomes relevant in a given class and at a given historical moment.

> Which is the source of *circularity:* the origin of social progress should be sought in *individuals in progress.* And inversely, the very idea, the first impetus of *personal* progress should be supported by social progress (society

of repetition without technical progress = suppression of progress. Progress = passage from the potentiality to the act. Nothing more.). (p. 423)

The fact that certain individuals can be grasped as making progress toward themselves depends on a widespread sense of social progress. But social progress is to individual progress as is "the organization . . . to the practical organism" (p. 423). In other words, the entire abstract and ahistorical discussion of human development as progress until now, Sartre is saying, must presuppose a specific sociohistorical world. Exactly how, and exactly what world, will not be made clear. This entire discussion seems to be meant only to apply in a society that has taken progress as its project, as mentioned in the *Cahiers*.

VERDI'S *DON CARLOS*

Sartre rapidly outlines an analysis of Verdi's creative project as an example of making progress by changing to stay the same. Verdi seems to go beyond the tensions he faces by integrating them into a new and original work. His ideological interest lay in being "the national representative of Italy as bel canto and theatre" (p. 423). Threatened by Wagner, chamber music, and musical internationalism, he sought to preserve and create – in distinction to Wagner the German symphonist and Gounod, the French composer of intimate music – a national music that kept the orchestra in a secondary role. "But precisely, *to save* his interest is to integrate the contradiction in the work: *Don Carlos*. Therefore *progress*" (p. 424). He finds it essential to keep lyricism and song, but also to integrate harmony and develop the role of the orchestra. Avoiding the Wagnerian solution of submitting voice to instrument, he creates a new tension – "and therefore *progresses*" – by doing the opposite: "In fact the preserved unity is enriched (growing complexity in tension and order)" (p. 424). And so he arrives at "total opera," with vocal predominance, which is both modern *and* Italian. Sartre mentions *Otello, Il Trovatore, La Traviata,* and *Falstaff* as stages along the way of Verdi preserving his *interest,* endangered by other composers. "Progress consists in preserving it as regulating ideal (it is my *project*) by introducing into it external modifications that risk destroying it. Progress: to interiorize the adversary in an undertaking that transforms interest (work already *done*) into an end (still affirming it by integrating the rest without making it explode)" (p. 424).

SOCIAL PROGRESS

Sartre now abandons the individual plane to sketch some striking notes for a discussion of *social* progress. He begins by speaking of societies without progress: those "without history" that live a life of repetition; those either lacking real progress or which lack awareness of it; and societies that *as such* are not organized to be affected by it – those investing tiny amounts in industry, whose production has leveled off, and which are regressing. "These societies cannot progress. Progress can only be installed on *their ruins*. This means that another society with other structures (and sometimes with, in part, the same men) is installed on the ruins of the first. And that it is *better*. Or more exactly, *more advanced* in the direction of the ultimate goal" (pp. 424–5).

But, he asks, "who determined the goal initially?" And "who benefits from progress?" Moreover, he insists on the necessity of distinguishing short-term and long-term progress. In the short term, one may never see real progress, because the second stage may be more catastrophic than the first. What progress is there from slavery to capitalism? Perhaps economic progress is visible, but do the people involved actually experience *human* progress? And in the long term, who, after all, are the subjects and beneficiaries of such progress? Sartre stresses these last points by noting that contemporaries may not experience progress, that its beneficiaries may be other people than its victims. He wonders what is the goal of the general movement, and asks, "Who can decide that it is this or that? And how?" (p. 425). And he also wonders whether progress is a "natural dialectical necessity or an action of praxis" (p. 425).

The answer to the social problem of progress appears in the question, Sartre now says elliptically. It seems to be the "organization of need" and the entire subsequent system of labor, practico-inertia, and counterfinalities and alienations that makes it hard to grasp progress that "masks it or puts it ceaselessly in question or deprives it of all possibility" (p. 425). In other words, "Is there progress?" no longer would seem to be a question of ontology or the philosophy of history, but rather now appears as a concrete political and social question, meaning "Progress for whom?" and "Progress controlled by whom?" "What makes progress true is the same organization of factors but viewed otherwise" (p. 426).

SCIENCE AND PROGRESS

Having discussed individual progress (as praxis and as human development) and having suggestively mentioned social progress, Sartre now returns to the theme of scientific progress discussed briefly in the *Cahiers*. Here his main concern is to explain why long-term and continuous, cumulative progress takes place in science but not in other areas of human praxis. Because it is a matter of pure exteriority – in other words, lacks the constant disruptive generational passage we have discussed from interiority to exteriority to interiority – scientific progress is a quantitative business and it is possible to accumulate its results. It is the "exploration of exteriority in exteriority" (p. 426). Why? he asks. Here, as in the text of *Critique* II, he describes the process of working on nature with tools – "acting from the exterior on the exterior to interiorize it" – and characterizes this as the moment giving rise to analytical reason.[18]

The relationship of all this to progress is that science, not the entire practical movement within which it occurs and which yields a practico-inert result rendering progress problematic at every moment, is continuous progress. Because the very stuff of science is inertia, it is not plagued by the practico-inert:

Science is the permanent dissolution of the practico-inert in its element of pure inertia. In this sense, it is the non-dialectical remedy for the anti-dialectic (therefore liberation of the dialectical movement). In the practico-inert, it sees only the inert. The inert is pure quantity. (Science) is inertia viewed by itself. (p. 427)

Sartre takes this quality of inertia as the explanation for the phenomenon of cumulative knowledge in science, insofar as the inertia of new areas is conquered and as it is divided. Why is this not the practico-inert obstacle it is for praxis? For science, it becomes "pure inertia of exteriority" whose fate is to be dissolved, for example to be measured, rather than practico-inertia that becomes an obstacle to praxis. Even if it can be said that science progresses by means of contradictions, they are resolved in terms "of the largest exteriority, the largest inertia" (p. 428). Unlike praxis, science does not totalize, is not intentional. Being exterior rather than interior, not being a matter of action, it remains *open*, "and this *openness* has for result its permanent progress. Accumulation – no scientific counterfinality" (p. 429).[19]

Who benefits from progress? Sartre's final reflection on progress returns to social issues and focuses on "the man of scarcity" (p. 430). He rapidly sketches a dazzling account of how the scarcity of the means of subsistence becomes an active element of history by being successively displaced to the point where a minority is conceded to possess rare abilities that give them the exclusive right to be rare people and dispose over a society's scarce goods. "One is what one has" (p. 431). Claiming the ability to satisfy one's needs by being one of society's "rare ones" implies "a system of constraints and myths keeping the majority (the *not-rare ones*) from demanding satisfaction, in short, requires exploitation, oppression, mystification. In a word, violence" (p. 432). Scarcity of the means of satisfaction becomes scarcity of a few rich people in a process that, indeed, *is* active violence. The scarcity of the rich is based on "need satisfied by the permanence of violence, which without violence would no longer be satisfied . . ." (p. 432). This holds true in a system based on profit. But what does this have to do with progress? To show the links of scarcity with violence Sartre notes that "progress toward abundance is hindered" by a system of profit that requires inadequate consumption. Its "man of scarcity" cannot pursue his privileges, indeed cannot even satisfy his very needs, without raising himself above others and pushing the system of scarcity to its conclusion.

Taken together, these reflections appended to the second *Critique* are even more inconclusive than those of the *Cahiers*. The latter added up to a strong case against the idea of progress as we know it; the former explored an abstract individual structure of action and possible instances of progress without clarifying ways in which individuals improve or advance over their starting points. Why use the term *progress* for Verdi's (to use the Sartrean terminology) interiorization of his situation and its tensions and their reexteriorization in *Don Carlos*? Progress over what? Even if we accept the distinction between science and social practice, in what specific sense is science's cumulative character regarded as progress? This issue returns us to the theme, mentioned in the *Cahiers* but not labeled as such, of counterfinality. But the one example of "improvement" Sartre cites when discussing individual progress winds up being deviated by the same weight of counterfinality: The machines I buy to protect my business transform me into someone who is wholly *other* than when I began. The more I transform, the more I become other. The instances Sartre cites of becoming other to stay the same are not successful intentions, but rather unintended results of praxes – domination by their products. How can these be regarded as progress in any usual sense of the term? If anything seems to militate against the usual notion of progress, it is Sartre's conception of practico-inertia. Sartre's final social reflections are sharp and suggestive but, alas, undeveloped.

PROGRESS AS IDEOLOGY

In raising the question about who benefits from progress Sartre suggests that those in power *stand in the way* of progress. Ten years later, in his longest discussion on progress intended for publication, Sartre describes technical progress as being used by those in power in pursuit of their own interest. He sees both the ideology and the reality of productive progress as being the "directing principle of *all* bourgeois ideology."[20] In the third volume of *The Family Idiot*, published in 1972, Sartre lays bare the roots of this ideological smokescreen by analyzing the historical situation following the bloody suppression of the workers in June 1848.

Eighteenth-century bourgeois ideology was universalist, concrete, and critical of existing social institutions. It was optimistic. This was because the prerevolutionary bourgeoisie, not yet in power, was able to see itself as a universal class, demanding the rights of everyone. When, on the heels of the February revolution and the fall of the July monarchy, the workers of 1848 made *their* demands, the bourgeois illusion of universality was punctured for all to see in the most dramatic of ways: Workers were massacred by the bourgeois national guard on the streets of Paris. How could bourgeois ideology continue to speak of the rights of *all* citizens?

Bourgeois ideology could no longer be universalist, humanist, and optimistic. The interest of the *patron* and the worker had fatally diverged. A "new humanism" (p. 273) is required that accommodates itself to the domination of man by man and yet can be accepted by all. And so we have the idea of progress: "submission to the thing, masked by an optimism." It is a new humanism characterized by dehumanization. All people, workers and capitalists alike, submit before the capitalists' self-interest. It is "thus manifested to the owner as a double alienation: to the others by manufacturing, to manufacturing by all the others; it is profit as objective truth of man and inhuman necessity, it is the ineluctable obligation to progress" (p. 276). This "new humanism," the myth of progress, contains "the hatred that the manufacturers believe they read in the look of the workers" (p. 278) since the June Days of the 1848 uprising. Although it is masked, the hatred of man in general becomes the core of the new ideology. Life becomes subordinated to an accumulation of things, worked-matter begins its reign over its creators. And yet the new ideology remains optimistic by projecting "the distant future – the world finally conquered, the embourgeoisement of the world – as the hidden end of all present undertakings" (p. 282).

Progress becomes both Platonic myth and Platonic idea. It is absolute demand – to promote mechanization, to lower costs. But self-interest and class interest are transformed into an ethical principle, dematerialized and stripped of all particular interest.

But this sole imperative is lived as if it were the manifestation, *here, now,* for *these* individuals, of an infinite imperative which will be manifested otherwise for others in future times but whose form will remain, in all circumstances, the same and whose variations of content will be rigorously linked one to another as phases of an immense development. (p. 283)

In this way, scientistic ideology presents, and hides, the bourgeois hatred of man, born out of a specific history, "as sacrifice to the *Ideal*" (p. 284).

As ideology, then, progress becomes both antihuman and raised above man. As a product of class struggle, it secretly expresses and hides the hatreds that spring from it. These strains are successfully contained within the idea's apparent optimism.

CONCLUSIONS: PROGRESS DEMYTHOLOGIZED

Taken together, these various reflections on progress complement the famous key terms of the rest of Sartre's writings. First, they confirm what we already know, namely that Sartre was perhaps the century's preeminent philosopher of individualism, action, and experience.[21] As such, we have seen him sketch decisive arguments against the idea of progress as we know it. Inasmuch as Sartre insists that progress can only be a human project and not some kind of law or objective trend, we see the central term of Sartre's thought underpinning his reflections: freedom. In other words, we cannot avoid making ourselves from what has been made of us. No matter what limits he is led to recognize by his postwar understandings of history, society, and politics, Sartre never abandons his original sense that individual humans make themselves. At the very least what remains is "the small movement which makes of a totally conditioned social being someone who does not render back completely what his conditioning has given him."[22]

This stress on our ultimate self-determination dashes the idea of an objective progress unfolding in and around us. We may indeed make ourselves on the ground prepared for us by the previous generation, but (to use the language of the *Critique* and *The Family Idiot*) we interiorize their results, which escaped them, and reexteriorize them as *our* project. Our own results, similarly, will escape us. This inevitable disjuncture from one generation to the next means that there can be no single transgenerational historical movement above and beyond the specific human beings inhabiting this world at any moment. Even as he absorbs Marxism Sartre insists that there are no "trends" or "forces" operating on their own: "*There are only* individuals and particular relations among them (opposition, alliance, dependence, etc.). . . ."[23]

This point is demonstrated by mass movements, analyzed in the first volume of the *Critique*, and the fate of the Bolshevik revolution, studied in the second. The fused group spontaneously gathers people together in pursuit of specific goals and in opposition to specific groups and situations. It does not preexist them nor can it survive their defection. And those who feel responsible for the group's survival know this. Menaced by this threat, almost from the beginning the group tries to find ways to compel adherence, launching the slow degeneration from group to institution. Its most oppressively stable forms result in the reappearance of serially isolated and thoroughly dominated individuals who are controlled by a bureaucratic central apparatus. But these are, strictly speaking, no more than ways of alienating the free practical activity of individuals. In the specific conditions of the Soviet Union in the 1920s and 1930s, a further alienation took place. Those in power deviated the original purposes of the revolution in struggling to carry them out, and in time, deviated their own consciousness of their goals. Not only does it seem difficult to talk of progress from generation to generation, but real history deviates the agents themselves from their original goals.

But what about the "trends" that actually seem to act upon us and carry us along? Here Sartre's discussions in both volumes of the *Critique* sharpen the points just made. Individuals may create and sustain such "trends" under forms of separation and alienation so that they take on a semiautonomous life (such as public opinion or the "Top Ten" or self-interest). But all such apparent products of "hyperorganisms" are in reality forms of organizing human activity under conditions of passive parallel separation and domination known as seriality. Taken together, praxes and their practico-inert products that come to set the terms for future praxes are described as *praxis-process.*

Elsewhere I have quarreled with Sartre's insistence that, ontologically, we can and must always return to individual praxis, arguing against him that the individuals are themselves always social, and that the (abstract) social layer of their being deserves a co-priority with the (equally abstract) individual plane: Every concrete individual and all individual praxes presuppose both planes.[24] We have seen Sartre give us stark alternatives: a single Mind *or* radically separated individuals; scientific accumulation without inertia *or* total generational discontinuity. But to indicate the usefulness and importance of Sartre's thrust it is only necessary to ask, What *is* society? Is it a hyperorganism that, ontologically existing independently of them, transcends individuals? I have said that it may be argued, against Sartre, that society is in some sense a substantive *being*, a sum of practices, customs, rules, and available praxes, including violence, that both become the identity of and impose themselves on every living individual. Nonetheless, Sartre helps us to understand that these require to be sustained *at every moment* by the specific praxes of social individuals. Above all, this sociality can never exist independently of the collectivity of individuals and their praxes – in the end, sociality is never any more than that. In some decisive sense, free and individual activity remains at the root of all history and all sociality, just as history and sociality remain at the root of all individuality.

Thus Sartre is correct to stress the absurdity of pointing to and talking about society as if it lives, acts, moves on its own. Society does not, history does not. *Moves:* proclaimed as existing across time, diachronically, this hyperorganic fiction, society, would become, change, evolve, irrespective of its individuals. Talked about as if it lived a life of its own, society could presumably be studied on its own; mystified, we could reify it and inquire about patterns of its autonomous development. We would indeed mistakenly claim to develop laws of its movement, such as the myth of progress.

Indeed, Sartre seems to be saying, alienated human praxis is precisely the meaning of nearly all the powers and forces operating *on* and *against* individuals in our world. Progress has been an ideology seeking to put the best face on this alienation. It hides the fact that any force of progress is collective human power, generally produced by individuals under arrangements of direct oppression or serial constraint, generally uncomprehended by anyone, controlled by a handful, imposed on the rest, policed by a few. All fetishisms of technology, from steam power to nuclear power, can be understood as alienated and collectively produced power.

CONCLUSIONS: BASES FOR UNDERSTANDING PROGRESS

Granted that progress is indeed ideology that distorts the real nature of human action in history, it might still be argued that one can observe genuine social and technological progress all around us. Does Sartre provide us with any tools for understanding, beneath the myth, secular trends of progress? Once we have stripped away the illusion about the world's inevitable movement toward happiness and plenty, an illusion that Sartre finds in both bourgeois and Marxist thought, how do we understand the many progresses that humans have made to improve their condition?

First, we can make use of Sartre's notion, in the *Cahiers*, that we are situated within a *project of progress*. Whatever may actually be true about the past, we inhabit a world so organized that not only its institutions and ideologies but virtually everyone living in it seeks to *make* progress. The past, the present, the future – all are seen through the lenses of scientific, technological, economic, social, and political amelioration. This sense of amelioration is broader and deeper than the technological and productive fetishism Sartre called the "directing Principle of all bourgeois ideology." We do not just change to stay the same; we seek to *improve*, relentlessly, restlessly, constantly.

Second, Sartre's brief sketches in the notes appended to the second *Critique* indicate how just staying the same involves a going beyond. *Negation* in *Being and Nothingness*, *praxis* in the *Critique*, and the *project* in *Search for a Method* suggest the constant transcendence that is human activity. Here Sartre talks directly and unequivocally about *progress*, stressing in yet another way that there is no human existence that does not go beyond. Whether the going beyond limits itself to slight, steady improvements, whether it effaces itself completely in simply restoring its starting points (and thus claims to stay the same), or whether it issues into social projects and ideologies of increasing productivity or social amelioration or more general progress, the goings beyond are based on something Sartre describes, however unclearly, as progress. If believing in full-blown social progress involves a special way of thinking about things, so does simply fulfilling one's essence – I claim to be simply adopting the skills already learned and used, and now passed down, by my father. As Sartre says, even to stay the same I must change.

A third Sartrean contribution to our thinking about progress grows directly from his discussions of alterity or otherness in history. Our efforts create results that are always other than we intend. We might, for example, recall a Spain bankrupted by the consequences of its New World mineral wealth, or a China denuded of trees and topsoil by the agricultural progress made by its peasants. The *Critique*'s pages lead us to the shipwreck imposed by the unintended consequences of human praxis. With the concept of the practico-inert, Sartre potentially illuminates another reality of our experience, indeed, another *trend:* negative progress. If we can point to cumulative improvements, so can we point to a world growing out of human control even as it is being brought under human control. "Necessity appears in experience when we are robbed of our action by worked matter, *not* insofar as it is pure materiality but insofar as it is materialized *praxis*."²⁵ If we design and build machines to increase human productive power, the machines in turn prescribe our behavior in relation to them: Men become a product of their product. This is where Sartre takes the discussion of alterity begun in the *Cahiers*. Strictly speaking, it offers insight not into how progress is made and unmade, but rather into antiprogress – in other words, the dehumanization of the humanized world.

But does matter dominate us to the *exact degree* and in the *exact ways* that we dominate it? Might not specific social and historical conditions influence the weight of practico-inertia? Another Sartrean contribution to our thinking about progress also turns on the concept of practico-inertia and opens a more optimistic answer to this question. It appears in the *Critique* and the latter part of the third volume of *The Family Idiot*. Above I asked whether there is not some space between the alternatives so starkly posed by Sartre: a single Mind *or* radically separated individuals; scientific accumulation without inertia *or* total generational discontinuity. We are helped to answer Sartre by his own notions of the practico-inert and of a practico-inert structure of practices, literary works, attitudes, and values known as the objective Mind. Each generation, we might say, has specific problems posed for it by the previous generation, and seeks to solve those problems both within parameters set for it by the previous generation and with the tools left for it by that generation. A generation does not have just any starting point but a specific set of them. To be sure, it may find it necessary to reject the problems bequeathed to it as midnineteenth-century French writers, who tended to withdraw from social life. This generation leaped over existing parameters, rejecting the notions of literary commitment and political universality bequeathed by its elders. A generation may feel it necessary to forge its own tools from scratch, inventing, for example, its own language. In any case, each generation inherits, and in one way or another, takes as its starting point the sedimented deposits left by the previous generation.

Certainly this does not imply progress as improvement, or even a tendency to progress. Two further things are necessary for that. First is a notion, alongside freedom and invention and indeterminacy, of some degree of common humanity, a sense of common needs posed as goals: food, shelter, and the pacification of existence, perhaps; freedom and self-determination, perhaps; the fullest development of human capacities, perhaps. Second is the sense of a *positive* practico-inert: practices, tools, institutions, habits, laws whose purpose is to meet those needs. At the end of the second *Critique* Sartre begins to speculate about the Soviet bureaucracy, and the Bolshevik revolution, so horribly deviated from their original goals, in precisely these terms. He is thinking about a *guided circularity* – controlling counterfinality so that it does not hopelessly deviate one's project. If so, practico-inertia is not hell; each generation does not simply face the endless prospect of "progress made and unmade." If so, human beings would be able to inscribe their purposes in matter, to be taken up by others alongside and after them. These others might select from what is given to them, might alter what they don't like and preserve what they value, passing *that* along to still others, along with their changes. *Need* would govern and limit the deviations from the original project. Each generation might still produce something other than what it anticipated, and each succeeding generation would have to transform the given situation into a project – with all the changes that might imply. Still, in the long run, might we not anticipate a next generation expanding its rights over the previous one, struggling on behalf of its hungers and against its limitations?

Struggling against whom? When Sartre comes to *need* near the end of the second *Critique*, he is trying to find a possible way out of the ultimate dialectical circularity that entraps all praxis by making its results other than intended. Need is a more-or-less fixed point, beneath or beyond all deviation. Similarly, at the end of his pages on progress attached to the end of the second *Critique*, Sartre focuses on the rare person whose need becomes effective, that is, who has the means and social power to satisfy it. Progress can hardly be discussed, he suggests here and makes explicit in *The Family Idiot*, without talking about relationships of domination and exploitation. Or, as Sartre wondered, in whose interest does progress take place? In *The Family Idiot* he attacked the idea of progress as ruling-class sleight-of-hand. Technological progress occurs, we might say, to head off *social progress*. Sartre never fully combined this later social and political emphasis with his earlier ontological speculations on progress. And he never did more than speculate about guided circularity. He never developed a sense of a positive practico-inert, say,

290 THE CAMBRIDGE COMPANION TO SARTRE

civil rights legislation or hard-won practices of mutual respect. If he had done so, he might have been able to provide us with a rich, complex analysis of the phenomenon that would do justice both to the mythology and its repressive social function, as well as to the the realities of amelioration and the ways they have been contested and won, as well as the negative curves of progress. As it is, he leaves us important insights, provocative suggestions, and the task of developing them further.

1 John B. Bury, *The Idea of Progress* (New York: 1932), p. 5.
2 Jean-François Lyotard, *The Postmodern Condition: A Report on Knowledge* (Minneapolis: 1984), p. xxiv.
3 Theodor W. Adorno, *Negative Dialectics* (London: 1973), p. 320.
4 "Existentialism Is a Humanism," tr. Bernard Frechtman, *Existentialism and Human Emotions* (New York: 1957), p. 44. Later Sartre was to explore a possible exception to this categorical statement: the building of socialism in the Soviet Union. In *The Ghost of Stalin* (1957) he speaks of successful *and* destructive aspects of Stalinism. The *Critique*'s second volume explores the relationship between the two, showing, most notably, how the two aspects are historically inextricable and indeed deviate the ultimate project. In the end, however, in this reflection the negative seems to overwhelm any amelioration.
5 *Cahiers pour une morale* (Paris: 1983), p. 31.
6 Sartre equivocates just a bit on this point: We are not happier than the Romans, but we can see that we have the capacities (perhaps even the spring of a greater unhappiness) to bring about a society that is happy and just (p. 48). And if we did bring it about, would we then be able to speak about an objective reality of progress? Sartre stops with the notion of *capacities*.
7 Later, Sartre mentions invention as another source of the "perpetual illusion of progress" (p. 61). The invention "transcends toward the *better*" and reduces what was before it to the state of preparation. In fact, a new situation is created "which is not better."
8 The notion of progress as development of order becomes freed from Sartre's attribution to "the philosophers" here and discussed for its own sake. The order is only partial, however, because it seems to be braked by a certain passivity that cannot be touched by our action. The *essence* is an example.

9 In these cases, progress means, once again, "the development of an original order" (p. 80) – an idea he will identify with Hegel (p. 115). This idea,
   which is optimistic at bottom, is rooted in the Hegelian conception that
   the "Whole is potentially present in isolated entities" (p. 95). This seems
   to be what Sartre has meant by essences, namely that the "particular is
   haunted by the totality" (p. 115).

10 American black elders, trying to keep alive *their* project, exhort their
   juniors to "Remember Martin Luther King." The younger generation is
   in a situation made possible by their elders, but they now create *their*
   goals. Similarly, there was no reason to think that, freed from Soviet and
   Communist domination, Eastern Europeans would want to continue
   along the lines of the 1945–89 period. Communism is not *their* project
   but the starting point they seek to reverse.

11 *Search for a Method*, tr. Hazel E. Barnes (New York: 1968), p. 92.

12 *Critique de la raison dialectique: II: L'Intelligibilité de l'histoire* (Paris:
   1985), p. 411.

13 Progress "is constituted, at least partially, by the games of counterfinalities which are not ours, in other words, insofar as matter serves
   as mediation between men" (p. 425).

14 See *Critique* II, 341–401; Ronald Aronson, *Sartre's Second Critique* (Chicago: 1987), pp. 210–18.

15 This *himself* he is to become "is an essence but contradictorily constituted by a past being (that of the fathers) and by a possible. The possible
   is *beyond* the transcended being but although rigorously given as *transcendence towards*, it does not have the precision of being" (p. 420). It
   envelops, transcends, and keeps this precision as it goes toward a new
   state yet to be defined by the agent himself.

16 "This can lead to a *rupture* by refusing Destiny. But then, refusal of
   oneself: oneself, this was the possible beyond being, but in breaking
   being, one finds oneself on the naked path of his own relation with the
   indetermination of a possible. What to become?" (p. 421)

17 Paul Nizan, for example, preserved to the very end a relationship with
   his father that manifested itself when he broke with the party and re-
   created his original alienation.

18 See *Critique* II, pp. 354–90.

19 Obviously, human, social situations can be studied scientifically in this
   way, externally, by searching their structures and laws, as Gandhi did in
   finding the untouchables to be the key element of the Indian caste
   system. Sartre does not here raise the fundamental question about "social science," namely that humans being studied are also centers of
   intentionality and totalization themselves, and thus inevitably remove

themselves from the efforts of external comprehension. Gandhi was not acting *upon* the untouchables but *with* them; the caste system was/is maintained by millions of individual praxes.

20 *L'Idiot de la famille*, Vol. III (Paris: 1972), p. 282

21 Not only does he disregard the traditional dominance of reason in philosophy, but even when he speaks of truth he seems to base it on individual experience and verification, and stresses again and again that each individual acts in such a way as to perpetually transcend his or her starting point. See the posthumously published *Vérité et existence* (Paris: 1989).

22 "Itinerary of a Thought," *From Existentialism to Marxism*, tr. John Mathews (London: 1974), p. 35.

23 *Search for a Method*, p. 162.

24 See my *Sartre's Second Critique* (Chicago: University of Chicago Press, 1987), pp. 234–43.

25 *Critique of Dialectical Reason, I: Theory of Practical Ensembles*, tr. Alan Sheridan-Smith (London: 1976), p. 224.

9 Sartrean Structuralism?

THE CURVE OF THE EPOCH

By the time of Sartre's death in 1980, Structuralism, as a movement, had evaporated, and various forms of Post-Structuralism were in full swing. At the beginning of his career, in the 1920s and 1930s, Structuralism was just beginning to be thought of, in a few localities remote from Paris and existentialism in disciplinary and in geographical space – for example technical linguistics in Prague. There is a sense, then, in which Sartre's life and that of Structuralism run in parallel, a tempting observation enough in the light of his theory of oracular lives, of the "curves" of epochs, in the third volume of *L'Idiot de la famille*.[1] The conjecture that Sartre and Structuralism might have had a serious affinity seems at first glance however to be a nonstarter, given the lack of apparent overlap between his concerns and those of the major structuralists (whether by avowal or attribution): Althusser, Barthes, Dumézil, Foucault, Lacan, Lévi-Strauss.[2]

What the structuralists had in common was a preoccupation with embodied relationships – whether political, literary, religious, historical, psychoanalytic, or ethnological – taken to be objective, sharing or borrowing the structure of language, and reflecting the unconscious structure of mind. What Sartre emphasized, in contrast, was the complete lucidity of the conscious subject as free to enter or not into relationships, and the responsibility of the agent for the constitution and maintenance in practice of the group structures to which he or she might belong. Because they all shared the discursive space of French intellectual life, encounters were of course inevitable, but the history of these serves further to undermine the conjecture in question, since Sartre was generally seen as disagreeing sharply with

Structuralism. In their discussion of the interview with Bernard Pingaud that closed the issue of *L'Arc* devoted to his work in 1966, Sartre's bibliographers (Michel Contat and Michel Rybalka) remark that "the oppositions between Sartrean philosophy and Structuralism, for all that they have been artificially inflated by journalists and insufficiently studied by scholars, are nonetheless essential and seem, up to this point, insurmountable. . . ."[3]

In that interview, nevertheless, Sartre responded to a direct question from Pingaud – "So you reject Structuralism?" – by saying "I am in no way hostile to Structuralism when the structuralist remains aware of the limits of his method."[4] And there is plenty of evidence in that interview and elsewhere in his work that he took the structuralists seriously, particularly Lévi-Strauss, so that the connection between his ideas and theirs seems worth a closer look. It will come as no surprise to find that the issues between them center on the conceptual relations between structure on the one hand and existence and history on the other.

The heroic period of Existentialism corresponded to a moment in which social structures, in France at least, were in effective dissolution. As the German occupation and the Vichy government collapsed together they left a void in which for a time there were no rules, so that existing subjects could have the experience of making their own, engaging in authentic praxis, standing forth toward things and one another in the heady and quasi-total freedom of the fourth part of *L'Être et le néant*. If there is, as I maintain, a relation of orthogonal reciprocity[5] between existence and structure, then this historical moment marked the limit of the swing toward existence at the expense of structure. Sartre was its prophet, its embodiment. Later in his career, when Marxism theoretically and the Cold War practically had forced him to acknowledge how tenuous and diminished human freedom often is, the swing was in the other direction, toward structure at the expense of existence, and it is in this light that his polemic against Structuralism is to be weighed. Later still, at the time of the events of May 1968, existence reasserted itself and there was less point than ever in cultivating structure as such, though the work on Flaubert that Sartre was writing at the time contains material of potential importance to Structuralism.

Even in the Marxist period, though, the period of overt criticism, there is evidence of Sartre's convergence with Structuralism. Marxism, along with psychoanalysis, literary theory, history, and anthropology, was of course one of the recognized domains of Structuralism in its moment of glory, though, as we shall see, this is not as significant a fact as we might at first be tempted to think. As far as that goes it should be noted that Sartre has some claim to contributions in each of these other fields as well: existential psychoanalysis; *What Is Literature?*; the long preoccupation with history in the *Critique* and the third volume of the Flaubert; the "structural anthropology" of *Search for a Method*. This last looks like a clear candidate for a Structuralism of his own, and under some reserve I shall accept it as part of an eventual package. The reserve derives from two observations: "anthropology" here does not mean Lévi-Strauss's discipline but rather what has come to be called "philosophical anthropology," while "structural" turns out to be *structurelle* rather than *structurale*; if this contrast of suffixes is construed as parallel to Heidegger's usage (of *existentiell* in opposition to *existential*) we would have to read Sartre's "structural" as connoting activity rather than system.[6]

But then "structure" as used by the structuralists themselves meant something more than "system," though it wasn't always easy to specify what the difference might be. In claiming a kind of Structuralism for Sartre I shall exploit this uncertainty. I have suggested that in the case of the major structuralists a plausible distinction between structure and system follows from an emphasis on relations rather than elements, "system" being taken to mean a set of elements, actually related in some way for a functional end, and "structure" being taken to mean a set of relations, potentially holding among the possible elements of one or more systems. An important feature of this difference (though not one insisted on by the structuralists themselves) is that if you have the relations, and a point of view from which they are intended (in the phenomenological sense), then you don't need the elements independently: They acquire the status of intentional objects, constituted out of the relations into which they are taken to enter. This insight is present in embryonic form in the early Marx, who in a brief text on the ontological argument summarizes it as asserting merely that " 'what I conceive for myself as actual (*realiter*) is an actual conception for me,' really matters to me." He goes on to point out that this by no means weakens the power of the object so conceived, whether a god or a social structure: "Humanity has incurred debts on the basis of its gods. . . . Real dollars have the same existence imagined gods have."[7]

Part of the appeal of Marx's conception of the world lies in his emphasis on this "for me," and not only in theology. One convenient way of escaping responsibility for unfortunate social facts (private property and wage labor, for example) is to regard them as relations between people and things: The capitalist is related to his property, so the expropriated worker vanishes from the equation; the worker is related to his work, so the factory owner similarly vanishes. Marx insists that both are disguised relations between people and other people: The owner of private property deprives, and the wage slave is enslaved to, human beings in flesh and blood, not economic abstractions. In the case of the worker there is *also* a relation with material, but that isn't what makes him a worker in the class sense and is beside the present point.

Sartre, in *Questions de méthode,* aligns himself firmly with this Marxian position: "We repeat with Marxism: there are only men and real relations between men."[8] These "real relations," however, can only be real from the point of view of the human individuals who establish or attend to them. All the categories so far invoked – God, money, property, wage labor – are relational, and are constituted and sustained from such a point of view. They are thus structuralist objects *par excellence,* Structuralism resting after all on the basic premise that "the reality of the objects of the human or social sciences is relational rather than substantial."[9] The question then must be how Sartre's treatment of them differs from that of the structuralists, and whether this involves an incompatibility or merely a difference.

Who, though, is to speak for the structuralists? The formulation of the basic premise in the preceding paragraph is my own, and while most of the structuralists might have agreed with it some of them would certainly have disagreed with my earlier claim that the relations in question can only be real from the point of view of human knowers or agents. For while "knower" surely implies "known," and "agent" similarly implies "act," there was a time in the heyday of Structuralism when its chief proponents quite happily suggested that these implications did not necessarily hold in the other direction; for example Barthes, in *L'Empire des signes,* speaks of "an act of knowledge without a knowing subject," and Lévi-Strauss, in *Le Cru et le cuit*, attributes to myth the power to think and act without the involvement of individual subjects. Cases could be multiplied, and the point will return below. The upshot is a theory of the human world that dispenses with humans. It was this sort of thing that Sartre could not stomach; in one way or another all his major criticisms of the structuralists turn on their failure to make room for human subjectivity and praxis.

It may be, however, that this particular aberration is not crucial to Structuralism, and that an essentially structuralist position might be sketched with which Sartre could have agreed, as the remark quoted earlier suggests he might have been disposed, within limits, to do. Here the question, an echo of the one in the preceding paragraph, becomes: Who is to speak for Sartre? or, which Sartre is to speak? For Sartre's commitment to Marxism did as much to exacerbate the polemic as the structuralists' hostility to subjectivity, and that commitment, while never flagging with respect to the importance of Marx's doctrines, changed considerably with respect to their truth. The risk here is of producing a Structuralism that is not Structuralism, subscribed to by a Sartre who is not Sartre. On the other hand I do not expect to produce a totalized Sartre who is a total structuralist, and what Structuralism is is nowhere canonically given, so that while the conjunction of the two positions may be glancing it will be authentic. If Structuralism could have survived May 1968 in better shape than it did, and if the Sartre of *L'Idiot de la famille* had chosen to interest himself in it explicitly, that conjunction would have been much stronger.

HISTORY, LANGUAGE, AND THE DIALECTIC

In the matter of Structuralism, especially that of Lévi-Strauss, and its relation to the Sartre of the 1960s, two red herrings surface at once and need to be disposed of. First, the fact that there is at this epoch a prominent Marxist structuralist, namely Louis Althusser, is (as suggested above) of less help than one might have hoped. Althusser, says Sartre, is disposed to "privilege structures in relation to history,"[10] and thus allows himself to be used by the structuralists, in sad contrast to Marx, who, "during his lifetime, was never used by other people."[11] But the structural transformations that produced the early Marx out of Hegel, the late Marx out of the early Marx, seem not to engage Sartre's attention directly, and presumably fall for him under his general reservation about the nonexplanatory status of structural analyses alone.

Second, there is in the literature a celebrated squabble between Sartre and Lévi-Strauss about the concept of dialectical reason, which, however, has very little to do with the issue of Structuralism as such. I have dealt with this exchange elsewhere;[12] Lévi-Strauss initiates it at the end of *La Pensée sauvage* with a chapter on "History and Dialectic" in which in his usual orotund way he takes Sartre to task for confusion about the relations between analytic and dialectical reason, and Sartre pursues it in an interview with Pierre Verstraeten on "The writer and his language" in the course of which he launches a furious attack against Lévi-Strauss. "Lévi-Strauss does not know what dialectical thought is. Not only that, but he is incapable of knowing," says Sartre; and there follows a lightning characterization of dialectical thought that is dazzling even by Sartre's own standards, yet completely lucid. As far as I know Lévi-Strauss – wisely, I think, if so – never attempted to respond directly to this outburst.

But there is another confrontation with Sartre in Lévi-Strauss, at the end of *L'Homme nu*, which is of consequence to Structuralism. It is a reply to Sartre's remarks in the interview with Pingaud, already cited, where he accuses the structuralists of cultivating structures so as to avoid confronting the Marxist imperative, and attributes the success of Foucault's *Les Mots et les choses* to a popular revulsion against the Marxist view of history. Contemporary historians recognize, says Sartre, that no serious history is possible that does not emphasize "material elements of the life of men, relations of production, praxis. . . ." But this does not necessarily mean the acceptance of Marxism.

Because Marxism cannot be "transcended," it is therefore to be suppressed. It will be said that history as such is elusive, that every theory of history is by definition "doxological," to adopt Foucault's term. Any attempt to justify [historical] transitions having been renounced, the analysis of *structures*, which alone permit of true scientific investigation, will be set over against history, the domain of uncertainty.[13]

Lévi-Strauss too is accused of practicing a Structuralism that "has contributed a great deal to the contemporary discrediting of history."[14] But the point of conflict between him and Sartre lies less in such rhetorical rebukes than in Sartre's positive conception of structure, which I cite at some length in the latter's own words:

There was a time when thought was defined independently of language, as something intangible and ineffable that pre-exists expression. Today people fall into the opposite error. They would have us believe that thought is only language, as if language itself were not *spoken*.

In reality, there are two levels. On a first level, language presents itself, in effect, as an autonomous system, which reflects social unification. Language is an element of the "practico-inert," a sonorous substance unified by a set of practices. The linguist takes this totality of relations as an object of study, and he has the right to do this because it is already constituted. This is the stage of structure, in which the totality appears as a thing without man, a network of oppositions in which each element is defined in terms of another, where there is no fixed point, but only relations, only differences. But this thing without man is at the same time matter worked by man, bearing the trace of man. You will not find in nature oppositions of the sort described by linguists. Nature knows only the independence of forces. Material elements are connected one to another, and act on one another. But this connection is always exterior. It is not a question of internal relations such as the masculine establishes in relation to the feminine, the plural in relation to the singular, that is, a system in which the existence of each element conditions that of all the others. If you admit the existence of such a system, you must also admit that language exists only as spoken, in other words in act. Each element of the system refers to a whole, but this whole is dead if nobody takes it up for his own purposes, makes it work.[15]

This passage clearly says, among other things and in other words, just what was said earlier about the indispensability of the subject, in this case the speaking subject: The relations that constitute the structure of language must be sustained from an intentional point of view.

Lévi-Strauss balks precisely at this point. Subjectivity and even individuality have always aroused his impatience (in *Tristes tropiques*, while generously admitting that he does in fact exist, he disclaims individual status for his existence on the grounds that there are many different things under his skull), and in the "Finale" of *L'Homme nu* the philosophical subject and its sympathetic critics get short shrift: ". . . misunderstanding the first duties of the scholar, which are to explain what can be explained and to leave the rest provisionally aside, the philosophers are above all preoccupied with furnishing a refuge where personal identity, a sorry prize (*pauvre trésor*), might be protected. And since the two things are conjointly impossible, they prefer a subject without rationality to rationality without a subject."[16] What they should have been doing of course was Structuralism after Lévi-Strauss's fashion, which not only "offers the human sciences an epistemological model of a power incomparable to those hitherto available to them," but also "reintegrates man into nature . . . [and] allows us to disregard the subject – that intolerable spoiled child who has occupied the philosophical stage too long, and prevented all serious work by demanding exclusive attention."

Lévi-Strauss's philosophical stage is thus set for the challenge: "So nothing seems less acceptable than the compromise sketched by Sartre in conceding a place to structure on the side of the practico-inert, but on condition that it be recognized that 'this thing without man is at the same time matter worked by man, bearing the trace of man.' " Here Lévi-Strauss quotes a large part of the long extracted passage given above, and continues:

These trenchant assertions leave one bemused. As if the opposition and complementarity of male and female, of positive and negative, of left and right – which since 1957 has been known to have objective existence – were not inscribed in biological or physical nature and did not bear witness there to the interdependence of forces! In contrast to a philosophy that confines the dialectic to human history and prohibits it from taking up residence in the natural order, structuralism willingly admits that the ideas it formulates in psychological terms may be nothing but tentative approximations of organic or even physical truths.[17]

Lévi-Strauss here appears as a more orthodox Marxist – a more faithful follower of the Marxism of Engels at any rate – than Sartre, in spite of the fact that Sartre in the passage under attack is defending Marxism against the structuralists.

These texts have the virtue, it seems to me, of presenting a completely clearcut opposition about which it is possible to argue to a firm conclusion – one that, in the event, will favor Sartre's view. However, the opposition is not one between Sartre and Structuralism. Two issues are in play. The first is an old split in Marxism itself, between materialism and the dialectic. Orthodoxy covers over the split, or attempts (as in the case of Engels and the "dialectics of nature") to wrench one side of it into the terms of the other. In fact there is absolutely no inconsistency between being a materialist on the one hand and having a dialectical view of history on the other. (The latter can't be sustained in any conclusive form, which is why Sartre gave it up after the *Critique*, but that does not affect the present argument.) But to suppose that this means a dialectical view *of materialism* is to make a fairly simple mistake.

Sartre's example of language is well chosen. Language requires the material substrate of sound waves, ears, larynxes, and the rest, but it isn't merely an arrangement of these, even though if they were eliminated it would be too. They make it possible for one person to address another and be understood. This isn't an organic or physical truth or even a tentative approximation of one; it belongs to a domain of intentionality that, anchored as it is in the material, *is nevertheless itself prerequisite to the distinction between the material and the nonmaterial.* By the same token intentionality is a condition of the dialectic and is not conditioned by it; the dialectic belongs in the domain of discourse, as its very name suggests, and to try to locate it in nature (except in the vague and general sense in which, assuming the rejection of the supernatural, everything is "in" nature, encompassed by it) is to miss an essential distinction between explanandum and explanans. If science is, as I have maintained elsewhere, "the explanation of nature in its own terms,"[18] that still does not mean that it is nature that does the explaining or benefits from the explanation.

When Sartre says that we do *not* find oppositions in nature, and Lévi-Strauss, bemused by this perversity, says that we certainly *do*, it is Sartre, I would maintain, who is the closer to the structuralist position — and also to the correct view of the matter. What we find in nature is the *material* for oppositions that *we* construct into intelligible systems, "signiferous" systems as I like to call them — that is, systems that are at once repositories of meaning and channels for its communication. The great insight of Structuralism (anticipated under another designation in Cassirer's philosophy of symbolic forms) is that differences in nature (between sounds, between species, between kindred) can be templates for cultural oppositions that are varied and multiple, and that the structures built up out of these oppositions stand in relations of mutual transformation to one another.

This is just what Lévi-Strauss is so good at showing in the contexts of mythology and kinship; it is only when he tackles the philosophical underpinnings that he gets confused. It might be said of him that he is a splendid structuralist but that his underlying theory of Structuralism carries unnecessary baggage. Of course this was true of most of the structuralists in one way or another – ideological baggage in Althusser, for example, semiological baggage in Barthes – and it was partly responsible for the failure of the central tenets of Structuralism to command the attention of philosophers like Sartre. But we are not obliged to accept features of these diverse views that can be shown to be superfluous with respect to the main doctrine, nor need we renounce the name Structuralism, as some people (Foucault for example) felt obliged to do, just because of having disagreed marginally with someone who claimed it.

The other issue that stands out in the passages cited concerns the relation between rationality and subjectivity. "Since the two things are conjointly impossible," says Lévi-Strauss – what could conceivably warrant such an extraordinary claim? and why should we let anyone get away with it? It is this sort of thing that makes those of us who work with Structuralism nervous about the company we keep: It seems to be a completely gratuitous assertion, thrown in for rhetorical effect. Rationality, I would want to say – if there is any point in using such an abstract category, as opposed to judgments that this or that assertion or argument or action is or is not rational, or an example or a product of reasoning – is precisely an attribute or disposition of subjects who organize the contents of their intentional domains in a structured way. There would be no intelligible objectivity corresponding to their subjectivity if it were not for rationality; conversely, no objectivity could be said to be rational if there were no subject to make this judgment. It might therefore be argued against Lévi-Strauss that the two things are, on the contrary, conjointly necessary.

Whether we want to say of the reason exhibited in a given episode of this organizational activity that it is analytic or dialectical is a separate question; the difference between analytic and dialectical thought, as I have pointed out, lies less in any categorial contrast than in the relative proportions of technical sophistication in the thought and self-awareness in the thinker; if the emergence of the *concept* of the dialectic (in the sense in which the term has come to be understood) was relatively late in the history of philosophy, that was no doubt because the practice did not depend on the concept. To quote an earlier formulation of my own,

thought must have been dialectical before it became analytic, since standards of precision could not have been conceived of except in reaction to a conscious sense of deficiency in that respect, i.e. by a negation of previous linguistic practice. But thought cannot be analytic without knowing that it is so – in the sense that notions of affirmation, denial, consequence, and inconsistency are necessarily parts of the conceptual repertoire, as a matter of practical if not theoretical awareness, of everyone who can be said to reason analytically – although it might well be dialectical without realizing this. It is natural, therefore, for those who think about reason to do so in analytic terms, and for the concept of the dialectic to be a later acquisition.[19]

STRUCTURE AND MEANING

To return, then, to Structuralism proper: What is of central importance to it and is that important for Sartre also? Sartre was in fact first enrolled by Lévi-Strauss as a possible supporter of his position as early as 1954, in an essay published by UNESCO in a collection on the university teaching of the social sciences, where the latter says:

Anthropology claims to be a *semiological* science, and takes as a guiding principle that of "meaning." This is yet another reason (in addition to many others) why anthropology should maintain close contact with linguistics, where, with regard to this social fact of speech, there is the same concern to avoid separating the objective basis of language (*sound*) from its signifying function (*meaning*),

and adds an end note: "Just after writing these lines, we came across very similar views expressed by Jean-Paul Sartre. After criticizing an out-of-date sociology, he adds: 'The sociology of primitive peoples is *never* open to this criticism. There, we study *meaningful wholes* [*ensembles signifiants*].' "[20]

What is the status of these "meaningful wholes," for Sartre and for Structuralism? Already in 1947–8, when as promised at the end of *L'Être et le néant* he was working at the promised *Morale*, Sartre is making excursions into what would prove to be structuralist territory, and finding social meaning in deep structures of exchange. In a passage remarkable for its anticipation of Lévi-Strauss he analyzes the potlatch ceremony, following Mauss's *Essai sur le don*, and observes that the gift is ambiguous and involves

a double structure: 1) deep structure of solidarity; 2) secondary and manifest structure of reciprocal subjection of the Other by the Other, with challenge. So that the ambiguity of the potlatch is that it leaves open the question whether it is a proposition of friendship or of defiance. . . . To a most exact degree the notions of friendship and enmity have the same originating source, like the notion of challenge and that of conflict, like that of war and of peace.[21]

And a little later on he says:

It is not a matter of two meanings that can be envisaged successively but of two simultaneous aspects of the gift. The structure "liberation–gratuitousness"[22] is the internal nucleus, it is the "nonthetic consciousness (of) the gift." Even in the element challenge there is the structure "protest," that is, the first and essential structure of protest is the nonthetic consciousness of being what I am not and not being what I am. Finally the structure "Destruction–Creation" brings to light the double aspect of freedom. And these three structures: gratuitousness, protest, to destroy – to create, are immediately intelligible to the Other on the same plane of nonthetic consciousness.[23]

This text bears the marks of its status as part of an unfinished project, one that Sartre deliberately left unpublished; the conceptual apparatus is rough and provisional. But it shows a direction in which Sartre might have gone if his attention in the postwar years had not been preempted by the political side of Marxism, with its emphasis on praxis rather than on its social-structural context.

"Structure" at the time of the *Morale* is not yet the articulated relational object it is to become, but it is already something apprehended and projected by subjects, having its origin in them rather than in their world even though it characterizes that world essentially. The structure of the world appears to us foundational, but this appearance is nothing but the echo of a hypothetical move of our own: "The hypothesis, pure nothingness-projecting-foundation, is founded by experience, which reflects it back to us as having-always-been-the-structure-of-being. If there is a law (a physical law established experimentally) it is because there is the thought of a law, but reciprocally, if there is the thought of a law it is because there is a law in the world. . . . If the structure of the foundation (*fondement*) is to-be-for-founding, the structure of the founded is to be (as founded) distinct from the foundation."[24] This is the sort of bootstrap operation that Sartre has used repeatedly in *L'Être et le néant*; it always marks for him the emergence of the human, of the *pour-soi* in one or another of its manifestations. The emergence of the human is the upsurge into the world of an intentional subjectivity, the contents of whose intentional domain are structured according to its own capacity for the positing and sustaining of relations.

Where Sartre's position in this matter differs from that of the classical structuralists is in the dynamic relation of the subject to its intended structures. The structuralist view sounds Kantian, in that it is the human mind that determines the structure of the human world. (Lévi-Strauss, at a conference of anthropologists and linguists in 1953 – thus a good five years after the Sartre passages quoted above – refers to the human mind as the "uninvited guest" at the conference, responsible for the common structure of language and culture.[25]) And this Kantian coloration seems right: While the structures of the structuralists are not Kant's categorial structures they play an analogous role, in more derivative, more complex, and more localized ways; the world they structure is not the phenomenal world of every rational being but the intentional world of some definite class of such beings, linked by kinship or a community of language or interest. But Structuralism looks for the synchronic relations that characterize such worlds, and its treatment of them stresses their stability and fixity; even diachrony, under the form of structural transformation, tends to be treated synchronically.

In one way this is quite inevitable, since every thought is here and now, contemporaneous with itself, so that any grasping of any intelligible content whatever can only be synchronic in this strong sense. But this synchronic representation remains merely schematic if it simply juxtaposes earlier and later states without exploring the human activity that produced the latter out of the former, if it "suppresses the human agent, making of him or her simply the transmission belt the system uses to produce internal modifications," as Sartre puts it in his critique of neopositivist historical pluralism.[26] "The system uses": This is what I have called the fallacy of misplaced agency, which violates the Marxist principle cited from Sartre earlier: There are only men and real relations between men.

STRUCTURE AND PRAXIS

The would-be Marxist in Sartre therefore argues, in the *Critique de la raison dialectique*, on the side of human praxis, but he is prepared to see this as balanced by structure, as unintelligible without structure – on condition that the reciprocal proposition be acknowledged, that structures are unintelligible without praxis. In this work he has a more complex view of what structures are–

those strange internal realities that are both organized and organizing, both synthetic products of a practical totalization and objects always susceptible of rigorous analytical study, both the lines of force of a *praxis* for every common individual and the fixed links between this individual and the group, through perpetual changes of both of them, both inorganic ossature[27] and everyone's definite powers over everyone else, in short, both fact and right, mechanical elements and, at the same time, expressions of a living integration into a unitary *praxis* of those contradictory tensions of freedom and inertia which are known as *structures*. Function as lived *praxis* appears in the study of the group as objectivity in the *objectified* form of structure. And we shall not understand anything of the intelligibility of organized *praxis* as long as we do not raise the question of the intelligibility of structures.[28]

These intelligible structures constitute a matrix for human action, which is therefore on the one hand confined within them – but on the other enabled by them. "We shall therefore call these structures, insofar as their inorganic materiality has been freely interiorized and reworked by the group, the necessity of freedom."[29]

One is reminded here of Saussure's principle of the "stacked deck": "We say to language: 'Choose!' but we add: 'It must be this sign and no other.' No individual, even if he willed it, could modify in any way at all the choice that has been made; and what is more, the community itself cannot control so much as a single word; it is bound to the existing language."[30] There is a typical Sartrean "tourniquet" in all this. Saussure evokes the necessity of freedom (though he leaves too little room for group reworking): Social structures once interiorized constrain and liberate at the same time, in that we are now free to communicate but only on the condition that we use available structures of communication. But in what sense have the structures been "freely interiorized"? We might remember the character in Sartre's "Erostrate," who resented having to use the common instrument of language: "words for example: I wanted *my own words*. But the ones I use have dragged through I don't know how many consciousnesses; they arrange themselves in my head by virtue of the habits I have picked up from the others and it is not without repugnance that I use them in writing to you."[31]

And yet if Paul Hilbert, the character in question, in fact uses these soiled words, there is a sense in which he has freely chosen to do so, since he had the choice of keeping silent. Having chosen to interiorize a common and (relative to the individual subject) objective structure is the condition of his membership in the social group, however antisocial his intentions toward it. And here Sartre appears to be completely in accord with Lévi-Strauss's basic structuralist doctrine: Structures – of language, kinship, political practice, and the like – ensure social solidarity by the exchanges they mediate. They make stable group formations possible. Sartre's statement of the point could almost be taken as canonical: "Thus structure, considered, by way of abstraction, as knowledge, is simply the idea which the group produces of itself (and of the universe insofar as it is practically determined as a field of objectification). And the content and foundation of this reflexive idea is simply the common organization as an objective system of relations; or rather, the organization conditions it and becomes its internal norm."[32]

But Sartre goes further than Lévi-Strauss in attempting, at this point in the *Critique*, to build praxis into structure:

the double character of structure (an inert object of calculation when seen as ossature without taking account of totalisation, or an effective power actualized by the *praxis* of each and all) implies a double character in the idea. In one sense, it is the free comprehension *everywhere* of functional activity in everyone. . . . It is at this still practical level that the group has a silent knowledge of itself through each common individual. . . . It is at this level that complex knowledges may disconcert a sociologist or ethnographer who encounters them in underdeveloped societies, because they conceive of them as theoretical knowledges derived from observation of an object, whereas they are really practical structures which are themselves lived in the interiority of a common action.[33]

In addition to "this implicit understanding – which is simply a structure *of power*" there is a structure that Sartre describes as *"the relational system as ossature,"* known to the "organisers and calculators" in the society; "the organiser therefore has an immediate, practical comprehension of the structures in all their complexity and this is the basis of the abstract analysis which he then performs on these structures as skeletons."³⁴ This "double character of structure" corresponds to a distinction I have dealt with elsewhere between "representational" and "operational" models in terms of which group structure is internalized.³⁵

The two dualities do not exactly match: For me everyone carries an operational *and* a representational model, externalizing the former in practice and the latter (if the occasion arises) in answering questions about practice. However, it is reasonable to think that the "organisers and calculators" will have a better articulated representational model than the others. Nor does either of these accounts quite match Lévi-Strauss's view of essentially the same complex in *La pensée sauvage:*

> . . . practices . . . are not to be confused with *praxis* which – and here at least I agree with Sartre – constitutes the fundamental totality for the sciences of man. . . . Without questioning the undoubted primacy of infrastructures, I believe that there is always a mediator between *praxis* and practices, namely the conceptual scheme by the operation of which matter and form, neither with any independent existence, are realized as structures, that is, as entities which are both empirical and intelligible.³⁶

Yet all three positions are recognizably structuralist, Sartre's no less than the other two. And Structuralism precisely does not, as we saw earlier, have a canonical expression (which is why a formulation of Sartre's could be offered in that role a few paragraphs back), so that it would be inappropriate to insist that the term apply in one case to the exclusion of another.

Once again, then, it is not on the issue of structures as such or their functioning in society that Sartre and Lévi-Strauss disagree, but on the ontological status of the structures and the situation of the subject and agent in relation to them. The two questions are interconnected. For Lévi-Strauss subjectivity and agency drop out in favor of an ontological objectivity of structure. For Sartre the elimination of the subject and the reification of the structure are equally unthinkable. In the interview with Pingaud in *L'Arc,* cited earlier, having pointed out that language exists on two levels, one practico-inert, in which it appears autonomous, the other in act, he insists that "on this second level it can no longer be a question of ready-made structures, which would exist without us. In the system of language there is something that the inert cannot provide by itself, the trace of a practice. Structure imposes itself upon us only to the extent that it is made by others."[37] In other words, behind the apparent objectivity of structure there lies the subjectivity of other agents – initiators, creators, above all *predecessors*, those countless subjects whose legatees and beneficiaries we are not only in language but in every social domain, whose praxis gave us the practico-inert by which we are surrounded and constrained but also empowered and enabled.

THE PRACTICO-INERT AS STRUCTURE

The concept of the practico-inert is central to a development in Sartre's views, from the *Critique de la raison dialectique*, including the posthumously published second volume, through to *L'Idiot de la famille*, especially the third volume (that extraordinary and as yet radically underestimated repository of what I take to be in many cases the most mature and definitive formulations of his main positions[38]), that would emerge into a full-fledged Structuralism if its emphasis were ever so slightly shifted. Sartre stands with respect to late Structuralism (for by the time of the *Idiot* we are in the 1970s and the winds of fashion since 1968 have been dissipating the movement) in an analogous position to Cassirer with respect to early Structuralism:[39] Each has the essence of the central doctrine, grasps it indeed more adequately than its more notorious exponents; neither sees its centrality. This more adequate grasp is easily enough explained by Sartre's and Cassirer's stature as philosophers, but in the absence of their own recognition of their relation to Structuralism it was not likely to be acknowledged by the self-proclaimed structuralists. Cassirer did, at the end of his life, perceive what was coming and align himself with it,[40] but Sartre's agenda remained, in principle at least, political rather than theoretical.

The practico-inert strikes me as one of the most useful additions to the conceptual repertoire of social philosophy in the last century at least, although it seems not to be much made use of outside Sartrean scholarship. It consists of everything we encounter as ready-to-hand, as *there* waiting for us, at our disposal, that has been devised and put in place by the praxis of our fellows and predecessors. So it includes not only tools and buildings, parks and fields, books and records, but also customs and traditions and language itself. Our life is conducted in its terms; we have a serial relation to it, in that each of us makes his or her own way in relation to the installations and expectations we encounter, and this has led to a perception of the practico-inert as alien and oppressive; but as we saw in the case of Erostratus the other side of this coin is its character as liberating and facilitating. Any given episode of that life is an intersection of our freedom with its fixity. Sartre begins the section of the *Critique* annotated by his French editors as "the intelligibility of structure" and subtitled by his English translators "Structures: the Work of Lévi-Strauss" with the remark that while socially organized activity may lend itself to exact scientific formulation it also involves the actions of individual agents: "in railways, for example . . . not only finished, 'crystallised' work – machinery, rails, etc. – but also the actual work of the railwaymen, from engine-drivers to ticket-collectors." It is, he goes on to say, "both an inert relation and a living praxis."[41]

The further development of these insights in the third volume of the *Idiot* has gone largely unnoticed because it is buried in a book that is perceived to be, and in the most flat-footed sense obviously is, about Flaubert. In fact it is about everything that thinking about Flaubert made Sartre think of, which – in view of the fact that he seems to have thought about Flaubert, off and on, for his whole life – covers a very wide tract of intellectual territory. In particular the social structures that Flaubert encountered, linguistic, institutional, historical, familial, psychoanalytic *avant la lettre*, lead Sartre into a consideration of what he calls, following Hegel, objective Spirit or objective Mind (*l'Esprit objectif*).

"Objective Mind," he says, "in a particular society at a given epoch – is nothing but Culture as the practico-inert."[42] Culture is a product of work, and at a given historical moment each worker finds that he or she has interiorized the structures of a received culture, primarily in linguistic form.

[Language] isolates and transforms into a finished product the knowledge that existed implicitly in the act of the worker. It confers names and hardens under the form of definite structures all the elements that interpenetrated one another in the cultural disclosure of work (mode of production, relations of production, institutional ensemble, morals, law, etc.). Named and, by that very fact, perpetuated, these fragments of reality becoming fragments of knowledge find themselves suddenly falsified.[43]

This false knowledge, mixed in with other opinions, is lived as "the subjectivity of class."[44] Sartre here is faithful to his political project; but that the structures he takes as paradigmatic should be those of oppression does not vitiate his insight. Structuralist theory needs to give an account of the way in which its structures are embodied, and such an account Sartre proceeds to offer, starting with an allusion to Lévi-Strauss that must I think be taken as entirely deliberate:

Primitive and unmediated thought (*la pensée sauvage et immédiate*) is nothing but the practical behavior of the worker.... it is born with work and disappears with it. All to the contrary, systems of value and ideologies when they are *verbalized* remain in the mind or at least in the memory because language is matter and their elaboration has given them material inertia. Written words are stones. To learn them, to interiorize their arrangements, is to introduce into oneself a mineralized thought that will subsist in us in virtue of its very minerality as long as some material work, exercised upon it from without, does not come to free us from it. These irreducible passivities I will call *as a whole* objective Mind. And this definition implies no negative intention on my part, no desire to belittle. To be sure, in an exploitive society these structured ensembles jeopardize the exploited classes to the extent that they intrude into each individual from without and impose themselves in the memory as ramparts against any coming to awareness. But to take them in themselves they simply manifest this necessary truth: Matter mediates between men just to the extent that, through their *praxis*, they make themselves mediators between different states of matter.[45]

The homely analogy of the chicken and the egg may be helpful in making clear what separates what I am reconstructing as Sartre's version of Structuralism from the version that animated the structuralist movement proper. The wit who said "A chicken is just an egg's way of making another egg" represented something familiar in an unfamiliar light but presumably didn't mean it (as far as that goes what might seem the more normal form of which this is an inversion, "An egg is a chicken's way of making another chicken," isn't a great deal more plausible, since there's no evidence that chickens have any idea of making anything). The structuralist inversion of Sartre's formula above would have matter (or a metaphorical equivalent – a structure perhaps) "make itself" the mediator; thus Lévi-Strauss's claim about myths' "thinking themselves through us." Sartre might quite comfortably think of a text as a writer's way of "making" a reader; for the doctrinaire structuralists, a reader/writer is a text's way of making another text.

That there is an alternation of structure and agency seems clear enough; the question is whether the structure is ever autonomous or whether it is not in the end a construction of agents. That many agents might, over a very long time, have constructed a structure that, as a whole, none of them intended to construct (in the sense of having purposed all of it consciously), would not confer autonomy upon it, or allow of its continuing in existence, without being intended by other agents (in the sense of being an object for a subject). As an agent I act in the context of structures handed down to me, that I have interiorized, for the most part unconsciously, in the course of my acculturation. They form the practico-inert of my culture: my language, my family, my economic circumstances, my group affiliations. An account of these, since I am a human subject and agent, will be a structural anthropology in the sense in which Sartre uses the term in *Questions de méthode*.

INDIVIDUAL AND SOCIAL STRUCTURE

It will be remembered that *Questions de méthode* was Sartre's opening move in the Flaubert project, and that the *anthropos* of its anthropology is essentially singular. The structures of the practico-inert in the second volume of the *Critique* permeate the society and seem sometimes to be sufficiently beyond control to be as good as objective – at any rate to change less than historical agents of change would like to think. For example, consider a transfer of sovereignty involving the overthrow of a previous regime: There will be, says Sartre, an "urgent *need* to dissolve the practico-inert, the legacy of the class that has been overthrown, because its very being – if it does not change – will always condition the same social structures, whatever they may be called."[46] However, he goes on to say,

in dissolving the inherited practico-inert the sovereign and, through him, the society interiorize the social structures it conditioned; and the transcendence of this interiorization, that is, its practical reexteriorization, has as its outcome, in a slightly different technical context, the constitution of another practico-inert that reconditions men, interpersonal structures and finally praxis itself. To the extent that the latter, turned aside, reverts unceasingly to the inert concretions in order to dissolve them, that it makes other concretions through counterfinalities that reexteriorize previous circumstances, that is, the dissolved practico-inert, circularity manifests itself as the internal structure of the practical totality and becomes under the form of spirals the movement of its temporalization toward the objective.[47]

"Circular" here means at once dialectical and recursive, a concept that in the adjectival form *récurrentielle* Sartre adopts to describe the structure of history in the third volume of the *Idiot*, where its principle is summed up aphoristically as "man is the son of man."[48]

In the *Idiot* however the main emphasis is no longer on the collective, and agency has a much greater role to play. I write, for example: Clearly I don't do so in a vacuum, I am conditioned in all sorts of ways, the process doesn't even deserve to be called "composition" but should be called "recomposition." But at the same time I am far from being a prisoner of structure, and I bring to the result contributions of my own:

the syntheses of recomposition operate at once according to objective rules (structures of language, explicit or implicit authorial intentions, judgments about the author on the part of other authors previously read, etc.) *and* according to idiosyncratic disposition of a singular interiorization (daydreams, associations, bad faith, ideological interests, etc.).[49]

This "singular interiorization," in an existing individual, represents Sartre's predictable refusal to give up existence in favor of structure. But this does not mean a refusal of structure; indeed structure is acknowledged as an essential component of the situation, without which the existing individual would be inarticulate. Only a perverse Structuralism would demand more.

Sartre never wished to be called an existentialist, and it is not clear why anyone would want to be called a structuralist. But Existentialism, in spite of what Sartre or anyone else might have wanted, came to be a marker in midcentury discourse, just as Structuralism did a generation later. We make of these movements what we can; my own claim with respect to the latter has been that it stood for something more important and more lasting than even its practitioners knew at the time.⁵⁰ Roland Barthes caught this slippage between ideas and their designations admirably when he said in 1971: "Structuralism, I do not renounce the word, but it has become uncertain."⁵¹ Sartre was the one contemporary philosopher whom Barthes did not renounce amid the general deconstruction of the 1960s and 1970s, to whom indeed he repeatedly referred as an admired influence; Barthes predicted a Sartre revival, saying that Sartre would be rediscovered "in a completely natural way" (Sartre, when asked to comment on this, said "I hope so").⁵² And Barthes would I suspect have been friendly to my assessment of some of Sartre's work not merely as compatible with a mature Structuralism but as making a genuine contribution to it, the essential feature of which lies precisely in its reconciliation of the social and individual aspect of structure, the articulation of the theoretical and the existential.

Barthes's expositor and critic, Annette Lavers, puts the matter in this way:

The dispute between structuralists and existentialists was not inevitable; the second of these two great postwar movements could have been conceived as a long overdue complement to the first to yield a total picture of man in society. . . . Structuralism's failure to recognize the central place of praxis was the object of Sartre's comment that "geology" would be a more appropriate description of Foucault's work than Foucault's own term "archaeology." And yet, Sartre had seemed in the late 1960s to be poised to add his structuralist *aggiornamento* to his earlier phenomenological, Marxist, and even psychoanalytical ones. And never more so than on the subject of structural approaches to the text, which he said he himself intended to use in his study on Flaubert. Controversy made him harden his positions, however.⁵³

Part of my argument in this essay has been that Sartre's refusal to be called a structuralist, like Foucault's, does not prevent the rest of us from enrolling him on the side of Structuralism. The human sciences, I continue to think, are best served at the present time by recognizing and cultivating the theoretical power of Structuralism. Too quickly abandoned by its own exponents in their rush to the new and "post-," it is capable, as Marxism was not, of playing the role Sartre ascribed to Marxism in *Questions de méthode* as the philosophy for our time. A thought out of season, perhaps, but one with which long immersion in the work of Sartre persuades me that he might, the hardening of controversy apart, have agreed.

NOTES

Translations from the French are my own, unless otherwise stated.

1 See Peter Caws, "Oracular Lives: Sartre and the Twentieth Century," *Revue Internationale de Philosophie*, 39, no. 152–3 (1985): 172–83.

2 I do not wish to enter here into the old question whether Foucault is properly called a structuralist, having dealt with it elsewhere (see my *Structuralism: The Art of the Intelligible* [Atlantic Highlands, N.J.: Humanities Press International, 1988], p. 32).

3 Michel Contat and Michel Rybalka, *Les Écrits de Sartre* (Paris: NRF/Gallimard, 1970), p. 430.

4 *Sartre Aujourd'hui, L'Arc*, no. 30 (1966): 88.

5 By this somewhat rebarbative expression I mean a relation between two quantities (loosely speaking – that is, attributes of which a thing can have more or less) which belong to different conceptual categories (that is, are measured along different dimensions and might be plotted on different axes) but which nevertheless vary mutually, one increasing when the other decreases and vice versa.

6 See Peter Caws, *Sartre* (London: Routledge and Kegan Paul, 1979), p. 143.

7 Karl Marx, tr. and ed. Lloyd D. Easton and Kurt H. Guddat, "Notes to the Doctoral Dissertation (1839–41)," in *Writings of the Young Marx on Philosophy and Society* (Garden City, N.Y.: Doubleday, 1967), p. 65.

8 Jean-Paul Sartre, tr. Hazel Barnes, *Search for a Method* (New York: Alfred A. Knopf, 1963), p. 135.

9 Caws, *Structuralism*, p. 1.

10 *L'Arc*, p. 94.

11 Ibid.

12 Caws, *Sartre*, pp. 147–8.

13 *L'Arc*, p. 88.

14 Ibid.

15 Ibid.

16 Claude Lévi-Strauss, *L'Homme nu (Mythologiques* ****) (Paris: Plon, 1971), p. 614.

17 Ibid., p. 616.

18 Peter Caws, *The Philosophy of Science: A Systematic Account* (Princeton, N.J.: Van Nostrand, 1965), p. 11.

19 Caws, *Sartre*, p. 150.

20 "The Place of Anthropology in the Social Sciences and Problems Raised in Teaching It," in Claude Lévi-Strauss, tr. Claire Jacobson and Brooked Grundfest Schoepf, *Structural Anthropology* (New York, Basic Books,

1963; Anchor edition 1967), pp. 362, 378. The quotation from Sartre is from *Les Temps Modernes* (October–November, 1952), p. 729, n 1.

21 Jean-Paul Sartre, *Cahiers pour une morale* (Paris, NRF/Gallimard, 1983), p. 389.

22 This particular structure, *libération–gratuité*, might be read as oppositional in the classical structuralist sense. *"Libération"* has the possible sense of "discharge from obligation," and the two conflicting desires that operate in the potlatch process are on the one hand to be freed of the burden of obligation imposed by previous donors and on the other to make a gesture of apparently unmotivated liberality.

23 Sartre, *Cahiers*, p. 389.

24 Ibid., p. 456.

25 Claude Lévi-Strauss, *Anthropologie structurale* (Paris: Plon, 1958), p. 81.

26 Contat and Rybalka, *Les Écrits de Sartre*, p. 744.

27 This is an unfortunate literalism in translation, since *ossature*, which has no homologue in standard English, does have a perfectly good equivalent – it means "framework" or even just "structure," as in *ossature sociale*, which my dictionary gives quite straightforwardly as "social structure."

28 Jean-Paul Sartre, tr. Alan Sheridan-Smith, *Critique of Dialectical Reason* (London: New Left Books, 1976), p. 480.

29 Ibid., p. 489.

30 Ferdinand de Saussure, tr. Wade Baskin, *Course in General Linguistics* (New York, Philosophical Library, 1959), p. 71.

31 Jean-Paul Sartre, tr. Lloyd Alexander, *The Wall* (New York: New Directions, 1948), p. 49.

32 Sartre, *Critique of Dialectical Reason*, pp. 499–500.

33 Ibid., pp. 500–1.

34 Ibid., p. 502.

35 Peter Caws, "Operational, Representational and Explanatory Models," *American Anthropologist*, 76, no. 1 (March 1976): 1–10.

36 Claude Lévi-Strauss, tr. anonymous, *The Savage Mind* (Chicago, University of Chicago Press, 1966), p. 130.

37 *L'Arc*, p. 89.

38 See for example Peter Caws, "Sartre's Last Philosophical Manifesto," in Hugh J. Silverman, ed., *Philosophy and Non-Philosophy since Merleau-Ponty. Continental Philosophy*, Vol. I (New York: Routledge, 1988), pp. 106–19.

39 See Caws, *Structuralism*, pp. 16–19.

40 See Ernst Cassirer, "Structuralism in Modern Linguistics," *Word*, 1, no. 2 (August 1945).

41 Sartre, *Critique of Dialectical Reason*, p. 480.

42 Jean-Paul Sartre, *L'Idiot de la famille: Gustave Flaubert de 1821 à 1857*, Vol. III (Paris, NRF/Gallimard, 1972), p. 44.

43 Ibid., p. 45.

44 Ibid., p. 46

45 Ibid., p. 47.

46 Jean-Paul Sartre, *Critique de la raison dialectique*. Vol. II, *inachevé: L'intelligibilité de l'Histoire* (Paris: NRF/Gallimard, 1985), p. 288.

47 Ibid., pp. 288–9.

48 Sartre, *L'Idiot* III, pp. 437, 440.

49 Ibid., p. 55.

50 Caws, *Structuralism*, p. xiv.

51 Roland Barthes, interview in *La Quinzaine littéraire* 68, March 1–15 (1971): 16.

52 "Sartre at Seventy: An Interview by Michel Contat," *New York Review of Books*, August 7, 1975, p. 13.

53 Annette Lavers, *Roland Barthes: Structuralism and After* (Cambridge, Mass.: Harvard University Press, 1982), p. 24.

CHRISTINA HOWELLS

Conclusion: Sartre and the deconstruction of the subject

SOME PRELIMINARY REFERENCE POINTS ON THE SUBJECT

Autonomous, independent, spontaneous foundation of knowledge, understanding, feeling, imagination? Alienating, idealist, bourgeois humanist, phallogocentric delusion? Does the subject lie between these two polar opposite descriptions of it, does it span them and, like a Pascalian paradox, fill all the space between, or does it lie elsewhere entirely, perhaps in a utopia? Is belief in the subject a necessary alienation, an *aliénation heureuse*,[1] a transcendental illusion of the Kantian kind? Is the subject an outmoded peg on which humanism used to hang its credentials and which can be abandoned along with the rest of the humanist paraphernalia? Or, to change metaphor, would such a rejection involve throwing the baby out with the bathwater? Is the concept of the subject necessary to any meditation on ethics, and, if so, need it be more than an "operational concept"?[2] Or should this idea be shunned as a manifestation of the worst kind of paternalism? Contemporary French philosophy returns incessantly to the subject – recent thinking on ethics and politics, and in particular on Auschwitz and on Heidegger, has made the issue a burning one once again – "through flame or ashes, but . . . inevitably,"[3] to use Derrida's concluding words in *De l'Esprit*. Having deposed the subject so firmly and with such apparent haste and delight in the 1960s and 1970s, French philosophers are now seeming to repent at leisure. The "death of man" (Foucault)[4] and the "ends of man" (Derrida)[5] are now seen to have lacked the radical finality with which their celebration endowed them twenty years earlier.

318

For our purposes, this revision of the subject, this disinterment of the human question, is all to the good, for it enables the interrogation of Sartre's position to be undertaken with seriousness, that is to say, not as a mere piece of historical inquiry, but as a genuine contribution to a vital philosophical debate. And it is in this spirit that the present chapter is conceived.

But before looking at Sartre's own views on the subject, let us consider briefly the bibliographical evidence for a change of attitude toward the subject in France. The published conference proceedings, special issues of journals, and multiple- and single-authored books of the last couple of years include the following:

> *Penser le sujet aujourd'hui*
> *Sur l'Individu*
> *L'Individu et ses ennemis*
> *Après le sujet, qui vient?*
> *L'Ère de l'individu*
> *L'Individualisme: le grand retour*
> *L'Ultime raison du sujet*
> *Hors Sujet*[6]

There are many more. Of course, the individual human being and the subject are not identical, they may even be opposed, though they are often conflated in the notion of the individual subject. The distinction has, however, no single or simple interpretation. The "individual" may be used in contradistinction to the "subject" to avoid the supposed metaphysical overtones of the latter – for example if the "biological individual" is at issue. But conversely, the term "subject" is employed in order to undercut the cozy, immediately familiar connotations that the "individual" may have when it is used to refer to separate, self-identical men and women whose status is self-evident and unproblematic. If the subject is berated as excessively theological, the individual is repudiated as insufficiently social. Both may appear to be attached to a lingering humanist heritage. But the barriers between them are far from clearcut, as is manifest in the fact that a work by the German philosopher Manfred Frank: *Die Unhintergehbarkeit von Individualität* is translated into French as *L'Ultime raison du sujet*. The text begins as follows:

A thesis is currently fashionable: In both theory and practice the "end" of the modern subject has come about, in all its forms, be it "apperception," "human reality," "person" or "individual."[7]

Frank's essay purports to be a refutation of this thesis, and thus provides further fuel for my contention that the subject is once again at the center of contemporary inquiry. Nonetheless, the slogan "a return to the subject" is rejected by both factions: Those held responsible for its so-called death – Derrida, Foucault, Lacan, Deleuze, among others – if not now dead themselves, refuse the implications of *volte-face*, revisionism, and regression contained in the notion of a "return." The question of the subject can, for them, be considered only on the basis of its prior decentering or deconstruction. There is no philosophically valid means of undoing or overlooking all the work that has already gone into the dismantling of the subject as a humanist, metaphysical concept. On the other hand, there are those who maintain that the "death of the subject" was itself a myth, so that again there can be no question of a *return:* The subject was never abandoned except as part of a polemical strategy that has finally lost all credibility. These two groups remain, it will be clear, ideologically opposed. But they have in common the aim of a thoroughgoing exegesis of the history of the concept of the subject, from Descartes through Kant and Hegel to Husserl and, for some, Heidegger.

Similarly, there is no current consensus concerning the individual. Indeed, the notion of the individual produces even less agreement than that of the subject. As Ricoeur (following Louis Dumont) argues, it has two very different, even opposed senses: an empirical sense, that of "an indivisible sample," and a moral sense, that of "an independent, autonomous, nonsocial being."[8] Simply equated by some with the individual subject –

We may understand in this context by individual a subject, a being attached to his own identity by self-consciousness or self-knowledge,[9]

"master of himself and marked by a personal history,"[10] incalculable, unstable, varied, irreducible,[11] autonomous, and independent[12] – it represents a stand against absorption by anonymous, faceless, mass-production, and nameless market forces. Alternatively, the individual is celebrated by others precisely as a single element in a subjectless flux, an atom, a "singularity,"[13] released from the humanist dress of earlier centuries. An undivided residue, without subjectivity or passions, without negation or otherness, an operational concept, unheroic, neutral, and synthetic. In this view, the individual represents precisely the *antithesis* of the subject, it is described even as an empty form, a specter haunting space after the death of the subject.[14] Some "individuals," then, are "subjects" and some are not. And some "subjects" are "individuals," but, similarly, some are not.

Etymologically, of course, the terms subject and individual have very different histories. The individual is undivided, at least with respect to the concept under which it has been individuated, and there is not much more to say about it in linguistic terms. The subject, on the contrary, may be divided, but this is not visible in its verbal formation. What is evident is rather the subject as *subjectum*, underlying ground or foundation (Greek: *hypokeimenon*). As *subjectus*, however, the subject may also be subject *to* something other – to laws, oppression, and so forth, but this is not the sense that the term carries as philosophical subject, though it provides fodder for some word play by certain philosophers.[15] Furthermore, the subject is opposed to the object, not merely in a linguistic sense, but also in the sense of being in contradistinction to the objective world that it perceives, knows, and, at some high points of hubris, paradoxically grounds.

The subject in its "modern" sense is traced back by its historians to Descartes and Kant, but the term is not ever used in this sense by the former, and is not used consistently by the latter. Nonetheless, Descartes is considered father of the modern concept of the subject insofar as he takes the *cogito* as logical foundation for all knowledge of the external world, as well as unifying principle underpinning the diversity of its objects.[16] It is in Descartes that Heidegger, for example, situates the origin of the subject–object split that he, together with other phenomenologists, sets out to heal.[17] The Cartesian subject is a kind of universal singular, common to all and yet specific to each and comparable to Kant's "bare 'I think'." Depending on whether the *Regulae* or the *Meditations* are focused on, Descartes may be seen as founding opposing conceptions of the subject as on the one hand individualist and on the other transindividual or even impersonal.[18] Furthermore, in the context of this chapter, it is also tempting to see Descartes as having founded a version of the split subject, although this interpretation is evidently open to accusations of anachronism. The mind–body split, at times conceived as a pure dualism, in which the subject is identified with mind, though it happens to be physically embodied,[19] has, at other points in the text, further implications. For Descartes envisages the body as origin of the passions, emotions, and sentiments that go toward the constitution of the *"vrai homme"* (true man).[20] If mind as thinking substance is radically distinct from human emotions, passions, and so on, then the Cartesian subject may be seen as potentially divided in a more far-reaching sense than the mind–body dualism would initially suggest. In any case, what is certain is Descarte's ambivalence with respect to the location of the subject, whether it lies in the "soul" alone or in an intimate union of body and soul.

The division of the Kantian subject is not merely potential, it is explicit and recognized to be problematic. There are several different possible interpretations of the subject in Kant, ranging at one extreme, perhaps, from a (Humean) bundle of sense perceptions to the transcendental unity of apperception, or from the temporal phenomenal subject to the atemporal noumenal subject. Kant's own recognition of the impossibility of clarifying the relation between the noumenal and phenomenal subject is well known. In his analysis of the paralogisms of rational psychology (that is to say, pure or speculative psychology, which attempts to understand and describe the essence of the self or subject analytically, by rational deduction rather than by empirical observation) he reveals the split at the core of the subject which prevents full self-knowledge, for the "I that thinks," the synthesizing subject, cannot be proved identical to the temporal subject of experience. Cartesian dualism was primarily that of the mind–body split. In Kant, the subject itself is dual. Knowledge for Kant is restricted to the phenomenal world, and the I that thinks is not part of that world, not subject to causal categories but rather responsible for causal structuring. The I that thinks is responsible for the constitution of the spatiotemporal world but is not part of it and cannot be known. The illusions of rational psychology all depend on "treating the subjective conditions of thinking as being knowledge of the object."[21] This tendency to confuse the conditions of representation of the subject with the subject itself leads rational psychologists to believe that the subject is simple, substantial, and personal. None of these assumptions is, in Kant's view, any more than the product of a false logic. In fact we can know nothing whatsoever about the transcendental subject:

We do not have and cannot have any knowledge whatsoever of any such subject. Consciousness is, indeed, that which alone makes all representations to be thoughts: and in it therefore, as the transcendental subject, all our perceptions must be found, but beyond this logical meaning of the "I" we have no knowledge of the subject in itself, which as substratum underlies this "I" as it does all thoughts.[22]

We are left with the paradox of an identity presumed between the "I that thinks" and the subject of experience, in the face of the impossibility of self-knowledge, and of the fact that the former is beyond causality, the latter subject to it. The distinction between, and yet identity of, the "I that thinks" and the "I that intuits itself"[23] is one of the great imponderables of the Transcendental Deduction, and one of the areas where, ultimately, in Kant's view, all that can "fairly be asked" of a philosophy that pushes reason to its very limits is that it "comprehend" the "incomprehensibility" of the paradox it has uncovered.[24]

Like Descartes and Kant, Sartre uses a multiplicity of different terms to discuss the vexed question of the subject. Like Kant and Descartes, he starts from the reflexive, thinking subject, and, like them, he wrestles interminably with the ensuing problems of dualism. Mind/body (Descartes), noumenal/phenomenal (Kant), *pour soi/en soi* (Sartre). And like both his predecessors, he makes various ingenious attempts to evade the implications of such a dualism, ultimately ruling the question out of court as metaphysical and irrelevant to phenomenological ontology! (*EN*, p. 719)

But this is not to say that Sartre's position may be assimilated to that of either Descartes or Kant. On the contrary. And his difference from them may become clearer if three figures of the intervening years are mentioned briefly at this stage – Nietzsche, Husserl, and Heidegger. Nietzsche and Husserl, I would suggest, polarize the warring tendencies at work in the subject of their predecessors and each relinquishes one half of the earlier problematic. Heidegger attempts (unsuccessfully?) to go beyond both.

Husserl's approach, expounded most clearly in the *Cartesian Meditations*, is to posit a transcendental ego, a unity underlying our actions, causal not caused. This transcendental ego is a self in a stronger sense than that of either the Cartesian *cogito* or the Kantian unity of apperception, and, not unexpectedly, Husserl views it as an advance on the subject. Descartes, he claims, mistakenly envisaged the ego as a separate *"substantia cogitans"* (*Méd*, 21), which made him the father of a misguided kind of transcendental realism. Kant's error was to posit the possibility of a noumenal world (p. 72), and to fail to follow through the notion of a "noematic a priori of sensible intuition" in his analyses of time and space in the *Critique of Pure Reason* except "in an extremely limited and unclear fashion" (p. 125). Phenomenology aims to avoid the subject–object cleavage and to close the gap between the abstract, rational, or noumenal subject and its concrete, empirical, phenomenal embodiment. But what in fact is produced is an unsatisfactory collage of the two, which re-introduces the empirical self along with the outside world and other people as "contents" of consciousness. Descartes and Kant both wrestled unsuccessfully with the problems of dualism that their philosophies engendered. Husserl's dismissal of these problems as deriving from misunderstanding merely replaces them with dog-matic simplifications that paper over the cracks rather than mend-ing them. Husserl seems bent on minimizing the difficulty of the problem he is dealing with, as is clear from his affirmation in the *Logical Investigations* that self-consciousness is "an everyday thing presenting no difficulties of understanding."[25] The "methodological twist"[26] of phenomenological reduction then permits him to con-sider this "unproblematic" immediate self-consciousness as provid-ing philosophical (rather than merely psychological) knowledge of a priori essences. But Husserl is far from having resolved the dilemma of his predecessors. In the first place, it is unclear how a phenome-nologist can consider himself as remaining within transcendental philosophy. And furthermore, from the point of view of transcenden-tal philosophy, it would appear that Husserl's attempt to describe the subject separate from its empirical manifestations (the *epoche* brackets off precisely the phenomenal spatiotemporal self in the transcendental reduction), although intended to *avoid* the illusions of rational psychology spelled out by Kant, nonetheless comes peril-ously close to a quintessential form of them in its conception of the "pure self" of the *Ideen*[27] and the *Meditations* (*Méd*, p. 18). The pure self certainly falls prey to two out of three of the "illusions" – it is simple and personal, though it is not substantial.

At the other extreme, Nietzsche is prepared to forgo the whole idea of selfhood. The paradoxes surrounding the subject in previous philosophy are, for him, mere traces of a language that divides experience into subject and object, giving the illusion of subjectivity and selfhood where in fact only an empty grammar is at work. The subject is a popular prejudice, a (Humean) fiction caused by grammar. It is an epiphenomenon of language. The Cartesian *cogito* proves nothing for Nietzsche other than that there is thinking: Descartes is a substantialist who is a victim of the "grammatical custom that adds a do-er to every deed."[28] And in *Beyond Good and Evil*, Nietzsche repeats that it is "a falsification of the facts to say that the subject 'I' is the condition of the predicate 'think'."[29] Indeed, in the *Genealogy of Morals* he considers knowledge to be fundamentally flawed by the pernicious effects of a belief in the subject: "Our entire science still lies under the misleading influence of language and has not disposed of that little changeling, the 'subject'."[30] Nietzsche's attack on the subject is fragmentary rather than systematic, but it is clearly related to his critique of individuation, with which it is ultimately combined in the notion of the *Übermensch* who is conceived precisely as a way of going beyond the individual human subject:[31]

The most cautious people ask today: "How may man still be preserved?" Zarathustra, however, asks as the sole and first one to do so: "How shall man be *overcome*?"[32]

In a sense, Heidegger may be seen as trying to move on from where Nietzsche and Husserl in their very different ways left off. On the one hand he apparently accepts Nietzsche's undermining of selfhood and personal identity, envisaging nonsingular *Dasein* as prior to the individuated self or subject. On the other, in *Being and Time* at least, Heidegger still considers himself engaged in a form of transcendental philosophy,[33] which he wishes to rid of the abstraction he associates with Husserlian phenomenology. If Husserl underplays the problems of transcendental philsophy by founding his description of the transcendental ego on intuition ("blind" without "concepts" in Kant's view), Heidegger ignores them entirely in his quest for a concrete description of *Dasein* that supposedly remains nonempirical. Viewed in this perspective, he could be considered to fall into the trap of rational psychology, in a generalized version that retains the illusions and paralogisms but applied now to a nonindividual nonpersonal Being (*Dasein.*) Given Heidegger's ambivalence toward the Kantian conception of the subject,[34] and his explicit aim of leaving behind all the metaphysics of subjectivity, it may seem ironic to use Kant to criticize Heidegger. However, the subject is not so easily abandoned, and a Kantian critique of Heidegger already has some respectable antecedents.[35]

Sartre's views on the subject are necessarily defined in response not only to the paradoxes of Kant and Descartes, but also to the polemics of Nietzsche, Husserl, and Heidegger. And the disaffection with Sartre in the 1960s is clearly related in its turn to his attitude to his German predecessors for, as the purpose of this chapter is to show, Sartre was one of the first French philosophers to think through some of the implications of what has been called the "divided subject" (or the "split subject" for Lacanians). But his writings of the 1930s and 1940s, though highly controversial in their day, have long since been absorbed, at least selectively, into the current philosophical doxa, constituting, indeed, a vital part of the formation of his structuralist and poststructuralist detractors. Rather than recognize Sartre as a forerunner, his immediate successors preferred to return directly to the German thinkers and – in their view at least – to radicalize still further their insights into the deconstruction of the subject. Sartre's own discussions became an embarrassment, coming so close in many ways to the points the philosophers of the 1960s and 1970s wished to make, but without the brutal iconoclasm then in favor. The solution was parricide. Only certain aspects of Sartre's thinking were recognized, his radicalism was almost willfully suppressed, and he was accused of that very bourgeois humanism and individualism he so profoundly and persistently attacked. Twenty years later (1992), Structuralism in its turn is out of favor, and its self-assessment as the farthest-reading critique of individual subjectivity and humanism is being put in question. In a review of a recent book on *Sartre and "Les Temps Modernes,"* a critic writes:

Certainly the structuralist concern with universals, synchrony and cultural pluralism stamp it as far less radical a philosophy than Sartre's which, with its sophisticated anticipation of the debates around orientalism in the analy-

ses of the political and ideological discourses of colonialism, emerges as a
much more far-reaching critique of humanism.[36]

The time is now surely ripe to leave aside competition for the post of
chief opponent to humanism, and to try to get beyond the vagaries of
intellectual fashion and the swings of the philosophic pendulum, in
order to pay some serious attention to Sartre's views on the subject.
For our purposes, the primary focuses will be Sartre's rejection of
humanist individualism in *La Nausée*, his insistence on the self as
an imaginary construct and an unrealizable limit in *The Transcendence of the Ego*, his refusal of human nature in *Being and Nothingness*, and of Man in the *Critique of Dialectical Reason*: "Man does
not exist" (*CRD*, p. 131).

We will look first at the 1936 essay on the *Transcendence of the Ego*
in which Sartre is attacking the Husserlian notion of the subject as a
transcendental ego. For Sartre there is no inner self or ego, source of
action, feeling, thought, will, and emotion. The self is an imaginary
construct, outside consciousness, object not subject of consciousness, a continuous creation held in being by belief. The self or ego, the
"I" and the "me" are synthetic products of consciousness, unified not
unifying, transcendent not immanent. Sartre is arguing against
Husserl that the ego is transcendent, not transcendental. A *transcendental* ego would be a personal core of consciousness, an original
unitary subject, source of meaning, center of personality, interior
foundation for my sense of self. For Sartre only consciousness is transcendental, and it is, properly speaking, originally impersonal or at
least prepersonal (*TE*, pp. 19, 79). (In his later writings Sartre will drop
the term "transcendental" entirely, possibly because of its Kantian
overtones.) A *transcendent* ego, on the other hand, is external to
consciousness, an ideal totality of states, qualities, and actions, a
construct that I tend to imagine as a source of my feelings and behavior but which is in fact a synthesis. In the terms of *Being and Nothingness*, the ego is *en soi* (*EN*, p. 147; *TE*, p. 55). For this reason a transcendental ego would be a "center of opacity" (*TE*, p. 25) in consciousness,
and would entail "the death of consciousness" (p. 23).

The "I," in Sartre's account, is not a unifying force; it is rather
consciousness that makes the unity and personality of the "I" possible (*TE*, p. 23). Not only is the ego external to consciousness, it is not
even permanently present to consciousness. Sartre's essay starts by

agreeing with Kant that "it must be possible for the 'I think' to accompany all my representations" (p. 13),[37] which he interprets as meaning that consciousness can always become reflexive, or in other words that self-consciousness is a constant possibility, and is the condition of possibility of experience. But it is the reflexive act itself that, for Sartre, brings the ego into being: "There is no *I* on the non-reflexive level" (p. 32); when I am reading or running for a train I am conscious of the book or the train to be caught, not of myself reading or running, though I may become self-conscious at any moment. Consciousness is always intentional, that is to say it always has an object; much of the time its object is the outside world, but occasionally I will turn my attention on myself. If this is momentary or incidental ("What are you doing?" – "I'm reading") the ego will appear fleetingly in the act of reflection. But if I want to capture that ego and analyze it I am doomed to disappointment. The self may be an object in the world, but unlike other objects it can be perceived only obliquely; I cannot ever observe my own ego at work: "The Ego appears only when we are not looking at it . . . by its nature, the Ego is fleeting" (p. 70). Since my self is not *in* consciousness, I cannot discover it by looking inward – introspection meets only a frustrating emptiness and opacity. By attempting to focus on the ego, consciousness passes necessarily from the simple reflexive mode in which the ego appears ("I'm reading") to a complex but nonetheless *non*reflexive mode that tries vainly to concentrate on an object that has already disappeared. This means that I can never *know myself* in any real sense (p. 69); I have no privileged knowledge of myself: My self-knowledge is similar to my knowledge of other people – that is to say, a result of observation and interpretation of behavior. And to take an external view of myself is necessarily to take a false perspective, to try to believe in a self that I have myself created: "so the intuition of the Ego is a perpetually deceptive mirage" (p. 69).

Independently produced as a conference paper in 1936, and first published thirteen years later, is Lacan's essay on the *mirror stage*. The similarity between the psychoanalyst's conception of the ego and that of Sartre is striking and its implications are manifold. In his essay, Lacan argues that the ego is an imaginary synthesis initially elaborated by the infant between six and eighteen months in response to his reflection in a mirror. The bodily unity and control that is visible in the mirror though not yet achieved by the young baby is identified by the infant with itself (E, p. 94). This impression of stable selfhood has two major implications: Firstly, it is imaginary, and second, it involves an alienation insofar as it depends on an identification with *another,* that is, the image of itself as other:

> It is sufficient to understand the mirror-stage *as an identification* in the strong sense which the term has in analysis: that is the transformation produced in the subject when he assumes an image.

> The jubilant assumption of his specular image by the child at the *infans* stage, still stuck in his motor incapacity and nursling dependence, would seem to exhibit in an exemplary situation the symbolic matrix in which the *I* is precipitated in a primordial form, before it is objectified in the dialectic of identification with the other, and before language restores to it, in the universal, its function as subject. (E, 94)

The self of the mirror stage is forever a fiction, a source of discordance and alienation that precedes language and social determinants. We may note that there is as yet no *subject* proper for this comes into being with and through language.

The mirror phase initiates and symbolizes for Lacan the "mental permanence of the 'I' " and its "alienating destiny" (E, p. 95). It anticipates the "eventual armor of an alienating identity" (p. 97) that the subject will assume. It is a *méconnaissance* (pp. 109, 832), a misrecognition; it is described as a "capture" by the image (pp. 113, 832), and it will come between the subject and his attempts at self-realization because of its "irreducible inertia" (p. 109). It is also the mirror phase that explains aggressivity in Lacan's view, rather than the "struggle for survival" of the classical Freudian picture, evoked in *Civilization and Its Discontents* (p. 344). In the specular image I am alienated from myself, constituted by internal tension and division (p. 113), by inner conflict (p. 344). What is more, the mirror image is more controlled, unified, and coordinated than the infant's own experience at this early stage, and one of his reactions is aggression toward his apparently superior rival self. Aggressivity toward others, rivalry, identification with others, ambivalence, all are *preceded* by the structure of my own relationship with myself: "The notion of aggressivity corresponds . . . to the division of the subject against itself" (p. 344). The child who identifies with another child, and cries when the other is hurt, for example, is merely manifesting his own previous constituted identification with an other, the other of his own self-image (pp. 113, 117, 181). Lacan remarks that Sartre described in striking terms the negativity and aggressivity underlying all human relations, even the most apparently loving and charitable, but that he was misled by an illusory notion of individual autonomous selfhood, and did not recognize the roots of such aggressivity as lying in the internally divided nature of the self (pp. 98–9). This is not quite an accurate view of Sartre who, as we have just seen, shares Lacan's conception of the ego as a fictional synthesis, but it is true that he does not consider this as the root of aggressivity toward others. Rather, as Juliette Simont shows in her essay in the present volume, Sartre attributes mutual oppression and aggressivity to the ordinary alienation of freedom in a material world that distorts it. But this archeology of alienation comes ten years after the *Transcendence of the Ego*, where Sartre's focus is purely on the necessity to view the ego as a synthetic construct.

If the ego is an imaginary construct, Lacan's opposition to ego psychology should come as no surprise. Ego psychology aims to strengthen the ego, to enable it to bring troublesome unconscious forces and instincts under control. Now, the unconscious has, for Lacan, nothing to do with instincts, and the ego is an illusion of identity, rather than a stable center that can be reinforced. The *subject* is riven, dislocated, and a strong ego can only involve it in an ever more inescapable alienation within a fixed objectification of itself in which it will be irremediably trapped. Ego psychology gives its blessing, unwittingly, to what Lacan calls the "formal stagnation" of "a permanent, substantial, self-identical entity" (*E*, p. 111). It sanctifies the series of ideal identifications in which the subject is ensnared (p. 178): "The ego . . . is frustration in its very essence" (p. 250). Ego psychology confuses the senses of ego – it deals not with the subject but with his *alter ego* (p. 374), and its attempts to help him toward social integration and adaptation are merely further stones on the grave of his chances of ever disentangling himself from his social (alienated) persona (cf. p. 399). Ego psychology has set itself not so much an impossible aim as a thoroughly *undesirable* one:

Certainly (Lacan writes), the reintegration of the subject with his ego is conceivable – all the more so because, contrary to an *idée reçue* of contem-

porary psychoanalysis, the ego (*moi*) is far from being weak . . . But this aim
would itself be an error, because it can only lead the subject to a further
alienation of his desire. (p. 453)

Ego psychology involves a total misunderstanding of analysis, it is
contradictory and retrograde (p. 454).

Lacan's explicit contrasting of the ego and the subject – to which
we will return – leads us back to the initial question of the nature of
the subject for Sartre. The *Transcendence of the Ego* gives only a
negative picture of the subject by demonstrating what it is not,
namely a transcendental ego that is *en soi* (*TE*, p. 55; *EN*, p. 147).
Indeed, the subject is almost entirely absent from the text, since
Sartre's argument is that "absolute consciousness, when it is puri-
fied of the 'I', has nothing of a subject about it" (*TE*, p. 87).

Consciousness is described as impersonal (p. 87), even if individuated (p. 78). But as Leo Fretz shows in his essay in this volume, there
has been at least a shift of emphasis by the time of *Being and Nothingness*. Here we see that although Sartre still believes that the
notion of a transcendental subject is "useless" and "harmful" (*EN*, p.
291), and maintains that consciousness is a "transcendental field
without a subject" (p. 291), this is not so much a denial of any kind
of subject as a consequence of his refutation of Husserl's identification of the subject with a transcendental ego. Sartre is clearly well
aware that a version of Husserl's view of the subject is commonplace, and indeed firmly inscribed in everyday (inauthentic) human
relations and social and legal institutions:

It is as Egos that we are subjects in fact and subjects in law, active and
passive, voluntary agents, possible objects of judgments of value and responsibility. (*EN*, p. 209)

But in *Being and Nothingness*, Sartre is for the first time prepared
to define what he himself understands by *subject* and *subjectivity*.
Subjectivity is defined as "consciousness (of) consciousness" (*EN*, p.
29), and the "instantaneous *cogito*" (p. 83). This means that subjectivity is an immediate, untheorized (self) awareness, neither positional nor thetic. Subjectivity is the spontaneous reflexivity of consciousness when it is directed toward something other than itself.
And it is precisely this reflexivity that stops consciousness remaining a "transcendental field without a subject" (p. 291). It is the reflex-

ivity of consciousness, its presence to itself, which constitutes the
pour soi, and which thereby personalizes it (p. 148). Consciousness
becomes personal because it is reflexive, present to itself. Only a
false hypostatization reverses cause and effect and transforms the
product of reflexivity into some kind of essential core of selfhood.
Clearly the *soi* cannot preexist consciousness if it comes into being
through the reflexive nature of consciousness.

It is this reflexivity, consciousness as it is for itself, as *pour soi*,
that constitutes the subject for Sartre. The *soi* is grammatically a
reflexive term, it indicates a relationship of the subject to itself, but
the subject cannot *be soi* or there would be no reflexivity and the *soi*
itself would disappear in self-identity and self-coincidence (*EN*, p.
119). The *soi* cannot inhabit consciousness, it is an ideal, a limit (p.
148). So the *pour soi* is only *soi* in an unrealizable sense: "over
there," "out of reach" (p. 148), "in the form of lack," as a "detotalized totality" (pp. 229, 718). It cannot have a "deep self" (a "*moi
profond*," p. 520). It is a relationship. The *pour soi* of consciousness
is fundamentally riven. It is present *to* itself and therefore always
separated *from* itself. "If it is present to itself, that means it is not
entirely itself" (p. 120). "Its being is always at a distance" (p. 167).

We must pause for a moment to look more closely at this idea of
the self-presence of the *pour soi*, for it provided Derrida with one of
the weapons to attack Sartre as part of the metaphysical tradition
that rests on an identification of being and presence. First of all it is
evident that *being* in the sense of the *en soi* is not "present" for
Sartre – indeed, in his view, "the *en soi* cannot be present" (*EN*, p.
165), "to be *there* is not to be *present*" (p. 166), "the present is
precisely this negation of being, this escape from being insofar as
being is *there* as something one escapes" (p. 167). We need not examine the refusal of presence to the *en soi* in this context. But what of
the *pour soi*? We have just seen the self-presence of the *pour soi* used
to deny its self-identity: "The *Pour-soi* has no being because its
being is always at a distance" (p. 167). *Présence à soi* is defined as "a
way of not coinciding with oneself, of escaping identity" (p. 119). It
is not plenitude, not "the highest dignity of being" (p. 119). Sartre
cites Husserl as evidence that even the most determined philosopher of presence cannot overcome entirely the reflexivity implicit in
all consciousness. Presence is precisely what prevents identity. "The

subject cannot be itself (*soi*). If it is present to itself, that means it is not completely itself" (p. 120). Consciousness is always elsewhere, "at a distance from itself" (p. 120). "The *pour soi* is obliged never to exist except as an elsewhere in relation to itself" (p. 121). It is "*diasporique*" (p. 182), dispersed.

Sartre's analysis of the self-presence of the *pour soi* anticipates Derrida's deconstruction of Husserl's *Logical Investigations* in *La Voix et le phénomène* (1967). Derrida also sets out to demonstrate that Husserl's own analyses undermine his insistence on the notion of self-identity: "The identity of lived experience instantaneously present to itself" (*VP*, p. 67). To this end, Derrida concentrates on Husserl's discussions of time and interior monologue and concludes that the phenomenologist cannot maintain consistently the self-coincidence of the present in either sphere:

If the present of self-presence is not *simple*, if it is constituted in an originary irreducible synthesis, then all Husserl's argument is threatened in its principle. (p. 68)

This is precisely Sartre's argument in the first chapter of Part II of *Being and Nothingness*. And even in the conclusion to *Being and Nothingness* where he is anxious to avoid an insurmountable dualism of *en soi* and *pour soi* and considers the question of the "being" of the *pour soi* insofar as it is nihilation (*néantisation*, EN, p. 716), the paradoxical nature of the formulations problematizes Being in a way far removed from Derrida's assertion that for Sartre "being in itself and being for itself were both *being*" (*M*, p. 137). The *pour soi* is not Being in any recognizable sense of the term: "the *pour soi* has no other reality than being the nihilation of being" (*EN*, pp. 711–12); it is like "a hole in being at the heart of Being" (p. 711), "it is perpetually founding its nothingness-of-being" (p. 713).

Its being is never *given* . . . since it is always separated from itself by the nothingness of otherness; the *pour soi* is always in abeyance, because its being is a perpetual deferring. (p. 713)

Sartre ultimately refuses to answer the question of whether it is "more profitable to knowledge" (p. 719) to consider Being as having two dimensions (*pour soi* and *en soi*) or if the old duality (consciousness/being) is preferable. Such questions, he argues, are metaphysical, not ontological. Nonetheless, the whole intention of the work is to insist "against Hegel . . . that being *is* and nothingness *is not*" (p. 51).

Derrida of course acknowledges that metaphysical discourse is inescapable even by those who attempt to deconstruct it. Of Heidegger, for example, he writes: "The fact remains that the being (*être*) which is nothing, which is not a being (*étant*), cannot be spoken of, cannot speak itself, except in the ontic metaphor" (*M*, p. 157). But in the case of Sartre, Derrida focuses on selected terminology of existentialism and contrives to ignore its real emphasis on negation. His rejection of Sartre's humanism relegates Sartre's own critique of humanism in *La Nausée* to a footnote (p. 138). Such a representation of his predecessor's thinking brings in its wake a refusal to recognize basic analogies between Sartre's philosophy and his own. I have argued elsewhere[38] that Derrida's notion of *différance* (with an *a*), while being radically impersonal and intended as a means of deconstructing consciousness – that cornerstone of humanism – is in fact clearly related to consciousness in the Sartrean sense. The relationship can be traced through at least three of the meanings of *différance:* first as a deferring and a noncoincidence, second as differentiation, and third as producer of differences and ultimately of meaning. In a fourth sense, that of ontico-ontological difference, *différance* could also be seen as analogous to consciousness insofar as it makes possible the difference between *l'Être* and *l'étant*, Being and beings. *Différance* may be intended as part of a radical deconstruction of the conscious subject, but its function at times appears remarkably similar. We shall return to the question of Derrida's attitude to the subject at the end of this chapter.

Sartre, then, from his earliest writings problematizes any easy understanding of the subject, casting doubt on all attempts at identifying it other than as self-divided and self-negating. And, as we have already seen to be the case for Lacan also, this lack of self-identity is less a curse to be disguised than an escape route from a noxious fixity. Lacan's intense opposition to ego psychology may be compared here to Sartre's analysis of role playing and bad faith in *Being and Nothingness*, in that both thinkers reject the alienation ensuant on any identification with a defined role. Even sincerity is a form of bad faith for Sartre since it involves an attempt to be true to what you really *are* (*EN*, p. 103). One might say that the drawback of ego psychology lies precisely in its "sincerity"! Sartre would concur with Lacan when he writes – perhaps in his most "existential" mood – of "the happy fault of life, where man, in being distinct from his essence, discovers his existence" (*E*, p. 345). Ultimately, Lacan may seem on this score more pessimistic than Sartre, for he envisages the possibility of a "devastating reintegration of the subject with his ego" in a "further alienation" (p. 453). In Sartre's terms, the equivalent integration of *pour soi* and *en soi* is impossible. Freedom cannot ever be combined with identity. This may make our yearning for selfhood a "useless passion," but it simultaneously protects us from the worst ravages of alienating self-identity.

But if Lacan and Sartre are in agreement in seeing man's original state as *dereliction*, *déchirement*, *lézarde* (split, *E*, p. 124), *manque à être* (*E*, p. 613), lack of being, flight from self (*EN*, p. 722), they remain irreconcilable in the 1940s over the question of the transparency of the subject itself. Sartre's rejection of the unconscious leaves him with a subject that can never *grasp* itself purely because it has no *self* to grasp, not because its truth might lie elsewhere. To use Lacan's image of the mirror – for Sartre, too, the self observable in a mirror is a mirage, an illusory and alienating synthesis. Consciousness is transparent and therefore not accessible to perception. But whereas, for Sartre, what consciousness may observe in an unalienated state is merely the outside world (and, in a sense, the past self), for Lacan matters are more complex. Consciousness may be transparent, the self may be a construct, but the truth of the subject lies elsewhere, in some other realm, *behind* the mirror, so to speak, in the unconscious.

Sartre's later rapprochement with Freud (through Lacan) and with Marx transformed his notions of consciousness and subjectivity to the point where he could say, in 1969, that he had replaced his old notion of consciousness with that of the *vécu* (lived experience), which is characterized by *oubli* (forgetting), opacity, unselfconsciousness, and lack of self-knowledge (*Sit* IX, p. 108). The subject, for the later Sartre, can no longer be unequivocally identified with the *pour soi* of consciousness. Let us see how Sartre arrived at this revised view and assess the significance of the change.

In his early philosophical works Sartre insists on the transparency of consciousness, but consciousness is not separable from its embodiment or its world. The transparency of consciousness is contrasted with the opacity of the body, with the facticity and finitude of the subject as instantiated in the world. The body represents "the facticity of the *pour soi*" (*EN*, p. 371). And when Sartre attempts to make clear the major differences and similarities between his views and those of Freud, he stresses that his own notion of consciousness includes the nonrational. Consciousness cannot be equated with knowledge. The subject may not understand himself, *despite* the self-transparency of consciousness.

It is not a matter of an unsolved riddle, as the Freudians believe: Everything is there, in the light, reflection has access to everything, grasps everything. But this "mystery in broad daylight" comes rather from the fact that the access enjoyed is deprived of the means which usually permit *analysis* and *conceptualization*. (*EN*, p. 658)

(Self-)consciousness is no guarantee whatsoever of self-knowledge, and for several reasons. The first is that the self is a construct not equatable with consciousness or the subject. The second is that the self is nonetheless *experienced* as innate and internal, and this provides a further hurdle to understanding – in the natural attitude, not reconstructed by purifying reflection, I reverse the order of cause and effect and attribute my behavior to my self rather than envisaging my self as a product, at least in part, of my behavior. Similarly, the "insights" of introspection are necessarily false since they are looking inward for a self who is an object in the external world (*TE*, p. 69). And finally, even purifying reflection cannot guarantee full self-knowledge and understanding: on the one hand, because there is no reason why I should have any privileged understanding of the world or of other people who have formed so large a part of my personal history; and on the other hand, because existential awareness always risks tipping me over into the reversed position from the *esprit de sérieux* so that I may fail to recognize the degree to which I am bound by the self I have constituted throughout my past life, and by the expectations others have come to place on me and I have come to place on myself (see *EN*, pp. 530, 542). Freedom does not enable me to escape finitude or facticity (p. 576). On the contrary: "Finitude is an ontological structure of the *pour soi* which determines freedom" (p. 631).

All this is already a far cry from the popular view of Sartre as a philosopher of unrestricted freedom and lucidity. But the Sartrean subject is to be further eroded by the alliance with Marx and Freud. The *Critique of Dialectical Reason*, *Words*, and the *Idiot of the Family* all extend the implications of Sartre's deconstruction of the subject as he reinterprets his philosophy within a Marxist framework. And Sartre's increasing sympathy for Freud and Lacan also encourages him to reduce the slender autonomy of the individual subject as the transparency and lucidity of consciousness are muddied by the murkier waters of the *vécu* or "lived experience," somewhat enigmatically described by Sartre as "the equivalent of conscious – unconscious" (*Sit* IX, pp. 110–11). The notion of the *vécu* demonstrates forcibly and paradoxically the impossibility for the subject of being *fully* self-conscious, or *fully* self-knowing, for the *vécu* is a "constant totalization" of the "dialectical process of psychic life" (p. 111), but one which – by the law of the hermeneutic circle – cannot include its own totalizing process in the totalization it effects. In this sense the *vécu* reveals the ultimately impossible regression of reflexive self-knowledge.

The *vécu* designates neither the refuges of the preconscious, nor the unconscious, nor the conscious, but the area in which the individual is constantly submerged by himself, by his own riches, and where consciousness is shrewd enough to determine itself by forgetting. . . . What I call the *vécu* is precisely the whole of the dialectical process of psychic life, a process that remains necessarily opaque to itself for it is a constant totalization, and a totalization *that cannot be conscious of what it is*. One may be conscious, in fact, of an external totalization, but not of a totalization that also totalizes consciousness. (pp. 108, 111)

In the same interview, Sartre claims to accept the Lacanian interpretation of the unconscious as the "discourse of the Other," a further threat to the autonomy of the subject who is determined and alienated by intentions other than his own:

As far as I'm concerned, Lacan has clarified the unconscious as a discourse which separates through language or, if you prefer, as a counterfinality of speech: Verbal structures are organized as a structure of the practico-inert through the act of speaking. These structures express or constitute intentions that determine me without being mine. (p. 97)

Sartre recognizes in Lacan's view of language elements that are compatible with his own, in particular the idea that we speak the language of others, that our speech is "stolen" from us, that it is second-hand, that we are born into a language that precedes us, alienates us, and determines us in ways of which we are often unaware. The essays of *Situations I* (especially that on Brice Parain), *Nausea, Saint Genet*, and the *Idiot of the Family* reveal this as a constant theme in Sartre's thinking, and I have discussed it extensively elsewhere.[39] Nonetheless, Sartre's agreement is in fact with the Lacan of the 1940s and possibly early 1950s, not with the more radical views of the later Lacan. Sartre might well accept the 1953 definition of the Unconscious as "that part of concrete discourse, insofar as it is transindividual, which is not available to the subject for him to reestablish the continuity of his conscious discourse" (*E*, p. 258). But already by 1956, the degree of human autonomy in Lacan's picture has been diminished to an extent Sartre would find unacceptable. The omission marks in the following quotation probably correspond to the point at which Sartre parts company with Lacan:

Man is, from before birth and beyond his death, taken up in the symbolic chain. . . . He is a pawn in the play of the signifier. (*E*, p. 468)

For Sartre this is only half the picture:

Man can only "be spoken" to the extent that he speaks – and vice versa. (*IF*, II, p. 1977)

The determinism apparent in the following passage is arguably the critical sticking point for Sartre's rapprochement with (Lacan's) Freud:

What Freud discovered was that . . . the displacement of the signifier determines the subjects in their acts, in their destiny, in their refusals, in their blindnesses, in their end and in their fate . . . and that, willingly or not, everything that might be considered the stuff of psychology . . . will follow the path of the signifier. (*E*, p. 30)

However, this view of the subject is perhaps best considered as part of the "reversal phase" of Lacanian theory, for its radical determinism is tempered by other of Lacan's discussions that show evidence rather of a "circular" determination of subject by signifier and signifier by subject (see *E*, p. 806). Nonetheless, this remains the vital issue on which Sartre and radical Structuralism are opposed: the question of determinism. For however fragile the Sartrean subject may appear, however far from the creative, self-determining human-ist ideal, a subject of sorts still remains: be it alienated or non–self-identical, its very fissures and cracks are what lets it *escape* the deterministic process.[40]

It is true that in the 1960s and 1970s Sartre conceives of the subject as predominantly formed by the opaque forces of family destiny and historical process. In the *Idiot of the Family* he describes how the infant internalizes the attentions of his mother, and is literally structured by her care, or the lack of it:

To begin with, the baby internalizes the maternal rhythms and tasks as the lived qualities of his own body. . . . His own mother, engulfed in the depths of his body, becomes the pathetic structure of his affectivity. (*IF*, I, pp. 57–8)

The prehistoric past comes back to the child like Destiny. (p. 55)

Personal characteristics that Sartre would previously have repre-sented as part of a freely chosen project are now interpreted as ineradi-cable structures of the infant's facticity: apathy, for example, "is in the first place the family experienced at the most elementary psycho-somatic level – that of breathing, sucking, the digestive functions, the sphincters – by a *protected* organism" (p. 54). But such structures form the basis of individual evolution and transformation; they ori-ent personal development rather than determine character:

Gustave assumes [his apathy] to make it into a more highly developed form of behavior and give it a new function: Passive action becomes a tactic. Preserved, overcome, traversed by new and complex meanings, its sense cannot fail to change. (p. 54)

The relation between freedom and conditioning is described in terms of a dialectic of chance and necessity: As individuals we make ourselves on the basis of structures and circumstances that we expe-rience as the natural texture of our existence, rather than envisaging them as limitations to a freedom that would otherwise be both unsituated and disembodied:

This dialectic of chance and necessity comes about freely without troubling anyone in the pure existence of each of us. . . . What we are seeking here is the child of chance, the meeting of a certain body and a certain mother . . . these elementary determinants, far from being added together or affecting each other externally, are immediately inscribed in the synthetic field of a living totalization. (pp. 60–1)

Gustave's original determinants "are *no more* at the outset than the internalization of the family environment in an objective situation that conditions them externally and *before* his conception as a singularity" (p. 61). And it is this "living totalization," this process of internalization of the outside world through the family that ultimately forms the subject for the later Sartre, just as it is the subject's reexternalization of what he has internalized that constitutes his praxis. In reply to the question of what has become of freedom, Sartre answers in 1969 that he now sees it as lying in the *difference* between conditioning and behavior:

That is the definition I would give today of freedom: the little movement that makes of a totally conditioned social being a person who does not reproduce in its entirety what he received from his conditioning. (*Sit* IX, pp. 101–2)

Subjectivity is similarly defined:

So, in *Being and Nothingness*, what you might call "subjectivity" is not what it would be for me today: the little gap in an operation by which what has been internalized is reexternalized as an act. Today, in any case, the notions of "subjectivity" and "objectivity" seem to me entirely useless. Of course, I may happen to use the term "objectivity" but only in order to emphasize that everything is objective. The individual internalizes his social determinants: He internalizes the relations of production, the family of his childhood, the historical past, contemporary institutions, then he reexternalizes all that in acts and choices that necessarily refer us to everything that has been internalized. (pp. 102–3)

So the subject seems to have been reduced to the play (the slight movement, the little gap) in the input–output process. What is more, the "output" is not clearly recognizable as my own:

The man who looks at his work, who recognizes himself in it, who, at the same time, does not recognize himself in it at all . . . is the man who grasps . . . necessity as the destiny of freedom externalized. (*CRD*, p. 285)

If man can never recognize himself fully in his actions and products (his objectification) this is because of the very nature of externalization: A subject can never identify with an object even if it is entirely of his own making; this is part of the radical split between consciousness and world, or between nothingness and being. "Each of us spends his life engraving on things his baleful image, which fascinates him and leads him astray if he tries to understand himself *through it*" (p. 285). The *project* is now defined as a "mediation between two moments of objectivity" (pp. 67–8) and praxis as "a passage from the objective to the objective through internalization" (p. 66) doomed to become part of the dead structures of the practico-inert.

There is no doubt that man . . . discovers himself as *Other* in the world of objectivity; totalized matter, as an inert objectification that perpetuates itself by inertia, is in effect a non-man, and even, if you like, a *counter-man*. (p. 285)

But if human agency is radically undermined in the *Critique* where Sartre writes of "acts without an author," "constructions without a constructor" (pp. 152, 754), nonetheless the subject has not been abandoned: "Only the project as mediation between two moments of objectivity can account for history, that is, for human creativity" (pp. 67–8). Subjectivity may be *nothing*, but it still retains a paradoxical absolute existence:

Subjectivity is *nothing* for objective knowledge since it is a non-knowledge, and yet failure shows that it exists absolutely. (*Sit*, IX, p. 166)

Sartre is not espousing Kierkegaardian irrationalism, but rather wrestling with the paradoxes attendant upon his attempt to maintain a working model of the subject within a nondeterminist materialism. And the subject is defined precisely in opposition to the "classical" subject of bourgeois humanism, forcibly rejected in texts as diverse as *Nausea* and the *Critique*: "Humanism is the counterpart of racism: It is a practice of exclusion" (*CRD*, p. 702). But this rejection of humanism is a complex matter. The preface to the *Critique* made clear that one of the primary questions to which the work would address itself was "Is there a Truth of man?" (p. 10). And *man* certainly remains Sartre's major preoccupation insofar as he wishes to affirm "the true humanism of man" (p. 102) in the face of "the dehumanization of man" (p. 58) brought about by neo-Marxist idealism and determinism. But this does not make Sartre a humanist in the traditional sense. Indeed, long before Foucault and the structuralists, Sartre argued that "Man does not exist" (p. 131);[41] the concept of man is described as a "singular universal" forged by history and "[with] no meaning outside *this* singular adventure" (p. 140). "The concept of man is an abstraction" (p. 183); "man is a material being in the midst

of a material world" (p. 196); "the history of man is an adventure of
nature" (p. 158). However, Sartre is equally far from dissolving man
into the structures that traverse him. His aim is to maintain *both*
poles of "the perpetually resolved and perpetually renewed contradiction between man-as-producer and man-as-product, in each individual and at the heart of each multiplicity" (p. 158). Furthermore, just as
his use of the notion of *man* is far from making him a humanist, so his
use of the notion of the *individual* is far from making him an individualist. He maintains several times in the *Critique* that "there is no
isolated individual" (p. 642):

The individual disappears from historical categories . . . the individual –
questioned questioner – *is I*, and is no one . . . we can see clearly how *I* am
dissolved practically in the human adventure. (pp. 142–3)

The paradox of "*I* am dissolved" ("je *me dissous*") is close to that of
the *Transcendence of the Ego*, "I is an other" (*"Je est un autre"* TE, p.
78). Marx has taken over from Rimbaud as master of alienation. But
Sartre is still resolutely refusing to slip into an easy acceptance of
either thesis or antithesis – and his dialectic seems to remain permanently in tension without synthesis. The subject may be deferred,
dissolved, and deconstructed, but it is not relinquished.

SOME REMARKS ON THE SUBJECT SINCE SARTRE

It would appear, then, that Sartre's constant tussle with the paradoxes endemic in the subject and the complexities of his evolving
views might well have been of interest to those other philosophers
who wished, in their various different ways, to deconstruct the classical humanist subject. But the polarization of French intellectual
life led to a very different situation, in which Sartre's views were
disregarded or dismissed by defiantly iconoclastic structuralists.
This drove Sartre, in turn, to make polemical statements, at least in
interviews, opposing Structuralism more strongly than his own
philosophical positions should properly have allowed. In the same
year (1966) that he commends Lacan for clarifying the linguistic
nature of the unconscious (*Sit* IX, p. 97), he attacks him in an interview with *L'Arc*, condemning the constructed nature of the Lacanian ego, and apparently rejecting out of hand the structuralist "decentering of the subject" according to which "man does not think,

he is thought, as he is spoken for certain linguists."[42] The attack was, however, made almost inevitable by the explicit purpose of the interview itself, in which Sartre was invited to counter the structuralists who were allegedly luring his followers from him. Sartre's real attitude to Lacan is in fact more positive than he reveals in the 1966 interview, just as Lacan's real position is more subtle than the presentation that Sartre gives of it in *L'Arc*. And in a less aggressive interview in *Le Monde* in 1971, Sartre recognizes that his own description of the *moi* of Flaubert corresponds fairly closely to Lacan's notion of the *moi* as "an imaginary construction, a fiction with which one identifies afterward" (*Sit*, IX, p. 99). We have already seen that this has been Sartre's consistent position since the *Transcendence of the Ego* in 1936. The fact is that Sartre welcomes Structuralism to the extent that its anti-individualism is part of an attack on bourgeois humanism, but he considers it one-sided:

There is no doubt that structure produces behavior. But what is wrong with radical Structuralism . . . is that the reverse side of the dialectic is passed over in silence, and History is never shown producing structures. (*Sit*, IX, p. 86)

Furthermore, Sartre's critique of Structuralism is readily comprehensible given the common structuralist misrepresentation of his own positions. In *La Pensée Sauvage* of 1962, for example, Lévi-Strauss launches into an attack on Sartre's conception of the subject that he provocatively assimilates to the most facile notion of personal identity:

He who begins by steeping himself in the allegedly self-evident truths of introspection never emerges from them. Knowledge of men sometimes seems easier to those who allow themselves to be caught in the snare of personal identity. But they thus shut the door on knowledge of man. . . . Sartre in fact becomes the prisoner of the Cogito; Descartes made it possible to attain universality, but conditionally on remaining psychological and individual; by sociologizing the Cogito, Sartre merely exchanges one prison for another. (*PS*, p. 249)

Later in the same chapter, Lévi-Strauss takes over from existentialism a theory of discontinuity of self, and uses to it to combat a notion of self-totalization that he wrongly attributes to Sartre:

There would be plenty to say about this supposed totalizing continuity of the self which seems to me to be an illusion sustained by the demands of social life and consequently a reflection of the external on the internal – rather than the object of an apodictic experience. (pp. 339–40)

Somewhat perversely, Lévi-Strauss combines his attack on the Sartrean subject – willfully distorted out of all recognition – with the notion of a *universal human mind*, envisaged as a hypothesis necessary to explain the recurrence of identical structures through different societies. Such structures are the product of "the unconscious activity of the human mind" (p. 329). This was presumably what Paul Ricoeur was referring to when he described Lévi-Strauss's ideas as "kantism without a transcendental subject."[43]

But if Lévi-Strauss retained the human mind while evacuating the human subject, there has since been a striking resurgence of interest in the subject in France that we will now examine briefly in an attempt to assess what relation it bears to Sartre's own positions as analyzed thus far.

In 1966 Foucault in *Les Mots et les choses* writes somewhat apocalyptically of "the disappearance of man" (*MC*, p. 397); Derrida, in 1968, refers in similar eschatalogical tone to "the ends of man" and "the shadows of humanist metaphysics" (*M*, p. 141); Lacan in his *Écrits* (1966) explicitly decenters the humanist subject, stating categorically that "the true center of the human being is no longer in the same place" (*E*, p. 401); Deleuze and Guattari in *L'Anti Oedipe* of 1972 replace the *je* (I, ego) with the *ça* (id, that), and the "I think, I speak" with "it shits" – the subject is decimated in the "desiring machines" of schizophrenic capitalism.[44]

But this is not the end of the subject. We have seen that Lacan, for example, never abandons the notion of subject, which, in a form of paradoxical *loser wins*, is constituted through a symbiosis with language, itself dependent on a *lack* of self-identity and an alienation to the imaginary:

Without that gaping lack that alienates man to his own image, the symbiosis with the symbolic, in which he is constituted as a mortal subject, could not have been produced. (*E*, p. 552)

Lacan's subject may be in exile, but its exile is what saves it from absorption into its imaginary identifications.

Foucault's relegation of "man" to the last years of the eighteenth century and the early years of the nineteenth makes it quite clear that *Les Mots et les choses* is analyzing a very specific and histori- cally restricted conception of man (see *MC*, p. 319), that is to say the "empirico-transcendental doublet" of the "analytic of finitude" (p. 329), in short, man as we know him since Kant. But if man is a "recent invention" (398), "in the process of dying," "a figure be- tween two modes of language" (p. 397), in this specific, narrow, historical sense, then his demise is hardly surprising, though the alleged brevity of the Kantian form of man is open to question. Concepts of man, like concepts of the subject, are necessarily histori- cally variable and evolving. And it is this that gave Foucault some credibility in his later attempts to interpret his earlier texts as part of a "history of the subject."[45] His presentation of his views in the 1960s was part of a polemical antihumanist strategy. As early as 1976, he expressed interest in the knowledge of the subject that had been accumulated through the centuries:

A knowledge of the subject; a knowledge not so much of its form, but of what splits it; of what determines it, perhaps, but especially of what makes it escape itself.[46]

And in an essay that appeared in 1982, he proposed the fostering of certain forms of subjectivity:

We must promote new forms of subjectivity while refusing the type of individuality that has been imposed on us for several centuries.[47]

Indeed, his aim in the 1980s was to explain how individuals, through their experience of desire, come to recognize themselves as sub- jects.[48] Foucault's 1982 lecture course at the Collège de France was entitled "*Herméneutique du sujet.*" However, the title of the writ- ten résumé was changed to "*Herméneutique de soi.*"[49] Foucault was evidently attempting to find a way around the centuries-old connota- tions of autonomy and unity (or, indeed, subjection?) that the term "subject" evokes, and to escape the personal, bourgeois implications of the "individual." The third person reflexive pronoun *soi* is not, in French, open to the same objections of totality and so forth associ- ated with the English "self." Foucault shows convincingly how the Greek formation of the *soi* is radically opposed to the "self" of some modern philosophies. It is *other-* not *self-*centered. In his terms it is exoteric.⁵⁰ However, in its constructed nature, as something to be constituted, the *soi*, despite its name, is closer to the Sartrean ego than to the *pour soi*, which, as we have seen, is precisely *not soi*.⁵¹

Deleuze and Lyotard are more resistant to a revival of the subject, though for different reasons. Deleuze wants to get beyond the debate in its entirety, to reach the point where it becomes irrelevant whether the term "I", for example, is still used.⁵² The question at issue is not to decide whether "desiring machines" are still subjects; this is simply to pour good new wine into bad old bottles. Deleuze envisages the history of the subject as part of the history of philosophy, to be spoken of in the past tense. The subject *served* the dual purposes of universalization and individuation, through the *je universel* and the *moi individuel*. It is, in his view, doubtless still of interest to examine how these are linked, or in conflict, and to approach the "subject" as it was conceived by Hume, Kant, Husserl, and others. But there is little sense in a contemporary critique of the subject. What is now of interest is what has replaced the concept. For Deleuze we are *eccéités* rather than *moi*, and the "subject" is less interesting than what he calls "preindividual singularities" and "nonpersonal individuations."⁵³ For Deleuze individuals are not necessarily persons, let alone subjects, and singular entities are not necessarily individuals. Individuals, persons, singular entities, and so forth all have to be distinguished. In the essay on Francis Bacon he maintains that "the form of representation expresses firstly the organic life of man as a subject."⁵⁴ The abandonment of the "subject" thus entails the rejection of artistic representation, and the dissolution of "figuration" in favor of "figurality" (to use Lyotard's terms⁵⁵). Bacon's "portraits," which "dehumanize" man, by presenting, for example, a series of studies of "heads" rather than "faces,"⁵⁶ exemplify Deleuze's own vision of modernity in terms of forces, rhythms, and bodies that lack the unity of the organism.⁵⁷ The "body without organs" is not easily reconcilable with even the most fragmented, decentered form of subjecthood.

Starting from phenomenology, Lyotard was slower than many to relinquish the subject in the first place, and now seems all the more determined to oppose its resurrection. Nonetheless, his recent preoccupation, in *L'Inhumain*, has been to distinguish between the "inhumanity" of the technological system in which we live, and another "inhumanity" that represents what, paradoxically, constitutes the essence of our humanity, and where, in Lyotard's terms, "the soul is at stake."[58] In a series of Pascalian paradoxes, Lyotard argues that childhood represents both our "initial poverty" (misère) and yet also what is "eminently human" in us, whereas educated adulthood is (merely?) a "second nature." However, it is tempting to use Pascal, together with Rousseau and Lacan, to attempt a deconstruction of Lyotard's human–inhuman model. Furthermore, it is only as subjects, indeed speaking subjects, that we can formulate the aim of a return to the prehuman infans stage from which, culturally at least, we have now emerged. Lyotard's essay reads as a somewhat unhappy blend of postmodernism and sentimentality. It is not so much a question of aesthetics, as Lyotard wants to claim, as of pathos.

Derrida, too, shifted position between the 1960s and the 1980s, from "the ends of man" to "the rights of man."[59] In 1968, having attacked Sartre for taking over Corbin's "monstrous translation" of Heidegger's Dasein as "human reality," he moves on to criticize Heidegger himself for his closet humanism, for "Dasein, if it is not man, is nonetheless nothing other than man" (M, p. 151). But Derrida's deconstruction of man and the subject has turned out to be something very different from the radical dissolution that it appeared in 1968. Already in L'Écriture et la différence, on the subject of writing, his position was complex:

The "subject" of writing does not exist if we understand by it some sovereign solitude of the writer. The subject of writing is a system of relationships between the layers in the magic writing pad, the mind, society, the world. Within this scene the "punctual" simplicity of the classical subject cannot be found. (ED, p. 335)

And when he was questioned about this by Guy Scarpetta in an interview published in Positions in 1972, he insisted that he had never maintained that there was no "subject of writing" any more than he had maintained there was no subject. He proposed that the whole operation of subjectivity needed to be reconsidered, by looking at it as an element in a relationship rather than as an original source. In 1980 the Cerisy Colloque Les Fins de l'homme took the phrase in a rather different sense from that of the 1968 article, and attempted to rethink the question of man, not ontologically (What is man?) but rather in terms of Heidegger's ethical reformulation of the question, "Who is man?" One of the explicit intentions of the conference was to reopen a question whose closure seemed likely to result merely in the reintroduction of a naive, reactive humanism:

Between a "disappearance of man," too well known today not to be badly known, a general critique of humanism too commonly accepted not to be, in its turn, worth questioning, and the shamefaced, naive, or reactive humanism on which so many discourses fall back in the end. . . . it may well be the case that the question of "man" needs to be asked afresh today, in a philosophical as well as literary, ethical, or political sense – and that it needs to be asked as a question of *ends*.[60]

Since then Derrida has frequently foregrounded the subject as focus for his thinking, in particular in *Psyche* and *De l'Esprit*. Their engagement with the humanist subject and their fascinating and self-avowed ambivalence toward it may be briefly glimpsed from the concluding pages of the essay on Heidegger:

I do not intend to criticize this humanist teleology. It is certainly more urgent to remember that despite all our refusals and avoidances of it, it has remained up till now . . . the price to pay for the ethical and political denunciation of biologism, racism and naturalism, etc. If I am analyzing this "logic," the aporias and limits, the presuppositions and axiomatic decisions, the inversions and contaminations especially, in which we see it trap itself, it is rather in order to reveal and formalize the terrifying mechanisms of this program, all the double constraints that structure it. Is it a matter of fatality? Can we escape it? . . . Can we transform the program? I don't know. In any case, we can't simply avoid it.[61]

Most recently and explicitly, in an interview with Jean-Luc Nancy for the issue of *Confrontation* entitled *Après le sujet qui vient?* (1989), Derrida takes Nancy to task for contending that the subject was ever "liquidated," insisting that it has rather been "reinterpreted":

For these three discourses (Lacan, Althusser, Foucault), for some of the thinking that they privilege (Freud, Marx, Nietzsche), the subject is perhaps reintepreted, resituated, reinscribed, it is certainly not liquidated. (*AS*, 92)

Furthermore, Derrida declares himself interested by a certain approach to the question:

The relation to oneself can only be one of *différance*, that is to say of alterity or trace. Not only does this in no way attenuate obligation, but on the contrary it constitutes its only possibility, which is neither subjective nor human. Which does not mean that it is inhuman or subjectless, but that it is

starting from this dislocated *affirmation* . . . that something like the subject, man, or whoever it may be, can be figured. (p. 95)

Derrida insists that it is naive to speak of "the Subject" as if it were a
mythical entity that has now been abandoned. Moreover, the "subjects" of Descartes, Kant, Hegel, Husserl are not themselves simple
but involve paradoxes and aporias that deserve renewed consideration. Derrida would like to "de-homogenize" the subject. Nobody,
he maintains, ever seriously believed in the so-called classical humanist subject, autonomous, self-sufficient, spontaneous. "The subject has never existed for anyone . . . the subject is a fable" (p. 97).
Furthermore, current work on the subject may well form part of a
deconstructive enterprise:

We were speaking of dehiscence, of intrinsic dislocation, of *différance*, . . .
etc. . . . Some might say: but precisely, what we mean by "subject" is not
absolute origin, pure will, self-identity or the self-presence of consciousness,
but rather this noncoincidence with self. Here is a response to which we
should return. By what right may this be called a subject? Conversely, by
what right may we forbid this to be called a "subject"? I am thinking of
those who want to reconstruct, today, a discourse on the subject that no
longer has the form of self-mastery, of self-adequation, center and origin of
the world, etc., but which would rather define the subject as the finite
experience of non-self-identity, of the inderivable interpellation that comes
from the other, from the trace of the other. . . . We will come back to this
train of thought later. (p. 98)

Unfortunately, Derrida does not return to this aspect of the subject
in the interview, but in the light of our analysis of the Sartrean
subject it is extraordinary to see what could well be a description of
the subject of *Being and Nothingness* envisaged as a possible attempt to come to terms with the subject in a way that does not fall
short of the work already carried out by deconstruction. As I have
indicated, *Voice and Phenomenon* repeated in part, and probably
unwittingly, Sartre's own deconstruction of the Husserlian subject.
Twenty years later, Derrida still seems unwilling to acknowledge
that Sartre is not merely a forerunner but a real originator of much of
what Deconstruction has to say on the subject. I have attempted to
show here that Sartre, like Descartes, Kant, and perhaps Husserl,
actually made a valiant attempt to grapple with the problems inherent in any theory of subjectivity – those of freedom/determinism,

350 THE CAMBRIDGE COMPANION TO SARTRE

praxis/structure, self/other, and so on, rather than merely acknowledging that such work is necessary, or even inevitable. The present climate of thinking about the subject may now perhaps enable us to reread Sartre and not merely take him as read.

Translations are my own except in the case of Lévi-Strauss and Lacan, p. 94. For details, see Bibliography.

1 A happy, or fortunate alienation. A term taken from Sartre's discussion of mother-love, and the illusion of necessity it bestows on the child (*IF*, I, pp. 140–3).

2 See Jean Baudrillard, "*Le Sujet et son double,*" in *Magazine littéraire* [henceforth: *Mag. litt.*], *L'Individualisme: le grand retour*, no. 264 (April 1989): 19–23.

3 *De l'Esprit*, p. 184.

4 *Les Mots et les choses*, pp. 396–8.

5 "*Les Fins de l'homme,*" in *Marges de la philosophie*, pp. 129–64.

6 For full details of publication, see the Bibliography.

7 M. Frank, *L'Ultime raison du sujet*, p. 7.

8 Paul Ricoeur, "*Individu et identité personnelle,*" in *Sur l'Individu*, p. 54.

9 Paul Veyne, "*L'Individu atteint au coeur par la puissance publique,*" in *Sur l'Individu*, p. 7.

10 Serge Moscovici, "*L'Individu et ses représentations,*" *Mag. litt.*, no. 263 (1988): 30.

11 Philippe Sollers, "*Lettre sur l'individualité littéraire,*" *Mag. litt.*, no. 264 (April 1989): 34.

12 Alain Laurent, "*L'Edifiante histoire de l'individualisme,*" *Mag. litt.*, no. 264 (April 1989): 36.

13 Gilles Deleuze, "*Un Concept philosophique,*" in *Confrontations*, no. 20 *Après le sujet qui vient* (1989), p. 90.

14 "Baudrillard: *le sujet et son double,*" interview in *Mag. litt.*, no. 264 (April 1989): p. 19.

15 See Etienne Balibar, "*Citoyen Sujet,*" in *Confrontations*, no. 20 (1989), pp. 23–47, esp. 23–7. See also J. Derrida, *De L'Esprit*, p. 34.

16 See Frédéric de Buzon, "*L'Individu et le sujet,*" in *Penser le sujet aujourd'hui*, pp. 17–29.

17 See Allan Megill, *Prophets of Extremity*, p. 139, referring to Heidegger's "The Age of the World Picture" (1938, 1952) and *The Question Concerning Technology and Other Essays* (New York: 1977).

18 Buzon, *L'individu et le sujet*, p. 21 (*Regulae*, 1628; *Méditations*, 1641).

19 R. Descartes, *Discours de la Méthode*, collected in *Œuvres et Lettres* (Paris: Pléiade, 1952), p. 148.

20 Ibid., p. 166.

21 *Critique of Pure Reason*, p. 361 (A, 396).

22 Ibid., 334 (A, 350).

23 Ibid., p. 167 (B, 155).

24 *Groundwork of the Metaphysic of Morals*, tr. H. J. Paton in *The Moral Law*, p. 123.

25 See Frank, *L'Ultime raison de sujet*, p. 44.

26 See Rüdiger Bubner, *Modern German Philosophy*, p. 19.

27 *Ideen* (1913), I, §80, p. 160. (See E. Levinas, *Hors Sujet*, p. 231.)

28 *The Will to Power*, fragment 484, p. 268.

29 *Beyond Good and Evil*, §17, p. 28. See Frank, *L'Ultime raison de sujet*, p. 9.

30 *The Genealogy of Morals*, first essay, §13, p. 179.

31 See G. Deleuze, *Nietzsche et la philosophie*, p. 108. See also J. Derrida, "*Les fins de l'homme*," in *Marges de la philosophie*, p. 163

32 *Thus Spake Zarathustra*, p. 297.

33 See Bubner, *Modern German Philosophy*, p. 24.

34 See Alain Renaut, "*Les Subjectivités: pour une histoire du concept de sujet*," in *Penser le sujet aujourd'hui*, p. 64.

35 For example Bubner, cited above, and A. Renaut, *L'ère de l'individu*.

36 Margaret Atack, reviewing Howard Davies in *Radical Philosophy*, 50 (Autumn 1988): 49.

37 The reference in the English edition is to *The Critique of Pure Reason*, tr. N. K. Smith, 1980, p. 152.

38 See "Sartre and Derrida: *Qui perd gagne*," *JBSP*, 13, no. 1 (1982). Reprinted in *Sartre: The Necessity of Freedom* (Cambridge: Cambridge University Press, 1989).

39 See my *Sartre's Theory of Literature*, MHRA, 1979.

40 See my "Sartre and Negative Theology," *Modern Language Review*, 74, no. 3 (1979).

41 See also *Les Mots*, where Sartre declares that "Man is impossible" (p. 211).

42 "Jean-Paul Sartre *répond*" in *L'Arc*, 30 (1966): 91–2.

43 See *Le Cru et le Cuit*, p. 19. Vincent Descombes, in *Le Même et L'Autre*, p. 95, attributes the origin of the notion to Sartre's *Transcendence of the Ego*. He also points out in respect of Althusser and Hegel that the absence of a personal subject is not equatable with the absence of a subject altogether, and derides Althusser for overlooking the Hegelian *Geist* in his characterization of Hegel as the first to see history as a process

without a subject. Lévi-Strauss's *Esprit,* with its unconscious, seems to be just as problematic.

44 *L'Anti Oedipe,* pp. 7–8.
45 See his interview in *Les Nouvelles Littéraires,* June 28–July 5, 1984.
46 *La Volonté de savoir,* p. 93
47 *"Deux essais sur le pouvoir et le sujet,"* in Hubert Dreyfus and Paul Rabinow, *Michel Foucault, un parcours philosophique,* p. 308.
48 *L'Usage des plaisirs,* p. 10.
49 See W. Schmid, "Foucault: *la forme de l'individu,"* in *Mag. litt,* no. 264, p. 55.
50 See Schmid, ibid., p. 56
51 Alain Renaut and Luc Ferry in *La Pensée 68* are less inclined to give Foucault the benefit of the doubt. They describe him as wanting to have his cake and eat it – as playing on the multiple meaning of the term "subject" in order to appear to be contributing to contemporary theories of the subject while at the same time attacking most modern forms of it. I am not sure myself whether such apparent ambivalence is avoidable. And in any case, Foucault's use of *soi* seems precisely part of an attempt to avoid the pitfalls of the *subject.* (See J. F. Lyotard in *La Condition Postmoderne,* p. 30. *"Ce* soi *est peu."*) Peter Dews, in *Radical Philosophy,* 51, "The return of the subject in late Foucault" also deems Foucault's later stance to be ultimately a failure, but he treats the attempt with more philosophical seriousness (pp. 47–51).
52 *Mille Plateaux,* p. 9.
53 *"Un concept philosophique,"* in *Confrontations,* 20, p. 90. cf; *TE,* p.78.
54 Deleuze, *Francis Bacon, Logigue de la sensation,* p. 81.
55 In *Discours Figure.* See *Francis Bacon,* p. 9.
56 Deleuze, *Francis Bacon,* p. 19.
57 Ibid., p. 33.
58 *L'Inhumain,* p. 10.
59 See discussion in *La Pensée 68,* p. 35.
60 *Les Fins de l'homme,* p. 20.
61 *De L'Esprit,* pp. 87–8.

Appendix: Hegel and Sartre

Even though Sartre repeatedly emphasized the divergences between Hegel and himself, this chapter discusses their convergences. It will be seen, moreover, that these often conflict with Sartre's own stress on the differences between them.

Sartre does not refer to Hegel in his early works; he seems to have become familiar with him only from *Being and Nothingness*[1] onward, where Hegel, along with Kant, Husserl, and Heidegger, is one of his chosen interlocutors and adversaries. This essay deals with certain specifically philosophical aspects of the debate: the conception of being-for-itself and being-for-others in Sartre and Hegel. *Being and Nothingness* also discusses the dialectical conception of nothingness. Juliette Simont has analyzed this question in an important footnote to her article "Sartre et Hegel: *le problème de la qualité et de la quantité.*"[2] I shall not therefore return to it directly.

In Sartre's analysis of being-for-itself and for-others, the most significant references are to the two *Logics* (the *Science of Logic* and the first part of the *Encyclopedia*) and to the *Propédeutique.*[3] Sartre's perceptiveness with respect to these dry texts leads one to conjecture that he had more than a merely academic knowledge of Hegel – did he perhaps discuss him with some of Kojève's pupils, with Jean Wahl, Lefèbre, and Hartmann, authors of a collection of selected texts from Hegel, Hyppolite, and Maurice de Gandillac? It is possible, but as yet unproven.

However, Sartre's reading of Hyppolite's commentary[4] on the *Phenomenology of Spirit*[5] and of his translations of Hegel certainly had a decisive impact on his *Cahiers pour une morale*[6] where Hegel's

Translated by Martine Jawerbaum.

presence may be felt throughout: There are no fewer than eighty references to Hegel without mentioning the numerous additional references to his dialectic. The discussion is more widespread in the *Cahiers* than in *Being and Nothingness*, being linked on the one hand to Sartre's internalization of the problematics of history, which will be clarified finally in the *Critique de la raison dialectique*,[7] and on the other to the struggle between master and slave, the analysis of which will change entirely in meaning in the *Critique*.[8]

The importance of Sartre's Hegelian "formation" has therefore become much more evident since the publication of the posthumous works, and does not appear so clearly in the works published during his lifetime. But the significance of Hegel is vital both in *Saint Genet* and in the later drama, not to mention *L'Idiot de la famille* and the posthumously published extracts from the *Mallarmé*.[9] In these later works, the major reference points are the figures of "individualism" (desire, the law of the heart, virtue) and the dialectic of the "beautiful soul" and of "evil and its forgiveness."[10] In *Saint Genet* explicit reference is made to the "animal reign of the spirit" (artists and intellectuals).

In the *Critique* on the other hand, where the intention was to use existentialism to found a materialist philosophy of history, the relationship to Hegel is evidently very ambivalent. It is of the same order as that of Marx to Hegel, if not that of Lenin to Hegel. The explicit argument of the *Critique* involves an overwhelming refusal (which I would call ideological) of Hegelian idealism. Nonetheless, an implicit undercurrent frequently borrows from, is inspired by, or simply reinvents Hegelian thinking. It is on this territory, the most fertile, that I have completed my analysis of the relationship of Sartre to Hegel, which began with *Being and Nothingness* – the territory of need, of action, and of the universal concrete.

THE LIMIT AND THE UNLIMITED

The notion of a "limit" may initially be used as a common point of reference. Both Hegel and Sartre reject its usual meaning and implications, if not its effectivity – that is, its instable and relative reality. Any limit is in fact a limit for anyone for whom it has a meaning, that is to say, for anyone who could equally well not take it into account, namely for a free being, for only a free being can be alienated and can measure the obstacles and prohibitions it encounters. Both philosophers suspect that freedom is self-limiting, even though its greatest temptation is nevertheless to rid itself of its own perpetual mobility, for fear of anxiety Sartre says. Likewise Hegel comments on the impossibility of escaping this anxiety of freedom: "If it wishes to remain in a state of unthinking inertia, then thought troubles its thoughtlessness, and its own unrest disturbs its inertia" (*PhSp*, p. 51).

Thus the limit, if it exists, is in league with the finite-recognizing-itself-as-such, and hence can only humble itself or declare its own modesty in simultaneous tribute to what appears to it to be the infinite; but, for the finite, it is an extravagant pretension to claim to know about the infinite: The finite, which is nothing, assumes the right to articulate the infinite, and moreover to do so indirectly, *through what it states about what is not the infinite: itself.* In this sense, even if it recognizes its finitude, it has in effect already overstepped its limits and must from the start be considered as indissolubly linked to the infinite, either because of its illusion of its difference from it, or because of its consciousness of their common connection.

Both Hegel and Sartre possess an acute consciousness of this dialectic: The finite cannot limit itself, or can do so only in the simultaneous consciousness of the limitlessness at stake in this decision. Sartre has coined aphoristic formulas for this dialectical tension of the finite and the infinite. He quotes Saint Paul: "It is the Law that creates sin," and goes on to explain: "Man cannot affirm without denying: If he poses a limit, it is necessary to infringe it. For he cannot pose it without posing the unlimited at the same time. If he intends to respect a social prohibition, in the same impulse his freedom suggests that he violate it, for it is one and the same thing to give oneself laws and to create the possibility of disobeying them. . . . The spirit, Hegel says, is unrest." (*SG*, pp. 29–30 of the French edition).

UNLIMITED AND INFINITE

The problematic of the infinite is thus at the center of this common reference to the dialectic of limits. This term, overdetermined if taken literally, nonetheless has the same meaning in Sartre and Hegel, namely the overstepping of the finite by itself. This will be repeatedly emphasized by both Hegel and Sartre.

Limitation is a *lack* inasmuch as a being *one* nevertheless contains the fact *to-be-over-and-done-with-it*, inasmuch as contradiction as such is immanent and posited in it. A being capable of containing and withstanding its own contradiction is the *subject*. This is what constitutes its *infinity*. When one speaks of a *finite* reason, it reveals itself infinite owing to the very fact that it determines itself as *finite*, for negation is a finitude, a lack, only for the *suppressed-being* of this negation, the infinite *self-relationship*. (*Enz*, §359, Remark)

This univocally corresponds to what Sartre calls "the unlimited" in the preceding quotation and, in *Being and Nothingness*, "the in-itself-for-itself, the Value, the Lacked, or the projected in-itself."

One could also account for this correspondence by what Hegel wrote in the Remark of §60:

Living beings, for example, possess the privilege of pain that is denied to the inanimate: Even with living beings, a single mode or quality passes into the feeling of a negative. For living beings as such possess within them a universal vitality, which overpasses and includes the single mode; and thus, as they maintain themselves in the negative of themselves, they feel the contradiction to *exist* within them. But the contradiction is within them, only insofar as one and the same subject includes both the universality of their sense of life and the individual mode that is in negation with it. This illustration will show how a limit or imperfection in knowledge comes to be termed a limit or imperfection only when it is compared with the actually present Idea of the universal, of something total and achieved. To call a thing finite or limited proves by implication the very presence of the infinite and unlimited and that our knowledge of a limit can only be when the unlimited is *on this side* in consciousness.

This time, we note the interchangeability of the term "infinite" with those of unlimited, universal, total, and achieved.

This is precisely what Sartre says of the projected in-itself: that it is or presumes to be totality, achievement, synthesis, beyond always already on this side, since it is it that *reveals* the lack and its determination – the lack revealing itself as such only with regard to its fulfillment synthesized with itself, thus anticipated and projected in its retroactive effect. But there is more in this than Hegel said: The projected in-itself does not only reveal the lack, it also fantasizes its removal by the projection or the sublimation of the finite effected in the synthetic ideality of the in-itself–for-itself. Two essential stages, at once complementary and, ontologically, con-

tradictory: the dynamic fecundity of the unveiling, and the fetishistic disaster of reified essentiality. On closer examination, however,
we recognize a similar tension in Hegel.

GENUINE AND BAD INFINITE

For the first stage (totalizing anticipation), there is the famous expression: "The living thing does not let the cause come to its effect"
(ScL, p. 562). This means that the world intervenes in the subject
only through the totalized and anticipated expectation effected upon
it by the subject. Hegel says: "The reason is that that which acts on a
living being is independently determined, changed or transmuted by
it" (ibid.).

The second stage (alienation) is the one that corresponds to Hegel's "bad infinite," the sempiternal critique he aims at Kant and
Fichte: that of the "real" dualism of the finite and the infinite, trying
to have it both ways so as to justify the thinker for his inability to
achieve their reconciliation, while taking his unceasingly renewed
effort to signify the legitimacy of his being encouraged by their separation. This critique is similar to the one made by Sartre of the in-
itself–for-itself in his discussion of bad faith: betting on immanence,
while aiming to reach transcendence, and, conversely, hoping each
time to reach the very being of consciousness . . . but reaching only
the barren repetitiveness of the relationship and the simultaneous
projection into the impossible of the infinite, which becomes all the
more haunting.

It must be noted that it is precisely at the turning point of his
critique of Kant and Fichte that Hegel introduces the genuine use of
the infinite. The connection between the two questions is thus obvious: It is the movement of anticipating self-idealization constituted
by the immanent "on-this-side" of the limit that can reveal "a failure
of discernment" as to the action of the immanent universality of the
Idea, that is of freedom. For how could one claim to separate finite and
infinite and, at the same time, have them meet by the must-be of the
finite if the infinite is not always on this side of the finite and connected to it? It is the same duplicitous backward and forward motion
between immanence and transcendence denounced by Sartre as the
very procedure of bad faith, and which can only be meaningfully
articulated by the simultaneous denial of the infinite of freedom act-

ing behind the duality – which will be more precisely denounced by Hegel in what he calls, with reference to the moral vision in the *Phenomenology of Spirit*, the perpetual "displacements" of the finite and the infinite. But here too, in the Introduction to the *Encyclopedia*, in the same §60, he speaks of this backward and forward motion: "At the very moment after their unification has been alleged to be the truth, we come upon the doctrine that the two elements . . . are only true and actual in their state of separation."

FROM THE BAD TO THE GENUINE INFINITE

To uphold this inspiration common to both authors, one should understand the ambiguous if not the ambivalent status of Value in Sartre, both as the possibility of determination of lack and as the alienation of wanting to be God according to the "useless passion" that overcomes man. For, if one can see the positive side of the project, in what exactly does the negative side of the bad infinite consist? That lack causes itself to be determined by the postulated totality of itself and of its object is a recurrent theme as far back as the *Carnets de la drôle de guerre*[11] and what makes its quest vain is the structure of consciousness as temporalizing ek-stasy: "The for-itself attained by the realization of the Possible will make itself be as for-itself – that is, with another horizon of possibilities" (*BN*, p. 101). This in itself already sanctions the impossibility of any self-coincidence through the mediation of the in-itself.

But at the bottom of this enterprise of failure is the ontological quest for the in-itself by the for-itself, as *redemption or absolution* of the contingency of the for-itself – the endeavor to transform the contingency of the finite into necessity, making it infinite in an attempt to reach what Sartre calls the Self: its transfiguration through the passion of being God. This is obviously the wrong way to "infinitize" the for-itself, to seek to invest it with a necessity that it lacks by its very origin, and by such means to seek to "raise" it from its initial deficiency; for it is *within* its finitude that the for-itself is infinite, due to the fact that it must constantly place its bet again, or carry on its never-ending game, all the while continuously inventing its rules and its meaning.

This inventiveness is the genuine infinite, veiled by the illusion of having grasped its meaning once and for all: "For nobody is allowed to say these simple words: I am me. The best ones, the most free, can say: I exist. It is already too much" (*SG*, p. 85 of the French edition). It is likewise veiled by the jeremiads of the unhappy consciousness, which Sartre declares to be the fate of every consciousness – meaning every consciousness within the regime of the bad infinite, of its phantasm, and accepting to measure its inanity . . . only so as to cultivate it.

The being of human reality is suffering because it rises in being as perpetually haunted by a totality which it is without being able to be it, precisely because it could not attain the in-itself without losing itself as for-itself. Human reality therefore is by nature an unhappy consciousness with no possibility of surpassing its unhappy state. (*BN*, p. 90)

It is true that the "unhappy consciousness" may appear as the nature of consciousness but, precisely because there is no nature of consciousness, this "nature" will be whatever consciousness makes of it: to complain of it, or to make it the unceasing springboard of its existence. It is clear, however, that if it complains of its unhappiness, then by cultivating it, it forbids itself to enjoy it other than perversely. That is, by satisfying itself with its own dissatisfaction – it is always something that one can count on! – in the constant renewal of the gap between finite and infinite, relative and absolute, immanence and transcendence, it forbids itself to enjoy it as a sense of the infinity of its finitude, or of a "total immanence" within itself and at the same time outside of itself, "as an absence, an unrealizable . . . achieved in total transcendence" (*BN*, p. 91).

A fillip suffices to pass from the "ugly" unhappy consciousness, suffering and grieving and glad to be unhappy, to the "beautiful" unhappy consciousness. The history of the unhappy consciousness shows us the genesis of this fillip, which distinguishes the one from the other. For its evolving meaning (historically assignable) will be Christianity – with which Hegel has grappled from his youth and which he will come to recognize as the genuine relationship between the finite and the infinite. From it he will derive his own dialectic of absolute immanence: post-Christian philosophical knowledge. Now Christianity – save for its original prematureness that will say everything without realizing its significance – will be condemned to go astray in an "unhappy" interpretation of its own consciousness: the fetishistic quest for the infinite in the Crusades, the naturalistic and

proprietary fervor of the nobility, who have returned and been re-
warded by the dispensation of lands to bear fruit, and finally the
mortifying asceticism that summons the infinite through the abso-
luteness of self-inflicted brutalities. All this until it becomes subject
to retroactive reinterpretation by Hegel, who annihilates it by saving
it, and who liquidates its transcendence and interiorizes its dialectic
in the immanence of consciousness. In this sense, what is reflected
history or thought genesis for Hegel becomes unfurled ontological
actuality for Sartre, but concerning the same object: the Infinite.

SARTRE'S DENIAL OF THE HEGELIAN INFINITE

From the outset, however, this poses a problem because, if Hegel
assumes the dialectic of the finite and the infinite, Sartre expressly
rejects its meaning and in *Being and Nothingness* the sole use of the
word "infinite" appears in a critique of Hegel:

> This structure of the reflection-reflecting (*reflet–reflétant*) [of conscious-
> ness] has disconcerted philosophers, who have wanted to explain it by an
> appeal to infinity – [either . . .] or by defining it in the manner of Hegel as a
> return upon itself, as the veritable infinite. But the introduction of infinity
> into consciousness, aside from the fact that it fixes the phenomenon and
> obscures it, is only an explicative theory expressly designed to reduce the
> being of consciousness to that of the in-itself. (*BN*, p. 76)

This creates at least two paradoxes.

The first paradox emerges from the additional argument at the end
of the paragraph:

> If we accept the objective existence of the reflection–reflecting as it is given,
> we are obliged to conceive a mode of being different from that of the in-
> itself, not a unity which contains a duality, not a synthesis which surpasses
> and lifts the abstract moments of the thesis and the antithesis, but a duality
> which *is* unity, a reflection (*reflet*) which *is* its own reflecting (*réflection*).

Sartre objects to the dualism inherent in Hegel's recourse to the infinite in the name of an immanent connection between duality and
unity. But in justifying this critique, he has recourse to an argument
that Hegel would not have disavowed; he opts for an objection, which
is Hegel's own, to all dualisms interpreted in terms of "real oppositions," on the grounds that they undergo reciprocal interaction in

vain because, insofar as the terms of the opposition "exist," they may perhaps influence one another but they will never pass one into the other by mutually suppressing each other through and within the movement of their respective self-assertion; if this were the case, they would cease to be "oppositions" and become "contradictions."

If the bad infinite is bad, it is precisely on account of this dualism. Hegel says of the infinite movement of this opposition that it is only "the perpetual repetition of one and the same content, one and the same tedious *alternation* of this finite and infinite" (*ScL-1812*, p. 84) and, for this reason, that "the infinite is itself finite" (p. 85) since, as the finite repetition goes on, it is absorbed in finitude . . . save when one realizes that this false unity of the finite and the infinite by the finite is de jure the real unity of the two. Indeed,

It is this unity alone that evokes the infinite in the finite; it is, so to speak, the mainspring of the infinite progress. This progress is the *external* aspect of this unity. . . . But the unity of the finite and the infinite is beyond them; for they are precisely finite and infinite only in their separation. . . . There is this to be said about the coming or going forth of the finite from the infinite: The infinite goes forth *out* of itself into finitude because, being grasped as an abstract unity, it has no truth, no enduring being within it; and conversely the finite goes *into* the infinite for the same reason, namely that it is a nullity. (pp. 85, 86, 90)

It is to this dialectic that Sartre appeals to account for the "phantom dyad" of consciousness insofar as it reveals an inseparable relationship between its self-totalizing unity and its detotalization, between self-consciousness and determined consciousness (belief, pleasure, joy, and so on):

At its origin we have apprehended this double-game of reference: consciousness (of) belief is belief and belief is consciousness (of) belief. On no account can we say that consciousness is consciousness or that belief is belief. Each of the terms refers to the other and passes into the other, and yet each term is different from the other. . . . [As a consequence] belief, owing to the very fact that it can exist only as *troubled*, exists from the start as escaping itself, as shattering the unity of all the concepts in which one can wish to enclose it. (*BN*, p. 75)

We now see that here the infinite is that which *troubles* any determined consciousness, the impossibility for consciousness to be without simultaneous self-consciousness, and at the same time its impossibility to be pure self-consciousness without finite determination.

The second paradox bears on the direct critique of Hegel who defines "the return upon itself" of the phantom dyad of reflection–reflecting "as the veritable infinite" (*BN*, p. 76). Sartre sees this both as an ad hoc explanation "to reduce the being of consciousness to that of the in-itself" (ibid.), and as a (perhaps not voluntary but in his eyes sure) means to "fix the phenomenon of consciousness and obscure it" (ibid.), in short, as a way of making consciousness opaque. But this critique is paradoxical since in Hegel the stage of the infinite is accompanied by the emergence of what he also calls the "for-itself" and which happens to be the stage that has the most in common with the Sartrean for-itself.

BEING "FOR-ITSELF" IN HEGEL AND SARTRE

In Hegel's *Logic,* "being-for-itself" appears as the truth that came out of the dialectic of the limit, which we have *already identified* with the dialectic of the finite and the infinite. The "for-itself" is the figure that supports this dialectic. "It is infinite being" Hegel affirms from the outset (*ScL-1812*, p. 91). Being-there has overstepped its limits (or its boundaries, which already are the limit, overstepped but irrepressibly recurrent as an element of real opposition) – which means that, incapable of existing without determination, it has interiorized its limits. It thus discovers itself to be its own negative, or rather it discovers within itself the negation that the limit opposed to it as well as the negation through which it referred itself to the limit. Hence these two negations prove to be only one and to constitute the very movement of infinity: "In being-for-itself, negation as being-inside-itself and negation as limit, as being-other, are posited as identical; being-for-itself is *self-related negation*" (ibid.). That is to say, denying its limit or its other in order to define itself as not being it, being-there has denied that which denied it, and thus carries it within itself as that-which-it-is-not; but, since the movement is simultaneous and reciprocal, one must say that it carries it within itself as that which in turn denies it to be the limit that it is.

Thus, through the mediation of its other, being-there denies itself – or asserts itself only within this double negation, which is really one and which it produces in order to exist. In Sartrean terms:

Being-there, by nihilating the in-itself, finds itself yet again nihilating itself through the mediation of the in-itself:

The for-itself has no reality save that of being the nihilation of being. Its sole
qualification comes to it from the fact that it is the nihilation of an individual and particular in-itself and not of a being in general. The for-itself is not
nothingness in general but a particular privation; it constitutes itself as the
privation of *this being*. . . . As a nihilation it is *made-to-be* by the in-itself;
as an internal negation it must by means of the in-itself make known to
itself what it is not and consequently what it has to be. (*BN*, p. 618)

This is what Hegel calls the "ideality of the for-itself." He defines it in the very same terms by which Sartre defines the dyadic
relationship:

Being-for-itself contains a separation, or being-other, but as disappearing
separation, as being-other sublating itself. The two moments are thus inseparable. The infinite self-relation is only a negation of the negation, and
this sublating of the being-other immediately is self-related unity. . . .
Ideality is thus the same thing as infinity, or it is its positive, reflected and
determined expression. What is infinite is ideal [*das Ideelle*]. (*ScL-1812*, p.
95)

THE MEANING OF THE GENUINE INFINITE FOR
SARTRE AND HEGEL (FROM DESIRE TO NEED IN
SARTRE: ANIMAL DESIRE IN HEGEL)

We have no hesitation in affirming the identity between desire in
Being and Nothingness and need in the *Critique de la raison dialectique*. But are their respective understandings of the infinite homogeneous? And, first of all, in what sense do they both claim to understand it? The overriding effect of desire, in addition to its function of
motivating behavior by the revelation of its lack with respect to the
in-itself–for-itself, is to cause the fetishization of Value, of ideality,
inasmuch as it seems to lack *being* more essentially than any particular *determinate object*. With need, there is a rehabilitation of the
object of satisfaction insofar as, in the context of scarcity, it is first of
all by the struggle for scarce goods that sociohistorical alienation
leaves its mark. In short: Satisfy people's needs and you will have
social peace. The issue is not simple organic needs of an elementary
and primordial kind, but needs that are sociohistorically defined by

the state of advancement of society. This appears as a significant difference between the *Critique* and *Being and Nothingness*.

It is at this stage, however, that we once again encounter the genuine infinite. Hence our interpretation of the ambivalence of *desire* retrospectively acquires a legitimacy. For indeed, what saves the apparently "materialistic" interpretation of need from a positivistic and utilitarian prosaicness? It is that in need the meaning of the quest of desire is at stake, in keeping with what Hegel says, that is, "that according to its content, it is in quest for itself" (*Enz*, §428), or that "self-consciousness is *Desire* in general. . . . the 'I' is the *content* of the connection and the connecting itself . . . self-consciousness is essentially the return from otherness" (*PhSp*, pp. 104–5). So desire returns to itself in that the object of desire is self-consciousness – that is, desire. And desire is the meaning of this return to itself, according to the distancing of the self from the world in which the object of its desire is chosen – that is, desire itself through whatever ensures its renewal. Desire has realized that what was at stake in its relationship to the world was its relationship to itself in its infinity.

As a matter of fact, the model of infinity has in a sense been given to us by Hegel in connection with the deficiency of sense-certainty, which amounts to always mistaking the prey for the shadow, or being for nothingness. In this connection, he praised the dog who seizes and assimilates his prey without further ado about sense-certainty. So it must be for desire which seizes its object, so that it may, *just like the dog, nourish itself and find the conditions of its reproduction*. For it is not a matter of the extinction of desire but of its *reproduction* by choosing in the world the complement that it lacks and needs to ensure its renewal.

Indeed, in *Being and Nothingness*, Sartre already said of desire that

concretely, each for-itself is a lack of a certain coincidence with itself. This means that it is haunted by the presence of that with which it should coincide in order to be itself. But as this coincidence in Self is always coincidence with Self, the being which the For-itself lacks, the being which would make the For-itself a Self by assimilation with it – this being is still the For-itself . . . the For-itself is a "presence to itself"; what this presence-to-itself lacks can fail to appear to it only as presence-to-itself. . . . Thirst – for example – is never sufficiently thirst inasmuch as it makes itself thirst; it is haunted by the presence of the Self, or Thirst-self. (pp. 100–1)

The positive and negative aspects of Value are here at their closest: The reproduction of itself is the very condition of existence of consciousness, but its reproduction as *Self* constitutes its alienating fetishization. The first kind of reproduction is at issue in the *Critique*, and the second in *Being and Nothingness*, but since the first is the truth of the second – in the sense of condition of possibility – one understands the retroactive effect of elucidation brought about by the *Critique*. It is for this text that Hegel provides the model in his works.

THE GOAL, OR THE STRUCTURE OF ACTION

In Hegel, it is "the native realm of Spirit" that is attained with the genuine infinite – not only "the native realm of Truth" attributed by Hegel to the Cartesian *cogito*, but also the remarkable benefit of "the native place of the Spirit-becoming-as-self-consciousness."

Sartre may reject the Hegelian infinite, probably because of its link with Christianity, but this rejection is less important than the identity of meaning underlying the genuine infinite for both authors: desire, project, and action. This meaning constitutes the structure of consciousness in its negativity, *practically* in its desire, that is to say its destruction-appropriation of the world with a view to reproducing itself in the impossibility of being satisfied with what is not its *self-reproduction* – self-reproduction not in a biologico-organic sense, but as the reproduction of its desire as desire, of self-consciousness as self-consciousness, or of freedom as freedom, that is, *with the aim of reproducing the possibility of the infinite creation of its relationship to the world.*

It is in the same sense that we could turn to the formula of Marx's dialectical materialism, namely to ensure the reproduction of one's workforce by the possibility of obtaining the goods sociohistorically necessary to the realization of this goal, goods themselves defined by the value of the working time socially necessary to produce them. Note the sociohistorical circularity of these two requirements: one of reproduction, and the other attached to the sociohistorical conditions under which the requirement of reproduction would be fulfilled. Thus there is no requirement external to its conditions, and there are no conditions external to the requirement of reproduction. The mediation between the two extremes is ensured by the determination of the biologicocultural goods of a determined state of civilization. This renewal of one's workforce is indeed the primary condition of the relationship-of-self-to-the-world-in-returning-to-self according to the indexation of the infinite, since it is freedom itself that is aimed at through the possible, the means or the object of its destruction-appropriation: freedom from self to self, mediated by the world.

The bad infinite would confine itself to the eternal renewal of the disappearance of the object in the unceasingly renewed quest for a new object, and will be sanctioned by bringing the infinite under the controlling rule of finitude: "Thus desire in its satisfaction is *destructive*, just as, according to its content, it is *in quest for itself*, and since satisfaction can arise only in what is singular and since that is fleeting, desire generates itself again in its own satisfaction" (*Enz*, §428). These are the three stages of desire insofar as it will submit itself to the "bad" infinite: destruction, reproduction, infinite recurrence.

If we wished to connect these three stages with Sartrean thought, we would only have to align three quotations, each corresponding to one of the Hegelian stages: (1) self-consciousness as lack and desire, (2) desire as desire to reproduce itself, (3) dissatisfaction with all finite satisfaction.

1. "The existence of desire as a human fact is sufficient to prove that human reality is a lack." (*BN*, p. 87)
2. "What desire wishes to be is a filled emptiness but one that shapes its repletion as a mould shapes the bronze which has been poured inside it." (p. 101)
3. "We know moreover that coincidence with the self is impossible, for the for-itself attained by the realization of the Possible will make itself be as for-itself – that is, with another horizon of possibilities." (p. 101)

We see that the difference in wording between Hegel and Sartre concerning the unceasing renewal of desire, its infinity preserving its "genuine" sense, is inessential compared to the identity of meaning. Hegel stresses the finitude of singular desire, the initial restlessness of freedom enlightened by the infinity of the relationship, freedom that persists as long as it is not recast into the self-experience of this relationship. Sartre indicates the unceasing openness of free desire through the insatiable dynamic of temporality that pretends to exhaust itself in an eternalized, successful synthesis of in-itself and for-itself.

In both philosophers, there is the same connection of desire to the infinity of its deployment in and its relation to the world, in Hegel, in accordance with what will be specified as free experience of oneself in relation to the finite satisfaction of desire. This will be reached by the denunciation of the "limit" constituted by the "objective Notion's own *view* of itself, which vanishes by reflection on what its actualization is *in itself*. Through this view it is only standing in its own way, and thus what it has to do is to turn, not against an outer actuality, but against itself" (*ScL*, p. 822). And in Sartre, in accordance with what will be denounced as a vain attempt to essentialize into eternity the finite obtaining of the object of desire, and is announced as "pure reflection" to come.

The reference to the genuine infinite has been supported (1) at the level of prereflective consciousness, (2) at the level of its "ontological" relationship to the other than itself, or of the infinity of its relationship to itself through the mediation of the other, and (3) by the finality of the practical content of desire as pursuing self-reproduction. The question of the Other has already been indirectly addressed in the interpretation we have offered of the self-reproduction of desire and more precisely of need as the criterion of determination of the biologicohistorical reproduction of man thus involves the question of others.

BEING-FOR-OTHERS AND THE RECOGNITION OF CONSCIOUSNESSES

Sartre and Hegel are faced with two problems. The first one is that of the *ontological status* of the recognition of consciousnesses. The second problem, internal to the first one, is that of the status of experience of recognition: is it a matter of intellectual or existential evidence?

As regards the first question, Sartre denounces Hegel's "ontological optimism," which seems rather to be that of his commentators. "Hegel places himself at the vantage point of truth – i.e., of the whole – to consider the problem of the Other" (*BN*, p. 243). *It* is the a priori position, be it that of an upsurge of the essence of desire or that of a "network of relationships" always already established with a man socialized from the outset. Hegel's famous formula concerning the recognition of consciousnesses seems to support this interpretation: "With this, we already have before us the Notion of *Spirit*. What still lies ahead for consciousness is the experience of what Spirit is – this absolute substance which is the unity of the different independent self-consciousnesses which, in their opposition, enjoy perfect freedom and independence: 'I' that is 'We' and 'We' that is 'I' " (*PhSp*, p. 110).

We shall return to the implosive tension of this phrase, but for the moment let us note that, in connection with it, Hyppolite demonstrates the ambiguity of the teleological thesis. According to him, Hegel "sees the quest for the recognition of man" (*GS*, p. 155) as the a priori of desire; yet, at the same time, he establishes the conditions under which this quest will be able to take place: "the condition of self-consciousness is the existence of other self-consciousnesses" (ibid.). This last clause (insofar as "conditions" must be searched for . . .) leaves open the possibility that the essence does not imply its actuality or its instantaneous convertibility into being. In other words, the essence of desire would in this case be mediated by *the possibility of its impossibility*, that is, by contingency, seeing that it comes into being in contingency and has no other necessity than this aleatory becoming which *has taken place* but which could just as well not have . . . unless we convert the transcendental analysis of a phenomenon into an ontology.

These are pincers in which Sartre does not want to be caught. For him, the question is neither one of admitting the a priori of an essence, be it founded in the brotherly humanism of Christianity, nor of admitting the a priori of a relational structure, of an intersubjective network. He thus has to understand human relationships according to the actuality of a content with no other essence than the "nihilating" reflexivity of desire with respect to its objects, that is, to consider desire as mediated by the *relative* necessity of each of its objects without any *absolute* necessity pinning down its contingency while pretending to reflect it – as if contingency mediated by the in-itself would sublimate itself in the in-itself–for-itself. It is precisely this which, in his eyes, would have as a consequence Hegel's "ontological optimism." With the realization of absolute knowledge, history would have conquered the titles of nobility of a becoming realized *through struggle and conflicts*; having thus interiorized the contingency of its possibility or the possibility of its impossibility, it would have done away with it by the synthesis of a reflexivity accomplishing itself according to the best of all possible worlds, the one which *is* what it *is . . . because* it is.

To escape from this temptation of an in-itself–for-ourselves – "The multiplicity of consciousnesses appears to us as a *synthesis* and not as a *collection*, but it is a synthesis whose totality is inconceivable" (*BN*, p. 301) – it is important to limit ourselves to the strict noetico–noematic correlation of lack (desire, then need) and its object. This means that, with the inert and the organic, need reproduces itself organically and that, with cultural needs bearing on man-made objects, it reproduces itself according to the sociality which attaches a historicocultural content to its objects. Which, if we were to follow to the letter the correlation between lack and object, places need in a revolutionary situation, at risk or in danger of extermination through the extermination of the series of which it is a term: It is in fact the circular threat brought by all to bear on everyone in the world of scarcity.

If, then, the series is consistent, the conversion of the self into a regulatory third can take place to create an ubiquity where, in the manner of the Hegelian substance but *this time wholly generated*, everyone will become all the others and the Whole simultaneously, or, in one word, the group in fusion via the regulatory third that everyone, rising up under the threat of dispossession, makes himself become – all this, as Hegel puts it, in "perfect freedom and independence . . . of the self-consciousnesses being-for-themselves" and aware of the fact that, beyond fusion, each one of them represents a danger for all the others through the opposition of their freedom "to the Substance that is their unity" (*PhSp*, p. 110).

Formally, this means that Sartre denies any a priori relationship (Christianity, Platonism, Kantianism, spiritualism), but also any relationship based *on exteriority* or *on an overview* that would be the very negation of the principle of relationship (Marxism of material conditioning, liberalism of the interaction of monads) in favor of an a posteriori intelligibility: in effect, the intelligibility that results from the actual encounter of several self-consciousnesses according to the nihilating and shifting comprehension by each person of everyone else's goals; that is to say, according to the interiorization by everyone of what he is on the basis of what he makes himself *not* be in his understanding of the other's goal. By not being the gardener I can observe from my hotel room, I become the intellectual on holiday that the gardener and the roadworker make themselves not be by doing what they do, and which they in turn become as what they are. So *an objective network of human relationships* is put in place *that owes nothing to any a priori whatsoever* apart from that of difference: We are all identical in that we all differ from each other, "no common nature, communication always possible" (*CRD*, p. 126). It is an identity of identity and difference that is thereby instituted, or in other words the regime of contradiction as the sole stability in intelligibility.

In consequence, human relations are defined by the state of mobile coexistence of the *instrumental* lines of force that support the material world, in that the roadworker's road is bordered by the wall behind which the gardener works, itself delimited by the window, worked materiality incarnating the sequestrated look of the intellectual on holiday, and this in an endlessly open circularity:

> The organization of the practical field into a world determines a real relationship for everyone but one that only the experience with all the individuals who feature in this field will define. This is nothing other than the unification by *praxis;* and everyone, unifying insofar as he determines a dialectical field by his acts, is unified within this field by the unification of the *Other*, that is to say as many times as there is *plurality* of unifications. (*CRD*, p. 217)

Once again we encounter the limit that Hegel had initially overstepped to go to the infinite: Here it is through the other that freedom can limit freedom. At the same time, we also reencounter its dialectic: the unceasing overstepping of any limit, and last, the limit of the dialectic of the limit because, as Hegel says, "the different self-consciousnesses being-for-themselves constitute the opposition to the substance that is their unity" (*PhSp*, p. 110).

The alleged epistemological optimism of Hegel disappears if the recognition of others is – for him as for Sartre – a shifting recognition. In Sartre, the complicity of each *praxis* with every goal, essentially mediated by the negative or the limit of being-for-others, constitutes the correlated intuition of the *praxis* of everyone, outside of any simultaneity but in the very unity of their struggle, battle, or fight – be it peacefully in the confrontation of meeting eyes. In a struggle intensified by the radicality of a rise to extremes, or the assumption of the *death risk* in Hegel, this will likely be intuited as the sense of nothingness arising when desire clarifies itself as freedom and is thus able to shut the door on the material conditions of life. Man is the being who dies for reasons to live (Aron said).

Of course, Sartre himself was not asking so much in order to attest the intuition of the freedom of others since, at any one time, with regard to his goal, it is truly the ordeal of death (of my freedom, of my possibilities, of my spatiotemporalization, etc.) that is lived as a confirmation of the other's freedom. Not, then, the intuition of the other's nihilation in itself, but the lived ordeal of the other as nihilation effected against me, the other not given in his freedom but his freedom tested by the gift of my alienation. It all amounts to the same thing since the other necessarily nihilates himself nihilating me and since I am myself nihilated only through the feelings induced in me by my shame or my pride, in short by my "being placed in danger in the world" – feelings that are recognitions at the same time as responses of my being-for-the-freedom-of-the-other.

Is there not an ultimate resurgence of the dialectic of the limit at the level of absolute knowledge in Hegel? And is there not a dialectic of the overstepping of the limits of everyone for all through the great moments of substantial universalization common to both authors – love, revolution, constitutional state, art, politics, and philosophy? For the random destiny of a universality in a state of perpetual becoming, there is the future of both works, which remain identically open.

NOTES

1 Jean-Paul Sartre, *Being and Nothingness, An Essay on Phenomenological Ontology*, tr. Hazel E. Barnes, (London: Methuen, 1969), hereafter quoted as *BN*.
2 *Revue Internationale de Philosophie*, Bruxelles, no. 152–3 (1985): 77.
3 *Hegel's Science of Logic*, tr. A. V. Miller, foreword by J. N. Findlay (London: George Allen & Unwin, 1969), hereafter quoted as *ScL*.
   For the first book of the *Science of Logic* ("Doctrine of Being"), however, reference is to the first German edition, hereafter quoted as *ScL-1812*.
   G. W. F. Hegel, *Enzyklopädie der Philosophischen Wissenschaften im Grundrisse* (Leipzig: J. Hoffmeister, 1949), hereafter quoted as *Enz*.

From §1 to §244 of the *Encyclopedia* ("The Science of Logic"), reference is to the existing English translation, namely *The Logic of Hegel*, tr. W. Wallace (Oxford: Clarendon Press, 1892), hereafter quoted as *Enc.*

G. W. F. Hegel, *Propédeutique philosophique*, tr. into French by Maurice de Gandillac (Paris: Editions de Minuit, 1963), from a text established by Rosenkrantz, Editions du Jubilé, Vol. 3 (Stuttgart, 1949).

4 Jean Hyppolite, *Genèse et structure de la phénomènologie de l'esprit* (Paris: Aubier Montaigne, 1946), hereafter quoted as *GS.*

5 *Hegel's Phenomenology of Spirit*, tr. A. V. Miller with analysis of the text and foreword by J. N. Findlay (Oxford, Clarendon Press, 1977), hereafter quoted as *PhSp.*

6 Jean-Paul Sartre, *Cahiers pour une morale* (Paris: Gallimard, 1983).

7 Jean-Paul Sartre, *Critique de la raison dialectique*, preceded by *Questions de méthode* (Paris: Gallimard, 1960), hereafter quoted as *CRD.*

8 Cf. Juliette Simont, "*La lutte du maître et de l'esclave dans les* Cahiers pour une morale *et la* Critique de la raison dialectique," *Études Sartriennes*, no. 4 (1990).

9 Jean-Paul Sartre, *Saint Genet, comédien et martyr* (Paris: Gallimard, 1952), hereafter quoted as *SG; L'Idiot de la famille* (Paris: Gallimard, Vols. 1 and 2, 1971; Vol. 3, 1972); *Mallarmé* (Paris: Gallimard, 1988).

10 I have discussed these dialectics implicitly or explicitly in *Violence et ethique, essai sur une morale dialectique à travers le théâtre de Sartre* (Paris: Gallimard, 1972); in "*Sens et structure de* Saint Genet *et de* L'Idiot de la famille," *Études Sartriennes*, 2–3 (1986); and in "*La vilaine belle âme*," *Yale French Studies*, 68 (1985).

11 "The future can exist only as a complement of a lack in the present. It is the very meaning of this lack. . . . What we call freedom of the human reality is the fact that it is never anything unless it motivates itself to be this thing. Nothing can ever happen to it *from the outside*. This is due to the fact that human reality is, above all, consciousness of being; it motivates its own reaction to the outside event and the event in it *is* the reaction. Moreover, it discovers the world only on the occasion of its own reactions. It is thus free in the sense that its reactions and the manner in which the world appears to it can be integrally ascribed to it" (*Carnets de la drôle de guerre* [Paris: Gallimard, 1983], pp. 280 and 138).

BIBLIOGRAPHY

There has been no attempt to impose standardization of references on contributors, some of whom have chosen to use the available English translations while others have preferred to translate Sartre's texts themselves. All editions referred to are cited in this Bibliography.

WORKS BY SARTRE

A full bibliography of Sartre's works up to 1969 is given by Michel Contat and Michel Rybalka in *Les Écrits de Sartre* (Paris: Gallimard, 1970). Later supplements are given in the English translation of the work, *The Writings of Jean-Paul Sartre* (Evanston, Ill.: Northwestern University Press, 1973), and in *Obliques*, no 18–19 (May 1979), edited by Michel Sicard.

Another good bibliography is given by Robert Wilcocks, *Jean-Paul Sartre, A Bibliography of International Criticism* (Edmonton: University of Alberta Press, 1975).

Editions cited: I give first the French original and then, if available, an English translation. Some contributors to this *Companion* have preferred to translate directly from the French. In this case, their page references are to the French originals.

Place of publication of all French texts is Paris.

SARTRE'S WORKS

La Transcendance de l'ego, Esquisse d'une description phénomènologique.
First published in *Recherches Philosophiques*, Vol. VI, 1936. Reprinted in edition by Sylvie le Bon, Vrin, 1965.
The Transcendence of the Ego. An Existentialist Theory of Consciousness.

Tr. Forrest Williams and Robert Kirkpatrick. New York: The Noonday Press, 1962.

L'Imagination. Alcan, 1936. Reprinted by PUF, 1969.
Imagination, a Psychological Critique. Tr. Forrest Williams. Ann Arbor: University of Michigan Press, 1962.

La Nausée. Gallimard, 1938.
Nausea, or The Diary of Antoine Roquentin. Tr. Lloyd Alexander. New York: New Directions, 1949. Tr. Robert Baldick. Middlesex (England): Penguin Books, 1965.

Esquisse d'une théorie des émotions. Hermann, 1939.
The Emotions: Outline of a Theory. Tr. Bernard Frechtman. New York: Philosophical Library, 1948.
also translated as:
Sketch for a Theory of the Emotions. Tr. Philip Mairet. London: Methuen, 1962.

L'Imaginaire, psychologie phénomènologique de l'imagination. Gallimard, 1940. Reprinted, *Collection Idées,* 1986.
The Psychology of the Imagination. Tr. Bernard Frechtman. New York: Philosophical Library, 1948, and Washington Square Press, 1966.

L'Être et le néant. Essai d'ontologie phénomènologique. Gallimard, 1943.
Being and Nothingness. An Essay on Phenomenological Ontology. Tr. Hazel E. Barnes. New York, Philosophical Library, 1956. Reprinted by Washington Square Press, 1972.

L'Existentialism est un humanisme. Nagel, 1946.
Existentialism. Tr. Bernard Frechtman. New York: Philosophical Library, 1947, and Citadel, 1957.
also translated as:
Existentialism and Humanism. Tr. Philip Mairet. London: Methuen, 1957.

Situations II: Qu'est-ce que la littérature? Gallimard, 1948.
What Is Literature? Tr. Bernard Frechtman. New York: Philosophical Library, 1949, and Harper Colophon Books, 1965.

"Orphée Noir." In *Situations,* Vol. III. Gallimard, 1949.
Black Orpheus. Tr. S. W. Allen. Paris: Présence Africaine, 1963.

Saint Genet, comédien et martyr. Gallimard, 1952.
Saint Genet, Actor and Martyr. Tr. Bernard Frechtman. New York, Braziller, 1963.

Critique de la raison dialectique, précedé de questions de méthode, I, Théorie des ensembles pratiques. Gallimard, 1960. Reprinted in new annotated edition, 1985.

Search for a Method. Tr. Hazel E. Barnes. New York: Knopf, 1963.
Critique of Dialectical Reason. Tr. Alan Sheridan-Smith. Ed. Jonathan Ree. London: New Left Books, 1976. Atlantic Highlands, N.J.: Humanities Press, 1976.

Les Mots. Gallimard, 1963.
The Words. Tr. Bernard Frechtman. New York: Braziller, 1964. Greenwich, Conn.: Fawcett Publications, 1966.

"Jean-Paul Sartre répond." L'Arc, 30 (1966): 91–2.

"Plaidoyer pour les intellectuels." In *Situations,* Vol. VIII. Gallimard, 1972.
"A Plea for Intellectuals." In *Between Existentialism and Marxism* (selected essays from *Situations,* Vols. VIII and IX). Tr. John Mathews. New York: Pantheon, 1974.

Situations, Vol. IX. Gallimard, 1972.
Situations, Vol. X. Gallimard, 1976.

On a raison de se révolter. Gallimard, 1974.

"Sur *L'Idiot de la famille."* *Situations,* Vol. X. Gallimard, 1976.
"On *The Idiot of the Family."* In *Life/Situations.* Tr. P. Auster and L. Davis. New York: Pantheon, 1977.

L'Idiot de la famille, G. Flaubert de 1821 à 1857. Gallimard, Vols. I and II, 1971; Vol. III, 1972. Revised ed., 1988.
The Idiot of the Family. Tr. Carol Cosman. Chicago: University of Chicago Press, Vol. I, 1981; Vol. II, 1987; Vol. III, 1989.

OEuvres romanesques. Pléiade, 1981.

Les Carnets de la drôle de guerre. Gallimard, 1983.
The War Diaries of Jean-Paul Sartre. Tr. Quintin Hoare. New York: Pantheon Books, 1984.

Cahiers pour une morale. Gallimard, 1983.

Le Scénario Freud. Gallimard, 1984.

Critique de la raison dialectique, Vol. II (inachevé), L'Intelligibilité de l'histoire. Ed. Arlette Elkaïm-Sartre. Gallimard, 1985.

Mallarmé, la lucidité et sa face d'ombre. Gallimard, 1986.
Mallarmé, or the Poet of Nothingness. Tr. E. Sturm. University Park: Pennsylvania University Press, 1988.

Vérité et existence. Ed. Arlette Elkaïm-Sartre. Gallimard, 1989.

BOOKS REFERRING TO SARTRE'S PHILOSOPHY

Aronson, R. *Jean-Paul Sartre. Philosophy in the World.* London: New Left Books. New York: Schocken Books, 1980.

Sartre's Second Critique. Chicago: University of Chicago Press, 1987.

and A. van den Hoven (eds.). *Sartre Alive.* Detroit: Wayne State University Press, 1991.

Barnes, H. *Sartre.* New York: J. B. Lippincott, 1973. London: Quartet Books, 1974.

Sartre and Flaubert. Chicago: University of Chicago Press, 1981.

Beauvoir, S. de *La Force de l'âge.* Paris: Gallimard, 1960.

La Cérémonie des adieux suivi de Entretiens avec Jean-Paul Sartre. Paris: Gallimard, 1981.

Burgelin, C. (ed.). *Lectures de Sartre.* Lyon, 1986.

Busch, T. W. *The Power of Consciousness and the Force of Circumstances in Sartre's Philosophy.* Bloomington: Indiana University Press, 1990.

Catalano, J. *A Commentary on Sartre's "Being and Nothingness,"* New York: Harper & Row, 1974.

A Commentary on Sartre's Critique of Dialectical Reason. Vol. I. Chicago: University of Chicago Press, 1986.

Caws, P. *Sartre.* London: Routledge and Kegan Paul, 1979.

Champigny, R. *Stages on Sartre's Way: 1938–1952.* Bloomington: Indiana University Press, 1959.

Chiodi, P. *Sartre and Marxism.* Tr. Kate Soper. Hassocks, Sussex: The Harvester Press. New York: Humanities Press, 1976.

Collins, D. *Sartre as Biographer.* Cambridge, Mass.: Harvard University Press, 1980.

Cranston, M. *Jean-Paul Sartre.* New York: Grove Press, 1962.

Cumming, R. (ed.). *The Philosophy of Jean-Paul Sartre.* New York: Random House, 1965; 3d ed., New York: Vintage, 1972.

Danto, A. *Sartre.* London: Fontana Modern Masters. New York: Viking, 1975.

Dempsey, P. *The Psychology of Sartre.* Westminster, Md.: Newman Press, 1950.

Detner, D. *Freedom as Value: A Critique of the Ethical Theory of Jean-Paul Sartre.* La Salle, Ill.: Open Court, 1988.

Derrida, J. *Marges de la Philosophie.* Paris: Editions de Minuit, 1972.

Desan, W. *The Marxism of Jean-Paul Sartre.* New York: Anchor Books, 1965.

Fell, J. *Emotion in the Thought of Sartre.* New York: Columbia University Press, 1965.

Heidegger and Sartre. New York: Columbia University Press, 1979.

Flynn, T. *Sartre and Marxist Existentialism*. Chicago: University of Chicago Press, 1984.

Fretz, L. *Het Individualiteitsconcept in Sartres Filosofie*. Delft University Press, 1984.

Fry, C. *Sartre and Hegel: The Variations of an Enigma in "L'Être et le néant."* Bonn: Bouvier, 1988.

Goldthorpe, R. *Sartre: Literature and Theory*. Cambridge: Cambridge University Press, 1984.

Grene, M. *Sartre*. New York: New Viewpoints, 1973.

Hartman, K. *Sartre's Ontology: A Study of "Being and Nothingness" in the Light of Hegel's Logic*. Evanston, Ill.: Northwestern University Press, 1966.

Howells, C. *Sartre's Theory of Literature*. London: Modern Humanities Research Association, 1979.

Sartre: The Necessity of Freedom. Cambridge: Cambridge University Press, 1988.

Jameson, F. *Sartre: The Origin of a Style*. New Haven, Conn.: Yale University Press, 1961.

Jeanson, F. *Le Problème moral et la pensée de Sartre*. Paris: Seuil, 1947. Tr. R. Stone as *Sartre and the Problem of Morality*. Bloomington: Indiana University Press, 1980.

Sartre par lui-même. Paris: Seuil, 1955.

Sartre dans sa vie. Paris: Seuil, 1974.

Jolivet, R. *Sartre, ou la théologie de l'absurde*. Paris: Fayard, 1965.

Kaelin, E. *An Existentialist Aesthetic: The Theories of Sartre and Merleau-Ponty*. Madison: University of Wisconsin Press, 1962.

King, T. *Sartre and the Sacred*. Chicago: University of Chicago Press, 1974.

König, T. (ed.). *Sartre's Flaubert Lesen: Essays zu Der Idiot der familie*, Reinbet bei Hamburg: Rowohlt, 1980.

La Capra, D. *A Preface to Sartre*. London: Methuen, 1979.

Laing, R. D., and D. G. Cooper. *Reason and Violence: A Decade of Sartre's Philosophy*. London: Tavistock Publishers, 1964. New York: Vintage, 1971.

Macquarrie, J. *Existentialism*. Baltimore: Penguin Books, 1973.

Manser, A. *Sartre: A Philosophic Study*. London: Athlone Press, 1966.

McMahon, J. *Humans Being: The World of Jean-Paul Sartre*. Chicago: University of Chicago Press, 1971.

Morris, P. *Sartre's Concept of a Person*. Amherst: University of Massachusetts Press, 1976.

Murdoch, I. *Sartre, Romantic Rationalist*. Cambridge: Bowes and Bowes, 1953.

Natanson, M. *A Critique of Jean-Paul Sartre's Ontology.* Lincoln: University of Nebraska Press, 1951. The Hague: Nijhoff, 1973.

Poster, M. *Sartre's Marxism.* London: Pluto Press, 1979.

Salvan, J. *The Scandalous Ghost: Sartre's Existentialism as Related to Vitalism, Humanism, Mysticism, and Marxism.* Detroit: Wayne State University Press, 1967.

Schilpp, P. *The Philosophy of Jean-Paul Sartre.* La Salle, Ill.: The Library of Living Philosophers, 1981.

Scriven, M. *Sartre's Existential Biographies.* London: Macmillan, 1984.

Silverman, H., and F. Elliston (eds.). *Jean-Paul Sartre: Contemporary Approaches to his Philosophy.* Pittsburgh: Duquesne University Press, 1980.

Stein, A. *Sartre, His Philosophy and Psychoanalysis.* New York: Liberal Arts Press, 1953. Rev. ed., New York: Delacorte, 1967.

Verstraeten, P. *Violence et ethique, esquisse d'une critique de la morale dialectique à partir du théâtre politique de Sartre.* Paris: Gallimard, 1972.

(ed.). *Sur les écrits posthumes de Sartre, Annales de l'Institut de Philosophie et des Sciences morales.* Editions de L'Université de Bruxelles, 1987.

Warnock, M. *The Philosophy of Sartre.* London: Hutchinson, and New York: Hillary House, 1965.

Existentialist Ethics. London: Macmillan, and New York: St Martin's Press, 1967.

Whitford, M. *Merleau-Ponty's Critique of Sartre's Philosophy.* Lexington, Ky: French Forum, 1982.

Wilcocks, R. (ed.) *Critical Essays on Jean-Paul Sartre,* Boston: G. K. Hall, 1988.

JOURNAL ISSUES DEVOTED TO SARTRE

Obliques, Sartre, 18–19, 1979.

Obliques, Sartre et les Arts, 24–25, 1981.

Yale French Studies, Sartre after Sartre, 68, 1985.

Études Sartriennes, II–III, *Cahiers de Sémiotique Textuelle,* 5–6, Université de Paris X, 1986.

Études Sartriennes, IV, *Cahiers de Sémiotique Textuelle,* 18, Université de Paris, X, 1990.

ESSAYS REFERRING TO SARTRE

Caws, P. "Oracular Lives: Sartre and the Twentieth Century," *Revue Internationale de Philosophie*, 152–3 (1985).

"Sartre's Last Philosophical Manifesto." In *Philosophy and Non-Philosophy since Merleau-Ponty. Continental Philosophy*, Vol. I, ed. H. J. Silverman. New York: Routledge, 1988.

Flynn, T. "The Role of the Image in Sartre's Aesthetic." *The Journal of Aesthetics and Art Criticism*, 33, no. 4 (Summer 1975).

"Praxis and Vision: Elements of a Sartrean Epistemology." *The Philosophical Forum*, 8 (Fall 1976).

"Merleau-Ponty and the Critique of Dialectical Reason." *Hypatia*, ed. W. M. Calden et al. Boulder, Col.: Associated Universities Press, 1985.

Howells, C. "Sartre and Negative Theology." *Modern Language Review* (July 1981).

Jopling, D. "Kant and Sartre on Self-Knowledge." *Man and World*, 19, no. 1 (1986).

Pucciani, O. "*Cet objet sartrien neuf: Un centre réel et permanent d'irréalisation.*" *Dalhousie French Studies* (October 1983).

Simont, J. "*Sartre et Hegel: le problème de la quantité et de la qualite.*" *Revue Internationale de Philosophie*, 152–3 (1985).

"*Morale esthétique, morale militante, au delà de la 'faribole'.*" *Revue philosophique de Louvain*, 73 (1989).

OTHER WORKS

Adorno, T. W. *Negative Dialectics*. London: Routledge and Kegan Paul, 1973.

Althusser, L., et al. *Lire le capital*. 2 vols. Paris: Maspéro, 1965.

Aristotle. *Nichomachean Ethics*. Tr. W. D. Ross. London: Oxford University Press, 1942.

Aron, R. *La Philosophie critique de l'histoire*. Paris: Vrin, Collection Points, 1969.

Introduction à la philosophie de l'histoire. Paris: Gallimard, Collection TEL, 1981.

Barthes, R. Interview in *La Quinzaine Littéraire*, 68 (March 1971).

Beauvoir, S. de. *La force de l'âge*. Paris: Gallimard, 1960.

Berofsky, B. (ed.). *Free Will and Determinism*. New York: Harper & Row, 1966.

Bubner, R. *Modern German Philosophy*. Tr. E. Matthews. Cambridge: Cambridge University Press, 1981.

Bury, J. B. *The Idea of Progress.* New York: 1932.

Cassirer, E. "Structuralism in Modern Linguistics." *Word*, no. 2 (August 1945).

Caws, P. *The Philosophy of Science: A Systematic Account.* Princeton, N.J.: Van Nostrand, 1965.

"Operational, Representational and Explanatory Models." *American Anthropologist*, 76, no. 1 (March, 1976).

Structuralism: The Art of the Intelligible. Atlantic Highlands, N.J.: Humanities Press, 1988.

Cumming, R. D. *Starting Point: An Introduction to the Dialectic of Existence.* Chicago: University of Chicago Press, 1979; 2d ed. in press.

Human Nature and History: A Study of the Development of Liberal Political Thought. 2 vols. Chicago: University of Chicago Press, 1969; 2d ed. in press.

The Dream Is Over: A History of Phenomenology. Vol 1. Chicago: University of Chicago Press, 1991.

Deleuze, G. *Francis Bacon, Logique de la sensation.* Paris: 1984.

Foucault. Paris: Éditions de Minuit, 1986.

Mille plateaux. Paris: Éditions de Minuit, 1980.

Deleuze, G., and F. Guattari. *L'Anti Oedipe.* Paris: Éditions de Minuit, 1972.

Dennett, D. *Elbow Room: The Varieties of Free Will Worth Wanting.* Cambridge, Mass.: MIT Press, 1985.

Derrida, J. *La Voix et le phénomène.* Paris, PUF, 1967; reprinted, 1972.

L'Ecriture et la différence. Paris: Seuil, 1967. Points, 1979.

Marges de la philosophie. Paris: Éditions de Minuit, 1972.

Positions. Paris: Éditions de Minuit, 1972.

De l'Esprit. Paris: Galilée, 1987.

Psyché. Paris: Galilée, 1987

Descartes, R. *Oeuvres et lettres.* Paris: Gallimard, Pléiade, 1952.

Descombes, V. *Le Même et l'autre.* Paris: Éditions de Minuit, 1979.

Dews, P. "The Return of the Subject in Late Foucault." *Radical Philosophy*, 51 (Spring 1989).

Dilthey, W. *Gesammelte Schriften.* Stuttgart: Teubner, and Göttingen: Vanderhoeck & Rurecht, 1914–77, Vols. VII and XVII.

Selected Writings. Ed. H. P. Rickman. Cambridge: Cambridge University Press, 1976.

Dreyfus, H., and P. Rabinow, *Michel Foucault: Beyond Structuralism, and Hermeneutics.* Brighton, Sussex: Harvester Press, 1982.

Michel Foucault, un parcours philosophique. Paris: Gallimard, 1984,

Engels, F. *Socialism: Utopian and Scientific.* Moscow: Progress Publishers, 1954.

Ermarth, M. *Wilhelm Dilthey: The Critique of Historical Reason.* Chicago: University of Chicago Press, 1978.

Foucault, M. *Les Mots et les choses.* Paris: Gallimard, 1966.

The Archaeology of Knowledge. Tr. A. M. Sheridan-Smith. New York: Harper & Row, 1972.

La Volonté de savoir. Paris: Gallimard, 1976.

L'Usage des plaisirs. Paris: Gallimard, 1984.

Le Souci de soi. Paris: Gallimard, 1984.

Frank, M. *L'Ultime raison du sujet.* Tr. from German by V. Zanetti. Paris: PUF Acts Sud, 1988.

Frankfurt, H. "Freedom of the Will and the Concept of a Person." *Journal of Philosophy,* 68 (1971).

Hampshire, S. *Morality and Conflict.* Cambridge, Mass,: Harvard University Press, 1983.

Thought and Action. London: Chatto and Windus, 1982.

Hare, R. M. *The Language of Morals.* New York: Oxford University Press, 1964.

Harre, R. *Personal Being.* Cambridge, Mass.: Harvard University Press, 1984.

Hegel, G. W. F. *Enzyklopädie de Philosophischen Wissenschaften im Grundrisse.* Leipzig: J Hoffmeister, 1949. §1–244, tr. W. Wallace as *The Logic of Hegel,* Oxford: Clarendon Press, 1892.

Hegel's Phenomenology of Spirit. Tr. A. V. Miller. Oxford: Clarendon Press, 1977.

Hegel's Science of Logic. Tr. A. V. Miller. London: Allen and Unwin, 1969.

Propédeutique philosophique. Tr. into French by Maurice de Gandillac. Paris: Éditions de Minuit, 1963.

Heidegger, M. *Sein und Zeit.* Tübingen: Niemayer, 1977. Tr. J. Macquarrie and E. Robinson as *Being and Time,* Oxford: Blackwell, 1967.

Hook, S. (ed.). *Determinism and Freedom in the Age of Modern Science.* New York: Macmillan, 1958.

Husserl, E. *Ideas I.* Tr. F. Kersten. The Hague: Nijhoff, 1983. Tr. W. R. Boyce Gibson, London: 1931.

Logical Investigations. Tr. J. N. Findlay. 2 vols. London: Routledge and Kegan Paul, 1970, and tr. Geach, Oxford: 1977.

Méditations Cartésiennes. Tr. G. Peiffer and E. Levinas. Paris: Vrin, 1986.

Hyppolite, J. *Genèse et structure de la "phénomènologie de l'esprit" de Hegel.* Paris: Aubier Montaigne, 1946.

Kant, I. *Religion within the Limits of Reason Alone.* Tr. T. Greene and H. Hudson. London: Open Court, 1934.

Critique of Pure Reason. Tr. N. K. Smith. London: Macmillan, 1980.

Groundwork of the Metaphysic of Morals. Tr. H. Paton in *The Moral Law,* London: Hutchinson, 1948; reprinted 1981.

Kierkegaard, S. *Either/Or.* Tr. D. F. and L. M. Swenson, and W. Lowry. Princeton, N.J.: Princeton University Press, 1944.

Lacan, J. *Écrits.* Paris: Seuil, 1966. Tr. A. Sheridan, *Ecrits, A Selection.* London: Tavistock Publications, 1977.

Laurent, A. *L'Individu et ses ennemis.* Paris: Hachette, 1987.

Lavers, A. *Roland Barthes: Structuralism and After.* Cambridge, Mass.: Harvard University Press, 1982.

Lee, S. H. (ed.). *Inquiries into Values.* Lewiston, N.Y.: Edwin Mellen Press, 1988.

Levinas, E. *Hors Sujet.* Paris: 1988.

Lévi-Strauss, C. *Anthropologie structurale.* Paris: Plon, 1958. Tr. as *Structural Anthropology* by C. Jacobson and B. Schoepf. New York: Basic Books, 1963.

La Pensée sauvage. Paris: Plon, 1962. Tr. as *The Savage Mind.* London: 1972 and Chicago: 1966.

Le Cru et le cuit. Paris: Plon, 1964.

L'Homme nu (Mythologiques ****). Paris: Plon, 1971.

Locke, J. *Essay on Human Understanding.* Ed. P. H. Nidditch. Oxford: Clarendon Press, 1975; reprinted 1988.

Lyotard, J. F. *Discours, Figure.* Paris: Klincksieck, 1971.

La Condition Postmoderne. Paris: Minuit, 1979. Tr. as *The Postmodern Condition: A Report on Knowledge,* Minneapolis: 1984.

L'Inhumain: Causeries sur le temps, Paris: Éditions de Minuit, 1988.

Marion, J.-L. *Généalogie de la psychanalyse.* Paris: 1985.

Marx, K. *Writings of the Young Marx on Philosophy and Society.* Tr. and ed. L. Easton and K. Guddat. Garden City, N.Y.: Doubleday, 1967.

Megill, A. *Prophets of Extremity.* London: Berkeley, L.A., 1987.

Merker, B *Selbsttäuschung und Selbsterkenntnis: Zu Heideggers Transformation der Phänomenologie Husserls.* Frankfurt: Suhrkamp, 1988.

Merleau-Ponty, M. *Phenomenology of Perception.* Tr. C. Smith. London: Routledge and Kegan Paul, 1962.

Sense and Nonsense. Tr. H. and P. Dreyfus. Evanston, Ill.: Northwestern University Press, 1964.

Adventures of the Dialectic. Tr. J. Bien. Evanston, Ill.: Northwestern University Press, 1973.

Mill, J. S. *A System of Logic.* New York: Bobbs-Merrill, 1965.

Mischel, T. *The Self.* Oxford: Blackwell, 1977.

Murdoch, I. *The Sovereignty of Good.* London: Routledge and Kegan Paul, 1970.

Myers, G. *William James: His Life and Thought.* New Haven, Conn.: Yale University Press, 1986.

Nagel, T. *Mortal Questions*. Cambridge: Cambridge University Press, 1979.
Nietzsche, F. *The Birth of Tragedy and The Genealogy of Morals*. Tr. F. Golffing. Garden City, N.Y.: Doubleday, 1956.
Thus Spake Zarathustra. Tr. R. J. Hollingdale. London: Penguin, 1961.
The Will to Power. Tr. W. Kaufman and R. J. Hollingdale. New York: 1968.
Beyond Good and Evil. Tr. R. J. Hollingdale. London: Penguin, 1972.
Pascal, B. *Pensées. Œuvres complètes*. Paris: Seuil, 1963.
Renaut, A. *L'Ère de l'individu, Contribution à une histoire de la subjectivité*. Paris: Gallimard, 1989.
Renaut, A., with L. Ferry. *La Pensée 68, Essai sur l'anti-humanisme contemporaine*. Paris: Gallimard, Folio, 1988.
Ricoeur, P. *Time and Narrative*. Tr. K. Balmey and D. Pellauer. 3 vols. Chicago: University of Chicago Press, 1984–8.
Soi-même comme un autre. Paris: Seuil, 1990.
Rorty, A. (ed.). *The Identities of Persons*. Berkeley: University of California Press, 1976.
Rorty, A. and B. P. McLaughlin (eds.). *Perspectives in Self-Deception*. Berkeley: University of California Press, 1988.
Saussure, F. de. *Course in General Linguistics*. Tr. W. Baskin. New York: Philosophical Library, 1959.
Schalk, D. L. *The Spectrum of Political Engagement*. Princeton, N.J.: Princeton University Press, 1979.
Schoeman, F. (ed.). *Responsibility, Character and the Emotions*. Cambridge: Cambridge University Press, 1987.
Strawson, P. "Freedom and Resentment." In *Proceedings of the British Academy*. London: 1962.
Taylor, C. *Sources of the Self*. Cambridge, Mass.: Harvard University Press, 1986.
Tugendhat, E. *Self-Consciousness and Self-Determination*. Tr. P. Stern. Cambridge, Mass.: MIT Press, 1986.
Velleman, J. D. *Practical Reflection*. Princeton, N.J.: Princeton University Press, 1989.
Wittgenstein, L. *On Certainty*. Tr. D. Paul and G. E. M. Anscombe. New York: Harper & Row, 1969.

COLLECTIVE WORKS AND JOURNALS

Confrontations. Après le sujet qui vient, no 20 (Winter 1989).
Les Fins de l'homme. Colloque de Cerisy, 1981.
Magazine littéraire. L'Individualisme: le grand retour, no. 264 (April 1989).
Penser le sujet aujourd'hui. Colloque de Cerisy. 1988.
Sur l'Individu. Colloque de Royaumont. 1987.

INDEX

385